ASPECTS

OF

THE OLD TESTAMENT

OTTLEY

THE BAMPTON LECTURES, *1897*
─────────────────────────

ASPECTS

OF THE

OLD TESTAMENT

CONSIDERED IN EIGHT LECTURES

DELIVERED BEFORE THE UNIVERSITY OF OXFORD

BY

ROBERT LAWRENCE OTTLEY, M.A.
SUCCESSIVELY STUDENT OF CHRIST CHURCH AND
FELLOW OF MAGDALEN COLLEGE
SOMETIME PRINCIPAL OF THE PUSEY HOUSE

'Caritas congaudet veritati.'—1 *Cor.* xiii. 6.

Wipf and Stock Publishers
199 W 8th Ave, Suite 3
Eugene, OR 97401

Aspects of the Old Testament
The Bampton Lectures, 1897
By Ottley, Robert Lawrence
ISBN 13: 978-1-55635-163-1
ISBN 10: 1-55635-163-1
Publication date 12/27/2006
Previously published by Longmans, Green, and Co., 1898

EXTRACT

FROM THE LAST WILL AND TESTAMENT

OF THE LATE

REV. JOHN BAMPTON,

CANON OF SALISBURY.

——"I give and bequeath my Lands and Estates to the
"Chancellor, Masters, and Scholars of the University of
"Oxford for ever, to have and to hold all and singular the
"said Lands or Estates upon trust, and to the intents and
"purposes hereinafter mentioned; that is to say, I will and
"appoint that the Vice-Chancellor of the University of Ox-
"ford for the time being shall take and receive all the rents,
"issues, and profits thereof, and (after all taxes, reparations,
"and necessary deductions made) that he pay all the re-
"mainder to the endowment of eight Divinity Lecture Ser-
"mons, to be established for ever in the said University, and
"to be performed in the manner following:

"I direct and appoint, that, upon the first Tuesday in
"Easter Term, a Lecturer be yearly chosen by the Heads
"of Colleges only, and by no others, in the room adjoining
"to the Printing-House, between the hours of ten in the
"morning and two in the afternoon, to preach eight Divinity
"Lecture Sermons, the year following, at St. Mary's in

"Oxford, between the commencement of the last month in
"Lent Term, and the end of the third week in Act Term.

"Also I direct and appoint, that the eight Divinity Lecture
"Sermons shall be preached upon either of the following
"Subjects—to confirm and establish the Christian Faith, and
"to confute all heretics and schismatics—upon the divine
"authority of the holy Scriptures—upon the authority of
"the writings of the primitive Fathers, as to the faith and
"practice of the primitive Church—upon the Divinity of our
"Lord and Saviour Jesus Christ—upon the Divinity of the
"Holy Ghost—upon the Articles of the Christian Faith, as
"comprehended in the Apostles' and Nicene Creeds.

"Also I direct, that thirty copies of the eight Divinity Lec-
"ture Sermons shall be always printed, within two months
"after they are preached; and one copy shall be given to the
"Chancellor of the University, and one copy to the Head of
"every College, and one copy to the Mayor of the city of
"Oxford, and one copy to be put into the Bodleian Library;
"and the expense of printing them shall be paid out of the
"revenue of the Land or Estates given for establishing the
"Divinity Lecture Sermons; and the Preacher shall not be
"paid, nor be entitled to the revenue, before they are printed.

"Also I direct and appoint, that no person shall be quali-
"fied to preach the Divinity Lecture Sermons, unless he hath
"taken the degree of Master of Arts at least, in one of the
"two Universities of Oxford or Cambridge; and that the
"same person shall never preach the Divinity Lecture Ser-
"mons twice."

PREFACE

THE following lectures are intended rather to illustrate than to defend exhaustively a view of the Old Testament which to the writer has long been habitual, and which, having some claim to be considered a *via media*, will, he hopes, commend itself to thoughtful Churchmen.

Mr. Goldwin Smith has recently asserted that those whom he calls 'rationalistic apologists' do but tamper with their conscience and understanding when they claim that the Old Testament contains both a divine and a human element. 'Far better it is,' he says, 'whatever the effort may cost, honestly to admit that the sacred books of the Hebrews, granting their superiority to the sacred books of other nations, are, like the sacred books of other nations, the works of man and not of God[1].' Such statements as this, and they are not infrequently made, seem to challenge the attention of loyal Churchmen, and to justify the attempt to deal dispassionately both with the undeniable facts that have been brought to light by

[1] *Guesses at the Riddle of Existence* (Essay on 'The Church and the Old Testament'), p. 95.

historical and critical research, and with the theories which they are supposed to support.

In writing these lectures I have had in view several different classes of persons.

There are those who, like Mr. Goldwin Smith himself, imagine that 'High Churchmen, having studied recent criticism, feel that there is a millstone to be cast off[1].' Speaking for myself, I am unaware of any 'millstone' other than the strange and inveterate misconceptions which are widely prevalent, and are apparently shared by the distinguished essayist himself, respecting the true place and function of the Old Testament in the life and system of the Christian Church. Those who have watched the course of religious thought on the subject will certainly feel that Mr. Goldwin Smith's strictures on the honesty and good sense of Churchmen are somewhat belated and irrelevant. I say confidently that the effect of a more strictly historical and scientific study has been to enhance the interest, reverence, and love with which we Churchmen regard the Old Testament. We deplore the comparative neglect of the Bible which has to some extent been the consequence of recent unsettlement, and we are anxious to enrich others as we have been enriched, by imparting to them a point of view from which the verdicts of criticisms can be justly appreciated.

It is a matter of simple experience that modern research has both enlarged our insight into the actual course and method of divine revelation, and has shed abundant light on many points which the pre-critical conception of Hebrew history left obscure or altogether unexplained.

Again, there are those whose dislike or suspicion of the critical movement has led them, as I think, to

---

[1] *Op. cit.* p. 50.

minimize the significance and value of its assured results. The main defect of some books written in defence of traditional theories is that while they endeavour, not without a measure of success, to discredit the results of an extreme, one-sided, and rationalistic criticism, they do not always appear adequately to recognize the importance of those conclusions which the research of 150 years has rendered inevitable, which sober critics of every school practically agree to accept, and which in any case have considerably modified the traditional theory of Hebrew history and religion [1].

My aim is to show that it is possible to regard as conclusive and to welcome with cordiality many verdicts of the 'Higher Criticism,' without necessarily accepting what is merely conjectural and arbitrary.

Once more, there is a class of persons to whom *maxima debetur reverentia*.

It may be asked whether I have seriously considered the probable effect on the simple faith and piety of ordinary Churchmen of statements which question cherished beliefs, and may possibly disturb or endanger faith itself. Certainly I recognize with sincere pain that certain assumptions and statements contained in this book may possibly cause disquiet and alarm to some devout Christians. But it is one of the difficulties of our present transitional position that each step in advance, while it brings relief to many, occasions distress or even scandal to some. We must face the inevitable cost involved in intellectual movement. The duty of a teacher is to weigh the perils of frank utterance against those of continued silence. On the

---

[1] I may mention such typical works as Prof. Robertson's *Early Religion of Israel*, Mr. Baxter's *Sanctuary and Sacrifice*, and Prof. Hommel's *Ancient Hebrew Tradition illustrated by the Monuments*.

one hand, he may know of many—clergy, students, schoolmasters, thoughtful laymen, highly educated women charged with the religious training of children, and others—who are deeply impressed by the solidity and weight of the case for the Higher Criticism of the Old Testament, and who, in view of its apparent results, are eagerly looking for guidance and reassurance. On the other hand, he is bound to consider carefully the danger of wounding or scandalizing those who have little or no opportunity of forming an independent judgment on matters of science or criticism, and who cannot be expected to part with convictions that are indissolubly bound up with their religious experience.

In view of this difficulty, a man is justified in committing himself to the guidance of God, and doing his best at once to aid the perplexed, and to deal tenderly with those whose faith has been hitherto undisturbed. I do not ask any reader to accept without due inquiry the particular conception of Hebrew history which has been adopted in these lectures; but I do desire to show that a Christian believer need not cast away his faith because his traditional view of the Old Testament has been shown to be inadequate or untenable. And if through any want of due reverence, caution, or consideration I have needlessly troubled any devout mind, I can only express my sorrow, and unreservedly submit what I have written to the judgment of the Church.

I must acknowledge a debt of gratitude to friends who have given me the benefit of their counsel and criticism, especially to Dr. Driver, Dr. Moberly, and Dr. Lock. To the governors of the Pusey House who granted me a Term's absence from Oxford, and to my friend Mr. Hutton of St. John's College who allowed me the use of his house at Burford, I am equally indebted. Mr. Rackham of the Community of the Resurrection, who has devoted unsparing pains to the revision and correction of the proof-sheets, has rendered a signal service both to the writer and to the readers of this book.

R. L. O.

WINTERBOURNE BASSETT,
August, 1897.

SYNOPSIS OF CONTENTS

LECTURE I.

THE CHRISTIAN CHURCH AND THE 'HIGHER CRITICISM.'

	PAGE
The Catholic spirit illustrated	1
Subject of the lectures proposed	6
Standpoint from which it is approached	11

I. The belief in the Incarnation 12
    The Incarnation illustrates the divine use of *media*, and the
        divine self-accommodation to human capacities . . . 13
    Analogy of the Incarnation applied to Scripture . . . 15
        (1) The unity of Scripture 15
        (2) Its twofold nature 17
        (3) Its self-witness 20

II. The belief in Inspiration 22
    The action of the Holy Spirit discernible—
        (1) In the formation of Scripture 26
        (2) In the writers themselves 27
    The meaning of Inspiration to be ascertained inductively . 29
    Its peculiar characteristics 30

III. The main results of historical criticism assumed . . . 32
    Summary of these results 33
    Special observations on the higher criticism—
        (1) Historical consistency of its results 36
        (2) Hindrances to their acceptance 40
        (3) The duty of deference to experts 44

IV. Factors determining the true use of the Old Testament—
        (1) The authority of Christ 46
        (2) The spiritual experience of Christians 49
    The doctrine of the Church: its bearing on our inquiry . . 51

LECTURE II.

DIFFERENT ASPECTS OF THE OLD TESTAMENT.

The special function of the Old Testament	53
General survey	55

SYNOPSIS OF CONTENTS

	PAGE
I. The Old Testament a history of redemption	56
The story of the 'origins,' its character and purpose	57
Special features of redemptive history—	
(1) The occurrence of miracle	61
(2) The principle of limitation or severance	63
Character of the historical narratives	65
II. The Old Testament the history of a progressive revelation	66
Different views of the evolution of the idea of God	67
Effects of the exodus	68
The foundations of monotheism	69
Of the idea of holiness	72
Of the idea of grace	75
The continuity of revelation	78
III. The Old Testament traces the history of a covenantal relationship	79
The divine requirement involved in it	81
IV. The Old Testament and the Messianic hope	82
The idea of a kingdom of God or 'theocracy'	84
Its history considered	85
Its characteristics proclaimed by the prophets—	
Universality	86
Spirituality	87
V. The Old Testament witnesses to a divine purpose for the individual	89
Growth of the sense of individuality	90
The teachings of spiritual experience and of national calamity	91
The general arrangement of the Hebrew Bible—	
Its correspondence with the five above-mentioned aspects of Old Testament theology	93

LECTURE III.

THE HISTORICAL ELEMENT IN THE OLD TESTAMENT.

Analogy of Scripture to physical nature	98
The Old Testament an historical book	100
Preliminary considerations—	
(1) Composite character of the narratives	101
(2) Probable results of archaeological research	105
(3) The *a priori* credibility of miracle	107
I. The patriarchal period relatively pre-historic	109
The narratives historical in substance	110
(1) A true picture of the general conditions of patriarchal life	113
(2) And of the main factors in Israel's religious development	115
(3) Element of idealization in the Pentateuch, its extent and characteristics	119
The 'priestly narrative': its character	121
Prophetic idealization in the older narratives	125
Considerations which appear to justify it	128
II. The Mosaic period—	
The work of Moses that of a prophet	131

SYNOPSIS OF CONTENTS

	PAGE
Main features of the Mosaic narratives	133
(1) They regard the exodus as a fundamental fact	134
(2) They aim at exhibiting the character and requirement of God	138
(3) They depict an ideal theocracy	140
(4) Typical significance of the narratives	142
General reflections	144

III. The historical books—
The materials forming their substratum, and their general features 145
Three elements in the prophetic theory of the history—
  (1) The reality of grace 151
  (2) The importance of critical epochs 152
  (3) Method of divine deliverances 154
The action of the Holy Spirit in Israel's history . . . 155
General summary 157

NOTE A. The patriarchal narratives 160

LECTURE IV.

THE PROGRESSIVE SELF-REVELATION OF GOD.

The continuity of revelation 161
I. General features of Hebrew revelation considered as progressive 162
  The method justified in Christ 164
  Illustrations of the tendency of Old Testament religion—
    (*a*) In the sphere of worship 166
      The principle of selection 167
      Circumcision 167
      Sacrifice 168
    (*b*) In the sphere of ethical ideas 170
      The idea of 'holiness' 171
      Mosaism and the Decalogue 172
      The idea of personality 175
      Human sacrifice : Gen. xxii. 176
      The slaughter of the Canaanites 178
II. The 'Name' of God progressively unfolded 181
  General names, '*El*, '*Eloah*, '*Elohim*, '*El 'Elyon* ; their meaning and use 183
  The patriarchal name, '*El Shaddai* 184
  The name *Jahveh* 185
  The titles *Adonai* and *Jahveh Tsebaoth* 186
  The Hebrew conception of revelation 187
  Theological significance of the different titles of deity . . 189
  '*El*, '*Elohim*, '*Eloah*, '*El 'Elyon* 190
  '*El Shaddai* and '*Adonai* 191
  Jehovah (*Jahveh*) 193
  Anthropomorphic language in the Old Testament . . 194
  The attributes of *Jehovah* 195
    (1) 'Righteousness' and 'truth' 198
    (2) 'Kindness' or 'grace'. 199
  The jealousy of *Jehovah* 200

xvi   SYNOPSIS OF CONTENTS

                                                                    PAGE
Jehovah Tsebaoth 203
The 'fatherhood' of God in the Old Testament . . . 204
Conclusion 205

LECTURE V.

THE ANCIENT COVENANT AND ITS WORSHIP.

The covenant between Jehovah and Israel inaugurated at Sinai . 206
I. The idea of the covenant: its history and conditions . . . 209
II. The moral requirement involved in the covenant . . . 213
    The Decalogue: its contents and characteristics . . . 215
        (1) Religion the foundation of personal morality and social
            duty 219
        (2) Absence of directions bearing on worship . . . 220
        (3) Moral symbolism of the Mosaic institutions . . 222
III. The sanctuary and the sacrifices—
    The prophetic idea that underlies them 224
    The description of the tabernacle an idealized sketch . . 226
    The levitical sacrifices 227
        (1) The sacrifices based on pre-existing customs . . 229
        (2) The attitude of the prophets towards sacrifice . . 230
        (3) Was the levitical system ever in actual operation? . 231
        (4) The development of piacular sacrifice 232
            Names and characteristics of the different classes of
              sacrifice 234
              General features common to all 236
              Features distinctive of each 238
IV. Symbolic and typical significance—
    Of the Tabernacle 247
    Of the sacrificial system 250
    Fulfilment of levitical types in Christ—
        The Burnt-offering 253
        The Sin-offering 255
        The Peace-offering 258
    Spirituality of the Law 259

NOTE A. The symbolic significance of the Tabernacle . . . 261

LECTURE VI.

PROPHECY AND THE MESSIANIC HOPE.

The use of the phrase 'The Law and the Prophets' . . . 265
Prophecy, the distinctive element in Hebrew religion . . . 269
I. The beginnings of prophetism—
    An institution common to the Semitic tribes 270
    The work of Samuel 272
    Elijah 273

SYNOPSIS OF CONTENTS

	PAGE
II. The prophets: aspects of their work—	
(1) Prophetic inspiration: its character. The name *Nabhi*	274
(2) The sphere in which the gift of prophecy was exercised	277
Function of the prophets	279
Social and political conditions of the eighth century	281
Social influence of the prophets	283
Their work that of proclaiming judgment	285
(3) The religious influence of the prophets	286
The prophets in relation to monotheism and universalism	287
The teaching of Amos: Jehovah the moral ruler of the universe	288
Hosea: the prophet of divine love	290
Two permanent elements in the prophetic conception of God	292
Teaching of the book of Jonah	293
III. The Messianic hope: its gradual growth	295
(1) The promise of spiritual victory—	
The *Protevangelium*	296
The 'Blessing of Jacob'	297
The prophecy in Deut. xviii. 15	298
(2) The hopes connected with David's house	299
The oracle in 2 Sam. vii.	300
'Figurative prophecy'	301
The Hebrew idea of royalty	302
Limitations of prophecy	306
(3) The self-manifestation of Jehovah—	
'The day of the Lord'	304
A day of judgment and of salvation	305
(4) The suffering people of God	308
Effects of calamity on the Messianic hope	309
'The servant of Jehovah'	310
(5) The new covenant	312
Teaching of Jeremiah and Ezekiel	313
(6) The post-exilic prophets	314
The apocalyptic literature	316
Ideal fulfilment of prophecy in Christ	318

LECTURE VII.

PERSONAL RELIGION IN THE OLD TESTAMENT.

Tendencies of the post-exilic age foreshadowed at an earlier period	323
Circumstances which gave an impulse to the development of personal religion	324
The post-exilic age spiritually fruitful	328
The *Hagiographa*: their character and contents	329
The foundation truths of personal religion—	
I. The idea of a future life	334
(1) The Law witnesses to the truth of man's personal relation to God	336
Hebrew conception of death	337
The dignity of human nature recognized	338

SYNOPSIS OF CONTENTS

	PAGE
(2) The anomalies of life and divine retribution	343
Doctrine of the Law	343
The 'era of difficulties': the book of Job	346
The 'era of quiescence': Ecclesiastes	348
II. The idea of a personal providence: the Psalms	350
Witness of other books: Cantica, Ruth, Esther, Daniel, Chronicles, Ezra, Nehemiah	355
III. The sense of the fruitfulness of suffering	359
Characteristics of the 'Wisdom literature'	359
The book of Job	361
The book of Ecclesiastes	364
Summary and conclusion	370

LECTURE VIII.

THE OLD TESTAMENT AND CHRISTIANITY.

The analogy between the incarnate Word and Scripture	373
I. The New Testament view of the Old—	
(1) The Old Testament revelation fragmentary	377
(2) Variety of methods in which God manifested Himself	378
(3) Rudimentary character of the old dispensation	379
The New Testament verdict on the Law	380
Unique authority of the Old Testament asserted by Christ	381
For Him there was 'a Bible within the Bible'	382
Principles observed by New Testament writers in their employment of the Old	383
Existing methods of interpretation: *Halachah, Haggadah,* and *Sodh*	384
Our Lord's employment of these methods	385
The New Testament exegesis of the Old—	
(i) Its breadth and freedom	389
Apostolic use of *Haggadah* and *Halachah*	390
Allegorism	392
(ii) Moral purport of the quotations	393
Contrast between Christ and the Scribes and Pharisees	394
(iii) Messianic use of the Old Testament	396
Summary	400
II. The permanent function of the Old Testament in the Church	401
Preliminary questions—	
The historical quality of the Old Testament narratives	401
The existence of a 'secondary' sense	405
(1) The sacramental view of the universe	406
(2) The organic relation between Judaism and Christianity	408
1. The Old Testament, a revelation of God's nature and character	412
The aim of God's moral government considered	413
Its methods and laws of action	414
The place of suffering	415
2. The Old Testament as witnessing to Christ	416
Its Messianic import	417
What is ideal is Messianic	419

SYNOPSIS OF CONTENTS xix

	PAGE
3. Function of the Old Testament in forming and training character	421
The 'morality of the Old Testament'—	
Theocentric	423
And altruistic	424
4. The Old Testament as a manual for the spiritual life	426
5. The Old Testament as an instructor in social righteousness	430
Social doctrine of the Old Testament—	
Not based on individualism	431
Recognizing moral forces in social progress	432
6. The Old Testament as an aid in New Testament exegesis	433
Summary of the lectures	436
Concluding reflections—	
The duty of individual Christians	437
Place of Scripture in the system of the Church	440

ASPECTS OF THE OLD TESTAMENT

LECTURE I

All things are yours.—1 Cor. iii. 21.

THERE are few terms the precise significance of which it is more difficult to fix than the word 'catholic.' As applied to the Christian Church it connotes primarily her world-wide extension. *The holy Church throughout all the world doth acknowledge Thee.* To the idea of extension the idea of doctrine is added. The Church is 'catholic' inasmuch as she is the teacher of all truth needful for man in the conduct and development of his spiritual and moral life; she is the home of all graces and virtues, and the school in which every variety of human character may find its appropriate discipline [1]. But there is another sense in which the Church of Jesus Christ is a 'catholic' society: to her most loyal children she is the imparter of spiritual breadth, she fosters a true catholicity of heart and temper. Faithfulness to the mind of the Church and submission to her discipline has sometimes been supposed, and with a show of justice, to involve hostility to the advancement of learning, cramped and petty views of things, and a one-sided estimate of human nature. And yet if the Church of God be the abiding-place of that Holy Spirit whose presence brings liberty, and the home of that charity which *rejoiceth with the truth* [2],

---
[1] Cyr. Hier. *Catech.* xviii. 23. Cp. Lightfoot on Ignat. *ad Smyrn.* viii.
[2] 2 Cor. iii. 17; 1 Cor. xiii. 6.

a faithful son of the Church will have a just sense of the infinitude and many-sidedness of truth. He will cultivate in himself the spirit of candour, and width of intellectual sympathy. He will be keenly alive to the strength of an opponent's case[1]. He will discriminate carefully between what is essential and what non-essential in the cause he defends. And here probably his difficulties will begin. Indeed every thoughtful Christian has sooner or later to face a practical problem, upon the right solution of which the advancement of truth depends. He has to combine the temper of restfulness with that of mobility, the stedfastness of a soldier with the detachment of a pilgrim. While he is the faithful and self-forgetful guardian of a precious heritage transmitted from the past, a heritage of belief and usage which necessarily moulds his thought and shapes his conduct; while he cherishes all those heavenly gifts which *pertain unto life and godliness*[2], he will yet be penetrated by the thought so simply and comprehensively expressed in the words, *All things are yours*. A Christian teacher or student will adhere jealously to the inherited rule of revealed truth, the immemorial tradition of the faith, and yet his utterances will be so far reserved, fragmentary, and incomplete as they correspond to the infinite *mystery of godliness*[3]. There was in Jesus Christ, *the Word of Life*, that which men could see with their eyes and handle with their hands[4]; but there was also more than they could fathom with the intellect or express in forms supplied by human speech. In the presence of His unveiled glory they were as men who stammered, *not knowing what* they *said*[5]. Accordingly in the earliest ages of Christianity at least, there was seldom absent from the minds of great teachers of

---

[1] Chrys. *Hom. in ep. ad Phil.* 246 C, D ῾Η γὰρ λαμπρὰ νίκη καὶ ἐκ περιουσίας γινομένη αὕτη ἐστίν, ὅταν τὰ δοκοῦντα αὐτῶν ἰσχυρὰ εἶναι μὴ ἀποκρύπτωμεν· τοῦτο γὰρ ἀπάτη ἐστὶ μᾶλλον ἢ νίκη.
[2] 2 Pet. i. 3. [3] 1 Tim. iii. 16.
[4] 1 John i. 1. [5] Luke ix. 33.

the Church a deep consciousness of insufficiency. In them, reverence was ever, so far as might be compatible with fidelity to truth, reserved and slow of speech. Even their most confident dogmatic statements were, so to speak, forced from them by the 'obstinate questionings,' whether of devout faith or of self-willed perversity, and they were advanced with manifold apologies and qualifying cautions[1]. It has often been remarked how unsystematic are many of the utterances of the early fathers; they felt themselves to be moving 'in worlds not realized'; they had presages rather than clear intuitions of the largeness and splendour of the divine revelation vouchsafed to man in Jesus Christ. This circumstance explains the grandeur, and yet the vagueness, of some occasional statements made by such a writer as Irenaeus. He knew that the Spirit of the living God had entered into the visible universe in order to possess, appropriate, and hallow it. The vision of God Himself was the true life of man[2], and human nature was already the receptacle of the grace and glory of God. Already man was a son of God, but it did not yet appear what he should be[3]. Only it was certain that man's destiny was a continual assimilation to his Creator. Irenaeus clung tenaciously to the deposit of faith, but he felt that only the progressive unfolding of the divine purpose for humanity would adequately interpret the full content of the rule of truth. In our day, when knowledge widens its range with such bewildering rapidity, we too have to discharge a twofold obligation. We are bound to guard the faith committed to us in its integrity, but with due

---

[1] See for instance Hilary's language in *de Trin.* ii. 2: 'Compellimur haereticorum et blasphemantium vitiis, illicita agere, ardua scandere, ineffabilia eloqui, inconcessa praesumere. Et cum sola fide expleri quae praecepta sunt oporteret, adorare scilicet Patrem et venerari cum eo Filium, Sancto Spiritu abundare; cogimur sermonis nostri humilitatem ad ea quae inenarrabilia sunt extendere, et in vitium vitio coartamur alieno: ut quae contineri religione mentium oportuissent, nunc in periculum humani eloquii proferantur.'

[2] Iren. *Haer.* iv. 20, 7: 'Vita hominis visio Dei.'

[3] Cp. 1 John iii. 2.

carefulness to discriminate between what is and what is not of faith; on the other hand we have to bear constantly in mind that to us Christians nothing achieved or discovered by human faculties is without its bearing on the Christian revelation; all things are ours in so far as they throw light on the destiny of man, on the ways of the eternal God, on the methods and conditions of His self-manifestation. We cannot divest ourselves of responsibility for the use of our judgment in bringing all things to the test of Christian reason and experience. *He that is spiritual judgeth all things, yet he himself is judged of no man. For who hath known the mind of the Lord that he may instruct him? But we have the mind of Christ*[1]. With the creed of the Catholic Church in his hands, a thoughtful Christian may look round upon the universe of things with eyes that penetrate deeper than the surface of life. The world may present to him a confused and bewildering spectacle, like that which Wordsworth studied so observantly in the London of his day:

> 'But though the picture weary out the eye,
> By nature an unmanageable sight,
> It is not wholly so to him who looks
> In steadiness; who hath among least things
> An under sense of greatest; sees the parts
> As parts, but with a feeling of the whole[2].'

The Christian knows that in his hands he holds the clue to this tangled maze; *the kingdoms of this world* are on the way to *become the kingdoms of our Lord and of his Christ*[3]. Thus the Christian slowly and gradually comes to recognize the inexhaustible significance of his creed. He finds in the Catholic Faith, 'loved deeplier, darklier understood,' that which will best minister to the intellectual and moral wants of the age in which he lives. To be truly catholic, in a word, is to be large-hearted; to be no mere votary of the past, but a student of the present; not a servile adherent of the creed, but a wise and sympathetic

---

[1] 1 Cor. ii. 15, 16. [2] *The Prelude*, bk. vii. [3] Rev. xi. 15.

intérpreter of it to living men. We Christians should set before us the task of endeavouring to understand our own age, its needs, its perils, its possibilities. We should ever look upward for light to see what knowledge, what aspect of truth, is most serviceable and necessary for the days in which we live. And cónversely each new development in human life or social organization, each gift of civilization, each discovery of science, each achievement of human toil, energy, and skill, each true *partus temporis*, will be of vital interest in so far as it interprets to us more luminously the clauses of our creed and the ways of divine wisdom; in so far as it gives us a truer sense of proportion and a larger insight into the things of faith.

Of this catholic heart, this spiritual versatility, the most conspicuous example is to be found in the writer of the Epistles to the Corinthians himself, whose vocation it was to preach to the world the mystery of a catholic Church. The great charter indeed of the Church's catholicity is contained not in the present passage, but rather in others which lie behind it: *All things are delivered unto me of my Father*[1]. *All power is given unto me in heaven and in earth*[2]. This truth of the Church's lordship in Jesus Christ is one which we are sometimes apt to overlook; this it is of which the Corinthians especially are reminded in the text. Accordingly St. Paul sets down what has been called 'an inventory of the possessions of the child of God': *All things are yours; whether Paul, or Apollos, or Cephas, or the world, or life, or death, or things present, or things to come; all are yours.* The Corinthians were absorbed in the disputes of the hour—disputes which turned largely upon personal preferences for this or that individual teacher in the Christian community. They were glorying, as St. Paul with a significant allusion to prophecy points out[3], not in God the Creator of the Church, but in men

---

[1] Matt. xi. 27; Luke x. 22.   [2] Matt. xxviii. 18.
[3] 1 Cor. i. 31. Cp. Jer. ix. 23, 24.

who at best were mere instruments of His providential purpose. To the Apostle, this blindness to the due proportion of things appeared disastrous and even intolerable. The Corinthians, he says in effect, are forgetting altogether the transcendent dignity of their Christian vocation, the ideal splendour of their privileges as saints. Not merely *one* scattered ray of the eternal light conveyed through one limited medium is theirs, but each 'bright beam of light' that God through His Apostles 'casts upon His Church.' Each teacher is a divine gift to the Church. St. Paul even manifests in his rapid transition from teachers, Paul, Apollos and Cephas, to *the world, or life, or death, or things present, or things to come,* a kind of noble impatience with the pettiness which is absorbed in discussing individual claims, and types of doctrine, instead of rising to the full recognition of sublime spiritual prerogatives. 'All things,' he seems to say, 'are yours; all are intended to minister to your spiritual growth; you are inheritors of the world, destined to be its judges, called to use for the highest ends its products, gifts, and opportunities. Angels minister to you as heirs of salvation; all things work together for your good. You are *heirs of God and joint heirs with Christ. He that spared not his own Son, but delivered him up for us all, how shall he not with him also freely give us all things*[1]?'

In the lectures which I am allowed to deliver here I propose to consider very simply and practically the present function of the Old Testament Scriptures in the Christian Church. Such an attempt, which is obviously beset with grave difficulty, is dictated by considerations which it may be well to indicate as briefly as possible. In the first place, a Christian teacher cannot fail to be seriously concerned at the

---

[1] Rom. viii. 32; cp. Rom. iv. 13, viii. 28; 1 Cor. vi. 2, vii. 31; Heb. i. 2, 14; and Firmil. *ad Cyp.* [*Epp. Cyp.* lxxv.] c. 4: 'Quoniam sermo divinus humanam naturam supergreditur, nec potest totum et perfectum anima concipere; idcirco et tantus est numerus prophetarum, ut multiplex divina sapientia per multos distribuatur.'

practical disuse into which for many ordinary Christians the Old Testament has fallen—a disuse which, whatever be its causes, must tend to impoverish the spiritual life of the Church [1]; and secondly, any one who is in contact with thoughtful persons younger than himself, or who is called to minister to the spiritual perplexities of devout Christians, is well aware that the real and apparent results of the 'Higher Criticism' have raised questions, a provisional answer to which cannot be indefinitely deferred without a certain breach of trust. In Germany many attempts have been made during the last few years to define anew the position of the Old Testament, and to bring the claims of Lutheran orthodoxy into harmony with those of historical inquiry. In England, however, the task of reconciliation has scarcely yet been attempted. Its peculiar delicacy lies in the fact, amply proved by experience, that while many are asking for guidance, many on the other hand are unwilling or unqualified to investigate the claims of criticism, or even to give a hearing to that which is believed in a vague and undefined way to threaten the foundations of Christian faith. A somewhat unintelligent conception of the Scriptures, and of their true place in the system of the Church, has also much to answer for. The result is that an attempt to guide and reassure troubled faith is beset with difficulties. The Christian apologist himself is suspected or even denounced; what he concedes appears to some to involve a virtual betrayal of essential truth; what he defends or maintains is thought by others to be an untenable remnant of exploded error. There seems indeed to be no subject in regard to which prejudice is more slowly dispelled,

[1] Some causes are discussed by Prof. Kirkpatrick in *The Divine Library of the Old Testament*, pp. 117 foll. Mr. J. Paterson Smyth in his useful work *How God inspired the Bible*, p. 15, quotes a typical letter from a young student in which the following sentences occur. 'There are hundreds ... like me, who do not want to lose our grasp of the Bible, but we can no longer view it as we have been taught to do. If there is any way by which we can still hold it and treasure it, do our teachers know it? and if they do, why do they not tell us?'

and passion more vehemently excited, than that which is to be considered in these lectures. The most necessary qualification for dealing with it is a certain tenderness of sympathy with those who are harassed by the breaking in upon them of new modes of thought and new collections of facts. A teacher must have realized in his own experience at least some of the pains of mental growth and the difficulties of self-adjustment to the claims of truth as it is progressively manifested [1]. We must not be surprised that mental versatility is a rare endowment, and that in the case of Holy Scripture the conflict is not merely between new knowledge and a traditional view, but between new knowledge and deeply-rooted spiritual experience. The real nature of the distress that agitates so many ordinary Christians at the present time is amply recognized by reverent criticism. 'It would argue,' writes the late Prof. Robertson Smith, 'indifference rather than enlightenment, if the great mass of Bible readers, to whom scientific points of view are wholly unfamiliar, could adjust themselves to a new line of investigation into the history of the Bible without passing through a crisis of anxious thought not far removed from distress and alarm [2].' Sympathy then with troubled faith should in any case guide the attempt to bring succour and relief to perplexed thought.

One ground of reassurance is to be found in a true apprehension of the exact conditions of modern inquiry. The battle, it has been well said, is not between rationalism and faith, but between true criticism and false [3]. Historical and literary criticism is to be regarded not as a foe to be held at bay, but as a good gift of God to our generation.

---

[1] Bernard, *in Cant.* xxxix. 3, makes a striking observation: 'Benignus est Spiritus sapientiae, et placet illi doctor benignus et diligens, qui ita cupiat satisfacere studiosis, ut morem gerere tardioribus non recuset.'
[2] *The Old Testament in the Jewish Church*, p. 1.
[3] Cp. Briggs, *Biblical Study, its Principles, Methods, and History*, p. 104.

It will be our duty presently to indicate at least in rough outline the considerations which appear to justify a cautious and provisional acceptance of at least the main results of modern critical investigation. Meanwhile let it suffice to remark that the traditional view of the Old Testament religion has in any case been profoundly modified, first, by the idea of historical development, which has given intrinsic reasonableness to the supposition that the Hebrew religion passed very gradually from a quite rudimentary stage to that of maturity; secondly, by the discovery or employment of facts and sources by which the results of literary criticism have been supplemented or confirmed. It is scarcely too much to assert that the century now verging to its close has witnessed the birth of a series of new sciences, if the title is strictly applicable to those fruitful departments of knowledge usually included under such names as 'Assyriology,' 'Egyptology,' and the like. The discovery of Phoenician inscriptions, systematic inquiry into the usages of early religions, the scrutiny of materials supplied by the mounds of Babylon, Egypt, Nineveh and Palestine —these have yielded a mass of data which have practically changed the conditions of Old Testament criticism [1]. It is often imagined that because many problems are apparently insoluble and many details are confessedly obscure or uncertain, the traditional view of the Old Testament remains virtually unaffected. But it is important to bear in mind that, even when all crude speculations and fantastic theories are excluded from view, there remains a mass of ascertained facts which the mere dislike of trouble may incline men to ignore, yet which deserve the most patient and painstaking attention of all educated Christians. In a famous sermon the late Archbishop Magee once pointed out the demoralizing effect of

---

[1] See J. Darmesteter, *Les Prophètes d'Israël*, pp. 158 foll. Cp. Renan, *Histoire du peuple d'Israël*, pref. p. xxiv [Eng. Tr.].

distorted or exaggerated preconceptions as to the nature of Scripture. The Church, he said, has too often 'attempted to evade the pressure' of criticism, 'by wire-drawn explanations, far-fetched harmonizings, ingenious hypotheses which do more credit to the ability than to the candour of those who have resorted to them[1].' We have surely been taught by the experience of the past that for a child of God candour is the first of duties, and the question has now forced itself to the front, whether or no something more is needed than *doubtful disputations* on points of detail; whether or no the present state of knowledge demands a reconstruction of our ideas respecting the mode of God's self-revelation in the sacred history. At the same time let us remember that the demand made upon our faith and courage is not a new thing. We are now facing, as the Hebrew Christians were called to face, 'the trials of a new age[2].' It has been pointed out that in their case the trials were such as sprang 'in a great degree from mistaken devoutness.' Those who live in an age like ours likewise need, it is true, *a word of consolation*[3]. New ideas, new phases of thought, new aspects of old problems, press upon us; ancient modes of statement seem sometimes to have become void of meaning; paths trodden by the feet of many generations seem to be outworn:

> ἅπανθ' ὁ μακρὸς κἀναρίθμητος χρόνος
> φύει τ' ἄδηλα καὶ φανέντα κρύπτεται·
> κοὐκ ἔστ' ἄελπτον οὐδέν[4].

But faith finds her solace in the history of the Church. She has the experience of nineteen centuries to support her, and to give her the assurance that God has been with His people all along, is with them now, and

---

[1] *The Gospel and the Age*, p. 322. Cp. the impressive words of Delitzsch, *New Commentary on Genesis*, vol. i. pp. 54 foll.: 'The love of truth, submission to the force of truth, the surrender of traditional views which will not stand the test of truth, is a sacred duty, an element of the fear of God.'
[2] Cp. Westcott, *Christus Consummator*, ch. i.
[3] Heb. xiii. 22. [4] Soph. *Ajax*, 646 foll.

will lead them even to the end. Scripture itself is the record of the struggles and conflicts through which human faith has long since triumphantly passed; it bears witness to a divine truth which has never failed, and a love which has never abandoned its purpose. Thus encouraged faith may calmly confront new problems, neither minimizing their importance nor exaggerating their difficulty. This at any rate is the temper in which our subject is to be approached. Our aim is to consider in a constructive and practical spirit some fundamental aspects of the Old Testament, regarded as a divine message to mankind for all time.

It has appeared after careful consideration, that the object in view might be most satisfactorily attained, not by attempting to reconstruct the history of Israel —a task which Mr. Montefiore has with striking ability achieved in his *Hibbert Lectures* — but by approaching the subject from the point of view of Old Testament theology. If we wish to reassure persons who suppose that Christianity itself is endangered by the results of Old Testament criticism, we shall find it advisable to start from the great religious thoughts and verities which Christianity has inherited from the Jewish Church and to look at them afresh in the light of modern research. It is not indeed as mere inquirers or searchers after truth that we approach the Old Testament, but rather as men of faith eagerly desiring to understand more intelligently the ways of One who has already made Himself known to us in Christ and who requires of men *truth in the inward parts*. We have to use our faculties honestly as in His sight. For St. Paul, as we have noticed, claims for Christians the judicial office; he implies that it is the function of Christian reason to pass judgment on the phenomena of human life and the products of human wisdom or skill. But Christian reason is synonymous with *the mind of Christ*[1]. The fixed standpoint from which a Christian

---
[1] 1 Cor. ii. 16.

approaches the consideration of all problems, ethical, social, or intellectual, is that of belief in the person of Him who by the presence of His Spirit inhabits and enlightens the Church. A true estimate of the Old Testament, its character, purpose, and teaching, is only possible on the basis of faith in Jesus Christ, the Son of God made man.

I.

First of all, then, we approach the Old Testament as believers in the Incarnation of the Son of God: that unique revelation of the glory and love of the Father, which lies at the root of all our Christian life and experience. *We know that the Son of God is come, and hath given us an understanding that we may know him that is true, and we are in him that is true, even in his Son Jesus Christ*[1]. In comparison with this fact all that foreshadowed it in the world's history, or in the literature which enshrined the expectation of good things to come, is of secondary importance and interest. *We know that the Son of God is come.* In their assurance of this divine gift, Christians can bear with much uncertainty and perplexity in regard to problems which lie on the fringe of God's self-revelation. But something is to be gained from a closer survey of the Incarnation in relation to the task which at present engages our attention, for it is a fact which necessarily illustrates the divine method of dealing with mankind. For example, the Incarnation is the perfect consecration of nature. It is the crowning example of the employment by God of *media*, of the appropriation of things visible and material as organs and vehicles of divine gifts to mankind. In the Incarnation, Almighty God reveals Himself as a being who wills to take things common and make them instruments of grace

[1] 1 John v. 20.

and power; to consecrate human nature, and elevate it into fellowship with the divine life; to convey spiritual blessings to the world through the mediation of human service and human suffering. Again, the Incarnation reveals to us a love which addresses itself to the actual conditions, and accommodates itself to the present needs, of mankind. 'Accommodation,' it has been said, 'is an essential principle in the method of a revelation of grace[1]'; and on a broad scale we are familiar enough with the exhibition of this principle in Hebrew history. In the election and education of a peculiar people, God is seen taking man as He finds him to make him what as yet he is not, adapting Himself to the existing capacities of a backward and untutored race. That this is the true inner secret of the Old Testament history we are assured when we study the life and work of the incarnate Son. If Jesus Christ were merely the last and most eminent of a line of prophets, there would be more to be said for that familiar type of criticism which represents Israel's religious development as a purely natural phenomenon, having its starting-point and controlling principle not in any intervention or guidance of a gracious and loving God, not in any supernatural revelation imparted to elect souls at different epochs in Israel's history, but in fetichism, or totemism, or polytheism, whence by a slow process of purely natural evolution it passed to its final stage in ethical monotheism[2]. Here we touch one of the distinctive features of Israel's religion, which separates it sharply from other contemporary religions of antiquity, namely, that it is a religion of revelation, whereas they are products of the ordinary development of man's religious and moral faculties[3].

The Incarnation, then, sets a seal of confirmation

---

[1] A. B. Bruce, *The Chief End of Revelation*, p. 113.
[2] Cp. Köhler, *Über Berechtigung der Kritik des A. T.* p. 66.
[3] Riehm, *Alttestamentliche Theologie*, § 4, pp. 26, 27.

to the general principle which was really at work in Israel's religious history; it reveals the secret of its upward tendency, namely, the condescending love and patience of God. And to that condescension who shall venture to prescribe limitations, considering what we now know of the depth to which divine love will stoop in order to win man from his sin and lead him to holiness? In the light of God's actual dealings with the world in the gift of His Son, we can appreciate better all that recent research has taught us respecting the close affinity between Israel's early faith and practice, and that of its heathen neighbours and kinsfolk. It no longer startles us to find the divine wisdom adopting, regulating, and consecrating to higher uses traditional customs or practices common to the entire Semitic race, in order to employ them as elements in a system of rudimentary instruction and of graduated moral discipline. We cannot be surprised even to find that very low and inadequate conceptions of the Godhead are accepted as the necessary basis of higher and more spiritual ideas. Indeed, not to enlarge upon so familiar a theme, it is enough to recall the saying of Wellhausen, that the religion of the Old Testament 'did not so much make men partakers in a divine life, as make God a partaker in the life of men [1].' If God really was, as we believe, preparing the world for such an event as the tabernacling of God with men, we have no occasion for wonder that He should, through long centuries of education, have accommodated Himself to what was partial, rude, and imperfect, while ever aiming at that which was perfect.

'God a partaker in the life of men.' Let us pause to consider the significance of this expression in its application to our subject. Does it not suggest that the divine action will inevitably transcend the range

---

[1] *Sketch of the History of Israel and Judah*, p. 17. The first volume of Renan's *Histoire du peuple d'Israël* is a striking illustration of this thesis, in spite of much in its pages that seems arbitrary, prejudiced, and fantastic.

of our experience, and possibly contradict the first suggestions, though not the ultimate conclusions, of reason itself? If the love of God be love indeed, it will not be deterred from self-manifestation. It will break down barriers. It will adapt itself to the actual situation. It will use the available material, the instruments ready to hand. There will be no limit to the range of divine condescension, except that imposed by the law of perfect holiness.

> 'What lacks then of perfection fit for God
> But just the instance which the tale supplies
> Of love without a limit? So is strength,
> So is intelligence; let love be so,
> Unlimited in its self-sacrifice,
> Then is the tale true and God shows complete.'

And, indeed, such a fact as the Incarnation, a mystery of which St. Paul and St. John have taught us the cosmic significance, inevitably suggests that in all departments of its operation, the love of God will exhibit a certain uniformity of method. Hence, we are only reasoning as serious Christians must necessarily reason, when we apply to the questions involved in the present day study of the Old Testament principles suggested by the acknowledged fact of the Incarnation. Let us follow out this line of thought somewhat in detail.

1. First let us bear in mind that in the Bible the Word of God comes to us[1], and addresses us as beings capable of moral response. The Bible appeals to us as an inspired book, a divine product. It is one as the person of Christ is one. Whatever conclusions may be ultimately ascertained as to its structure and the mode of its formation, it presents itself to us as a whole, possessed of a certain unmis-

---

[1] We must not without caution *identify* the 'Word of God' with 'Scripture.' Such an identification is not biblical and is open to serious objections. 'In the Old Testament the term *Word of God* is applied chiefly to particular declarations of the purposes or promises of God, especially to those made by the prophets; in the New Testament it denotes commonly the gospel message.' (Driver, *Sermons on Old Testament Subjects*, pp. 158, 159.)

takeable unity of function[1]. Like the human eye, or the trained conscience of a human being, the Bible is an organism respecting which we may reasonably think that we can in some degree trace the stages of its growth and development. And just as the question of the manner in which an organism or faculty is developed is entirely distinct from the question of its true function and capacities when in a developed state[2], so in the case of Scripture, the question of the nature and use of the complete organism, the product viewed in its entirety, is one, comparatively speaking, unaffected by inquiries relating to its structure and formation. The mystery with which we are face to face in Scripture is that of a message or word from God, a divine book, which, as a matter of age-long experience, has actually produced in every period which has followed its completion spiritual results of infinite magnitude and importance. It is the total product, the complete work, which fulfils such vast and varied functions in the spiritual history of mankind[3]. Questions in regard to the mode of its formation are secondary. When the different oral accounts of Christ's life were first committed to writing, there can be little doubt that the earliest narrative was that which recorded His public acts and utterances during the

---

[1] An ancient expositor of the Psalms, Didymus of Alexandria, compares Scripture to the seamless robe of Christ : οὐ γὰρ βεβιασμένην ἕνωσιν, ἀλλὰ συμφυῆ ἔχει· ἔστιν δὲ καὶ ἄνωθεν διὰ τὸ θεόπνευστος εἶναι· ὑφαντὸς δι' ὅλου, διὰ πάσης γὰρ δυνάμεως ἡ γραφὴ ἄνωθέν ἐστιν (*in Psalm.* xxi. 19).

[2] Cp. Wace, *Boyle Lectures*, ser. i. p. 18.

[3] Cp. Sanday, *Bampton Lectures*, p. 402 : 'If we take a wider range, and look at the diversified products of this individual inspiration, and see how they combine together, so as to be no longer detached units but articulated members in a connected and coherent scheme, we must needs feel that there is something more than the individual minds at work ; they are subsumed, as it were, in the operation of a larger Mind, that central Intelligence which directs and gives unity of purpose to the scattered movements and driftings of men.' Dalman, *Das A. T. ein Wort Gottes*, p. 10, observes that for our Lord and the New Testament writers, 'im Grunde liegt der Nachdruck nicht auf der Weise der Entstehung der biblischen Bücher, sondern auf dem Resultat des litterarischen Processes dem sie entstammen.'

period of His sacred ministry; the mystery of His birth was one in which the Church was keenly interested, but for an answer to her questionings she could, it would seem, afford to wait. The point of primary importance to the earliest believers was not whence our Lord came, but what He *was*, what He *did*, what He claimed of man when He actually appeared. By analogy we may regard the Bible as a book in which the continuous spiritual experience of mankind has recognized the very presence of the Word of God: the declaration of His whole mind and will concerning His creatures, the unveiling of His character and of His everlasting purpose of grace[1]. Here is something which historical and critical study cannot impair. A leading critic of the Old Testament has used words which admirably express the result of Christian experience on this point. 'Of this I am sure . . . that the Bible does speak to the heart of man in words that can only come from God—that no historical research can deprive me of this conviction or make less precious the divine utterances that speak straight to the heart. For the language of these words is so clear that no re-adjustment of their historical setting can conceivably change the substance of them. Historical study may throw a new light on the circumstances in which they were first heard or written. In that there can only be gain. But the plain, central, heartfelt truths, that speak for themselves and rest on their own indefensible worth, will assuredly remain to us[2].'

2. This point which we have barely touched upon here will be recalled at the close of the present lecture. Meanwhile we pass on to consider some further teachings suggested by the fruitful analogy of the Incarnation. We have seen that it illustrates

---

[1] Cp. Iren. *Haer*. iv. 5. 1 : ' Quoniam impossibile erat sine Deo discere Deum, per verbum suum docet homines scire Deum.'
[2] Robertson Smith, *O. T. in J. C.* lect. i. p. 19. The whole of this admirable lecture is worthy of careful study.

C

the divine unity of Scripture as fulfilling a special function in the spiritual history of mankind. But the same analogy reminds us of a duality of natures [1]. As Christ was at once divine and human, so Scripture is found to have a twofold aspect. We shall be prepared to recognize frankly that on one side it is perfectly human, when we remember that about the incarnate Son when He appeared on earth all was simple, plain, natural, common. He was *found in fashion as a man.* The great trial indeed for our Lord's contemporaries —the trial under which average Jewish faith actually broke down—was the simplicity and the plainness of His outward appearance. *Is not this*, they said, *the carpenter, the son of Mary, the brother of James and Joses, and of Juda and Simon? and are not his sisters here with us? And they were offended at him* [2]. Now similarly Scripture is found to have a literary history, exceptional indeed in certain respects, but by no means entirely mysterious or inexplicable. In proportion as critical science advances, we recognize that in its letter, in its *prima facie* appearance, Scripture is, if I may so say, more human, more ordinary. It displays to a certain extent the same traces of human workmanship, human compilation, even human limitation and fallibility, as are discoverable in other products of oriental literature. The Pentateuch for example, or at least a considerable portion of it, proves to be a collection of fragments gathered together no one can certainly say how, when, or by whom. If we take a more general survey of the Old Testament, we find that, in spite of the impressive unity of purpose which pervades the whole, there is a remarkable diversity in the types of literary production incorporated in it. All species of composition known to the ancient Hebrews would seem to have been utilized, in so far as they

---

[1] This thought is worked out with admirable skill in Abp. Magee's sermon on 'The Bible human and yet divine.' See *The Gospel and the Age*, pp. 311 foll.
[2] Mark vi. 3.

were capable of becoming adequate vehicles of spiritual teaching. We have in fact to deal with a library in the Old Testament—a library containing history, poetry, proverbs, philosophical discussions, annals, genealogies, semi-historical folk-lore, and primitive myths. It is evidently a literature which, as Ewald has remarked, has shaped itself just as freely as that of all other ancient nations. It is distinguished by an extraordinary simplicity, vigour, and naturalness— a simplicity which is owing not to any deficiency of refinement or culture in the periods which produced the several books, but to 'the dominant power of a true religion[1],' or rather to the continuous and controlling guidance of the self-revealing Spirit of God.

There is then admittedly a human side to Scripture, and the condescension which we witness in the Incarnation of the Son of God prepares us to find that in the Old Testament God has left to the human instruments of His will more than we had once supposed[2]. He has employed different types of mind and character to execute or advance His purposes. In the recording of His acts and words He has sanctioned the employment of literary methods which in a higher stage of culture might be judged inappropriate. He has consecrated individual peculiarities or special intellectual endowments to ends of His own. The result is that to the critical eye Scripture wears an ordinary and occasionally even humble exterior; it is not free from such incidental defects, limitations, and errors, as are incident to all human composition; but under this lowly form is concealed a special divine presence[3]. Here, as in the Incarnation, may be discerned the self-unveil-

---

[1] H. Ewald, *Revelation, its Nature and Record* (Eng. Tr., T. & T. Clark), p. 320.
[2] See Sanday, *The Oracles of God*, serm. ii.
[3] Jukes, *The Types of Genesis*, p. xvi, 'Christ the incarnate Word of God seems to me, not an illustration only, but a proof, both of the preciousness of the letter, and of the deeper spirit which everywhere underlies the letter throughout the word of God.' The same point underlies Origen's distinction between the 'flesh' and 'spirit' of Scripture (*de Princ.* iv. 11 and 14).

ing of a divine Spirit, the operation of divine power, the appeal of divine love. These I repeat are great realities of the spiritual world, which have been put to the test by a thousand generations of Christians. Their experience has shown that the highest office of Scripture is one that transcends the range and sphere of critical investigation. The appeal of the Spirit who speaks in Scripture is to man's spirit; the appeal of power is to man's sense of need; the appeal of love is to the faculties of man's heart and will.

3. For there is one further point in this fruitful analogy which may be profitably mentioned. We may consider the importance of the self-witness of Scripture. On the one hand, like our Lord's human body, the Bible is a thing *in rerum natura*, a book among books; on the other, its self-witness challenges us to acknowledge a higher claim; it speaks as having authority; it claims to be something more than a mere human compilation. Just as Jesus Christ arrested the attention of men, drew them to Himself by the exercise of an incomparable moral authority, and put forward superhuman claims to their allegiance, so Scripture appears to challenge inquiry and to claim authority in virtue of its direct bearing on conduct and character, its continual appeal to faith and its express testimony to the divine purpose for humanity. A book that touches human life at every point cannot be of merely human origin. It bears the impress of a controlling mind; it displays the action of an informing Spirit, who knows what is in man. St. Paul even speaks of the Old Testament as a living personality: it *sees beforehand* the purpose of God's electing grace; it *preaches the gospel* to Abraham[1]. This aspect of Scripture is one which lies outside the scope of critical inquiry.

[1] Gal. iii. 8; cp. Rom. ix. 17.—'For us and for all ages,' says Bishop Westcott, 'the record is the voice of God; and as a necessary consequence the record is itself living. It is not a book merely. It has a vital connection with our circumstances and must be considered in connection with them. The constant use of the present tense in quotation (λέγει τὸ πνεῦμα τὸ ἅγιον, λέγει ἡ γραφή κ.τ.λ.) emphasises this idea.' (*The Epistle to the Hebrews*, p. 475.)

True criticism indeed never dissects the Bible as if it were a dead body. It treats each book of the Old Testament, for instance, as 'a fragment of ancient life,' not to be fully comprehended or justly appreciated without a sincere effort to enter into sympathy with the thought and circumstances of the age in which it was written[1]. Yet criticism after all moves on the plane of human science; it is concerned mainly with the natural and historical side of Holy Scripture; it deals with that which Origen aptly calls 'the flesh of the word.' But the Christian student will ever bear in mind that beneath the outward veil which with the aid of the critic he reverently scrutinizes, there breathes a living Spirit, who directly appeals to conscience, will, and faith. There is the living word of God, the word that quickens and converts, that pierces and heals, that enlightens and guides the spirit of man; the word that claims to be the food of souls, the light of the conscience, the sword of the Spirit, the mirror of humanity, the unchanging witness to the work and office, the authority and glory of the Son of God[2].

II.

Our inquiry then presupposes and takes as its foundation the fact of the divine Incarnation, and so far we have been engaged in considering some of the features which such a fact, supposed to be true, would lead us to anticipate beforehand in the written records of revelation. Students of the history of doctrine will further notice that there has been a tendency in regard to Scripture analogous to that which may be observed in some stages of the evolution of Christology. The human element has occasionally been minimized or altogether forgotten. Men have been tempted, says

---

[1] Cp. Robertson Smith, *O. T. in J. C.* p. 16.
[2] Cp. Heb. iv. 12; 1 Pet. ii. 2; 2 Pet. i. 19; Jas. i. 25; Eph. vi. 17; John v. 39.

Archbishop Magee, to make of the Bible 'not a supernatural book, which it is, but an unnatural book. . . . They were determined to find the whole Bible as it were in every text of the Bible. . . . They were for ever turning rhetoric into logic, vision into history, poetry into hardest and most literal prose.' They forgot that in the Bible Almighty God 'was using human hearts, human thought, human knowledge, human peculiarities of character, in order that in and through them His word might be conveyed to us [1].' Rabbinical methods of scriptural exegesis supply one example of this tendency; the theory of verbal inspiration another [2]. But without further enlarging on the subject I proceed to mention another truth presupposed in these lectures, namely the fact of the inspiration of Scripture [3]. What, speaking generally, ought we to understand by this term? To this inquiry some provisional answer at least is necessary at this point. It shall be as brief and clear as the conditions of the subject will allow.

It is to be observed in the first place that the doctrine of inspiration is designed to explain a fact which is quite independent of human theories. It is an attempt to give a rational account of the unique religious influence which has been exercised by the Bible. That influence is not dependent upon a particular doctrine, the form of which may have varied at different periods. 'The word,' it has been finely said, 'which is like a fire and like the hammer that breaks

---

[1] *The Gospel and the Age*, p. 321.
[2] e. g. the theory expressed in the *Formula consensus Helvetica* (1674), can. 2: 'Hebraicus V. T. codex . . . tum quoad consonas, tum quoad vocalia, sive puncta ipsa sive punctorum saltem potestatem, et tum quoad res tum quoad verba θεόπνευστος . . . ad cuius normam, ceu Lydium lapidem, universae quae extant versiones, sive orientales sive occidentales, exigendae et sicubi deflectunt revocandae sunt.' See the passage in Augusti, *Corpus Librorum Symbolicorum*, p. 445.
[3] Driver, *Introduction to the Literature of the Old Testament*, pref. p. xix : 'Criticism in the hands of Christian scholars does not banish or destroy the inspiration of the Old Testament ; it *presupposes* it ; it seeks only to determine the conditions under which it operates, and the literary forms through which it manifests itself.'

in pieces the rocks, does not need to be accredited by any human theory as to its origin[1].'

Next we should bear in mind that inspiration in its primary sense does not properly describe the character of a sacred book, but rather denotes the living action of God on the faculties of men. Revelation takes the form on the one hand of an outward historical movement. It implies an actual movement towards man on the part of a living Being, possessed of perfect freedom to act, to intervene, to manifest Himself on behalf of His good purpose[2]. Revelation, in a word, means the historical self-manifestation of God in redemptive action, and it may be remarked in passing that miracle is an antecedently probable element in such action. Divine will and purpose must have at least the same scope in the universe that is open to the mind and energy of man. But parallel to this outward action of God is an internal operation of His power upon human faculties. The outward course of history is accompanied, so to speak, by the Spirit of prophecy, which acts upon the constitution of man in such a fashion as to enlarge his capacity to apprehend and to correspond with the outward self-manifestation of the divine character and mind. The New Testament takes it for granted that there have existed *prophets since the world began*, men indwelt by the Spirit, organs of revelation who were enabled to apprehend and sympathize with the purpose of God while it was in actual process of historical realization. 'Israel's religious teachers,' says Prof. Schultz[3], 'are prophets, not philosophers, priests, or poets. Hence the Old Testament religion can be explained only by revelation, that is by the fact that God raised up for this people men whose natural susceptibility to moral and

---

[1] Oettli, *Der gegenwärtige Kampf um das A. T.* (1896), p. 5.
[2] Phil. ii. 13.
[3] *Theology of the Old Testament*, vol. i. p. 54 [Eng. Trans.]. Cp. J. Darmesteter, *Les Prophètes d'Israël*, p. 220, and Ewald, *The prophets of the O.T.* [Eng. Tr.], vol. i. pp. 3-8.

religious truth developed by the course of their inner and outer lives, enabled them to understand instinctively the will of the self-communicating, redeeming God regarding men; that is, to possess the religious truth which makes free, not as a result of human wisdom and intellectual labour, but as a power pressing in upon the soul with irresistible might. Only those who frankly acknowledge this can be historically just to the Old Testament.' When in fact we examine the Old Testament religion, and ask ourselves how out of the rude polytheistic nature-worship which was common to the Semitic race, there arose a religion which so evidently contained the secret of a lofty spiritual development, we are practically forced to find the explanation in the fact of inspiration; in the immediate action of the living Spirit of God, arousing at least in the leading figures of the Hebrew race a consciousness of God[1]. For it is not necessary to assume—indeed the Old Testament itself contradicts the supposition—that a lofty conception of God was at any time, at least before the exile, a paramount force in the life or thought of the masses of the Hebrew people[2]. Certainly however, the unique development of Hebrew religion, and its constant elevation above the level of kindred faiths surrounding it, irresistibly suggest the conclusion that there were from the very earliest dawn of the history, individual men on whom the Holy

---

[1] Observe the importance of the *religious genius* in revelation. 'It is a defect,' says Pfleiderer (*Gifford Lectures*, i. 183), 'of the present realistic theory of development, that it underestimates or entirely overlooks the significance of *personality* in history, and endeavours to find the active forces of progress only in the masses. The masses however are never spiritually creative. All new world-moving ideas and ideals have proceeded from individual personalities, and even they have not arbitrarily devised them or found them out by laborious reflection, as men find out scientific doctrines by investigation; but they have received them by that involuntary intuition which is also participated in by the artistic genius, and which everywhere forms the privilege of original genius, to whose eye the essence of things and the destination of men are disclosed ... yet ... the revelation of the religious genius is the expression of what the best men of their time have divined and longed for, the unveiling of their own better self, the fulfilment of their own highest hopes,' &c.

[2] See Riehm, *Alttestamentliche Theologie*, p. 11.

AND THE 'HIGHER CRITICISM'

Spirit of God was directly acting, leaders of religion of the true prophetic type, quick to apprehend the meaning of those successive acts in which Almighty God revealed His own character, His control of history, and His purpose for mankind at large. Inspiration then in the first instance is an idea correlative to that of revelation. It means a divine action on man's faculties, by which his intellect is continually trained to more intelligent apprehension of divine purposes, his conscience to deeper knowledge of moral requirement, his heart to worthier love, his will to more exact response. For He who is the object of knowledge Himself imparts the faculty to know; and it follows that 'the essence of a revealed religion is absolutely dependent on prophecy. Without it we have only natural religion or philosophy [1].' Indeed the fundamental characteristic of Hebrew religion is the conviction that God is a self-communicating Being, who does not isolate Himself from the world, but by His Spirit awakens in His creatures the capacity to know and execute His will. That a true knowledge of God is possible, that it depends upon His self-imparting grace, that the word of God actually comes to individual men, making them messengers of the divine will to their fellows, that God speaks to them in modes and under conditions of His own choice and appointment, that He admits them to communion and converse with Himself—this is indisputably an axiom of Israel's faith, and indeed of any supernatural religion [2].

Now, believers in inspiration maintain that in regard to the Bible there can be apprehended by the spiritual mind a special action of the Holy Spirit akin to that which manifests itself in the prophets. This action is discernible, partly in the providential formation and preservation of the Scriptures, partly and chiefly in their intrinsic quality and characteristics. Inspiration

---

[1] Schultz, *op. cit.* i. 237.
[2] *Ibid.* ii. 118. Cp. Sanday, *Bampton Lectures*, pp. 124-128.

implies on the one hand the continuous direction and over-ruling guidance of the Spirit, acting apparently, as Dr. Liddon pointed out in his last sermon from this pulpit, on the principle of selection [1], and so controlling the entire process of the Bible's formation, as might best serve the spiritual interests of mankind. In regard to this providential action of the Holy Spirit, Origen makes a far-seeing observation in his *Letter to Africanus*. Dealing with the question of variations in the Hebrew and Septuagint text of the Old Testament, he appeals boldly to what we might call a self-evident principle of a revelation of grace. 'Can it be,' he asks, 'that the divine providence, having given in holy Scriptures material for edification to all the churches of Christ, was unmindful of those who had been bought at a price, those for whom Christ died [2]?' Origen evidently means that in Scripture a divine regard for the spiritual interests of mankind is abundantly manifested. Certainly the Old Testament is very far from being the kind of volume which human ingenuity would have compiled for religious purposes; but experience has shown that nothing less expansive, less full, less varied, less mysterious, would have satisfied the needs and yearnings of human nature. Further, the spiritual experience of Christians warrants the belief that the action of the Holy Spirit, while it has controlled the formation and selection of such writings as should best serve the providential purpose of God, has also protected them from such defects as might be injurious to that purpose. An inspired Bible does not mean a book free from a large admixture of imperfect elements, but it does mean a book perfectly adapted to fulfil the function it was intended by God to discharge.

On the other hand, inspiration is primarily a quality

---

[1] See his University Sermon on *The Inspiration of Selection*, preached May 25, 1890.
[2] Orig. *ad Afric*. iv. So Aug. finds providential purpose in the obscurities of Scripture (*de doc*. ii. 6).

of the writers or compilers to whom we owe the several books of Scripture. Men of different types were moved to write, and enabled for their special work, by the Holy Spirit, who employed the products of their pen in His own way and for His own purposes[1]. In considering this matter, however, we are bound to remember that critical analysis of the Old Testament books has somewhat altered the conditions of the problem. In the case of writings which have passed through a prolonged literary process, it is somewhat misleading to speak of the writer as if he were a single person[2]. Waiving this point, however, let us inquire wherein the inspiration of the biblical writers consists? Chiefly it would seem in a gift of special moral and religious insight[3]. The inspired writer is one who is spiritually enlightened. He is alive to the character, requirement and purpose of the All-Holy. He gives prominence to spiritual truths and laws. He reads history in the light of his present spiritual knowledge. He looks upon the world as God's world; in history he traces the dealings of God with various types of character, individual or national. He reads in the events of the present, a divine commentary on the past; in the records of the past he finds laws of future development. It is indeed signi-

---

[1] Sanday, *Bampton Lectures*, p. 227: 'The authority of the word written was precisely the same as that of the word spoken.... It was inherent in the person who wrote and spoke, and was derived from the special action upon that person of the Spirit of God.' Driver, *Serm. on O. T. Subj.* p. 136: 'The divine thought takes shape in the soul of the prophet, and is presented to us, so to speak, in the garb and imagery with which he has invested it; it is expressed in terms which bear the external marks of his own individuality, and reflect the circumstances of time and place and other similar conditions, under which it was first propounded.'

[2] Cp. Dalman, *Das A. T. ein Wort Gottes*, p. 18.

[3] Driver, *Serm. on O. T. Subj.* pp. 146, 147: 'We may, I suppose, say that what we mean by it [inspiration] is an influence which gave to those who received it a unique and extraordinary *spiritual insight*, enabling them thereby, without superseding or suppressing the human faculties, but rather using them as its instruments, to declare in different degrees, and in accordance with the needs or circumstances of particular ages or particular occasions, the mind and purpose of God.'

ficant that the larger part of the Old Testament books are ascribed by Jewish tradition to prophets, that is to men who were regarded as specially assisted by the Holy Spirit, whether in reading aright the lessons of national experience, or in divining correctly the providential course of events in the future. Indeed this tradition is so far correct that beyond any question prophetism seems to have been the distinctive element which made Israel's religion what it was[1]; and as a matter of fact nothing was introduced into the canon which was not believed tô be in some sense prophetic[2]. For the prophetic faculty alone could enable the biblical writers to interpret the true drift and meaning of the events or experiences which they described. In this lies the present importance of their work. Without being either perfect in form or free from error, the writings of Old Testament sages and historians give us such a representation of the mighty works and gracious revelations of God as can best minister to the education of faith in every age. For under the guidance of the Holy Spirit, Hebrew literature took a direction, and attained to a height, peculiar to itself. 'Just as we have here a nation,' says Ewald, 'wholly different from any other elsewhere upon earth, so we have also a literature shaped and fashioned under a spirit, and thence also with results, wholly different from those of foreign or other Semitic nations,' and this in spite of the fact that, 'in external literary forms Israel followed the old models of earlier Semitic culture[3].'

The above discussion of the term 'inspiration' will suffice to make clear the standpoint presupposed in

---

[1] Cp. J. Darmesteter, *Les Prophètes d'Israël*, p. 210; Driver, *Serm. on O. T. Subj.* p. 101; Meinhold, *Jesus und das A. T.* pp. 103, 104.

[2] Cp. Josephus, *c. Apion.* i. 8; Girdlestone, *The Foundations of the Bible*, p. 17; Sanday, *Bampton Lectures*, p. 254. The Jews appear to have supposed 'that books composed during the prevalence of Prophecy were inspired in the strict and true sense, and that those composed after the cessation of Prophecy were not.'

[3] *Revelation, its Nature and Record*, p. 308.

the following lectures. A merely mechanical theory of inspiration is untenable for this reason amongst others, that it ignores the possibility of degrees in inspiration; nor does it adequately recognize God's providential action in regard to the sacred literature of other religions [1]. Further, the history of the canon is instructive as reminding us that the relative value of the different books contained in the Old Testament varies somewhat widely [2]. The very fact that there was hesitation in reference to the inclusion of several disputed books is sufficient evidence that the precise spiritual function of a particular writing might not always be obvious or certain, and in any case if the true bearing and import of the divine message in each book is to be correctly understood, it can only be by patient effort to enter into the historical conditions under which it was produced, and the state of mind or culture to which it was addressed.

We arrive then at a true conception of inspiration inductively by careful study of the Bible itself. The term 'inspiration' includes on the one hand the providential superintendence or guidance which controlled the formation of the canon, on the other that supernatural influence which heightened the faculties, or directed the genius, of the biblical writers. Inspiration has been admirably described as ' an influence within the soul, divine and supernatural,

[1] Cp. Sanday, *Bampton Lectures*, pp. 398 foll. Observe, the true conception of inspiration does not require us to regard the inspiration of non-Israelites as impossible or imaginary. What distinguishes the biblical writers is the character of their knowledge of God and their peculiar insight into His requirement of man. Schultz, i. 255, points out that in its earlier parts, the Old Testament itself 'goes upon the supposition that even a Balaam is inspired by the true God, and that his curse or blessing takes effect (Num. xxii. 6; xxiii. 5; xxiv. 3 f. Cp. Mic. vi. 5); that Moses has a certain resemblance to the wise men and the sorcerers of Egypt; that even heathen kings have dreams of a truly divine significance (Gen. xx. 6; xl. 5 f.; xli. 1, 25, 28); that the prophets of the Philistines prophesy truly (1 Sam. vi. 2 f.); in a word, that God speaks even beyond the bounds of Israel,' &c.

[2] Sanday, *op. cit.* p. 259: 'Just as there is a descending scale within the canon, there is an ascending scale outside it.' Cp. Driver, *Serm. on O. T. Subj.* p. 153.

working through all the writers in one organizing method, making of the many one, by all one book, the book of God, the book for man, divine and human in all its parts; having the same relation to all other books that the person of the Son of God has to all other men, and that the Church of the living God has to all other institutions[1].' That this influence works mainly in the direction of moral illumination is the view of many ancient Christian thinkers on this subject. Thus while Tatian and Justin Martyr lay stress upon the affinity in character, which makes men suitable instruments of the divine Spirit[2], Origen declares that the Holy Spirit 'enlightened the ministers of truth, the apostles and prophets, to understand the mysteries of those things or causes which take place or act among men or concerning men[3].' 'By the contact of the Holy Spirit with their soul,' he elsewhere says, 'they became more clear-sighted in their faculties, and more lustrous in their souls[4].'

This view of inspiration is to be distinguished from the popular notions, which undoubtedly influenced other ancient writers. There were some who failed to discriminate between inspiration in the moral sense described above and the passive reception of a divine *afflatus*. This latter idea was characteristic of Greek 'mantic'; it exercised considerable influence upon the mind of Philo, and of those fathers who were penetrated by Hellenic modes of thought[5]. Such a conception,

---

[1] From a sermon quoted by Briggs, *Biblical Study*, p. 161.
[2] See Tatian, *c. Graecos*, §§ 13, 29 (quoted by Westcott, *Introd. to the Study of the Gospels*, p. 424). Cp. Justin, *Cohort.* 8, and *Dial. c. Tryph.* 7.
[3] *de Princip.* iv. 14.
[4] *c. Cels.* vii. 4 διορατικώτεροι τὸν νοῦν καὶ τὴν ψυχὴν λαμπρότεροι.
[5] Cp. Sanday, *Bampton Lectures*, p. 75. Philo and apparently Josephus seem to have considered inspiration to consist in a species of frenzy or ecstasy, an actual suspension of the reasoning faculties in man, so that he was simply a passive instrument or mouthpiece of the divine Spirit. Substantially the same view was held by some ecclesiastical writers, e. g. Athenagoras, *Leg. pro Chr.* § 9; Hippol. *de Antichr.* ii.; Clem. Alex. *Protrept.* i. 5; &c. See generally passages quoted by Westcott in his essay on 'The primitive doctrine of inspiration' (*Introd. to the Study of the Gospels*, pp. 417 foll.).

however, must obviously be corrected by investigation of the Old Testament itself. There is nowhere a trace that the writers of the historical books for example were conscious of being supernaturally informed of facts ascertainable by ordinary means, or of not enjoying entire freedom and power of independent judgment in their selection and arrangement of materials. They appear simply to use the historical sources open to them in their own way, and they nowhere advance any claim to have worked in a fashion different from that of ordinary profane writers. We may go further, and maintain that the very idea of a 'special revelation' of past facts, e.g. the process of creation, or the origins of tribal history, is contradicted by analogy. Revelation in no case undertakes the task of imparting information in regard to the events of past history. It ever proclaims God's will and requirement in the present, and to that end *interprets* the past or unveils the future [1]. The popular idea that a fact, because it stands in Scripture, is strictly historical and infallibly true results from an untenable theory as to the true meaning and purpose of inspiration and implies a real confusion of thought. The question at issue is, *What is the nature* of that inerrancy which all Christians alike ascribe to Scripture, when they acknowledge that it is a divine book? For on this point the teaching of Jesus Christ and the experience of Christendom may suffice to guide us [2]. In the Old Testament He, who afterwards spake to us by a Son, spake beforehand by the mouth of prophets *in many parts and many fashions*. Modern research, however, is throwing new and startling light on the *modus operandi* actually followed by the Holy Spirit in His self-communication to man, and in

---

[1] This is well stated by A. Köhler, *Über Berechtigung der Kritik des Alten Testamentes*, p. 14.
[2] Orig. *de Princ.* iv. 9 maintains μὴ ἀνθρώπων εἶναι συγγράμματα τὰς ἱερὰς βίβλους, ἀλλ' ἐξ ἐπιπνοίας τοῦ ἁγίου πνεύματος βουλήματι τοῦ πατρὸς τῶν ὅλων διὰ Ἰησοῦ Χριστοῦ ταύτας ἀναγεγράφθαι καὶ εἰς ἡμᾶς ἐληλυθέναι.

His superintendence of the process by which a sacred literature was gradually formed. The consequence is that the best we can do is to describe in general and somewhat vague terms what we mean by inspiration; it would be perilous to attempt any formal definition. We should certainly define at the expense of overlooking some vital element of divine truth. Inspiration is our mode of denoting the influence of a Spirit whose operation is manifest in two or even three distinct but closely related spheres. We may trace that operation, first, in the personality of those great religious leaders whose ministry or testimony was employed as a medium of divine revelation; secondly, in the community whose spiritual life, rather than that of single individuals, is reflected in such great literary products as the Psalter; thirdly, in the providentially guided action of those who so compiled, edited, and collected the records of revelation, as to impress on the total product of their labours a peculiar uniformity of tone and character[1]. *All these worketh that one and the self-same Spirit, dividing to every man severally as he will*[2].

III.

There is yet another subject in regard to which some preliminary explanation is desirable, namely, the extent to which the results of historical criticism are to be taken for granted in the following lectures. There is, however, the less need for any lengthened statement because it has been a constant practice with Bampton lecturers to presuppose the labours of their predecessors. Briefly stated, the position provisionally accepted in these lectures is one of substantial agreement with the cautious and well-considered summary of Prof. Sanday in the second and third of his lectures

---

[1] Cp. Dalman, *Das Alte Testament ein Wort Gottes*, p. 19.
[2] 1 Cor. xii. 11.

on Inspiration. He has with characteristic fairness and clearness stated what may be taken as the established results of nearly 150 years' investigation of the Old Testament[1]. It seems scarcely necessary to give any complete account of those results. Broadly speaking, the outcome of historical criticism has been a modification of the traditional view respecting the order of the successive stages in Israel's religious development. It has been rendered most probable and even morally certain that the active ministry of the prophets preceded the discipline of the law, at least in its completed form. 'The great change of perspective,' says a French writer, 'which recent criticism introduces in the sacred history is that it assigns the central place in this history no longer to Moses on Sinai, but to the choir of the prophets[2].' This is not in reality such a revolutionary statement as might appear at first sight, for on the one hand the activity of the prophets certainly presupposes the stage of Mosaism, that term being carefully guarded so as to imply not a fully developed system of ritual and law, but an historical movement that laid the foundations of a divinely organized polity and suggested the ideas, religious and moral, by which that polity was afterwards moulded[3]: an element of law was thus present as a working factor in Israel's progress from the time of Moses. On the other hand, Moses himself is regarded by the prophets as one of their number[4], nor can there be any question that he is the most distinguished figure in that long line of inspired men who appeared at the turning-points

[1] See especially Sanday, *Bampton Lectures*, pp. 116-121, 172 foll. For a sketch of the progress of criticism in relation to the Pentateuch, see Delitzsch, *New Commentary on Genesis*, introd.
[2] Darmesteter, *Les Prophètes d'Israël*, p. 11.
[3] Mosaism would be based on the 'Book of the Covenant' and perhaps the 'Decalogue.' Prophetism developed Mosaism on its ethical side. Judaism was a period of education and discipline in which sacrifice was almost the sum total of obedience. Cp. A. B. Bruce, *Apologetics*, p. 170.
[4] See Hos. xii. 13; cp. Deut. xviii. 15.

of Hebrew history as representatives and exponents
of a higher religion than that of their contemporaries.
The work of the prophets, then, preceded the prolonged
and strict discipline of the Pentateuchal law. At the
same time, the history of the canon justifies us in
continuing to speak of 'the law and the prophets'
so long as we are referring not to the order of
historical appearance, but to those great divisions of
the Hebrew Scriptures which are respectively known
by these titles, and which were successively compiled
in their present shape during and after the Exile.
The completed Pentateuchal law may still be regarded as a principal factor in Israel's spiritual
discipline—only it was an instrument employed in
a manner, and at a stage of the history, other than
was once supposed [1]. The prophets are still to be
reverenced as the great leaders of religion who, in
due succession, laboured to keep alive in Israel *the
light of the Lord.* It is a reassuring circumstance
that, in regard to the history and work of the great
Hebrew prophets, there is substantial accord between
the defenders of the Hebrew tradition and the
adherents of the higher criticism [2]. But the compilation and redaction of their oracles was the work
of a later age than that in which the prophets
themselves flourished, and there is good ground for
thinking that some anonymous pieces were inserted
in the volume of their collected works and assigned
to different great names, in accordance with a well-
known literary practice of the time. It might also
seem that the collected record of prophetic teaching
acted more powerfully on a later age than the living

---

[1] Robertson Smith, *O. T. in J. C.* p. 310: 'The time when [the law] became God's word, i.e. became a divinely sanctioned means for checking the rebellion of the Israelites and keeping them as close to spiritual religion as their imperfect understanding and hard hearts permitted, was subsequent to the work of the prophets. As a matter of historical fact the law continues the work of the prophets, and great part of the law was not yet known to the prophets as God's word.' Cp. Hunter, *After the Exile*, part i. pp. 273 foll.

[2] Cp. Darmesteter, *Les Prophètes d'Israël*, p. 121.

voice of the prophets had acted on their own contemporaries. To conclude, we have here a fixed point which is amply confirmed by an investigation of the Old Testament itself: the work of the prophets preceded the discipline of the completed law. In some shape or other this proposition is admitted even by opponents of the higher criticism. No person capable of judging can refuse to recognize the fact that the levitical code only became a powerful and regulative influence in Israel's national life after the return from Babylon. Nor need we find any difficulty in supposing that prophetism was followed by a stage relatively lower— that of law. The question however is not whether the legal stage was inferior to the prophetic, but whether or not it served an indispensable purpose in the religious education of Israel [1].

Literary criticism and analysis has also rendered necessary a new view as to the composition of the Old Testament documents. In particular it has shown with unquestionable clearness and force that there are at least three main strata of laws incorporated in the Pentateuch, strata which are not all of one age, but 'correspond to three stages in the development of Israel's institutions,' stages still clearly recognizable in the narrative 'of the historical books [2]. It is important, however, that we should not

---

[1] See the suggestive remarks of Dr. Bruce, *Apologetics*, p. 262.
[2] Robertson Smith, *O. T. in J. C.* p. 388. These strata of laws are—
(1) The first legislation, contained in the so-called 'Book of the Covenant' (Exod. xxi-xxiii), which, roughly speaking, belongs to the age of Moses himself.
(2) The law of Deuteronomy (Deut. xii-xxvi), which reproduces but expands the first legislation.
(3) The levitical legislation, which includes the ancient 'Law of holiness' (Lev. xvii-xxvi) and represents the usage of the priests as codified and supplemented during and after the exile in Babylon.
A careful comparison of these three bodies of law makes it evident that they belong to different periods of Hebrew history; on one point there is practical unanimity, viz. that the book of the law discovered during the eighteenth year of Josiah's reign (621) in the temple at Jerusalem, was none other than the Deuteronomic law (cp. Cornill, *Einleitung in das A. T.* § 9; Ryle, *Canon of the O. T.* chap. ii.). At any rate the influence

exaggerate the significance of this and other similar discoveries. The fact that a continuous divine revelation was made to the Hebrew people remains unaffected by inquiry into the nature and origin of the records which embody either the history or the spiritual products of that revelation. At what period these records were severally committed to writing, out of what materials they were compiled, under what conditions they were produced and reached their present shape—all these are matters of secondary importance [1]. To the same category belong most questions of authorship. It will probably never be precisely settled how much of the great literary or legislative creations which tradition assigns to Moses, David, Solomon, Isaiah, or Zechariah, can be truly attributed to them. It is not vitally important that we should ever attain to definite knowledge on such points, and certainly it is a great mistake to overrate the need of exact information in regard to matters which do not affect the substance of revelation. At any rate a Christian apologist may conscientiously claim the right to retain a perfectly open mind on the purely literary questions that may from time to time be under discussion among experts in criticism.

I have given some bare illustrations of the changes which our present knowledge involves in current conceptions of the Old Testament. But in order to anticipate objections it is necessary to add two or three observations bearing upon the whole subject of criticism.

First, the results of the higher criticism commend themselves to students of the Old Testament on broad grounds of historical probability and consistency [2].

---

of the book of Deuteronomy on the course of the history and on the historical books *begins* at that point of time.

[1] Cp. Westcott, *The Ep. to the Hebrews*, p. 493.

[2] Robertson Smith, *O. T. in J. C.* p. 234. 'The results [of Old Testament criticism] are broad and intelligible, and possess that evidence of historical consistency on which the results of special scholarship are habitually accepted by the mass of intelligent men in other branches of historical inquiry.' Cp. Sanday, *Bampton Lectures*, p. 414.

As a branch of historical science, biblical criticism concerns itself with the interpretation of facts which lie open to the observation of every attentive reader of Scripture. This task has been pressed upon scholars partly by the results of mere literary analysis of the Old Testament, and partly by the accessions to our knowledge which have been gained in departments directly or indirectly illustrative of Hebrew life and religion, in the special fields covered by archaeological and ethnographical research, or by the comparative study of religions. The critical method of dealing with Hebrew history is that of comparing the actual working institutions described or implied in the historical books, with those contained in the legal parts of the Pentateuch; its aim is to reconstruct the story of Israel's development in accordance with all the available evidence. Now in regard to this reconstruction of the history, it is obvious that to a non-expert that theory will ultimately commend itself which supplies the most satisfactory and comprehensive explanation of the divergent phenomena [1]. Attempts to defend the traditional view of Israel's history are too often entirely unsatisfying. The detailed and sometimes forced interpretation of innumerable points of difficulty cannot be regarded as an adequate answer to a massive and consistent argument based on historical facts and supported by analogy. We have seen that the most noticeable point in which criticism revises the traditional view of the Old Testament is the relative position to be assigned to the prophets and the law. According to the critical view the Pentateuch embodies the legal code not of Mosaism properly speaking, but of post-exilic Judaism. In proof of this position it is pointed out that in the historical books we find a state of things prevailing which strikes at the very root of the full-blown levitical system [2]. For while the

---

[1] Cp. Sanday, *op. cit.* p. 215.
[2] See Robertson Smith, *O. T. in J. C.* pp. 271, 317.

levitical law rigidly restricts sacrificial worship to a single central altar and shrine, the custom practised and sanctioned till a late period in the history of the divided kingdom is freedom of sacrifice. It appears, in fact, that the central principle of the Pentateuchal legislation was either unknown or ignored before the age of Josiah. It has been shown, with what seems to many unanswerable force, that the centralization of worship and its limitation to a single sanctuary was a result only gradually achieved; that during the period previous to the erection of Solomon's temple a totally opposite state of things prevailed, which was apparently sanctioned by judges, kings, priests, and prophets alike; that the tendency towards limitation was encouraged by the great prophets of the eighth century, who perceived and denounced the abuses which had grown up in connexion with the popular cultus; that a doubtful attempt was made by Hezekiah, and a somewhat more successful effort by Josiah, to abolish the local sacrificial worship, but that until Josiah's reign scarcely a trace can be discovered of the observance in fact of the Deuteronomic law by which sacrifice was restricted to a central sanctuary[1]. In this case the references found in the historical books to a centralized worship do not appear to be nearly sufficient to outweigh the argument drawn from silence and from plain facts which justifies the critical theory[2]. It is plain indeed that the general conception of Israel's previous history formed by the compilers of the historical books does not entirely correspond with the conclusions suggested by the narrative itself; and that we have to deal not merely

---

[1] Wellhausen, *Prolegomena to the History of Israel* (Eng. Tr.), ch. i.
[2] The traditional theory is well stated by Dr. Robertson Smith, *O. T. in J. C.* pp. 231 foll. Its weakness is (1) that 'the standard which it applies to the history of Israel is not that of contemporary historical records'; (2) 'the account which it gives of the work of the prophets is not consistent with the work of the prophets themselves'; (3) in general, there is a serious discrepancy between the traditional view of the Pentateuch and the evidence of the historical books in regard to the freedom of sacrifice allowed by men like Samuel, David, and Elijah.

with a great mass of important historical materials in the Old Testament, but with theories and interpretations of history which themselves demand close and reverent attention, but must not be supposed to foreclose independent scientific investigation of recorded facts.

But further, in regard to the literary composition of the Old Testament writings, and especially of the legal and historical portions, the critical view falls in with the analogy presented by the phenomena of other ancient literatures. 'Modern research,' we are told by a very candid friend of the higher criticism, ' has shown that a considerable part of the most ancient literature of all nations was of composite origin, more especially when it was of a historical or a religious character. Older documents were incorporated into it, with only so much change as to allow them to be fitted together into a continuous story, or to reflect the point of view, ethical, political, or religious, of the later compiler. The most ancient books that have come down to us are, with few exceptions, essentially compilations [1].' Accordingly if the literary analysis of the Old Testament points to such phenomena as these: gradual accretions added to the national annals, frequent assumption that institutions of comparatively late date go back to an earlier age, groups of writings of different style and date connected with certain historic names, the uniform ascription of laws to a primitive legislator—we are only required to recognize in Hebrew literature the operation of the ordinary laws observable in that of other ancient nations.

Speaking broadly, the modern reconstruction of the history can justify itself on the one hand by its general accordance with the results of a purely literary analysis of the Old Testament, since the conception which historical criticism has formed of the general course of

[1] Prof. Sayce, *The Higher Criticism and the Monuments*, p. 3. See a good description of the phenomena common in secular writings of antiquity in Sanday, *The Oracles of God*, pp. 27, 28.

Israel's history is one that explains almost innumerable discrepancies and confusions which the traditional view left unsolved, or dealt with in a superficial and unsatisfactory manner. On the other hand, it harmonizes with the knowledge acquired in other branches of scientific research [1]. Further, it is worth while to note, that the admissions even of conservative writers on Old Testament subjects occasionally suggest inferences more far-reaching than those actually put forward by their authors [2]. We may welcome these admissions as indicating a tendency among Christian scholars towards cautious acceptance of at least the main positions of the critical theory, a theory which is favoured not only by a mass of positive and negative evidence, but also by a striking degree of *a priori* probability [3].

Secondly, it must be frankly admitted that the acceptance of the higher criticism has been hindered, not only by the mistaken fears and *a priori* prejudices of believing Christians, but also by the undisguised hostility to supernatural religion with which conspicuous foreign critics have conducted the investigation of Old Testament subjects. Critical theories have been occasionally advanced in the interests of avowed

---

[1] The general study of history throws light not merely on the formation of the Old Testament books, but on the character of their contents. In all early history there is a stage of myth, and a stage of prehistoric legend or saga. 'I hold,' wrote the late Prof. Freeman, 'and I see nothing in our formularies to hinder me from holding—that a great part of the early Hebrew history, as of all other history, is simply legendary. I never read any German books on these matters at all, but came to the conclusion simply from the analogies supplied by my own historical studies.' (*Life and Letters of E. A. Freeman*, by W. R. W. Stephens, B.D., vol. i. p. 345.)

[2] See for instance Girdlestone, *The Foundations of the Bible*, p. 42 (on the work of the Chronicler); pp. 138, 139 (on the ideal character of the Mosaic legislation); p. 193 ('concessions and convictions').

[3] For example, the late codification of the Priestly code (P) falls in with the evidence that among the Semitic tribes ritual and ceremonial were generally a matter of unwritten *usage* and traditional *practice* (*O. T. in J. C.* p. 332); it also explains the object of Ezekiel's *Torah* (Ezek. xl–xlviii), and its relation to the levitical legislation; moreover, it falls in with all that we know from other sources of the temper of the Jewish people after its return from exile. Cf. Bruce, *Apologetics*, pp. 264–266.

naturalism; they have often been dictated by disbelief in the possibility of miracle. Further, distrust has naturally been excited by the arrogance, the patronizing temper, the dogmatism, the overweening confidence of tone, displayed by some critics. These faults are noticed by a brilliant French writer in a noteworthy passage which many Old Testament students would endorse. Speaking specially of German criticism, M. Darmesteter says, 'It has generally been wanting in flexibility and moderation. It has insisted upon knowing everything, explaining everything, precisely determining everything. It has claimed to arrive at the primal elements of formations which have been repeatedly modified and of which we have only the remains. It has introduced into the work of reconstruction, which ought to sacrifice facts that are indifferent or devoid of historical significance, the scruples of an analytic method which has no right to ignore or neglect anything. Hence complicated and obscure theories, provided with odd corners in which all the details may be sheltered, and which leave the mind little opening or leisure to observe the tendency of facts and the general currents of history[1].' Indeed, a conspicuous fault of the critical temper is its disinclination to make allowance for the immense range of our ignorance, and for the consequent difficulty of attaining completeness and precision beyond a limited sphere[2]. Further, we cannot fail to notice a certain want of spiritual sympathy with the age and writers of the documents which are from time to time under discussion, yet such sympathy is absolutely necessary if we are to avoid shallowness and presumption in estimating the evidence[3]. It is

---

[1] *Les Prophètes d'Israël*, pp. 4, 5. The same writer speaks severely of rationalism in the sphere of criticism. 'Le rationalisme, cet épouvantail de l'orthodoxie, est une chose bien différente de l'esprit historique qui seul est fécond, et auquel il est peut-être plus contraire que la critique croyante.'
[2] Cp. Sanday, *Oracles of God*, p. 74.
[3] Cp. Sayce, *op. cit.* pp. 5, 15. Girdlestone, *op. cit.* pp. 195, 196, says: 'They (critics) write as if they expect everything to be brought up to the critical style of the present century, regardless alike of the age of the books,

the want of it which formerly led some critics to cast imputations on the moral probity of the Old Testament writers.

While however we allow that there was much which seemed to justify the uncompromising hostility with which Christian men of the last generation met the advance of criticism, we must in fairness acknowledge much fault on our own side[1]: much slowness of heart, much want of faith and undue timidity, much unreasoning prejudice, much disproportioned and misdirected zeal, much unwillingness to take trouble, much readiness to explain away unwelcome facts, whereas 'explaining away is a process which has no place in historical inquiry[2].' We have failed to do justice to the laborious and patient thoroughness, the exact and profound erudition, the sagacious insight of the great scholars of Germany. We have seldom made due allowance for the immense difficulties of their self-imposed task, we have exaggerated the deficiencies of their method and the insecurity of its results[3]. If however in the past suspicion and dislike have been carried too far, there are welcome indications that such a temper is gradually disappearing, and that Christians are learning to distinguish more accurately between what is essential and what is non-essential to their faith[4]. And if it should be objected that we of this

of the genius of the people, and of the spiritual intent of the writers.' Cp. Robertson Smith, *O. T. in J. C.* p. 329.

[1] For a frank admission of faults on the traditional side see Girdlestone, *op. cit.* p. 196.

[2] Robertson Smith, *O. T. in J. C.* p. 421.

[3] As Darmesteter justly remarks (*Les Prophètes d'Israël*, p. 232): 'Inégalités d'érudition et témérités de méthode sont le prix nécessaire dont se paye toute synthèse surtout au début de la science. Ces synthèses prématurées . . . n'en sont pas moins d'incomparables instruments de progrès,' &c.

[4] The following passage from one of Professor Freeman's letters is interesting in this connexion:—

'It seems to me that the Old Testament history falls into the hands of two sets of people. There is one that thinks itself bound to defend everything at all hazards—or, what is worse, *to put something out of their own heads instead of what is really in the book.* And there is another set who take a nasty pleasure in picking every hole they can: the small German critic, generation are unfaithful to the traditions of those venerated teachers in whose place we are allowed to stand, we can but reply that *wisdom is justified of all her children.'* We whose training has been in many respects diverse from theirs, whose difficulties and responsibilities are altogether different, cannot fairly plead their example as an excuse for evading the task specially assigned to us, or for refusing to consider the claims of that which presents itself to us in the name of truth. It is not impatience, or love of novelty, or self-confidence, or a mere wish to be abreast of recent thought that has led to the changed attitude of younger men; it is the desire to follow humbly and honestly the guidance of the Spirit of Truth. There comes a time when suspense of judgment, indefinitely prolonged, may become a breach of trust or at least a failure in courage. We should be untrue to the high traditions of Christian theology were we simply to reject the conclusions of criticism on the ground either that they conflict with private preconceptions, or that they occasionally emanate from quarters hostile to the Christian Faith. For while it is scarcely necessary to point out that a believer in the Incarnation will not share those antecedent objections to the supernatural, or those *a priori* theories in regard to the origin and growth of religious ideas, which have doubtless biassed some continental critics in their discussion of Old Testament problems, it is reassuring to remind ourselves of at least one conspicuous instance in which a great conception bearing vitally on religion reached us from a non-Christian source, I mean the idea of evolution. Christians have welcomed that idea; it has profoundly modified and enriched our knowledge of the creative methods employed by Almighty God, and of His present relation to the universe. Yet this idea at first sight appeared to threaten cherished

or rather *guesser*, grown smaller and nastier because he thinks it fine. From neither of them will you ever get truth.' (*Life and Letters*, &c., vol. ii. p. 412.)

Christian beliefs. Accordingly we have abundant reason for anticipating that the critical sagacity which for nearly a century and a half has been devoted to the literature of the Old Testament, will in the long run enlarge our knowledge of the ways of God, and promote His glory; we may therefore appropriate all that true criticism has to teach us with the confidence and trustfulness of those who believe that *All things are* theirs. Since Christian faith has welcomed the theory of development in nature, it has no reason to fear an evolutionary account of Hebrew religion[1].

Once more, if we are told that the time has not really arrived for a verdict on the results of the critical movement and that nothing can be more foolish and short-sighted than premature concessions, we can only be guided by the opinion of experts in regard to the actual point which Old Testament inquiries have reached. Many competent authorities think that we have now entered on the period of reconstruction[2]. This does not mean that the time has arrived for pronouncing a comprehensive and final judgment on the labours of criticism. We must decline altogether to be deeply committed on critical questions; we may even hold that some points which are now confidently assumed to be settled beyond dispute are either insoluble, or still highly uncertain. But it is maintained, and as it seems to me with justice, that certain critical conclusions are practically established which, even on the lowest estimate of them, profoundly modify the traditional view of the Old Testament. Although in the matter of minor details we may regard these conclusions as tentative and provisional, we must not exaggerate the importance of such divergences of

---

[1] Cp. Bruce, *Apologetics*, p. 173.
[2] e.g. Prof. Sayce, *The Higher Criticism*, &c., p. 24. Robertson Smith, *O. T. in J. C.* p. 16: 'The true critic has for his business, not to destroy but to build up. The critic is an interpreter, but one who has a larger view of his task than the man of mere grammars and dictionaries—one who is not content to reproduce the words of his author, but strives to enter into sympathy with his thoughts, and to understand the thoughts as part of the life of the thinker and his time.'

opinion on minor points as may exist among critics at the present time. The question is whether there is not a solid body of ascertained facts on which they are substantially agreed [1]. Even if we maintain that some critical verdicts need to be revised or altogether rejected, or that the preconceptions on which they are based are arbitrary and untenable, yet the right and duty of scholars to inquire into the history of the Old Testament literature cannot be gainsaid. Erroneous criticism cannot be corrected by dogmatic theology, but only by a better, more searching, and less prejudiced criticism [2]. We must be careful not to give occasion for the reproach that the maintenance of a tradition is of more consequence to us than the acceptance of the results of scientific inquiry. Attempts to dispute the importance, or minimize the significance of the higher criticism are no longer of any avail, but rather do injury to the cause of Christian truth, inasmuch as they excite the justifiable suspicion that we Churchmen have not the courage or the moral force to look facts fairly in the face. It is right to raise the question whether our general unwillingness to accept critical conclusions is due to an honest disbelief in their validity, or whether it results from indolent dislike of taking trouble, from a narrow and inadequate theory of inspiration, or from a tendency to force the Bible into a false and untenable position—'a position perilous to its authority, unwarranted by its own statements, and, worst of all, in a great measure obscuring the real power and beauty of its teaching [3].'

[1] Sanday, *Bampton Lectures*, p. 120: 'We may reasonably say that what they [the results of criticism] offer to us is a minimum which under no circumstances is capable of being reduced much further, and that the future is likely to yield data which are more, and not less, favourable to conclusions such as those adopted in these lectures.' Cp. Cheyne, *Aids to the Devout Study of Criticism*, p. 172.

[2] Cp. Köhler, *op. cit.* p. 68. Delitzsch, *New Commentary on Genesis*, vol. i. p. 54, observes: 'Believing investigation of Scripture will not subdue this nuisance of critical analysis unless it wrests the weapon from its adversary's hand, and actually shows that analysis can be exercised without thereby trampling under foot respect for Holy Scripture.'

[3] J. Paterson Smyth, *How God Inspired the Bible*, pp. 15, 16.

IV.

Having now cleared the ground by a definite statement of the presuppositions with which we approach our subject, I shall endeavour in the following lectures to illustrate the positive functions which the Old Testament, viewed in the light of modern research, is intended to fulfil in the Christian Church. It may be useful to illustrate the way in which a servant and disciple of the Lord Jesus Christ may still continue to use the Old Testament, even though inevitable changes have passed over his conception of its origin, structure and character. I cannot, however, conclude the present lecture without a brief consideration of two factors which determine the true use of Scripture and specially of the Old Testament: first, the authority of our Lord Jesus Christ; and secondly, the collective experience of the Christian Church.

1. Nothing is more certain to a devout Christian than the fact that the Old Testament comes to us solemnly commended by the express authority of the Lord Jesus Christ. Hence the danger of ignoring and misunderstanding its special teaching, or of omitting to devote to it honest, reverent, and intelligent study.

But our study must be discriminating. We must draw a careful distinction between the inspired teaching of the Old Testament in regard to divine and spiritual things, and those many matters contained in it which fall within the sphere of natural knowledge. Christ did not come into the world to teach history or science, but to make sinful men children of God and heirs of eternal life. How carefully He warns us in the Gospels that there are tasks and functions the fulfilment of which formed no part of His mission. *I am not come to call the righteous. I came not to judge the world, but to save the world. I came not to do mine own will. Man, who made me a judge or a divider over you*[1]*?* It was surely not the purpose of His coming to teach us the exact course of Israel's history, or the origin and nature of the sacred books which recorded it, but rather to point men to the sources from which they might learn necessary truth about the nature and character of God, His requirement of man and His purpose for the world. *Search the Scriptures,* He said to the Jews; *for in them ye think ye have eternal life*[2]. Considering, however, that both Christ and His Apostles represent Israel's history as a preparation for His coming, and refer to the Old Testament as God's express word concerning His previous dealings with humanity, a Christian cannot be satisfied with any representation of the history which denies that it was throughout its whole course a continuous preparation for the coming of Christ. At the same time he will ever bear in mind that the Incarnation completed the self-revelation of God which, *in divers parts and in divers manners,* had been communicated to mankind from the first. He will remember that our Lord nowhere claims for the Old Testament that it is an infallible authority in regard to such points as the course of primitive history or of Israel's national development. To grasp correctly and present adequately the actual incidents of a long historical movement falls within the sphere of men's natural faculties, and is a proper subject of scientific investigation according to the recognized laws of historical research[3], and consequently any appeal to Christ's authority on such points is dangerous in so far as it mistakes the true purpose of His coming. He came to reveal

---

[1] St. Matt. ix. 13; St. John xii. 47 and vi. 38; St. Luke xii. 14.
[2] St. John v. 39.
[3] Cp. Köhler, *Über Berechtigung der Kritik des A. T.* pp. 24, 25. Valeton, *Christus und das A. T.* p. 27, speaking of the appeal to Christ's authority on points of scientific or historical research, well remarks: 'Es wäre ein wenigstens teilweises Übertragen seiner Bedeutung von dem Gebiete, wo sich alles dreht um Leben, Errettung, und Seligkeit, auf ein ganz anderes und für diese Dinge neutrales Gebiet, wo bloss Fragen wissenschaftlicher Art verhandelt werden.'

God to men, and He points to the Old Testament Scriptures as the source whence an adequate, if not an altogether perfect, knowledge of God and of His kingdom may be derived. And we shall find that criticism in no way impairs this function of the ancient Scriptures. We approach them as of old, only with a heightened consciousness of the divine operation which has brought the Old Testament into its present and final form. That form has been reached under the providential guidance of One who foresaw our circumstances, and who so controlled the tongue of the seer, the imagination of the poet, and the pen of the chronicler, that their utterances possess an abiding and progressive significance, speaking with fresh meaning and power to each successive generation of God's children. We must not lose in any literary or scientific investigations the characteristic Christian spirit. We may be keenly interested in the researches of critics; we may ourselves approach the Old Testament as students of literature, as philologists, as historians, as linguists, as archaeologists; but, after all, the main interest must not, cannot, be merely scientific or technical; it must be ethical and spiritual. The distinctively Christian temper is that which approaches the Bible as the record of a real and continuous revelation of God—His mind, His character, His moral requirement, His disciplinary dealings with mankind. We need to place ourselves on a level with believing students of all ages who, apart from the accidental circumstance that their critical knowledge or their exegetical methods were less perfect than ours, do nevertheless set before us an example of the true spirit in which Scripture should be approached and used. They do not allow personal tastes or predilections to blind them to the real purpose of Scripture. They do not suffer any subordinate interest to interfere with the primary object of biblical study, which is to make us *wise unto salvation*[1], to teach us about man

---

[1] 2 Tim. iii. 15.

and his need of Christ, about God and His purpose for humanity, about the conditions of acceptable worship and the attainment of perfect character.

2. It remains to estimate briefly the importance of Christian experience. It might be asked why Christian faith is more or less independent of critical controversies in regard to the Old Testament? The answer is because the Bible is 'a book of experimental religion[1]'; it depicts in each of its various stages the history of an actual friendship between God and man. The most potent factor in the formation of the canon was undoubtedly religious experience. The Old Testament books gained their authority and their place in the sacred library because, as a thoughtful critic has said, 'they commended themselves in practice to the experience of the Old Testament Church and the spiritual discernment of the godly in Israel[2].' The Mosaic dispensation did, as a matter of fact, educate in devout Israelites a certain faculty of spiritual insight; it produced a high level of religious knowledge and affection; it trained powers of discrimination which could be entrusted with the delicate task of gradually selecting or determining the contents of the Old Testament canon. At the period when the necessity for collecting a canon was realized, most of the Old Testament books were already familiar to the faithful, who found in them the light of their consciences and the food of their spiritual life. In fact, the canon assumed its final shape and gradually attained to authority as the result rather of an experimental process, than of theological reflection or discussion. For the canonical books, sufficiently at least for all purposes of religious edification, illustrated the great evangelical truths by which faith is kept alive[3]. They gave adequate expression

---

[1] Robertson Smith, *O. T. in J. C.* p. 8. [2] *Ibid.* p. 162.
[3] On this point, so far as it bears upon the Jewish limitation of the Old Testament to the 'canonical' books and the exclusion of others, see an excellent passage in Buhl, *Canon and Text of the O. T.* [Eng. Tr.] § 22.

to the vital needs which divine revelation satisfied. Indeed in large part that which we call with some freedom of expression the word of God is actually the word of man, since it gives utterance to the appeals, the supplications, the questionings, the yearnings after God, which make the Bible a universal book, reflecting the experience and the wants of humanity[1]. And the authority of the Bible, like that of Jesus Christ Himself, lies in the directness of its response to man's needs. Like the Lord's own teaching, Scripture is self-evidencing. Like Him, it speaks directly to the hearts and consciences of men, and its divine origin and authority is vindicated by the continuous testimony of Christians who have verified its message; and let us remember that its appeal to our generation is 'strengthened incalculably by the results of that same appeal to the minds and hearts and consciences of every preceding generation[2].'

Spiritual experience then lies behind the record in which it is enshrined, and this leads us to the observation that, after all, Christian faith is essentially independent of the Old Testament. The great fundamental verities are not learned by us from the pages of the ancient Scriptures. For instance, the writer of the Epistle to the Hebrews reminds us that we learn the fact and the true significance of the world's creation, not from the pages of Genesis, but as the result of Christian faith[3]; we find the verification of the fall of man in universal experience; we infer the pity of God for the human race from the upward movement which has marked its development and which culminates in the advent of the Son. In the Old Testament, Christian faith puts itself to school with the saints of the preparatory dispensation; it enters into their hopes and fears; it takes their language of love or trust on its lips; it learns how they regarded those great acts of God to which their whole history bears

---

[1] Cp. J. Paterson Smyth, *op. cit.* p. 122.
[2] *Ibid.* p. 27. Cp. pp. 21, 22.
[3] Heb. xi. 3.

undying witness. But faith carries with it a religious test learned in the school of Christ: it appropriates everything in the Old Testament which can edify the conscience, while it passes by all that falls short of Christ's teaching; thus it sometimes sets aside what the ancient saints extolled—the vengeance of Jael, for instance, or David's treatment of Moab—discriminating freely between what is profitable for the spiritual life and what belongs to a lower stage of human development[1].

There is one final reflection specially appropriate in this connexion. We have noticed the attestation which is given by Christian experience to the function of the Old Testament, but what has been said after all amounts to the assertion that the Old Testament Scriptures are an integral part of a treasure which peculiarly belongs to the Church of God—that divine society which exists as the living witness of God's continuous self-revelation in the world and which appeals to the Scriptures as corroborating her own primary testimony to God's truth. Believing then, as we do, that new and impressive views of God's providence are being opened out to us by the gradual advance of critical science, and that a revelation is being made to us respecting God's word in Scripture parallel to that which is already familiar to us in the sphere of physical nature, we shall realize the far-reaching importance of that foundation doctrine of the Church which God seems to have restored to us in time to enable us to deal with the critical question dispassionately and fearlessly. We, in this University, are not likely to forget the honoured names of those great spiritual leaders to whom, under God, we owe the recovery of this doctrine; nor can we easily over rate its vast significance. The doctrine has a plain bearing on our present inquiry. The Church of God!

---

[1] Cp. Köhler, *op. cit.* pp. 64, 65. Aug. *de doctrina*, ii. 8, gives a rule for determining the canonicity of different books which presupposes the guidance of organized experience.

—we belonged to her, her message was delivered to us, her powers were at work upon us before we were able to read a line of the Bible. She taught us that in the Bible God's voice was to be heard, but the manner in which it speaks she did not define. Thus the way has been left open for those who might competently instruct us in regard to the methods actually employed by the Holy Spirit. We certainly are not true to the mind of the Church, nor to that lofty temper which St. Paul commends to the Corinthians as specially characteristic of Christians, if we fail to appreciate and worthily use the gift of new knowledge with which this age of scientific criticism has enriched us. We approach the Old Testament with reverent interest as believers in the incarnation of the Son of God; with a deep sense of our own insufficiency as believers in the mystery of inspiration, and finally with the quietness and confidence of those whose feet are planted on the rock of the Holy Catholic Church, that city of God which claims as her own all that is good in human character, all that is precious in human life, all that is true in human knowledge. *All things are yours, whether Paul, or Apollos, or Cephas, or the world, or life, or death, or things present, or things to come; all are yours; and ye are Christ's; and Christ is God's.*

LECTURE II

But continue thou in the things which thou hast learned and hast been assured of, knowing of whom thou hast learned them; and that from a child thou hast known the holy scriptures, which are able to make thee wise unto salvation through faith which is in Christ Jesus.—2 Tim. iii. 14, 15.

IN this passage St. Paul at once indicates the scope and purpose of the Old Testament, and prescribes the condition of using it profitably. He begins by stating the reasonable ground on which the authority of the Christian Church is based. *Continue thou*, he says to Timothy, *in the things which thou hast learned and hast been assured of, knowing of whom thou hast learned them.* The acceptance of authority in itself implies an act of the moral judgment. The individual submits himself to the guidance of the Christian community mainly because it exhibits an impressive *consensus* of belief in regard at least to certain fundamental truths, but the testimony of the Church is commended and enforced by the spiritual life and character which lie behind it. The neophyte can venture upon an act of self-committal, because his reason tells him that the highest type of human excellence within the sphere of his observation has its roots in the creed of Christendom. In verse 15 the apostle appeals to Timothy's personal experience and training. *From a child* he has been taught to study the 'sacred writings' of the Old Testament and to find in them the necessary guidance of his religious thought and conduct. The peculiar function of these Scriptures is to *make wise unto salva-*

tion. The very phrase conveys a warning that men may approach Holy Scripture not only in a wrong temper and spirit, but under a positive misconception as to its true purpose. The study of the Old Testament is calculated to impart 'wisdom'—the knowledge, that is, of the great principles of divine action in the world, of the conditions under which man can be admitted to fellowship with his Creator; knowledge which is contrasted, on the one hand, with the intelligence or insight (σύνεσις) which apprehends the immediate purpose of God, on the other hand, with the practical wisdom (φρόνησις) which dictates right courses of action. The condition of acquiring this wisdom is faith resting on Christ Jesus. The true function of the Old Testament can only be rightly estimated from the standpoint of faith in one whose coming was from the first destined to crown the entire history of revelation.

Leaving on one side the exegesis of this particular passage, let us pass on to consider some general aspects under which the Old Testament presents itself to the Christian student. Viewed historically, the Old Testament is the sacred book of Judaism, the charter so to speak of the community which was organized by Ezra and Nehemiah on the basis of the levitical law and of the sacrificial cultus of the post-exilic sanctuary. It embodies the account, first, of the origin, historical career, and peculiar character of the holy community and of its sacred institutions; secondly, of the divine communications imparted to it from time to time through the agency of the prophets. Thirdly, it contains products of religious emotion and reflection, which illustrate the spiritual influences that prevailed in the Jewish Church and helped to mould its character. Lastly, the Old Testament depicts the external circumstances and conditions under which Judaism grew to maturity[1]. But the interest of a Christian in the ancient scriptures cannot be merely

---

[1] Cp. Dalman, *Das A. T. ein Wort Gottes*, p. 13.

literary or archaeological. He will be concerned with other aspects of the Old Testament, and of these five especially seem to deserve attention.

The Old Testament is to be studied, in the first place, as a record of the history of redemption. It contains the account of a continuous historical movement of which the originating cause was the grace of God and the aim the salvation of the human race. It scarcely requires to be stated that this aspect of the Old Testament opens very serious and urgent questions in regard to the precise character and extent of the strictly historical element in the ancient narratives. Secondly, the Old Testament is the authentic record of a divine revelation. It describes the course of a progressive self-manifestation of God, of the unveiling to man according to his needs and capacities of a supreme personality to whom he finds himself standing in necessary and intimate relationship. Thirdly, the Old Testament may be treated as the history of a covenantal relationship between man and God, of a continuous converse or friendship which from the first depended on moral conditions, and ever tended towards a more perfect mode of union between the divine and human natures. Fourthly, the Old Testament is to be regarded as the record of a growing anticipation or hope, the hope which we call Messianic, and which found expression not merely in ancient oracles and prophecies, but also in the symbolic institutions of the chosen people. This expectation was rooted in spiritual experience, outlived even the most formidable disasters which overtook the Hebrew nation, and found its accomplishment in an event of which only a chosen few were able to recognize the true significance. Lastly, the Old Testament is to be studied as the revelation of a divine purpose, not merely for a particular nation or even for humanity at large, but also for the individual soul in its frailty and solitariness, its sense of accountability, its presages of immortality.

In the present lecture these five aspects of the subject will be dealt with in general outline. The ensuing lectures will elaborate each in somewhat fuller detail. The classification does not pretend to be exhaustive, but it will probably be found to embrace the main points which are of special interest to Christian students of the Old Testament, and which are more or less affected by the discoveries of recent criticism and research. At any rate, ample scope will be provided for illustrating the new points of view in regard to scripture which we owe to the labours of modern scholarship. Our ideas of the methods actually employed in divine revelation will perhaps be enlarged, while some misconceptions may be removed which have hitherto hindered some minds from profitably studying the Old Testament. On the other hand, we may be led to a more intelligent use of the materials that are now available for those who desire to form a true estimate of Israel's place and function in the history of religion.

I. In the first place, then, we are to study the Old Testament as a history of redemption. This point of view enables us at once to discern the significance and purpose of that sublime statement of fundamental truths which forms the vestibule, so to speak, to the edifice of the Old Testament[1]. The early chapters of Genesis contain the presuppositions which alone could render welcome and intelligible the thought of a redemptive movement on the part of God for the salvation of men. They describe the creation of the world by God, the formation of man in the Creator's own image, the entrance of moral evil, and the divine purpose of restoration.

It will be convenient at this point to discuss these wonderful narratives, which are essentially poetical in

---

[1] Cp. Dillman, *Comm. on Genesis*, p. viii : 'Die Genesis ist die Vorbereitung zu den folg. Büchern oder gleichsam die Vorhalle zu dem Tempel der Theokratie dessen Errichtung in den folg. Büchern dargestellt wird.'

their form, and clearly stand on a different level from the historical books properly so called, which are to be considered separately in a subsequent lecture. They deal not with the substance of redemptive history, but rather with the facts of human nature which lie behind it; and consequently any prolonged discussion respecting the nature, sources, or scientific value of the 'narrative of the origins' is for present purposes irrelevant, or at least of very secondary importance. Even a slight observation of the characteristics of the Hebrew mind will suffice to show us that the scientific interest, if it existed at all, occupied an entirely subordinate place in the religious thought of an Israelite[1], and thus the story of the origins, though cast in a quasi-historical or mythical form, is in fact instinct with a religious aim. It does not appear to have had any peculiar or special connexion with Israel, but was in some form or other common to other branches of the Semitic race. The current traditions of the Creation, the Fall, and the Flood, are employed as a suitable medium for expressing the fundamental thoughts of true religion: the distinctness of God from the created universe; the immediate dependence on Him of all being at each stage of its development, and the essential goodness of that which owes its existence to Him. To the student of comparative religion it is no doubt of great interest to notice that in the story of the origins we have a narrative which shows clear traces of connexion with Phoenician and Chaldaean traditions; to the believer in divine inspiration it is of chief importance to notice how primitive myth is consecrated to spiritual uses, and how in the process it is purged of all that is puerile or immoral, the main outlines of the original story being retained, while the lower elements in it are entirely overmastered by the sublime spiritual thoughts

---

[1] Cp. Schultz, *Old Testament Theology* [Eng. Tr.], ii. 180; Köhler, *Über die Berechtigung der Kritik des A. T.* pp. 25, 26; Driver, *Serm. on O. T. Subj.* No. 1.

of a lofty religion¹. Such elements are indeed only
survivals, like the survivals in natural history, serving,
for aught we know, some beneficent purpose, showing
that Israel's religion had its roots in a Semitic
paganism, from which under the impulse of the Spirit
of God it gradually emancipated itself. No student
of the Old Testament will find serious difficulty in the
existence of mythical or even polytheistic elements
which have in fact become the medium of pure
religious ideas, and which have been so far stripped
of their original character as to serve the purposes
of a monotheistic system². 'Where the Assyrian or
Babylonian poet saw the action of deified forces of
nature, the Hebrew writer sees only the will of the
one supreme God³.' It is only necessary to remark
in passing that we have here the earliest, and in some
respects the most striking, illustration of a law which
pervades the entire religious development of the
people of God. The higher faith retains elements
derived from the lower stages of religion, but only to
regulate and to purify them, or in some cases even to
pass explicit judgment upon them. While in fact it is
abundantly clear that the religion of Israel presupposes
the nature-worship of the ancient Semitic peoples, it
is equally certain that it displayed from the very first
an upward tendency in the direction of a spiritual
monotheism. The ultimate outcome of Israel's long
discipline manifests the reality of that continual and
delicate divine pressure which lifted a rude and
barbarous tribe above its surroundings and raised it
to the throne of spiritual influence, in reference to
which Athanasius declares that Israel was 'a sacred

---

¹ Cp. Wellhausen, *op. cit.* pp. 304, 305, 314.
² Schultz, *op. cit.* i. 118.
³ Sayce, *The Higher Criticism and the Monuments*, p. 71. Cp. Renan, *Histoire du peuple d'Israël*, bk. i. ch. 4. Renan illustrates at length the influence of Babylonia on the Hebrew story of the origins, and points out how 'A free will, as implied by the words *He created*, substituted for ten thousand capricious fancies, is a progress of its kind' [Eng. Tr. p. 67].

school of the knowledge of God and of the spiritual life for all the world¹.'

The account of creation is followed by other fundamental statements relating to man's nature and destiny, the entrance of sin, and its culmination in death and divinely inflicted judgment. Distinctive of the Old Testament is the view that man was created in the divine image, that by the law of his original constitution he was a personal, self-conscious, and spiritual being, designed for communion with his Maker², and endowed with faculties enabling him to fulfil a spiritual destiny. Here again we do not look for scientific anthropology, but rather for a conception of human nature based upon experience and reflection. The narrative of the Fall is to be regarded as a particular solution, in poetical form, of a problem which at a very early period presented itself to human thought. In its essence the Fall consists in man's conscious choice of something lower than God Himself, something antagonistic to His revealed will. It is the perversion or defect of *will*; it is aversion from God³. The inspired story of Genesis suggests profound spiritual truths in regard to the character rather than to the origin of human sin. It presents a picture entirely true to nature of the awakening of moral consciousness and of that which is its ordinary sequel: the recognition by man that his will is out of harmony with the requirements of the moral order; the instinctive dread of severance from the source of all life; the discovery of the true significance of death for a spiritual being; the consciousness of physical evil as an impediment and obstacle in the way of human development. The biblical narrative is, in fact, the Hebrew solution of a fact which is quite independent of the scriptural evidence and is attested by the moral experience of

---

[1] *de Incarn.* c. xii.
[2] Schultz, ii. 238: 'The seal of the *Elohim* nature is stamped as it were on the substance of the fleshly nature.'
[3] Ath. *c. Gent.* v ἡ τῶν κρειττόνων ἀποστροφή. Greg. Nyss. *Orat. Catech.* v ἡ ἀπὸ τοῦ καλοῦ τῆς ψυχῆς ἀναχώρησις.

humanity[1]. The narratives then are apparently intended simply to justify and render credible the revelation of a divine love displayed in man's restoration. It is noticeable that they tell us nothing in regard to the conditions of primitive civilization. They merely indicate that man's original state was not what it is now. They do not suggest that he was perfect in the sense that he attained at once to complete development. They imply 'a living commencement which contained within itself the possibility of a progressive development[2].' Man was destined to develope upwards, and a certain measure of communion with his Creator was intended to guide and condition his progress, by giving to it impulse, direction, and stability. But the interest of the earliest compilers is primarily soteriological. Original sin is for them the starting-point of a divine purpose of recovery — of an historical movement passing through stages of orderly development and working mainly from within the fallen race itself[3].

The story of the Flood brings into view the principal factor in salvation—the gracious action of God crowning and rewarding the faith of man. The details of the story may appear to curious inquirers contradictory or even impossible[4]; nevertheless, the narrative gives expression to the religious thought that while God in His wrath visits sinful man with unsparing calamities, even at the very moment when he least expects it, yet in the midst of His judgments He guides and protects His own elect. Christians

---

[1] Coleridge, *Aids to Reflection*, aphorism cix; Mozley, *Lectures and other Theological Papers*, ix, x. Observe, in his allusions to the fall St. Paul does not always connect the fact with Adam. He rather insists that 'all have sinned' (Rom. iii. 23). So Athanasius (e. g.) describes the fall in *plural* terms. See *c. Gent.* iii; *de Incarn.* v. It is the apostasy not of *a man*, but of *mankind*, that is the occasion of redemption. Rom. vii. 21 shows that the point of importance is the existence of a uniform *law*, which in the Hebrew story is represented as resulting from the physical connexion between the human race and its first progenitor.

[2] Martensen, *Christian Dogmatics*, § 78.

[3] Cp. Oehler, *Theology of the O. T.* § 7.

[4] Cp. Meinhold, *Jesus und das A. T.* p. 114, &c.

accordingly are not concerned to maintain that the narrative as it stands is literally correct. It is enough to learn from it those true conceptions of God's character and action which formed the basis of Israel's faith, and which have been verified by the subsequent religious experience, not of Israel only, but of mankind.

The Old Testament, then, regarded as a history of human redemption, starts with certain necessary presuppositions which, though embodied in a primitive and childlike form, find their verification ultimately in the moral experience of mankind. The precise value and importance of the historical books will occupy our attention later. Meanwhile, it will be appropriate in this general survey of the subject to notice briefly two particular features which give a distinctive character to the sacred history.

In the first place, the course of redemption is marked at various points by the occurrence of the supernatural. In the Old Testament history divine action or intervention is represented as having been specially conspicuous at certain great crises or epochs, particularly it would seem on occasions when Jehovah willed to manifest Himself as unique or supreme among the supposed deities of heathendom, and accordingly miraculous powers are usually attributed only to a few leading instruments of revelation, such as Moses, Elijah, and Elisha [1]. Now it cannot be questioned that a complete self-manifestation of the divine nature demands action as well as utterance, and that miracles of grace and power are constitutive elements that may be antecedently expected in any authentic revelation of God [2]. The abstract possibility of miracle seems to be necessarily implied in the religious conception of God as a free, spiritual being, to whom the moral interests of the universe are of higher importance than the uninterrupted maintenance of physical law.

---

[1] Oehler, *The Theology of the O. T.* § 63.
[2] Cp. Bruce, *The Chief End of Revelation*, p. 168.

Miracle is also a natural element in any revelation of grace which takes the form of action rather than speech, for, as Dr. Bruce observes, 'the maximum of gracious possibility cannot be manifested without miracle [1].' A logical theism must claim for God the power to intervene in His own universe *on behalf of His good purpose* [2], and to display His entire exemption from any bondage to the present order of nature or to the past course of history [3]. In point of fact it is *creative* epochs in the history of religion that seem generally to be signalized or heralded by an exceptional coruscation of miracle. Indeed, if the Old Testament be the record of a divine movement destined to culminate in the Incarnation and Resurrection of the Son of God, a miraculous element in the history seems to be not only antecedently probable, but even necessary, as indicating the special purpose, direction, and moral quality of the divine action [4]. This general defence of the Old Testament miracles does not, however, imply a belief that every supernatural occurrence related in the different books literally happened exactly as it is described. Since it is admitted that the majority of the historical books only attained their present form centuries after the occurrence of many of the events recorded in them, we may—at least while the date of the original materials out of which they were compiled remains uncertain—safely allow the possibility of cases in which poetical or hyperbolical language has been hardened into concrete fact. It has been suggested that this is a probable explana-

---

[1] *The Chief End of Revelation*, p. 175.   [2] Phil. ii. 13.
[3] See Isa. xliii. 18, &c. Cp. the remarks of A. Ritschl, *Unterricht in der christlichen Religion* (Bonn, 1886), § 17: 'Die religiöse Betrachtung der Welt ist darauf gestellt, dass alle Naturereignisse zur Verfügung Gottes stehen, wenn er den Menschen helfen will. Demgemäss gelten als Wunder solche auffallende Naturerscheinungen, mit welchen die Erfahrung besonderer Gnadenhilfe Gottes verbunden ist, welche also als besondere Zeichen seiner Gnadenbereitschaft für die Gläubigen zu betrachten sind. Deshalb steht die Vorstellung von Wundern in nothwendiger Wechselbeziehung zu dem besonderen Glauben an Gottes Vorsehung, und ist ausserhalb dieser Beziehung gar nicht möglich.'
[4] Cp. A. L. Moore, *Science and the Faith*, pp. 98, 99.

tion of the narrative which describes the standing still of the sun at the command of Joshua[1]. Nor is it a matter of crucial importance to contest the opinion, whatever it may be worth, that even in the case of great personages belonging to a much later age, there has been a somewhat free ascription of symbolic miracles. Thus, in the case of Elijah and Elisha it is sometimes maintained that the analogy of secular history points to a possible growth of popular tradition, filling up or adding to the record of their mighty deeds. Differences of opinion in regard to the precise extent of the undoubtedly historical nucleus contained in the narratives relating to such heroic figures may reasonably be admitted. In any case the miracles, whether actually performed or popularly ascribed, foreshadowed the redemptive works of the incarnate Son. To lay equal stress on the miracles of the Old Testament and on those of our Lord not only involves a serious confusion of thought; it implies misapprehension of the true character of the Old Testament and forgetfulness of the principle expressed in Augustine's maxim, *Sicut Veteri Testamento, si esse ex Deo bono et summo negetur, ita et Novo fit injuria si Veteri aequetur.*

Secondly, we may notice a general principle which underlies the redemptive action of God, namely, the principle of limitation or severance. The tendency of Hebrew history is towards specialization: the action of a *purpose of God according to election*[2] is observable. The entire story of Genesis, for instance, consists in

---

[1] Kittel, *History of the Hebrews*, vol. i. p. 303 [Eng. Tr.], says of Joshua x. 12–14: 'This [event] can signify nothing but an extraordinary duration of the day of battle which allowed Joshua to finish his martial day's work. The daylight held out till the work of vengeance on the enemy was completed. Joshua has poetically glorified this in the song as a standing still of the sun, because he knew of no other explanation.' Kittel implies that a miracle did take place, but the reviser of the book of Joshua turned the song 'into matter-of-fact prose.' Renan, *Histoire*, &c., bk. ii. ch. 3, gives a simple literary and linguistic explanation of the passage, on which Judg. v. 20 sheds some light. A parallel instance is perhaps to be found in Num. xxii. 28.
[2] Rom. ix. 11.

a series of separations. Even the account of creation itself begins by recording an act of severance as if it were a constant law of the divine action: *God divided the light from the darkness*, the waters above the firmament from those below, the dry land from the seas[1]. In the actual history this law of severance meets us in a new form as the principle of election, according to which the few are set apart and educated in order that, by their means, blessing may be extended to the many. The account of the patriarchs is so framed as to give special prominence to the idea of election[2], but it already emerges in Gen. iv. 26, where a contrast is implied between the world-power and the worshippers of the true God. And there can be no doubt that the same principle gives us the true key to the significance of Israel's entire history. It is uncertain at what point in its career the truth of its election was fully realized by the nation, but it is clear that the divine purpose was in process of fulfilment from the first. *This people have I formed for myself; they shall show forth my praise*[3]. At the earliest stage of its national existence Israel was reminded of the purpose for which it had been separated from the nations of the world. Even in the primitive forecast of its great destiny a universalistic element was present[4]; in Abraham and his seed all the nations of the earth were to be blessed; and subsequently Israel was taught that He who had brought the nation to Himself, with the design of making it *a kingdom of priests and a holy nation*, was no merely national God like the deities of the heathen, but *the Lord of all the earth*[5]. Israel was chosen, as we may well believe, in prefer-

---

[1] Gen. i. 4, 6, 10.
[2] See Gen. xii. 3; xiii. 14; xv. 5; xvii. 5; xviii. 17-19; xxii. 16, &c.
[3] Isa. xliii. 21. The doctrine of Israel's election seems to be most clearly brought out by the prophets of the eighth century, and a stimulus was given to the conception by the publication of Deuteronomy. See Montefiore, *Hibbert Lectures*, p. 124; Sanday, *Bampton Lectures*, p. 163.
[4] Cp. Bruce, *Apologetics*, pp. 198, 199.
[5] Cp. Exod. xix. 5, 6; Joshua iii. 11.

ence to other nations 'because in genius and temper it was best fitted to realize God's purposes towards man, to be the channel of His grace, and to develope, through many failures, an ideal of godliness and faith [1].' But if Israel was called to be the medium of a blessing designed for humanity at large, the privilege imposed high obligations. For the Hebrew people was chosen to be the depositary of a purer faith and loftier morality than that recognized by other races. Hence the necessity of Israel's isolation from the surrounding heathen and its subjection to a special moral discipline. It was the task of the eighth-century prophets to bring home to the nation the ideal purpose of its separation from the world and the bearing of God's elective action on the spiritual destinies of mankind. There is true discernment in the fine remark of Irenaeus, 'Jehovah brought His people out of Egypt in order that man might once more become a disciple and follower of God [2].' The ultimate object of the divine grace was not Israel, but humanity.

In speaking of the Old Testament as a history of redemption, we do not mean that it furnishes a complete history of Israel. It has been said with truth that the Old Testament rather 'supplies the materials from which such a history can be constructed [3].' It is indeed a record of God's action in history, but one that is marked by special purpose and character, interpreting what it narrates, and selecting facts according to some inner principle of fitness. The historian may justly require that the record in its main outlines should be adequate and that Israel's interpretation of its own history should be in essential points trustworthy. But we shall see that it is unwise to over-estimate the extent of the strictly historical element in the Old Testament. The selection of facts and the mode of their presentation are dictated not so much by a merely

---

[1] Driver, *Serm. on the O. T.* p. 57.
[2] Iren. *Haer.* iv. 16. 3. Cp. Bruce, *Apologetics*, p. 182.
[3] Robertson Smith in his preface to Wellhausen's *Prolegomena*, p. vii.

historical interest as by a sense of the religious import of what is narrated. 'It has not pleased God,' says a recent writer, 'to convey to us instruction concerning the ancient period [of Israel's history] in the form of indisputably historical documents; consequently the external details of the narrative cannot be for us the matters of chief significance. Occasionally the prophetic elucidation of material not in itself religious may be the important thing in a particular book. For example, to a historian the narratives in the book of Judges which relate the exploits of Hebrew heroes are more important than the Deuteronomic framework; yet it is precisely this framework that gives the book its canonical character. The historical and the canonical valuations of a book follow different laws, and go in different directions [1].' The evident aim, generally speaking, of the writers and compilers of the sacred history is to convey and emphasize a certain religious impression, not to give a complete or rigidly accurate picture of events.

II. The second of those general aspects of the Old Testament which will occupy our attention is by far the most important. The Old Testament does not merely contain the history of a divine redemptive movement: it is also the record of a self-revelation of Almighty God; it describes the gradual disclosure of the divine name and attributes. The permanent interest of Israel's history for mankind lies in the fact that in the history a supreme moral personality is unveiled. Israel's sacred literature is primarily a school of divine knowledge for the whole world.

Now, that the Old Testament exhibits a gradual evolution of the idea of God is, of course, indisputable. Naturalistic criticism gives its own clear, plausible, intelligible account of the gradual advance of Israel's belief. In the earliest stage of Semitic thought the divine nature is vaguely conceived in polytheistic fashion as distributed among a plurality of beings

[1] Dalman, *Das A. T. ein Wort Gottes*, p. 15.

whose operation lies hidden behind the various processes of nature. As the consciousness of tribal unity is developed, each tribe recognizes a special deity, linked to itself by ties of interest and natural affinity. When different tribes coalesce and realize something of national unity, the deity is elevated to the position of a national god, united by a special bond to one particular people and land. Presently, when the nation comes into conflict with neighbouring peoples and their gods, the dignity and importance of the deity is enhanced in proportion to the measure of national success in warfare. He is honoured as the mighty god whose power extends even beyond the limits of his own special sphere of influence. With the advance of culture and civilization, men recognize moral qualities in their god, attributing to him the virtues which they fear or reverence in their fellowmen. As the horizon of human thought widens, the deity is acknowledged to be a righteous being who controls and guides the destinies, not only of his own subjects, but also those of alien nations. Finally, when the faculties of abstraction and reflection have reached a certain point of development, the conception is formed of one God, the creator of all things, reigning in solitary majesty over all the nations of the earth. The whole process is thus represented as one of simple natural development, and the idea of special revelation is set aside as unwelcome and unnecessary.

As is usually the case, the same set of facts is capable of being interpreted in two distinct ways and from two opposite points of view. The real question at issue in our present-day controversy with naturalistic criticism is whether or no God is a living being[1], to whom the spiritual interests of mankind are of supreme importance, and who at each stage of development, physical or moral, is Himself present in the universe

---

[1] See Oettli, *Der gegenwärtige Kampf um das A. T.* p. 13; Valeton, *Christus und das A. T.* p. 1.

as an impelling, directing and overruling cause[1]. The distinctive feature of Israel's religion is prophetism, and where the voice of inspired prophecy is heard, God is specially at work in history; the purely naturalistic account of the phenomena breaks down. It is no part of our present task, however, to discuss so fundamental a point as this. There can be no question in regard to the belief of those who felt themselves to be not chance discoverers of interesting truths, but inspired organs of divine revelation. We may observe, however, that the idea of a gradual evolution in the conception of God is expressly recognized by the Old Testament itself. One main object of the priestly narrative which forms the basis of the Pentateuch seems to be that of indicating successive stages in the self-revelation of God, each stage being apparently marked by some new declaration of the divine name, in other words, by some express manifestation of His character. It will be our duty to examine hereafter the theological import of these several names. At this point it is only necessary to notice the general outlines of the Old Testament doctrine of God, surveyed as a whole. The divine self-revelation, be it remembered, was chiefly embodied in action and history. Indeed the Bible contains very little of mere abstract teaching or formal doctrine; the character of God and His relation to the universe are rather left to be inferred from His action. To the prophets the supreme interest of human history lies in its being a sphere of observation in which the attributes, purposes and methods of God may be studied. And the very foundation of Israel's national history was constituted by an event to which in later times the religious mind of the people continually reverted,—a signal historical deliverance, an act of divine intervention, which in itself implied a unique manifestation of God's nature and character. The incidents of the exodus could scarcely fail to suggest some general ideas about God which the whole subse-

[1] Cp. Oettli, *op. cit.* p. 4.

quent history was destined to elucidate, confirm, and enlarge; even at this early stage there emerged, so to speak, the ideas of the divine unity, the divine holiness, the divine grace, that is, the willingness and power of God to redeem.

We should be passing beyond the limits of probability if we insisted that the exodus did more than *suggest* these ideas. It will scarcely be disputed that they can have been apprehended, perhaps not very distinctly, only by a few leading spirits in the newly-formed nation; and they were not openly preached, so far as we can judge, until the period of the eighth-century prophets. In the book of Deuteronomy they may be said to be leading and characteristic theses. Take, for instance, the first of the ideas now in question—that of the divine unity. An unbiassed study of the Old Testament discloses to us the gradual development of the conception. It is practically certain that in its earlier stages the worship of the ordinary Hebrew was not monotheistic but monolatrous. Till a comparatively late period the average Israelite seems to have believed in the existence of other gods than Jehovah—deities who stood in the same relation to foreign tribes and nations, as that in which Jehovah stood to Israel. Prof. Riehm draws attention to the tendency, common apparently among tribes of Semitic descent, to acknowledge a special tribal god. The natural basis on which a true monotheism could be securely built up was formed by monolatry or henotheism[1]. Israel's earliest religious lesson was, in fact, learned on the Red Sea shore. In the marvellous deliverance of His people from the tyranny of Egypt, Jehovah was already proved to be at least incomparable, or unique, among gods[2]. It was not as yet distinctly perceived, at least by the mass of the

---

[1] *ATl. Theologie*, p. 45. Renan, *Histoire du peuple d'Israël*, bk. I, ch. I, remarks that 'even from the most ancient times the Semite patriarch had a secret tendency towards monotheism, or at least towards a simple and comparatively reasonable worship.'

[2] Exod. xv. 11. Cp. 1 Sam. ii. 2; Isa. xl. 25.

ransomed people, that Israel's God was the Lord of all the earth. He was regarded as the tribal god of the Hebrews, fighting its battles, and claiming its allegiance, in opposition to the gods of surrounding nations. It has been thought by some critics that the idea of Jehovah's uniqueness only appears in the early period of the monarchy [1]; but it is more probable that it arose as a direct consequence of the events of the exodus. That solemn crisis in Israel's history signally manifested the impotence and insignificance of other gods in comparison of Jehovah. Thus the foundation of a consistent monotheism was laid, not in any definite declarations of the divine unity—such as we find at a later period—but in a practical proof that other *Elohim* were powerless to resist the will of the Deity who had chosen Israel for Himself and had wrought its salvation [2]. The exodus manifested the incomparable glory and irresistible might of Israel's God. And indeed during the period of its conflict for the possession of the promised land Israel was too deeply absorbed in practical tasks to feel any special interest in the question whether other gods 'had or had not metaphysical existence. The practical point was that Jehovah proved Himself stronger than they by giving Israel victory over their worshippers [3].' And so long as other supernatural beings were regarded as merely

---

[1] Cp. Darmesteter, *Les Prophètes d'Israël*, pp. 23, 24: 'Avec les victoires de David, avec les splendeurs de Salomon, avec la construction du temple qui donne enfin à Jéhovah une demeure fixe et à son culte un centre de plus en plus absorbant, Jéhovah devient définitivement le dieu propre d'Israël. Les triomphes de David prouvent qu'il est plus puissant que les dieux voisins : Qui est comme toi parmi les Élohim, ô Jéhovah ? '

[2] Cp. Oehler, *Theol. of the O. T.* § 43 ; König, *The Religious History of Israel* [Eng. Tr.], p. 74.

[3] Robertson Smith, *The Prophets of Israel* (ed. 1), p. 60. Darmesteter, *op. cit.* pp. 217, 218, seems to state the case correctly : 'La tribu . . . est polythéiste, puisque le croyant reconnaît la multiplicité des forces et des volontés divines et croit à plus de dieux qu'il n'en adore ; mais elle est monothéiste en ce qu'elle se livre spécialement à un seul, monothéisme chancelant, qui se concilie parfaitement avec l'idolâtrie et transportera aisément son obéissance et ses offrandes de Jahvé à Molokh, Baal ou Camoch, etc. . . . Mais ce monothéisme incertain, idolâtrique et sans morale, contient en germe le monothéisme strict.'

relative, and incapable of resisting the one God of Israel's allegiance, a naïve belief in the existence of other *'Elohim* did not necessarily conflict with the idea of the divine unity. Prof. Schultz justly observes that ' Where it is a matter of religion, not of philosophy, the first and necessary thing always is the conviction of having God as one's own, and of being also God's—not the consideration of how this God stands related to the possibility of there being other gods[1].' At the same time there is ample reason for supposing that there was a constant tendency in the spiritual leaders of Israel, or at least in the special organs of divine revelation, to combat the popular notion that Jehovah was merely one God among many. Certainly the whole drift of the chapters in which the events connected with the exodus are narrated, is the exaltation of Jehovah as the one being whose existence, influence, and righteous will it behoved the chosen people to acknowledge[2]. It is probable on *a priori* grounds that, though the age of what may be called theoretic monotheism was introduced by the teaching of the eighth-century prophets, the idea of the divine unity was an inference, so to speak, from premisses which the exodus had suggested to reflective minds. Such an event could not fail to give birth to the thought, on the one hand, of Jehovah's irresistible might, on the other, of His moral transcendence. Here we seem to have the historic basis of the doctrine of the divine unity[3].

There are, then, good reasons for the supposition that a strictly monotheistic belief does not date from the earliest period of Israel's national existence. On the contrary, there are unmistakeable indications that a belief in the actual existence of other deities survived to a comparatively late age. The existence of heathen gods was not uniformly denied. They were either

---

[1] *O. T. Theology*, i. 180.
[2] See Exod. viii. 10; ix. 14, 16; x. 2; xv. 2, 11, 18.
[3] Montefiore, *Hibbert Lectures*, pp. 134, 135.

regarded as *'Elilim,* 'nothings'[1]; or they were supposed, if existent at all, to be subordinate instruments of the one God: Jehovah alone was *God of gods and Lord of lords*[2]. The ascription however of unique majesty to the national Deity tended towards His elevation to the dignity of an only existent Lord of the universe[3].

The facts of the case thus justify the idea of evolution in religious thought which historical analogy itself might antecedently suggest. We have no interest in maintaining that Israel's religion sprang to the birth, perfect and complete, in the age of Moses. The monotheistic idea had a long history even within the limits of the chosen race whose mission it was to teach mankind the knowledge of God. But the idea seems to have been closely connected with another which next claims our attention, namely, that of the divine *holiness.* 'The belief that Jehovah was the only God,' says Prof. Kuenen, 'sprang out of the ethical conception of His being[4].' The question is at what period such a conception first appeared. What is contended is that the events of the exodus could not fail to introduce certain moral elements into the idea of God which Israel inherited from its Semitic ancestors.

The truth of the divine holiness, in its developed form, is one of those ideas which impart a unique character to Israel's religion. It was a truth which other religions were constantly striving to express, and which the universal human conscience instinctively anticipated in external institutions of worship. But Israel alone was enabled to lift the idea of holiness from the purely outward and ritual, into the inward and ethical

---

[1] אלילים Lev. xix. 4; 2 Kings xvii. 15; Jer. ii. 5; viii. 19. See also Deut. iv. 19; x. 17; Ps. xcv. 3; xcvi. 5. Cp. 1 Cor. viii. 5, 6.
[2] Cp. Pfleiderer, *Gifford Lectures*, vol. ii. 48; Ritschl, *Unterricht in der Christlichen Religion*, § 11. The belief in the existence of other gods seems expressly indicated in such passages as Exod. xv. 11; Judges xi. 24; Ruth i. 16; 1 Sam. xxvi. 19; 2 Sam. xiv. 16.
[3] Cp. Darmesteter, *op. cit.* pp. 213, 214.
[4] *Hibbert Lectures*, p. 119; ap. Montefiore, *op. cit.* p. 135.

sphere, and thereby gave to its religion a distinctness from all other faiths not only in degree but in kind[1]. What then is the historical *genesis* of this idea? If the date of the documentary evidence is disputed, we are left to a balance of probabilities; and there are at least some considerations in favour of the view that the process by which the notion of holiness was, so to speak, *moralized* began at the period of the exodus. Jehovah is first described as 'holy' in the Song of Moses, and the term apparently implies merely the negative notion of 'separation,' or possibly 'transcendence[2].' The 'holy' God is He who is raised absolutely above the world, and is thereby separated from the creature. Of earthly things, every object or being is holy in so far as it is appropriated to religious service, or is withdrawn from common uses. Originally therefore holiness, even as applied to persons, was not in any sense a moral attribute; it implied only ritual separation[3], and we can almost trace the process by which, under the influence of prophetic teaching, the idea of holiness passed from an outward to an inward sphere, from the notion of external consecration or dedication to that of moral sanctity. But it is in relation to the divine Being Himself that the word 'holy' is specially remarkable—not only because the conception of holiness was constantly elucidated by every fresh stage in the self-revelation of God, but also because it was the basis of that peculiar consciousness of Israel's function in the world which is characteristic of the later prophets and of the priestly school who impressed upon Israel its permanent and ineffaceable stamp of separateness. *Ye shall be holy; for I am holy.* Israel, as belonging

---

[1] Cp. A. L. Moore in *Lux Mundi*, p. 72 foll.
[2] Exod. xv. 11. Cp. Isa. xl. 25; Ps. xcix. 2 foll.
[3] On 'holiness' see Robertson Smith, *Prophets of Israel*, pp. 224 foll.; Oehler, *op. cit.* §§ 44, 45; Riehm, *A Tl. Theologie,* § 12. As is well known, the idea of 'holiness' (separation) was common to the heathen neighbours of Israel, and might incidentally, e.g. in the case of the 'holy' persons of Canaanitish nature-worship, imply consecration to immoral purposes. See Robertson Smith, *Religion of the Semites*, pp. 90, 192.

to Jehovah by redemptive right, must necessarily participate in His character, and look upon itself with something of the reverence due to what is divine. We are justified in believing that the idea of its holiness, its call to consecration, is the secret of that fine spirit of self-respect which has never abandoned Israel even in the most stormy and sorrowful vicissitudes of its subsequent history.

Holiness, then, seems to be a conception which had its roots in the circumstances of the Mosaic age. It was a keynote of national polity and organization from the first. In calling God 'holy' Mosaism guarded the truth of the divine transcendence; it protested, as it were, against the religious error of contemporary heathendom, Egyptian or Canaanitish, which confused nature with God, and as it were degraded God into the region of the creature. In calling things or persons 'holy,' Mosaism lifted them, so to speak, out of the region of what was profane or unclean into a divine sphere. But the whole tendency of Mosaism was to develope and extend the idea. True, holiness in the ethical sense was far from being Israel's present character; rather it was the nation's ideal goal and destiny[1]. While then the 'holiness' of the newly-formed nation was in the first instance a mark or character impressed from without on its physical and social life, and found embodiment in visible ordinances relating to external and ceremonial purity, 'holiness' was ultimately destined to be transformed into an inward quality or attribute, a real separateness not from mere bodily uncleanness but from spiritual and moral defilement; aloofness not from the idolatrous pollutions of Egypt, but from sin. Thus the character of Jehovah's chosen people was to be conformed to that of Him who had sealed them as His own.

There was yet another idea which the exodus

---

[1] As God's own people Israel is קָדֹשׁ, Exod. xix. 6; Lev. xx. 26, opposed to חֹל Lev. x. 10; 1 Sam. xxi. 5 foll.; Ezek. xxii. 26.

suggested, and which subsequent periods of reflection served to impress permanently on the mind and imagination of Israel, viz. the idea of Jehovah's redemptive grace. In the deliverance of His people God had manifested Himself as one who is able and willing to redeem; able because He is almighty[1], free from anything like entanglement in the processes of nature, and having perfect liberty to intervene with direct personal energy in the history of men and nations. The Old Testament writers look back with awe and exultation to the days of the nation's birth, signalized as it was by a mighty display of supernatural force; but the occasion of Jehovah's intervention made it manifest that His power was guided by love and gracious willingness to redeem. The God who had espoused the cause of an enslaved and oppressed people must needs be a Being full of pity and rich in mercies, faithful to His promises and righteous in His judgments[2]. The exodus was indeed a supreme display of character, and we are even justified in holding with Ewald that the very keynote of the Pentateuch is the conception of Jehovah as a merciful deliverer. That idea, as he points out, is embodied in the sanctions affixed to the first five commandments of the Decalogue. In each case the divine precept is based on some feature in the beneficent character of God. Thus in the first word Jehovah proclaims Himself as the Saviour who has ransomed Israel from the house of bondage; in the second as a jealous God, good to them that love, severe to them that hate Him, yet even in sternness remembering His mercy; in the third as a glorious God, who will by no means clear the guilty or give His glory to another; in the fourth as a God who has thoughts of peace and refreshment for His 'desert-wearied' people and leads them to blessedness and rest; in the fifth as a God who gives bounteously to the poor, and prepares for them a land to dwell

---

[1] Exod. vi. 1. [2] Exod. iii. 7, 8; vi. 5, 8.

in. Israel's obligation to obedience is rooted in Jehovah's character. His redemptive acts on behalf of His elect people stand in the forefront of the moral law, and supply the motive of love and service.

Grace is, in fact, a prominent element in the divine self-revelation from the first point in Israel's history to the last. And, in accordance with the whole course of man's religious history, a stage of external manifestation precedes that of inward realization. Grace is first revealed in the sphere of history and providence,—God working for the redemption of a downtrodden people; 'doing for Israel what she could not do for herself, in love and pity redeeming a helpless enslaved race from a state of bondage,' and throughout its history ever renewing the manifestation of his goodness. *In all their affliction he was afflicted, and the angel of his presence saved them; in his love and in his pity he redeemed them; and he bare them, and carried them all the days of old* [1].

At a later period, grace came to be regarded by the prophets as an internal operation of divine love, 'a beneficent power working within men, enabling them to fulfil the divine will [2],' a power subduing sin, cleansing the conscience, and renewing the heart. So the historical and external enfranchisement was acknowledged to be the type of a spiritual deliverance; and as religious affections became more perfectly developed, devout Israelites became ever more alive to the true significance of Jehovah's mighty acts on behalf of their fathers in the time of old; witness the tenderness of such a passage as the following extract from the fourth book of Esdras. *Thus saith the Almighty Lord, Have I not prayed you as a father his sons, as a mother her daughters, and a nurse her*

---

[1] Isa. lxiii. 9.
[2] Bruce, *Apologetics*, p. 249. Riehm, *A Tl. Theologie*, p. 35, remarks that in the Old Testament as in the New we have a redemptive act of God: 'Im alten Bunde eine Erlösung des Volkes von äusserlicher Knechtschaft, im neuen eine Erlösung aller einzelnen von geistlicher Knechtschaft.'

young babes, that ye would be my people, and I should be your God; that ye would be my children, and I should be your father? I gathered you together, as a hen gathereth her chickens under her wings[1]. Indeed the most essential characteristic of Old Testament religion is its unshaken conviction, that the Holy God who manifested Himself to His chosen people was above all else a God of grace: Israel's election, and redemption, and its preservation throughout the perilous vicissitudes of its chequered history, were standing proofs that the most fundamental and enduring element in the divine Being is Love [2].

It will be our business in a later lecture to investigate more particularly the main points of the Old Testament revelation of God. Meanwhile, let it suffice to remark that we only do justice to the labours of criticism when we acknowledge the fact of a long and slow development in Israel's conception of deity. Some have supposed that the knowledge of God was originally simple and pure, and that the religion of Israel was merely the re-establishment of a primitive monotheism. But, in spite of the admitted possibility of degradation as a factor in religious history, it must be frankly owned that there is a lack of evidence for the existence of an original monotheistic religion among the Semites, and indeed the Old Testament itself contains indications that even in Abraham's family there was a survival of idolatrous practices and beliefs [3].

The history of Israel seems, as a matter of fact, to show us clearly marked stages in the development of the idea of God, the prophets from Moses onwards being the leaders of religious thought. In the earliest period, Jehovah is popularly conceived as a national God, opposed to the gods of surrounding nations, having the same attributes as they, chiefly wrathful-

---

[1] 4 Esdras i. 28 f. The date of this book is thought to be circ. 90, A.D.
[2] Cp. Riehm, *ATl. Theolog.e*, § 11, pp. 62, 63.
[3] Cp. Gen. xxxv. 2; Joshua xxiv. 2. Cp. Riehm, *op. cit.* pp. 31, 32.

ness and jealousy, worshipped with similar rites and making the same demands. But, as we have seen, higher and purer ideas were impressed by the marvels of the exodus on at least the more receptive minds. Step by step the evolution of thought proceeds. The narrative of Israel's conflicts is the story of *the wars of Jehovah*[1], of a struggle between Israel's national God and the deities of alien tribes. The work of the prophets was to moralize the conception of Jehovah; to show that His essential attributes were ethical, His necessary requirement of man, holiness. Finally, in the great overthrow of the nation the national conscience was led by the Holy Spirit to recognize that which the loftier spirits had already discerned ages before; it acknowledged the triumph of the divine righteousness; it rose to the conception of a God one, holy, and gracious [2].

With one general remark we leave the subject of progressive Revelation. It has been already pointed out that belief and unbelief are confronted by the same facts; they are distinguished by the divergent account which each gives of the facts. The process of evolution in Israel's faith lies on the very surface of the Old Testament, and is verified by all that we know of God's dealings in every department of His action. We recognize then the progressive development of Old Testament religion: but we look upon it not as 'a spontaneous upward movement of the human mind, whereby it passes from crude errors to purer forms of thought, but as a progressive self-unveiling of Deity in the sphere of revelation, as a divine work of education, dealing with stubborn and

---

[1] Num. xxi. 14.
[2] Cp. Darmesteter, *op. cit.* pp. 165 f. It is very important to bear in mind the contrast between the mass of the Hebrew people and the inner circle which responded to the teaching of prophetic leaders. There is every ground for asserting with Riehm, *op. cit.* p. 11 : 'Die Masse des Volkes, insbesondere auch die Priesterschaft, blieb immer im Grossen und Ganzen auf jener ersten Stufe der volkstümlichen Ausgestaltung der alttestamentlichen, Religion stehen, während die höhere Entwicklungs-gestalt des Prophetismus sich auf einen engeren Kreis beschränkte.'

intractable material¹.' The contrast between these two views is profound, and we owe a debt of gratitude to the historical criticism which has enlarged our sense of the continuity observable in divine revelation. We have learned to apprehend more clearly what has been an axiom of Christian thought since the principle was vindicated by Irenaeus in opposition to the Gnostics². 'It is the same God,' says a recent writer, 'who made Himself known to Abraham, Moses, Elijah, and Isaiah, who revealed Himself as our Father in the person of Jesus Christ. He is the same with the fathers as with the children: but He condescends lovingly to submit Himself to those limitations of man's spiritual life which He Himself ordained. He reveals Himself to children, according to their capacity, to men in such wise as is suitable to men; He does not at one sweep get rid of all obscurities and all obstacles, but overcomes them gently and patiently by acting on them from within; He does not annihilate with one magic stroke all alien elements, which His revelation finds already present in the minds of its recipients, but allows the measure of divine knowledge and experience which can be imparted to work as a ferment which in time will sever the defective elements from the good³.'

III. A third point of view from which the Old Testament may be studied will have to be considered. It traces the history, and states the conditions, of a covenantal relationship between God and man; of a life of friendship or communion which grows out of the original relation in which the Creator stands to the creature. This life of love begins historically with God's election of the patriarch Abraham: and the deliverance of his descendants from servitude became the basis of a 'covenant' between Jehovah and those whom *He took by the hand to lead them*

---

[1] Oettli, *op. cit.* p. 19.
[2] Cp. Iren. *Haer.* iii. 3. 3, &c.; also Novat. *de Trin.* viii.
[3] Oettli, *op. cit.* p. 20.

out of the land of Egypt[1]. For the present it is desirable to waive the question when the unique relationship of God to His ransomed people first came to be regarded in the light of a covenant, a question of which Wellhausen seems to dispose somewhat too confidently. At this point it will suffice to touch upon some leading features of the settlement which was traced back by Hebrew faith to the time of the exodus.

First, it is noticeable that the 'covenant' is rather a matter of divine institution or disposition than a contract between two equal parties[2]. The initiation is taken by Jehovah, and is purely an act of grace. He who establishes a bond of union between Himself and man also fixes the necessary conditions of it. This is tantamount to saying that behind the covenant lies Israel's election, a thought which is specially characteristic of the book of Deuteronomy[3]. Again, we find that the covenant is formally ratified by sacrifice, in accordance with the principle universally recognized—διαθήκη ἐπὶ νεκροῖς βεβαία[4]. The death of a sacrificial victim on the one hand secured the immutability of the terms laid down in the covenant, and on the other symbolized the surrender of man's natural life, which must be freely yielded up if it is to be brought into contact with the divine nature. Only by accepting death can human nature enter upon a higher sphere of active serviceableness in the kingdom of God. Further, the sprinkling of the victim's blood upon the people was an emblem of their consecration to the life of covenant-fellowship. It was a kind of baptism by which Israel was translated into a spiritual kingdom, and endued with the sanctity of the divine life. It was a seal of that act, or series of acts, by which

---

[1] Jer. xxxi. 32. Cp. Heb. viii. 9.
[2] Διαθήκη rather than συνθήκη. Cp. Westcott, *Ep. to the Hebrews*, pp. 222, 299.
[3] Deut. vii. 7; viii. 18.   [4] Heb. ix. 17.

Jehovah had appropriated the nation to Himself and made it His own[1]. Finally—and this is the main point —the covenant necessarily involved a divine requirement. Accordingly, in Exod. xxiv. the newly-formed nation binds itself to Jehovah's service, *All that the Lord hath said will we do, and be obedient*[2].

Thus at the very outset of its national career Israel is pledged to moral obedience, and it is forewarned that a special character is the condition of union with the holy God[3]. *Ye shall be a holy nation* — such is the divine command; *Ye shall be holy, for I am holy*;—words which point to the future rather than the present; to a predestined purpose rather than an accomplished fact. 'From the first the people were told of their calling . . . what they existed for, what their existence pointed to[4],' and the position of the Decalogue, both in Exodus and in Deuteronomy, is a significant token of the principle so emphatically insisted on by the prophets that the *moral* law is the essential bond of union between God and man, and that ethical obligations transcend those of the ceremonial and ritual law. So Jeremiah insists[5]: *I spake not unto your fathers, nor commanded them in the day that I brought them out of the land of Egypt, concerning burnt offerings or sacrifices; but this thing commanded I them, saying, Obey my voice, and I will be your God, and ye shall be my people; and walk ye in all the ways that I have commanded you, that it may be well unto you.* It is, as Irenaeus points out, the Decalogue which fixes the eternal conditions of fellowship between God and man; and consequently its precepts are extended and enlarged, rather than dissolved, by the personal advent of the Redeemer[6].

---

[1] Cp. Ezek. xvi. 8: 'Then becamest thou mine.' See Oehler, *Theol. of the O. T.* § 121.

[2] Exod. xxiv. 3, 7.

[3] This is already implied in Gen. xviii. 19. Cp. Exod. xix. 6; Lev. xi. 45, xix. 2.

[4] R. W. Church, *Discipline of the Christian Character*, p. 30.

[5] Jer. vii. 22, 23. These verses have naturally played an important part in the history of criticism. [6] Iren. *Haer.* iv. 16. 4.

The thought, then, of a covenant uniting man to his Creator may be said to pervade the Old Testament, and it cannot be adequately accounted for apart from some actual divine movement towards man. For the express object and end contemplated in the covenant, in each stage of its history, and on each occasion of its renewal, is ever the same, and is achieved by the same method of divine action. By a process of limitation, by a severance at once physical and moral, the God of Israel sets apart a peculiar people to be the instrument of His purpose and the organ of His praise[1]. But though the initiative belongs to the God of grace, the very institution of a covenant-relationship implies the recognition of the freedom and dignity that belongs to human nature. 'Man in relation to God,' observes Prof. Schultz, 'is not a being without rights, or one to be treated in an arbitrary way or merely with lenity. He stands to God in a relation of personal and moral fellowship[2].' Thus, as a being created in the image of God, man is not only called to correspond to the moral law; he on his side may claim to share in a measure the thoughts and purposes of God. The notion of a covenant involves a certain relationship of equality, and an element of mutual obligation. In the Old Testament are laid the foundations of a spiritual connexion between God and His creatures which was destined to be perfected in the mystery of the indwelling Spirit. Man already becomes in a sense *an heir of God* and a joint-heir with His Christ[3].

IV. Yet another aspect of the Old Testament will engage our attention. It is a record which unfolds in successive stages the growth of a unique anticipation or hope concerning the future, not of the elect race only, but of mankind. The Israel of the Spirit was ever waiting, throughout the long ages of the national history, for the manifestation of the kingdom of God[4]. In the days that immediately preceded the first Advent

---

[1] Cp. Riehm, *op. cit.* p. 35.
[2] *O. T. Theology*, ii. 5.
[3] Rom. viii. 17.
[4] Cp. St. Luke xxiii. 51.

this was the hope to which Israel passionately clung—
it was indeed the only hope that remained. And the
history of Israel is unlike that of any other nation in
that the chosen people was divinely destined to fulfil
a peculiar mission to the world. The sense of mission
was at first, no doubt, dim and obscure, but in the
prophets it became powerfully developed, and in it
originated the hopes that we call 'Messianic.' If we
wished in a single phrase to describe the ideal destiny
of Israel, we might select the term, *Servant of Jehovah*[1],
since the mission of the chosen people was, in fact, to
proclaim to the nations in Jehovah's name the kingdom
of God. In the momentous events of the exodus,
as they were interpreted by the piety of later ages, the
foundations of a visible kingdom of God among men
were laid. *Ye have seen what I did unto the Egyptians,
and how I bare you on eagles' wings, and brought you
unto myself. Now therefore, if ye will obey my voice
indeed, and keep my covenant, then ye shall be a peculiar
treasure unto me above all people: for all the earth is
mine: and ye shall be unto me a kingdom of priests, and
an holy nation*[2], that is, a people bearing the marks of
special consecration to Jehovah, and entrusted with
a spiritual mission, extending to all the nations of the
earth. It is highly doubtful whether the nation at
the time of its foundation was conscious of its vocation.
There can be no question, however, that in looking
back on its wonderful past, the spiritual Israel of
a later period rightly interpreted the significance of its
redemption from Egyptian servitude. Through painful
discipline a remnant at least of the nation became conscious that it was called to be a vehicle of divine
knowledge and salvation to the world; it was com-

---

[1] Cp. Edersheim, *Warburton Lectures*, p. 45; and Wellhausen, *Prolegomena*, p. 400. Observe the title 'Servant of Jehovah' implies a call to special service or obedience. It is used of Abraham (Gen. xxvi. 24), Caleb (Num. xiv. 24), Moses (Deut. xxxiv. 5, &c.), Joshua (Joshua xxiv. 29), David (2 Sam. vii. 5, &c.), Job (i. 8), Isaiah (xx. 3, &c.). The phrase, in its collective sense applied to Israel, is first used by Jeremiah (e.g. xxx. 10) and Ezekiel (e.g. xxviii. 25), and is common in Deutero-Isaiah.
[2] Exod. xix. 4-6.

missioned to proclaim the sovereignty of God. *Thy saints give thanks unto thee,* sings a psalmist, *they show the glory of thy kingdom and talk of thy power; that thy power, thy glory, and mightiness of thy kingdom might be known unto men*[1]. Hence the keynote of Moses' song is the reign of God on earth: *Jehovah shall reign for ever and ever* [2]; and the thought thus expressed becomes the one 'pervading and impelling idea of the Old Testament[3].'

Now of this kingdom of God the polity of ancient Israel was a kind of external and visible embodiment. Although the religion of the Old Testament from the first contained the potency of becoming a world-religion, yet in its beginnings it bears all the marks of a purely national or tribal religion. The kingdom of God is seemingly confined within the limits of an organized nationality; fellowship with God means participation in the chosen people[4]. The divine sovereignty is not conceived as a relation in which Jehovah stands to the whole created universe; it is rather the dominion which He exercises over the special people of His choice. Hence Israel's polity might be called a 'Theocracy,' a term apparently invented by Josephus to denote the immediate, personal sovereignty of Jehovah in Israel[5]. When the primitive covenant between Jehovah and the people was ratified, God became *King in Jeshurun*[6], the fountain-head of all authority and governance, all civil and religious enactments. He became the sovereign, the law-giver, the judge, the champion, the protector of His people.

---

[1] Ps. cxlv. 10-12.   [2] Exod. xv. 18.
[3] Keim ap. Edersheim, *op. cit.* p. 48.
[4] Cp. Riehm, *op. cit.* pp. 27, 28.
[5] Cp. Oehler, *Theol. of the O. T.* § 91.
[6] See Josephus, *c. Apion.* ii. 16 (quoted by Oehler, *l. c.*). Robertson Smith, *The Prophets of Israel* (ed. 1), p. 52, remarks that 'The word theocracy expresses precisely that feature in the religion of Israel which it had in common with the faiths of the surrounding nations,' but Stanton, *The Jewish and the Christian Messiah*, p. 100 note, points out that the word 'does describe very happily what *became* distinctive of Israel. . . . The idea was preserved among them when other nations had lost it' in a very elevated form.

He went before them to battle as their leader; their triumphs were victories won by *His holy arm*[1].

It would be a mistake however to suppose that the idea of a theocracy was completely realized in the primitive Mosaic institutions. We must remember that they are described to us by writers who are dominated by the theocratic idea, and whose conceptions of ancient Hebrew history are coloured by the facts and ideals of their own time. Nevertheless, there is no reason to doubt that Moses planted a seed which the lapse of time was destined to bring to maturity. The position of utter dependence on their God and His appointed mediator in which the newly enfranchised Hebrews found themselves contained the essential germ of theocratic ideas. Researches into the primitive religion of the Semites give support to this view. Wellhausen maintains that in ancient Israel the theocracy never existed in fact as a form of constitution; it only came into existence in the strict sense after the exile, and was transported in an idealized form to early times. But this statement must be qualified by the consideration that among the Hebrews, as among other Semitic tribes, it would be obvious and natural to address the tribal god as king, and the belief in such a sovereignty would carry with it the conviction that the supreme guidance of the state was actually in the hands of the deity, and that the whole sphere of ordinary social and civil life was subject to His control and direction[2]. Under the monarchy the theocratic idea was gradually recognized, developed, and expanded. The reign of David and his successors had very far-reaching consequences in this connexion. The monarchy 'drew the life of the people together at a centre, and gave it an aim'; it developed a 'national self-consciousness'; while political developments necessarily affected the

---

[1] Ps. xcviii. 2.
[2] Wellhausen, *Prolegomena*, c. vii. p. 256, and c. xi. p. 411 [Eng. Tr.]. Cp. Robertson Smith, *Religion of the Semites*, p. 31.

growth of religious ideas. The kingship of Jehovah was, as it were, visibly realized under the monarch; the reigning king of David's line was reverenced as Jehovah's representative, reigning by His grace and in His name; and to the prophets of the eighth century the kingdom of Jehovah became practically identical with the kingdom of David. Isaiah, observes Wellhausen, 'is unconscious of any difference between human and divine law: law in itself, jurist's law in the proper juristic sense of the word, is divine, and has behind it the authority of the Holy One of Israel . . . Jehovah is a true and perfect king, hence justice is His principal attribute and His chief demand [1].' On the whole, it is probable that the kingship of Jehovah was a conception belonging indeed to the Mosaic age, but under the monarchy consciously acknowledged and taken as the foundation of ideal hopes for the future. The conquests of David and his successors over the tribes bordering on Palestine appeared to the prophetic eye to signalize a gradual extension of the victorious sway of Jehovah. Kingship appears to have invariably suggested to a Hebrew mind the notion of conquest over foes, and extension by victorious conflict of a rightful dominion. Thus the prophetic picture of the Messiah represents him as an ideal ruler, filled with the spirit of Jehovah, and adorned with all the virtues of a just and powerful prince.

As time went on, however, the ideas of the prophets were at once expanded and spiritualized [2]. They were inspired to proclaim two truths respecting the kingdom of God which the mass of the nation had peculiar difficulty in apprehending: viz. its universality—the kingdom was to embrace mankind; and its spirituality—it was to be a kingdom of holiness. Each of these ideas was suggested by the events, or by the needs of the present. The thought of universal dominion resulted in part from the disasters

---

[1] Wellhausen, *Prolegomena*, c. xi. pp. 413-415.
[2] See Kuenen, *Hibbert Lectures*, pp. 126 foll.

which overtook Israel on the broad stage of secular history. The outcome of contact or collision with the great world-powers of Egypt, Asshur, and Babylon, was the conception of a world-wide empire of Jehovah, embracing the very nations which threatened or oppressed the defenceless kingdom of God. The temptation of the average Israelite was to mistake a portion of the divine kingdom for the whole; but prophecy rose to the sublime thought of a worldwide kingdom of God, into which all the nations of the earth should flow and bring their glory, in which a Prince, enthroned as Jehovah's representative and vicegerent, should reign in peace and righteousness over a universe redeemed from all elements of moral or physical evil. Certainly the constitution of the visible theocracy, as we find it fully developed in Judaism after the exile, seems at first sight to mark a retrogression from the ideals of Messianic prophecy; but here also *wisdom is justified of her children;* and we can see now that the legal stage of Israel's development was the means of keeping alive and deepening those great spiritual ideas which alone could give to the religion of the Old Testament a true universality.

Again, the prophets proclaimed the spiritual character and purpose of Jehovah's kingdom. It was to be a kingdom of righteousness. The obstinate and cherished belief of ordinary Israelites was that the divine favour had been pledged to them unconditionally, and that Jehovah would under any circumstances intervene on His people's behalf; it was thought to be self-evident that any difficult or dangerous crisis would certainly end in Israel's favour. On the other hand, it was the work of the prophets to combat this delusion. In season and out of season they were the preachers of God's moral requirement. They insisted that the holy God could be Israel's God only in so far as the laws of social righteousness were recognized and fulfilled. They refused, as Wellhausen finely expresses it, 'to allow the conception of Jehovah to be involved in the ruin of the kingdom. They saved faith by destroying illusion[1].' Their function, in a word, was to vindicate the spirituality of God's kingdom; to proclaim the indefeasible conditions of the divine covenant. Moreover, they perceived that a spiritual kingdom must necessarily outgrow nationalistic limitations: its dominant tendency and its irresistible impulse must be to embrace universal humanity.

The kingdom of God, then, began with the founding of the Mosaic state. Israel was welded into a compact community by uniform laws, customs, and ordinances of worship. It became a nation not by growth from within but by a kind of constraint from without. It was bound together by the truth which it cherished. Thus organized, the nation was in due time launched into a tumultuous sea of heathen peoples—as the object of a 'relative, temporary, economical preference[2],' in order to become the vehicle of revelation to the whole earth. Isolated Israel certainly was: *lo, the people shall dwell alone, and shall not be reckoned among the nations*[3], but only with a view to the ultimate accomplishment of a definite purpose of grace towards the world. The Gentiles are accordingly summoned by Jehovah to *rejoice with his people*[4], while Israel, the covenant people, with its spiritual mission to the world, is hailed as the *firstborn, the light of the Gentiles, the head of the heathen*[5]. Such was Israel's ideal calling, and all the prophecies that relate to the conversion of the world through Jacob or the 'Servant of Jehovah' are primarily applicable to the ideal Israel. We know how these great and precious promises became gradually narrowed to a remnant and only received final fulfilment in the representative personality of one, who was himself the true Israel, the true Prince

---

[1] *Sketch of the History of Israel and Judah*, p. 89.
[2] Bruce, *Chief End of Revelation*, p. 116.
[3] Num. xxiii. 9.
[4] Deut. xxxii. 43; Rom. xv. 10-12.
[5] Exod. iv. 22; Isa. xlii. 6; Ps. xviii. 43.

of God. But what was fulfilled in Him had primary reference to the people of whose stock He willed to be born; through Him the Church of the Old Testament was destined to fulfil its prophetic and priestly calling; in Him all the glories and sufferings predicted by prophecy for the chosen people were to find full accomplishment; and thus in the historical fulfilment a single individual embodied and represented the race from which He sprang[1].

The Messianic hope of the Old Testament will therefore occupy our attention. We shall attempt to study the elements which history contributed to it and the stages of its progress; we shall also have to notice the limitations of prophetic foresight, and the strictly historical conditions of prophetic prediction. But the point of highest interest is the steady growth of the universalist idea of salvation; of the thought that Israel's God is the God of all the earth, that in the last days the people of God is destined to be surrounded by a world of converted nations, that in Zion, the city of His choice, the Lord *will destroy the face of the covering cast over all people, and the vail that is spread over all nations; that He will swallow up death in victory, and wipe away tears from off all faces* [2].

V. The Old Testament is to be studied, in the last place, as witnessing to a divine purpose for the individual soul. It continually directs attention to the importance of personality in the development of the kingdom of God. It sets before us at each stage of a progressive movement the figures of men, sometimes pliable and passionate, sometimes commanding and majestic, on whose ready will, prompt obedience, or bold ventures of faith, nothing less depended than the cause of God in the world. The Old Testament is indeed from one point of view a history of vocations, either accepted by faith or neglected by indolence; either awakening the response of human will or forfeited by human sin. In self-

---

[1] Riehm, *Messianic Prophecy*, p. 218.   [2] Isa. xxv. 7, 8.

surrender and submission to the call of God the soul of man became conscious of itself and of the contrarieties which religion alone explains, the strange blending in human nature of weakness and misery with greatness and strength[1]. Again, the Old Testament repeatedly illustrates the fact that man's obedient response to vocation is followed by a consciousness of personal inspiration which enhances the sense of individuality: the soul recognizes the illuminating or strengthening influence of a power higher than itself, educating the intellect, expanding the heart, and quickening the conscience; it becomes aware of a divine operation which does not constrain man 'mechanically to receive the truth, but enables him to know it'; does not merely reveal to him what God would have him believe and practise, but raises him into intelligent sympathy with His mind and will[2]. The sense of personal union with Deity however did not override or overpower individuality, but rather developed and stimulated it. The inspiration of prophets and saints was no mere possession of the soul by a divine influence, no ecstatic ebullition of irrepressible feeling, but a power which added dignity to its subject, awakening at once his consciousness of divinely appointed mission, and his perception of the heights to which human frailty might be exalted by divine grace. 'It belongs to the notion of prophecy, of true revelation,' says Wellhausen in a memorable passage, 'that Jehovah, overlooking all the media of ordinances and institutions, communicates Himself to the *individual*, the called one, in whom that mysterious and irreducible *rapport* in which the deity stands with man clothes itself with energy. Apart from the prophet, *in abstracto*, there is no revelation; it lives in his divine-human *ego*[3].'

---

[1] Cp. Pascal, *Pensées*, art. iv.
[2] J. Caird, *Philosophy of Religion*, ch. iii. Cp. Meinhold, *Jesus und das A. T.* p. 139: 'Es findet ein mit dem Steigen der geistigen Entwickelung gleichlaufendes Anwachsen der Aufnahmefähigkeit für religiöse Dinge statt.'   [3] *Prolegomena*, p. 398.

But again beyond the quickened sense of personal dignity and worth which resulted from conscious inspiration, the preciousness of the individual soul seemed to follow from the very thought of a God who was willing to communicate Himself to His creatures. The goodness of God, manifested in His readiness to bring man into a relationship of sacred intimacy with Himself, formed as it were an implicit premise whence the hopeful conclusion might be drawn that a creature so favoured was not destined to extinction, but rather to a life of fellowship with his Maker, not to be interrupted even by death. Thus the evolution of the sense of individuality depended upon the spiritual experience of elect souls. There arrived a stage in Israel's religion when good men found their only solace in the life of communion with God. In the troublous and dreary period of Israel's permanent subjection to a foreign yoke, personal religion became the strength and stay of the devout. To the psalmists, for example, the thought of God is a refuge in any trouble; He alone is the object of the soul's confident trust, its adoring joy, its sacred thirst, its supreme exultation, its limitless love. And the soul which was capable of such yearnings and aspirations, felt itself ennobled by the reflected majesty of Him to whom it clung. With strong confidence it rested in the assurance that what God had so highly favoured and blessed, He would not despise. *Thou wilt not leave my soul in hell*—such was the cry of the human heart. *God will redeem my soul from the power of the grave: for he shall receive me. My flesh and my heart faileth: but God is the strength of my heart, and my portion for ever*[1]. The man whose portion is this life clings to what is vain and transitory; and he passes away with that to which he clings. But the soul which holds to God discovers in its very love the pledge of an undying life.

The hope which is fulfilled in Christianity is thus foreshadowed and anticipated in the Old Testament:

[1] Pss. xvi. 10, xlix. 15, lxxi. 26.

the hope, namely, of a kingdom of God which is also a kingdom of personality; a sphere in which, with the advancing development of the community, the individual also arrives at the plenitude of liberty, perfection, and blessedness [1].

There remains yet another factor which tended to develope the life of personal religion. Just as the dissolution of the Greek states gave a certain impulse to the spread of Stoicism with its characteristic doctrine of the αὐτάρκεια of the individual, so the disasters which darkened the later stages of Judah's history inevitably suggested some fundamental moral problems, to the solution of which the wisdom of the time devoted its energies. At the same time the pressure of national calamity roused in individual men doubts and questionings respecting their personal relation to the God of their fathers. In fact in the sacred literature of the Hebrews we have an example of a phenomenon familiar in secular history. One consequence of political disorganization was that Hebrew sages devoted themselves to inquiries concerning the duties of life and the conditions of personal well-being, either by way of compensation for the loss of a sphere of public activity, or as a solace amid the troubles of a declining state. The prevalence of violent social anomalies and contrasts, combined with the corruption and decay of public religion, quickened the spirit of inquiry into the deeper mysteries of the divine dealings with mankind. Such fundamental religious ideas as those of personal responsibility, of the need of atonement for sin, and of the efficacy of repentance were the fruit of sorrowful meditation on the causes of Israel's national ruin. These ideas took their place as permanent elements in the religious character; they practically marked an advanced stage in the growth of the human mind. Ancient theories of human suffering and of divine retribution upon wrong-doing had become too strait to satisfy the needs of an enlarged

---

[1] Cp. Martensen, *Christian Ethics (General)*, § 63.

experience. They failed to provide a resting-place for thought, or an adequate explanation of indisputable facts. Man's perplexities, in short, drove him to find refuge in the inscrutable power and changeless character of God. Thus the Old Testament is a history of the education of faith; it ends with a presage of a divine self-manifestation which alone can solve the riddle of the universe and throw light on the destiny of man.

We have now reviewed in a summary fashion the main topics which will be severally considered in subsequent lectures. It is worth while to observe, in conclusion, how closely the general arrangement of the Hebrew Bible appears to correspond with those five aspects of Old Testament theology which have been briefly described.

In the Pentateuch and the historical books, the two most prominent ideas are those of redemption and revelation. The book of Exodus contains the account of a redemptive movement on God's part which forms a kind of creative period in the history of Israel and of mankind[1]. The deliverance of the chosen people laid the foundation of that view of history which is characteristic of the Bible: it gave birth to the conviction that God is in very truth a living God; that His hand is at work in the universe, controlling the destinies of nations and using the faculties of individual men; that He manifests Himself in the world in order to further moral purposes of His own, in ways that are relatively to us supernatural. But the deliverance of Israel from bondage was also the starting-point of a higher revelation. The character of Jehovah was displayed both in the fact of the deliverance, and in the manner of its accomplishment. The God of Israel's salvation revealed Himself as a being of transcendent beneficence, long-suffering, and pity for the oppressed[2]. And the evidence for the actual events of the exodus is parallel

---

[1] Cp. Wellhausen, *Sketch of the History of Israel and Judah*, p. 7.
[2] Cp. Bruce, *Chief End of Revelation*, pp. 193, 194.

to that which attests the resurrection of Christ. The testimony lies in Israel's national life and historical career, which cannot be satisfactorily explained apart from some great original impulse that can only be attributed to divine power. The deliverance itself called into existence a church or witnessing body, which cherished the recollection of its wonderful past in living hearts and memories. The testimony to the fact of the exodus was thus independent of any written record; such a record was quite possibly formed at a period contemporaneous with the events, but as it is impossible to say whether any portion of it survives in its original shape, so it is important not to overestimate our dependence on documentary evidence.

To resume, in the Pentateuch we find a history of redemption and a revelation of Jehovah, together with that which necessarily accompanies such revelation, namely the institution of a new relationship between God and man, which in the book of Exodus is conceived as a covenant based on moral conditions. The historical deliverance was the foundation of a higher religion, marked by a higher standard of morality. There can be no doubt that this new morality was an original element in Mosaic religion, whatever may have been its precise extent in the earliest legislation. The object of Israel's redemption was proclaimed from the first, though it was only very gradually and slowly brought to fulfilment. The original law of Israel, says Professor Robertson Smith, 'is pervaded by a constant sense that the righteous and gracious Jehovah is behind the law, and wields it in conformity with His own holy nature. The law, therefore, makes no pretence at ideality.... The ordinances are not abstractly perfect and fit to be a rule of life in every state of society, but they are fit to make Israel a righteous, humane, and God-fearing people, and to facilitate a healthy growth towards better things[1].' In a word, the undoubted tendency of the first legislation was

[1] *O. T. in J. C.* p. 343.

towards the development of a higher morality. The character of the divine kingdom was ethically determined even in the earliest stage of its history.

The next division of the Hebrew Bible—the book of the prophets, former and latter—is mainly concerned with the actual history of the covenant relationship which Jehovah had established between Himself and Israel. In these books history is described or interpreted from the theocratic point of view; events are regarded as worthy of record in proportion as they illustrate the advance or the retrogression of the theocratic idea. The writers of the earlier books make it their chief aim to illustrate the blessings which follow faithful observance of the covenant conditions and the loss that follows unfaithfulness. The great prophets themselves have two main themes: judgment and redemption. Their mission is to denounce Israel's unfaithfulness, and to vindicate the spiritual conditions of the divine covenant; but their warnings and rebukes alternate with promises of a glorious future—promises which reach their climax in the prediction of a new covenant[1] unlike the ancient covenant of the exodus—a covenant under which the spiritual blessings for which the heart of man waits and longs shall be effectually attained. From one point of view, at any rate, this passage may be regarded as the culminating point of Messianic prophecy; so at least it seems to be treated by the writer of the Epistle to the Hebrews. The characteristic blessings of the Messianic age are virtually summed up in three promised spiritual gifts: power to do God's will, knowledge of His character, remission of past sins.

Lastly, the writings classed as Hagiographa illustrate in various forms the subjective apprehension of the blessings of covenant fellowship. They are the product of religious emotion and religious reason. Accordingly in this group of books there is something that gives us the sense of a 'many-sided sympathy' in

[1] Jer. xxxi. 31 foll.

the Old Testament [1]; there belongs to some of them at least an interest not merely national but universal, while others seem specially adapted to enter into the circumstances and minister to the needs of individual souls. There are some elements in the Hagiographa which appear to constitute a link of connexion between Judaism and the heathen world; and others which witness to the providential care of God for the individual soul, and to the divine regard for every variety of conditions in human life.

With this brief indication of the way in which the different aspects of the Old Testament find each its peculiar expression in different parts of the sacred volume, we may close the preliminary survey of our subject.

[1] Ryle, *The Canon of the O. T.* p. 182.

LECTURE III

We have heard with our ears, O God, our fathers have told us, what thou hast done in their time of old.—Ps. xliv. 1.

An inspired book, such as we believe the Old Testament to be, cannot be designed merely to record the religious experiences or promote the spiritual interests of one favoured nation; still less can it be intended for special and particular groups of individuals—leaders, priests, antiquarians, or scholars. It is meant for universal humanity. It must be adapted to serve world-wide purposes; it must be capable of being to all men everywhere a source of the same divine power, guidance, grace and encouragement which it supplied of old to members of the covenant-people. We need not pause to dwell on the fact that Christian experience has vindicated this high estimate of the practical purpose which the Old Testament was destined to fulfil. I will only notice that the universality of their scope helps us better to appreciate the inexhaustible variety which characterizes the Scriptures—a variety not only in the style and tone of the different books, in their subject-matter, point of view, and mode of treatment, but a variety also in respect of their canonical value and function. It has been suggested that if we regard the Bible as an organism in which every particular book has its distinct office and function, the analogy justifies us in considering some books to be more important than others, some more essential to the integrity of the whole than others. This way of regarding the Bible is intended to reassure the perplexed by reminding them that there may be questions raised in regard to certain books 'without vital consequence to faith ensuing [1].' We may, however, somewhat extend the analogy, and observe how the phenomena of physical nature, viewed in their totality, illustrate the diversity which is so noticeable in the contents of Scripture. For nature also is a book in which, as in Scripture, we study the manifestation of a divine life. We observe that nature is in a mysterious way bound up with the fortunes of man: *the day of the Lord* comes upon it as upon him, in judgment or benediction. When man is glad, nature also rejoices *with joy and singing*. It has an inner sympathy with him; it is the sphere of his labour; it is in a great measure subject to his control; it is the medium of God's dispensations of power or blessing concerning him. Nature, then, may be expected to give us a clue to the right view of Scripture. It is infinite in its variety—a variety so vast that thought has to partition off one department after another for the purposes of special investigation. Indeed, the extent of variation seems to outrun the requirements, so far as our human faculties can judge, of adaptation to particular ends. Again, nature is fragmentary in appearance. It continually suggests—even in the scenes of waste and devastation with which the surface of the universe is overspread—that God employs means and aims at results which lie beyond the range of our present powers of perception. And yet there is in nature an inner unity and completeness—the sense of which partly arises from our instinctive transference to nature of the unity which underlies our own sense of personality and partly follows from our conception of God as the single sustaining cause of all

---

[1] Bruce, *Apologetics*, pp. 314, 315. It is noteworthy that in the First Prayer Book of Edw. VI (1549) the following rubric was inserted: 'The Old Testament is appointed for the first lessons at Matins and Evensong, and shall be read through every year once, except certain books and chapiters which be least edifying, and might best be spared, and therefore are left unread.' This direction was omitted in the revised Book of 1662.

things, *rerum tenax vigor*[1]. This harmony is taken for granted in our blessed Lord's parabolic teaching. It is the harmony of a consentient witness. Thus by its completeness and by its fragmentariness, by its sternness and rigour no less than by its softness and loveliness, by what it is and by what it is not, nature witnesses to the indwelling and sustaining presence of its Author. And when we turn to Scripture we are prepared to find that God adapts Himself to the diversity of human needs in ways analogous to His operations in nature. We find Scripture also marked by an infinite variety, yet by a clearly felt harmony. We find it to be fragmentary, yet in one view complete. It exhibits strange features of apparent imperfection and anomaly, yet it is manifestly an organic whole. Scripture is analogous to nature also in this: that while its general aspect is stern and sombre, its promises and suggestions point to an unearthly glory and perfection of things yet to be revealed. Further, the interpretation of Scripture, as of nature, is seen not to belong exclusively to any one age or time. Each generation reads it with the aid of fresh light, and finds in it a new significance. It contains much that can only be apprehended and interpreted in the light of an acquired knowledge of the whole and an enlarged acquaintance with human nature and its needs. The attentive reader of the Old Testament, like the student of nature, has moments of insight when he perceives 'gleams like the flashing of a shield.' For Scripture, like nature, points persistently beyond itself to a uniform purpose pervading the multiplicity of historical events which it

---

[1] Cp. Briggs, *Biblical Study*, p. 359. 'The Bible is a vast organism, in which the unity springs from an amazing variety. The unity is not that of a mass of rocks or a pool of water. It is the unity that one finds in the best works of God. It is the unity of the ocean, where every wave has its individuality of life and movement. It is the unity of the continent, in which mountains and rivers, valleys and uplands, flowers and trees, birds and insects, animal and human life, combine to distinguish it as a magnificent whole from other continents. It is the unity of the heavens where star differs from star in form, colour, order, movement, size and importance, but all declare the glory of God.'

describes, and of spiritual moods which it reflects. It unveils, even while it partially conceals, a presence for which the human heart instinctively yearns, towards which it stretches out hands—a presence which speaks and appeals to man as spirit to spirit and heart to heart.

And if it should be asked what led to the formation and eventual completion of a 'canon' of the Old Testament, the answer is perhaps something of this kind. The conviction arose after the overthrow of the Hebrew state that it was desirable to secure in a permanent form the spiritual forces which had built up and moulded the characteristic life of the Jewish Church, and that there already existed writings sufficiently qualified to fulfil this function. In regard to the methods by which canonical problems were gradually settled we are very much in the dark, but in the total result we can trace the action of religious experience, guided by divine wisdom to select those particular writings which had proved themselves best adapted to develope and educate religious faith.

Regarded in its entirety, the Old Testament is the record of man's communion with his Creator; it traces through all its successive stages the history of a friendship between God and man which reaches its climax in the spiritual life of Christian saints. It tells the chequered story of that sacred mutual love: on the divine side, the disappointments of love—its constancy, its patience, its tenderness, its hopefulness; on the human side, the fallings away and vanishings of love—its recoveries, its heroisms, its ventures of faith, its perpetual tendency towards consummation in a perfect union between God and man, in the Incarnation of God and the presence in human hearts of the indwelling Spirit. In the Old Testament the story is all but completed, and it is enshrined in enduring forms of typical value and significance, for in the retrogressions and advancements of one particular nation lies hidden the whole spiritual history of mankind, in so far as Israel represents that instinct of communion with Deity which belongs to man as man.

We come, then, to the Old Testament as to an historical book. 'The Bible,' says Ewald [1], 'is through and through of historical nature and spirit. Standing conspicuous amid all the efforts of antiquity, the most profound as a work of mind, the loftiest in elevation and sweep of thought, a product of noble pains, compact in itself and finished, it bears upon its face, looked at as a whole, the clearest impress of historic truth.' Ewald goes on to draw an obvious contrast in this respect between the sacred book of Islam and the Bible. In this there is no need to follow him, but I would take the above passage as a keynote of the discussion on which it is our business to enter to-day, respecting the nature and extent of the historical element in the Old Testament. For certainly the primary and most important subject of investigation in regard to the Old Testament is its claim to be a trustworthy history of redemption. The fullness and the diversity of its contents serve to fill with life and colour the outlines of a vast historical picture, in which the progress and perfection of all true religion is included [2].

The historical element in the Old Testament: how vast and how difficult a theme! It is obvious that we must begin by suggesting a few considerations essential to the inquiry.

1. In the Hexateuch and the historical books we are dealing, as will be allowed on all hands, with highly composite narratives, in which the oldest historical traditions have been revised, developed, supplemented, and to some extent remodelled in a religious spirit and from a point of view in some cases priestly, in others prophetic. In the Hexateuch, primitive traditions and later conceptions as to the course of Israel's early history have been woven together in

---
[1] *Revelation, its Nature and Record*, p. 407.
[2] *Ibid.* p. 408.

a double or threefold cord, so as to present to critical eyes the appearance of a highly ingenious and elaborate mosaic constructed out of materials of very different historical value. In the prophetic books of Judges, Samuel, and Kings, early traditions have been at different times selected or revised in such a way as to impress on the narrative a uniform stamp or quality and to infuse into it certain strongly marked religious ideas[1]. There are plain tokens in these writings that both the original selection of facts and the mode of estimating them are determined by particular religious preconceptions, and it would even appear that in some cases the special standpoint from which events and incidents are regarded, and the framework in which they are set, are of more importance for religious purposes than the facts recorded. The peculiar character of the books of the Chronicles will be noticed later. It is sufficient at this point to say that owing to their late date they cannot claim to be placed on the same level of historical value as the earlier authorities on which they are manifestly based.

What has been now said amounts to the assertion that the written documents available for constructing the history of Israel are, when tested by a modern standard, of unequal value and of very divergent quality. They contain fragments of contemporary records and annals which would satisfy any modern tests; but these are intermingled with elements of quite another kind: quasi-historical narratives which clothe religious thoughts in a poetic and symbolic garb[2], and popular stories or traditions which owe their vivid beauty to the creative genius of a race singularly gifted with imaginative power[3]. Embedded in them we find considerable fragments of ancient songs and of very early narratives, borrowed apparently from the archaic *Book*

---

[1] Cp. Wellhausen, *Prolegomena*, pp. 293, 294.
[2] This of course applies to the history of the origins. Cp. Meinhold, *Jesus und das A. T.* pp. 112, 118, 132.
[3] Cp. Schultz, *O. T. Theology*, i. 21.

of Jashar, or the *Wars of Jehovah*, which extolled the exploits of primitive Hebrew heroes. There is also, in the Hexateuch at least, a considerable element of apparent history, which really consists of law embodied in the form of historic precedents. We have perhaps been accustomed to regard the early books of the Bible merely as historical records; but critical inquiry has reminded us that to every species of literary composition natural to the ancient Hebrews has been assigned by the overruling Spirit of God a place in the sacred volume, and we must be prepared to part boldly with exclusively modern prejudices in dealing with this wonderful literature. The trained historical sense of western minds is apt to take offence at the notion that the faculty of poetic or historic imagination should be employed as a suitable medium of instruction by the Spirit of truth. But to those who study the Old Testament in the temper of sympathy and reverence, no genuine and natural product of the human mind will appear common or unclean or incapable of consecration to lofty and divine uses. Speaking broadly, the documents now under consideration seem to have a twofold value. On the one hand, without themselves professing to give an account of the exact course of Israel's history, they supply materials with which historical investigation may successfully work. On the other hand, they furnish a valuable means of ascertaining the point of view from which Israel regarded its past career, and the religious conceptions which influenced the literary treatment of ancient traditions. An attentive student of the Old Testament cannot fail to notice how profoundly the records of Hebrew history are penetrated by religious ideas. The ideals and conditions of the age in which the books attained to their present form are projected into antiquity, and the problem of the modern historian is to disentangle from its ideal or imaginative embodiment the genuine historical nucleus which unquestionably underlies the record. As it now stands, the sacred history has been aptly compared to an epic poem[1], and there is no reason for denying that a certain epic character belongs to Israel's historical documents in common with other ancient literature. The Semitic mind seems in fact to have been distinctly wanting in the purely scientific interest which loves historical precision and accuracy of detail. Its interest was confined to the discernment of religious principles; it was inclined rather to interpret the spiritual significance of events than to lay special stress upon exactness of detail. To certain great facts of past history the Hebrew mind clung with unwavering tenacity. These were cherished as constant objects of devout contemplation; they were the support and joy of faith; they were the favourite theme of sacred poetry; they were the commonplaces, so to speak, of prophetic preaching. And we cannot wonder that the mighty acts of Jehovah on behalf of His people were idealized and invested with a sacred halo of glory or even of romance. In admitting the action of impassioned imagination, we neither question the occurrence of the historical facts themselves nor detract from their religious significance. The present point, however, is that the historical writings of the Old Testament reflect the characteristics of the race that produced them. Their historical quality is modified and coloured by the peculiar genius of the writers, and it is accordingly undesirable and imprudent to attach *overmuch weight* to historical details for which corroborative evidence is not forthcoming[2]. We must be content to possess a narrative which in its main outlines is demonstrably authentic, but we must

---

[1] See Renan, *Histoire du peuple d'Israël*, bk. ii, ch. 4 s. fin. and Kittel, *A History of the Hebrews*, vol. i. p. 40 (Eng. Tr.). So Hofmann ap. Köhler, *Über Berechtigung der Kritik des A. T.* p. 41. Cp. J. Darmesteter, *Les Prophètes d'Israël*, p. 240: 'Ainsi se forma cette merveilleuse épopée publique, exemple unique d'une histoire refaite à coup d'idéal.'

[2] Mr. Schechter, *Studies in Judaism*, p. xviii, refers to the interesting fact that some Jewish scholars have substantially accepted the above view of the historical portions of Scripture. Zunz, for instance, holds that the early history is presented ' in an ideal light,' in accordance with a 'traditional interpretation adapted to the religious needs' of a particular age.

not allow ourselves to reason as if all the sources available for ascertaining the true course of Israel's history were of equal value. And in endeavouring to arrive at a general estimate of the historical trustworthiness of the records, we must distinguish between the various strata of the ancient tradition, which are either left in juxtaposition or have been fused together into a single narrative. It is here that we shall in the long run be bound to submit to the guidance of experts in criticism, accepting their verdict where they agree, and suspending judgment where they differ. Thus a cautious student will recollect that the early history of the Hebrews, as of other races, is involved in great obscurity; he will therefore be on his guard against the *idola tribus* which occasionally influence the critical mind—the passion for positive results, for finality, for systematization even in spheres where these are, from the nature of the case, unattainable. He will not be unduly impatient of necessary distinctions, and of a certain complexity and obscurity in problems which he might antecedently have expected to find simple and straightforward.

2. A second consideration relating to our present subject is the fact that a mass of evidence, which bears upon the primitive history of the Hebrews, is being gradually accumulated in other fields of inquiry, and it is accordingly a plain duty to make allowance for actual or probable results of archaeological research as a modifying factor in our estimate of the Old Testament narratives, corroborating or correcting the conclusions that might be drawn from the internal evidence of the written documents[1]. The Hebrew Scriptures after all form only one fragment of a vast literature, of which other portions are gradually coming to light in different parts of the East. These discoveries prove

[1] In the *Bampton Lectures* of 1859 by the Rev. G. Rawlinson, an attempt was made to state anew 'the historical evidences of the truth of the Scripture records, with special reference to the doubts and discoveries of modern times.' Clearly the attempt must be repeated from time to time in the history of the Church.

not only that the art of writing is of far greater antiquity than was once supposed, but also that a certain degree of literary culture prevailed throughout western Asia, even at a period preceding the exodus of Israel from Egypt[1]. Hence it is not more than reasonable to expect that they may modify some of the conclusions which had been reached by literary criticism respecting the most ancient periods of Hebrew history. It would, however, be unwise to overrate the extent to which critical results are likely to be modified by this branch of knowledge. There are no doubt discoveries which lead us to defer our acceptance of certain critical verdicts; there are others which have to some extent qualified or corrected the axioms on which literary criticism has at times too confidently insisted. But there is an agreement between literary critics and archaeologists on at least two points: they are at one in their estimate of the general character, as distinct from the intrinsic value, of the Old Testament documents; and they seem also to be agreed in acknowledging that we have reached a period of reconstruction[2]. This may well encourage us in an attempt to deal not merely critically but constructively with the literature and theology of the Old Testament. The real value of sacred archaeology is that it enables us to enter into the circumstances of those to whom the Word of God came, with that intelligent sympathy which alone can appreciate the quality of their writings and the conditions which moulded or influenced their thought. Indeed, the change which has come over our conception of the Old Testament documents seems to be due not merely to the results of research into special points of history, but also to the fact that there has been a development of the historical *sense*, and an enlargement of the power of insight into the peculiar characteristics of the Hebrew

---

[1] See generally Sayce, *The Higher Criticism and the Monuments*. On the antiquity of writing in the East, Cornill, *Einleitung in das A. T.* § 4.
[2] Sayce, *op. cit.* p. 24. Cp. Robertson Smith, *O. T. in J. C.* p. 16.

mind. When we are asked why we hesitate to ascribe to the early books of the Old Testament a uniformly historical character, we can only reply, first, that there is no sufficient reason for assuming that Hebrew history has been exempted from the ordinary conditions observable in all other primitive annals; and secondly, that in any case the ancient Scriptures are a genuine product of the Semitic mind, guided and controlled no doubt by the wisdom of the divine Spirit, but clearly reflecting the characteristics of the oriental temperament—its imaginative capacity, its passionate moral fervour, its intuitive perception of spiritual laws and realities.

3. Once more it is necessary to repeat with all possible emphasis that a Christian reader of the Old Testament will feel no *a priori* difficulties in regard to the occurrence of miracles [1]. On the contrary, he will be prepared to find in the course of redemptive history creative epochs at which the moral character and purpose of Almighty God manifest themselves in a manner relatively to our ordinary experience supernatural. The possibility of miracle in point of fact logically follows from the belief which is everywhere conspicuous in the Old Testament—the belief in the living personality of God. The anthropopathic expressions which are so frequently applied to Jehovah—the ascription to Him, for example, of love, hatred, wrath, jealousy, scorn, and repentance—do tend to inculcate, perhaps in the only possible form, a fundamental truth of religion, namely that the Creator and Ruler of the universe is akin to man in the essential characteristics of His being—in the possession of will, character, and moral freedom. Inadequate of course as descriptions of the divine nature, anthropopathic modes of speech reflect this conviction which dominated the Hebrew mind and which gained strength and clearness in proportion to the advance of Israel's religion. But, as was previously pointed out, a general acknowledgment of

[1] See Rawlinson's *Bampton Lectures* (1859), pp. 27 foll.

the *a priori* credibility of the Old Testament miracles does not bind us to regard every supernatural occurrence recorded in the Old Testament as literal fact. In regard to this point we may the more confidently claim freedom because, on the whole, miracle is kept in the background in the Old Testament, while in some passages (such as Deut. xiii. 1–3) a comparatively low estimate of its evidential value is expressed. Indeed, it would appear that it was only in the age of Judaism that there arose a kind of passion for the miraculous, in some respects anticipating the temper of mind which sought after a sign and was rebuked as evil and adulterous by our Lord[1]. Miracles may justly be believed to have accompanied a momentous creative act of God, such as that which brought into being the nationality of Israel[2]; but, after all, their chief significance in the view of the Old Testament writers is that they constitute an unmistakeable sign of Jehovah's presence among His people at particular crises of their history[3]. They do not seem in the old dispensation any more than in the new to have been a normal part of the divine method under normal circumstances[4]. So far as we can judge from the records, the closing stage of the journey from Egypt to Canaan appears to have been marked by a gradual cessation of miracle[5], a fact which illustrates the action

---

[1] Cp. Robertson Smith, *O. T. in J. C.* p. 409.
[2] Cp. Deut. xxxii. 6, Isa. xliii. 1, &c.
[3] Cp. Joshua iii. 10. Schultz, *op. cit.* vol. ii. pp. 193 foll., has some admirable remarks on the O. T. view of miracle. He points out how the Hebrew mind, with its vivid consciousness of God's immediate action in nature, would view a miracle: regarding it not as an unnatural or supernatural event, but rather as a striking proof of God's power and freedom. To the Hebrew a miracle 'does not stand out as an irregular individual occurrence in contrast with a differently ordered whole; but it stands out as a specially striking individual occurrence in contrast with other single events, which, being less striking owing to their frequency, are less calculated to produce the impression of God's almighty power in executing His purposes.' It is a significant fact, and consistent with his treatment of the Gospel narrative, that M. Renan attributes the miracles of the wilderness-journey to imposture (*Histoire du peuple d'Israël*, bk. i, ch. 13).
[4] Cp. Mason, *The Relation of Confirmation to Baptism*, p. 477.
[5] Cp. Joshua v. 12.

of what has been called a 'law of parsimony' in revelation—of a principle of restraint and limitation, avoiding both waste and extravagance.

We may now pass to the special subject of this lecture, prepared by what has been already said to be contented with broad general conclusions only, and remembering that in this matter, as in many others, it is possible to overrate the importance of completeness and precision. For convenience' sake we shall do well to limit our survey of the history of Israel to three distinct epochs: (1) the patriarchal age, (2) the Mosaic period, (3) the period of the Judges and of the early monarchy. From the nature of the case it is plain that the evidence available for the history of each epoch is different in quality, but this need not deter us from attempting to form some conception of its value that may be practically serviceable in the study of the Old Testament.

I.

In dealing with the patriarchal period we must bear in mind that the age to be investigated is, relatively speaking, prehistoric. The available documents, in their final shape at least, belong to an age removed by an interval of several centuries from the events. The narrative which is generally held by critics to be the earliest, that of the Jehovist, seems indeed to be based on ancient popular tradition, but it describes the age of the patriarchs as in some essential respects so closely similar to later periods, that it can only be regarded as a picture of primitive life and religion drawn in the light of a subsequent age. We have here to do with the earliest form of history, traditional folklore about primitive personages and events, worked up according to some preconceived design by a devout literary artist[1]. The question at once naturally arises how

[1] Cp. Wellhausen's *Prolegomena*, pp. 295, 296.

these narratives are to be employed and interpreted. As is well known, some very extreme conclusions have been advanced by critics, as for example that the patriarchs are not real historical personages at all, but mere personifications of particular Semitic tribes[1]. Some writers maintain that 'Abraham,' 'Isaac,' and 'Jacob' are titles of primitive tribal deities[2]. It is not my business to investigate these theories, which in their extreme form are never likely to pass beyond the stage of unverified hypothesis. It may at once be pointed out that while no convincing reasons have ever been alleged for doubting the historic personality of the great patriarchs, there are some considerations which materially support the traditional view. There are of course historical points respecting which the verdict of a purely literary criticism cannot be final, and its more or less provisional conclusions need to be supplemented or even corrected by archaeological *data*. The discoveries of recent years have admittedly shown that during the age in which Hebrew tradition places the patriarchs, there was much more intercourse between Palestine and the far East than was formerly suspected, —a circumstance which increases the probability that a genuine historical *substratum* underlies the patriarchal narratives[3]. Again, there is a striking element of internal consistency in the story of the patriarchs. It fits in with known facts; it accounts for subsequent developments. The entire course of events in the Mosaic period seems to presuppose the nomad and migratory stage which tradition connects with the person of Abraham and his immediate descendants.

---

[1] See Kuenen, *The Religion of Israel*, vol. i. p. 111. For a similar but slightly modified view see Wellhausen, *Prolegomena*, p. 320. Cp. Renan, *Histoire du peuple d'Israël*, bk. i, ch. 8.
[2] See Kittel, *History of the Hebrews* (Eng. Tr.), i. 171.
[3] Cp. Sanday, *Bampton Lectures*, p. 221. The importance of Gen. xiv, which seems to lie outside the recognized sources of the Pentateuchal narrative, must not be over-estimated. It renders credible, but cannot be said actually to prove, the facts related in the patriarchal narrative. See some judicious remarks of Meinhold, *Jesus und das A. T.* p. 124. Cp. Kittel, *op. cit.* i. 175-180.

As Professor Kittel, following Dillmann, points out, 'the religious position of Moses stands before us unsupported and incomprehensible [1],' unless we accept the tradition which traces to the patriarchs the rudiments at least of a higher religion and the first tentative occupation of the promised land. The fact-basis which underlies the story of Abraham's call may be his migration from Chaldaea, dictated by motives of ' vague dissatisfaction with prevalent religious beliefs and practices, rather than a new clearly conceived idea of God [2].' Thus we may hold it to be intrinsically probable that so unique a history as that of the elect people had precisely such a beginning as the book of Genesis relates. The circumstances indeed of the patriarchal age may not have been in all points what they afterwards appeared to minds trained in the school of levitical piety and imbued with strict theocratic ideas; but it may be confidently claimed for the patriarchal narratives that they give the true ideal significance of the events summarily, and perhaps obscurely, described in them.

While, however, in receiving the narrative as substantially true, though coloured by later prophetic conceptions of Israel's history, we are accepting an account which is entirely consistent with all that we otherwise know respecting the redemptive methods of Almighty God [3], we have no interest in denying a certain element of idealization in the description of the primitive period. There may possibly be an element of truth even in the view that the figures of the patriarchs are tribal personifications. We may agree with Baethgen that Abraham, Isaac, and Jacob are historical persons, but that ' these personalities are invested with the characteristics which afterwards marked the tribes descended from them [4].' It is likely enough that the

---

[1] *History of the Hebrews*, vol. i. p. 174.
[2] Bruce, *Apologetics*, p. 199.   [3] Cp. *ib'd.* pp. 195-199.
[4] Baethgen, *Der Gott Israels und die Götter der Heiden*, quoted by Meinhold, *Jesus und das A. T.* p. 120: 'Die hervorstechenden Eigenschaften, durch welche ein Volk sich vom andern unterscheidet, werden auf die Helden der Vorzeit übertragen, so dass diese zu typischen Gestalten

great figures of the remote past were made the subjects of many popular legends and traditions[1]; and it is no doubt possible that to a certain extent a tribal history may have been expressed in a personal and individual form[2]. It might be admitted, for instance, if it could be made to appear historically probable, that Joseph was a prominent chieftain belonging to a tribe which bore his name, and that the story of his personal career conceals the record of a tribal migration from Canaan to Egypt[3]. There is ample scope for speculation on this and kindred points, nor does a general acceptance of the Hebrew tradition in its main outlines preclude a certain latitude of view in regard to such minor details. We have indeed no reason for abandoning, even though we may be required to modify, our ordinary view of the patriarchal narratives; but we should be open to the charge of misconceiving altogether the spirit and intention with which they were compiled if we insisted, as some are inclined to do, on their possessing a character which cannot justly be attributed to them. We are dealing with stories which are probably derived for the most part from oral tradition, and are unlikely to have been based to any great extent on contemporary records, though the existence of such documents is admittedly possible. It has been sometimes asserted that oral tradition was more likely to be preserved in a state of integrity among the Hebrews than elsewhere, but the grounds

---

werden.... Mir steht es fest dass Abraham, Isaak und Jakob... geschichtliche Persönlichkeiten sind; ebenso sicher ist est mir, dass diese Persönlichkeiten zu idealen Trägern der Charactereigenschaften geworden sind, welche das Volk als seine eigenen erkannte.'

[1] Cp. Darmesteter, *Les Prophètes d'Israël*, pp. 220 foll.

[2] In the Book of Judith (v. 6 foll.) the movement of Abraham from Chaldaea is described as a *tribal* migration.

[3] So, for instance, Renan and Kittel. Montefiore, *Hibbert Lectures*, pp. 12, 13, follows Kuenen and Renan in regarding all the patriarchs as legendary heroes 'individualized *heroes eponymi*,' whose family story represents the early career of the Beni-Israel. On similar grounds it has been held that names like 'Mamre' and 'Eshcol' are collective and represent tribes. See however a criticism of the theory in Robertson, *The Early Religion of Israel*, pp. 123 foll., and note xi (p. 499).

urged in support of such a belief are precarious and sometimes arbitrary. Accordingly, while there are sufficiently good reasons for holding that the main outlines of the pre-Mosaic history are trustworthy, it would be unwise to insist particularly on more than the following points, which are unlikely to be disputed.

1. The narratives of Genesis present in the main a faithful picture of the general conditions of patriarchal life, especially in respect of its moral characteristics. A Hebrew writer, we must remember, would be continually in a position to observe with his own eyes the habits and customs of primitive civilization; among the tribes of Bedawin Arabs on the east side of the Jordan, some of the unchanging features of nomadic shepherd-life may be witnessed to this day. The oldest narrative, though coloured by prophetic idealism, gives a vivid portrait of patriarchal life: its simple forms of worship, its family priesthood, its sacrificial feasts, its sacred customs and social institutions. Moreover, there are features in the story which point to a comparatively low standard of ethical and religious development, especially the use of cunning and violence, together with a certain element of sexual licence. We notice also obvious traces of the close affinity that existed between the religion of the Hebrew patriarchs and the common ideas and practices of the neighbouring Semitic tribes: the notion, for instance, that the revelation of deity was confined to certain definite spots, such as Sichem, Bethel, Hebron, and Beersheba; the reverence paid to sacred pillars, trees, and other emblems which were regarded as monuments and tokens of a special presence of God; and the use of *teraphim* for oracular purposes, a custom which apparently lingered to a comparatively late period [1].

[1] See Riehm, *ATl. Theologie*, pp. 51, 52. Cp. Gen. xxi. 33, xxviii. 18 foll., xxxi. 19, xxxv. 2, 14, &c. *Teraphim* were still found in the time of David (1 Sam. xix. 13). On the general characteristics of the patriarchal age see Renan, *Histoire du peuple d'Israël*, bk. 1, chh. 2 and 3. M. Renan forms a high estimate of the book of Genesis regarded as 'the idealistic description of an age which really existed.' A book, he adds,

These indications of a very rudimentary religious condition are valuable, not only as enhancing the credibility of the narratives, but also as deepening our consciousness of the divine influence which actually guided the Hebrew race from the first, controlling the development of faith, accepting what was rude and primitive as a needful stage in a constant upward movement, and gradually raising the ancestors of Israel above the general level of their age. It is not, I think, too strong to assert with Schultz that 'we cannot, in point of fact, picture to ourselves the rise of the Hebrew religion in any other way than Hebrew legend does,' when it represents God as entering into converse and communion with primitive man in modes suited to his present capacity. The whole subsequent course of revelation tends to confirm the idea that at some point in early Hebrew history there actually took place such an event as we believe the 'call' of Abraham to have been: a self-manifestation of Almighty God and a vocation addressed to a particular man, on whose response to the divine call the future development of the redemptive movement was allowed to depend. This is the important point, and there are many extraneous matters in regard to which we can well afford to be neutral or indifferent. All that we are told by literary critics respecting other internal features of the early narratives—for instance, respecting the presence in them of mythical details or euhemeristic elements [1]—only serves, if modern theories can be substantiated, to illustrate more vividly, first, the antecedently probable fact that Israel's religion was rooted in the natural soil of Semitic usage and worship; secondly, the fact that it contained, even in its most rudimentary stage,

which is not strictly historical, may well supply a perfect historical picture. Elsewhere, he remarks (pref. p. xiii, Eng. Tr.) that 'nothing in the history of Israel can be explained without reference to the patriarchal age.'

[1] Such elements are probably to be discerned in the traditions of the antediluvian period. Such names as Tubal-cain, Jubal, Enoch, Lamech, &c., point to the possibility of figures originally mythical becoming human. See the cautious remarks of Schultz, vol. i. pp. 112 foll.

a divinely implanted germ or element, which by perpetual upward pressure ultimately attained to complete predominance, and imparted to the faith of Israel its capacity in the fullness of time to welcome and adore the Son of God himself, manifest in human flesh.

2. In the patriarchal tradition we may reasonably contend that we have a faithful representation of the two principal factors which determined the distinctive character of Israel's religion: namely, a personal and redemptive operation of God in history on the one hand, and the response of human faith on the other. If we wished to select the master-thought of the Old Testament, we should be justified in saying that it is belief in the providence and direct action of the living God. Certainly this was the point of view from which the writers of the Pentateuchal narratives described the early stages of the history; it was the standpoint from which the prophets reviewed and interpreted Israel's wonderful past. It was the living experience of Jehovah's might that made Israel unique among nations: *Unto thee it was showed, that thou mightest know that the Lord he is God; there is none else beside him. Out of heaven he made thee to hear his voice, that he might instruct thee: and upon earth he showed thee his great fire; and thou heardest his words out of the midst of the fire. And because he loved thy fathers, therefore he chose their seed after them, and brought thee out in his sight with his mighty power out of Egypt*[1]. *Whatsoever the Lord pleased*, says the psalmist, *that did he in heaven, and in earth, and in the sea, and in all deep places*[2]. In the Old Testament Jehovah is not merely represented as one who controls the course of natural events ; He interposes, He actively operates, He brings mighty things to pass, He makes Himself known in acts that display the tenacity of an invincible will, the splendour of a spiritual purpose, the reality of redemptive power. And although in early times the mass of the nation probably thought

---

[1] Deut. iv. 35-37.   [2] Ps. cxxxv. 6.

of Jehovah as one who worked only on behalf of His own elect people, yet the prophets and those who were imbued with their spirit recognized the divine hand in universal history. They teach that the sovereignty of Jehovah is co-extensive with human life and society, and that His moral purpose embraces all the nations of the world. They magnify His power to initiate, to impel, to control, to overrule[1]. *Is anything too hard for the Lord?* they ask[2]. *Ah Lord God!* cries Jeremiah, *behold, thou hast made the heaven and the earth by thy great power and stretched out arm, and there is nothing too hard for thee ... the great, the mighty God, the Lord of hosts is his name, great in counsel, and mighty in work: for thine eyes are open upon all the ways of the sons of men*[3]. That the Most High ruleth in the kingdom of men[4] is, in short, a primary axiom of the highest Hebrew faith, and any expressions, however anthropomorphic, which serve to convey an idea of the living personality of God are employed by the sacred writers without any fear of misconception.

It is scarcely necessary to point out that this idea of deity pervades the narratives of Genesis. The living God Himself is ever at work controlling and judging the deeds of men. On the other hand, the book teaches in the most striking and emphatic way the necessity and significance of man's response to the revealed will and electing love of God. It is noticeable that Kuenen who questions the historical existence of the patriarchs, explicitly rejects the idea of a divine election to which their faith was a response. 'Is,' he asks, 'the belief in Israel's selection still tenable in our days? That the first Christians—who knew but a small portion of the inhabited world, and could hope that within a comparatively short time the true religion would have reached that world's uttermost bounds—

---

[1] Amos ix. 7; Deut. ii. 12, 22; Isa. v. 26 foll., vii. 20, viii. 7, ix. 11, x. 5 foll., xxiii. 9, xlv. 1; 2 Kings v. 1.
[2] Gen. xviii. 14.   [3] Jer. xxxii. 17 foll.
[4] Dan. iv. 17.

should have acquiesced in this view is most natural. But we? Is this belief in harmony with the experience which we have now accumulated for centuries together, and with our present knowledge of lands and nations? We do not hesitate to reply in the negative.... We now perceive that the means of which God was formerly thought to have made use are altogether disproportioned to the end which in reality was to be attained. So long as we yet knew but little of "the heathen," and formed but an indistinct idea of their number, their characteristics, and their development, we could reasonably believe that God had *suffered them to walk in their own ways* in order, with a view to them and their future, to manifest Himself first of all to one nation. Now this idea seems to us a childish fancy. Israel is no more the pivot on which the development of the whole world turns than the planet which we inhabit is the centre of the universe. In short, we have outgrown the belief of our ancestors[1].'

Now the Old Testament, it need scarcely be said, assumes precisely the contrary state of things to be the fact. The principle of election is obviously conceived to be a primary element in the divine method, and accordingly the whole story of Genesis describes the response made to God's action by successive individuals—men in whom had been awakened a certain susceptibility to the divine self-revelation. There were *holy prophets—that is, men of spiritual genius—since the world began*. The religion which was to embrace mankind could only find an entrance through some solitary soul, quick to apprehend and to welcome the promises of God. This is tantamount to saying that the progress of the race in religion, as in other things, has depended upon individuals; and even if it could be shown that the name of Abraham is merely a mythical abstraction, or a tribal personification, it would yet be reasonable and indeed necessary to assume that

[1] *Religion of Israel*, vol. i. pp. 8, 9.

at a certain point in history an individual man appeared, capable of so entering into communion with God as to be the true father of the faithful. In point of fact, does not the whole history of religion show that there are critical moments when everything turns on the fidelity, the simplicity, the courage, with which some individual soul surrenders itself to obey the will of God? The only adequate explanation of the rise and growth of Hebrew religion is the supposition that God actually made known His will to some individual human spirit, and manifested Himself to him singly and alone. Abraham's history, says Dean Church, 'is marked as the history of a man, a soul by itself in relation to Almighty God; not as one of a company, a favoured brotherhood, or chosen body, but in all his doings single and alone, alone with the Alone, one with One, with his Maker as he was born and as he dies, alone: the individual soul, standing all by itself, in the presence of its Author and Sustainer, called by Him and answering to His call, choosing, acting, obeying, from the last depths and secrets of its being[1].' Belief in God, belief that what He promises He is able to perform, faith—this is the second essential factor in the religion of the Old Testament. It is easier to believe that this faith was born in the heart of an individual than that it was the simultaneous impulse of a tribe; but even this latter supposition would not necessarily conflict with the principle of election, nor with the great prominence assigned to faith by the Old Testament as a vital element in the spiritual history of mankind. I say then confidently that the early narratives do faithfully present the conditions and factors which alone account for the rise and onward movement of Israel's religion. Thus there seems to be no just reason for doubting the main incidents of Abraham's traditional career. The rite of circumcision may well have been selected

---

[1] Church, *Discipline of the Christian Character*, p. 20.

as a fitting sign of the higher relationship with God to which Abraham and his tribe felt themselves called [1].

3. It will be convenient here to touch upon a delicate and difficult point suggested by the special characteristics of the Pentateuchal narrative, a point to which some reference has already been made. I allude to the fact that the Pentateuch unquestionably exhibits an element of what may be called idealization. The character of the ancient patriarchs and their manner of worship, the story of the Egyptian plagues, the experiences of the Israelites in the wilderness, their movements to and fro, their conflicts, their tribal arrangements, their internal polity and order, above all, their sanctuary with its ordinances of sacrifice— all these not only must be supposed, but can actually, as I believe, be shown, to have been to a considerable extent idealized by the pious reflection of a later age. It has been pointed out that a special tone and tendency characterizes each of the principal documents which appear, so far as our present knowledge extends, to form the substance of the Pentateuch. The Elohist writer, for example, seems to narrate the history of Israel's origins from a prophetical standpoint; he interprets in a religious spirit what he records, and aims at bringing out the didactic significance of events [2]. The Jehovist, on the other hand, displays an inclination towards profound theological reflection. He is penetrated by the thought of Jehovah's mercifulness, long-suffering, and covenant-faithfulness. He delights to trace the successive stages in the development of faith. It is he who tells how Abraham *believed in the Lord, and he counted it to him for righteousness*; how a heavenly benediction ever crowns the response of human faith to the electing grace of God [3]. The Jehovist appears in fact to survey the field of history

---

[1] See the section in Riehm, *A Tl. Theologie*, on 'The Religion of the Patriarchs,' § 9.
[2] See e. g. Gen. l. 20.
[3] Gen. xv. 6. Cp. Exod. xiv. 31, xix. 9; Num. xiv. 11.

with the eye of mature spiritual experience; in the lowly beginnings of Hebrew history he discerns the divinely intended consummation—the ultimate purpose which from the first filled the incidents of ordinary life with solemn significance [1]. Once more, the author of the priestly document evidently purposes to give a systematic and circumstantial sketch of the sacred institutions of the theocracy, and from this standpoint he regards the entire career of the nation. In effect he presents us with an ideal picture of the Mosaic age. 'His representation as a whole,' says Dr. Driver, 'seems to be the result of a systematizing process working upon the [ancient] materials, and perhaps also seeking to give sensible expression to certain ideas or truths [2].' Of this ideal sketch there is beyond reasonable doubt an historical basis, but the facts and institutions described are so conceived as to exemplify ideal theocratic principles. It is no part of my plan to enter at length into the well-known characteristics of the priestly code. By way of illustration it will suffice to refer to one point. It would appear that the dominant thought of the priestly writer is that of Jehovah's abiding presence in the midst of His people. That sublime prophetic idea was, as it were, visibly realized in the local position and organized *cultus* of the second temple. But the writer seems to project back into the Mosaic age an ideal system which was only realized in fact at a period several centuries later than the exodus. He accordingly describes the tabernacle as occupying a central position in the camp of the Israelites, whereas the earlier composite narrative (JE) regularly represents the 'tent of meeting' as *outside* the camp. Moreover, the writer's usual conception of the collective people is as a 'congregation [3],' a term that does not occur in the non-priestly portions of the Hexateuch.

---

[1] Gen. ix. 22 foll.; xvi. 12; xix. 31 foll.; xxv. 25 foll.; xlix. 9 foll.
[2] *Introduction to the Literature of the Old Testament,* p. 120. See generally Wellhausen, *Prolegomena,* ch. viii; Robertson Smith, *O. T. in J. C.* lect. xiii. [3] עדה.

Now it is to be observed that there is absolutely no question of the writer's good faith; he does not carry his idealizing tendency to the point of overlooking the sins by which the divine purpose, either for the people or for Moses himself, was thwarted or abrogated[1]. But in historical details, especially those which relate to chronology, the priestly writer is evidently more concerned with ideal conceptions than with actual facts. His work is interwoven with the older writing, which represents a different tradition, in such a way as to make the total result unique: a kind of blending of fact with theory, of actual institutions with an imaginative conception of their original form and ideal significance.

It may assist us to form a clearer notion of the idealizing process under consideration if we endeavour to depict to ourselves the motive and purpose of the priestly compilers of the Pentateuch, and the method of procedure which they appear to have adopted. The facts are probably somewhat as follows. At a late stage in Israel's history, apparently during the exile in Babylon, when the process of national development seemed to be arrested, and an age of enforced inactivity and reflection succeeded a period of tumult and disaster, an unknown priestly writer, or possibly a school of writers, took in hand the task of framing a compendious and concrete picture of the early history of the Hebrew people. They were guided, no doubt, by the light of that divine purpose for Israel which the oracles of prophecy and the teachings of calamity had at length brought home to the national conscience. To a devout Jew placed in these circumstances the lessons of history would appear unmistakeable. It was plain that from the first Jehovah had formed Israel to be a holy community, bound together by sacred institutions of divine appointment and by the presence of God Himself dwelling in the national sanctuary. The authors of the priestly code evidently entered on their

---

[1] See Exod. xvi. 2; Lev. x. 1; Num. xx. 12, 24; xxvii. 13 foll. &c.

task filled with precise legal conceptions of what an ideally holy community should be, and accordingly their theory of Israel's history is entirely religious. 'To the community is assigned a purely religious end: political aims are ignored, for the people lives for God's sake and not for its own[1].'

On the whole it cannot, I think, be fairly disputed that Prof. Robertson Smith's general description of the writing in question is correct. 'It is only in *form*,' he says, 'an historical document; in substance it is a body of laws and precedents having the value of law, strung on a thread of history so meagre that it often consists of nothing more than a chronological scheme and a sequence of bare names.' From the fact that 'the supposed Mosaic ordinances and the narratives that go with them are,' practically and at least in their developed form, 'unknown to the history and the prophets before Ezra... to the Deuteronomic writers and... to the non-priestly parts of the Pentateuch,... it follows with certainty that the priestly recasting of the origins of Israel is not history (save in so far as it merely summarizes and reproduces the old traditions in the other parts of the Hexateuch) but *Haggada*, i.e. that it uses old names and old stories, not for the purpose of conveying historical facts, but solely for purposes of legal and ethical instruction[2].'

Such is the theoretical point of view from which the priestly narrative of Israel's early history and sacred ordinances is compiled. The object of the writers is not to supersede the work of the prophetic narrators, but to supply a counterpart to it. Before the captivity a fusion of the two main historical documents of the Pentateuch (the Jehovistic and the Elohistic[3]) had in all probability taken place; the combined narra-

---

[1] See Montefiore, *Hibbert Lectures*, No. vi. p. 319. This lecture gives an admirable account of the influence under which P was compiled.
[2] *O. T. in J. C.* p. 420.
[3] For a good account of the different documents see Dillmann, *Comm. on Genesis*, pp. ix-xiv. Observe, Dillmann uses for P, E, J, the symbols A, B, C.

tives had been revised from the Deuteronomic standpoint, and had already, as it seems, been united with the book of Deuteronomy [1]. At the close of the exile, writers of the priestly school completed what had been already begun, combining the materials already extant, and piecing them together in a framework which in form is historical, but is really little more than a continuous exposition of the legal and religious ordinances of Israel, tracing them for the most part to Moses himself.

Such, then, seems to have been the literary process towards which the available evidence distinctly points. Without unduly insisting on the accuracy of details, we may attempt to describe summarily the view which our present knowledge may lead us to form of the Pentateuch in its final shape. The work viewed in its entirety as a single product contains two expositions of Israel's history which stand side by side, separate and distinct in origin, purpose, and internal characteristics, forming together a combination of different elements, of prophetic narrative with priestly *torah*. It contains history idealized, the actual historic traditions and the ideal goal towards which the history was tending being presented in juxtaposition. In estimating, therefore, the evidential value of the narratives, it is essential to bear constantly in mind the two elements they contain: on the one hand, the ancient traditions of Israel's past, moulded in forms of rare grace, dignity, and simplicity under prophetic influence; on the other, side by side with these, and often interwoven with them, the idealistic and imaginative sketch of the priestly writers, whose chief interest lay not in tracing the actual course of Israel's primaeval history, but in exhibiting the spiritual and theocratic consummation towards which it was advancing from the first.

---

[1] Robertson Smith, *O. T. in J. C.* p. 425. The history of the ancient 'law of holiness' (Lev. xvii–xxvi) is obscure. It comes to us embedded in P, but the process by which it was taken up, expanded, and accommodated to P's standpoint cannot be traced. The antiquity of many of the injunctions contained in this law, especially in chh. xviii–xx, is undoubted.

Some writers have spoken with undisguised contempt of the authors of the priestly document, but it would be absurd to charge them with wilful desertion or falsification of the historical tradition. Even while they 'reshape the narrative in order to set forth later laws under the conventional form of Mosaic precedent[1]' they leave the ancient tradition of JE substantially in the form handed down to them. How shallow and unjust are those criticisms of the narrative which ignore its essential character! how futile is the attempt to measure them by the standard of modern historical literature! To treat the priestly narratives as worthless fictions is anachronistic; to treat them as literal and undiluted history is to ignore the distinction between history and *Haggadah*[2]. The *Haggadistic* treatment of history implies a certain amplification of incidents recorded or alluded to in the original narratives, according to the views and necessities of later times. It admits the play of fancy; it manipulates the details of sacred history in such a way as may best serve the purpose of instruction or edification. It was in Judaistic times at least a recognized mode of dealing with the early narratives which probably had passed through a long process of development. Since criticism has discovered so much that illustrates the mind and intention of the different contributors to the Pentateuch, we are bound to study it not only with more intelligence and sympathy, but also with more discrimination than was formerly possible.

The importance of the priestly writing from a religious point of view is certainly great. The Pentateuchal law played a significant and necessary part in the development of true spiritual religion. It preserved and sheltered some of the loftiest and most beautiful ideals of prophecy: e.g. the idea of a holy people dedicated

---

[1] Robertson Smith, *O. T. in J. C.* p. 387.
[2] *Ibid.* p. 430. Obs. P is essentially a *law-book*, and cannot be used as an independent source for the actual history of the Mosaic and pre-Mosaic period. Cp. Kittel, *op. cit.* i. pp. 96 foll.

to God, and of the divine consecration of its natural life; the idea, in a word, of an indwelling presence of God among men. What criticism justly questions is whether, in view of our present knowledge, we have a right to go to the priestly literature for historical information; whether such use of it does not imply an entire misconception of its essential character.

But an element of idealization in the stricter sense is to be found even in the older prophetic narratives. The primitive story describes the ancestors of the Hebrew people with an evident intention to represent them as types of spiritual character. It is true indeed that there is a vivid reality, and faithfulness to human nature in the narratives of Genesis which strengthens our impression of their general truth to fact. These life-like figures—so entirely human both in their weakness and in their strength—cannot be mere creations of pious fancy. But even in these vigorous delineations of actual men and women we are able to recognize the overruling guidance of Him to whose purposes the narrators unconsciously ministered. The figure of Abraham especially, *the friend of God*, is to a certain extent idealized. He is represented as a prophet, a saint, a servant of God, a priestly intercessor, a hero of faith, a recipient of splendid promises; his outward prosperity and wealth correspond to his spiritual dignity; it is manifest that he is pourtrayed from the standpoint of men who fully recognize his transcendent importance in the history of religion—an importance which eventually seems to overshadow even that of the great lawgiver of Israel himself. Further, the very fact that in the New Testament Abraham reappears as the most sublime figure in the past history even of all mankind[1], confirms the impression that we have here a case of legitimate and profitable idealization. Abraham is an historic personage, but he is also a spiritual type: he is the ideal representative of the

---

[1] Cp. Rom. iv; Gal. iii; Jas. ii. 21 foll.; Heb. xi. 8 foll., besides the passages in the gospels, Luke iii. 8; John viii. 33 foll.

life of faith and of separation from the idolatries of an evil world. He prefigures 'the ideal character and aims of the people of God[1].' His descendants, too, are typical figures: Isaac is a type of the life of spiritual sonship, Jacob of the spirit of service, Joseph of the purifying power of suffering and of the glory that follows it. The spiritual purpose of the narratives is manifest; they are literally penetrated with religious ideas. In fact, as Origen forcibly insists[2], the Pentateuch was intended to serve higher purposes than merely that of supplying historical information. It was *written for our learning; it is profitable for doctrine, for reproof, for correction, for instruction in righteousness*[3]. It was intended to be a mirror of human life, not only as it is, but as it should be and is hereafter destined to become; a glass in which a man may behold *the face of his genesis*[4] and go his way, ready not to forget, but to fulfil what he has learned.

Considering indeed the real function of Holy Scripture, we cannot fail to appreciate the value of the ideal element which we have been illustrating. If the object of the Bible be to teach us the outlines of religious character and the true knowledge of God, to instruct us *how* we *ought to walk and to please God*[5], it might be justly maintained that these Old Testament portraits of human character, faithful in general outline but idealized in colour, are most suitable for the purpose of edification. The peculiar features and essential elements of the religious life are in fact nowhere so vividly pourtrayed as in the living and

---

[1] Driver, *Sermons on the Old Testament*, p. 127. Cp. Aug. *serm.* ii: 'Quicquid scriptura dicit de Abraham et factum est, et prophetia est.'
[2] See A. Jukes, *The Types of Genesis briefly considered as revealing the development of human nature*, esp. pref. p. xiii. Cp. Orig. *Hom.* 2 *in Exod.* § 1: 'Nos omnia quae scripta sunt non pro narrationibus antiquitatum, sed pro disciplina et utilitate nostra didicimus scripta.' *Hom.* 1 *in Exod.* § 5: 'Non nobis haec ad historiam scripta sunt neque putandum est libros divinos Aegyptiorum gesta narrare, sed quae scripta sunt ad nostram doctrinam et commonitionem scripta sunt.'
[3] Rom. xv. 4; 2 Tim. iii. 16.   [4] Jas. i. 23.   [5] 1 Thess. iv. 1.

breathing pictures of the patriarchs. The fundamental conditions of the life of communion and converse with God find here an entirely adequate expression. In the hands of the inspired writers who narrate them, the simple incidents of the patriarchal story become parables of the spiritual life. The call of Abraham, the trial of his faith, Isaac's willing self-surrender, the vision of Jacob at Bethel, the sorrows and exaltation of Joseph and his self-discovery to his brethren—these and such-like incidents may be accepted as historical, but in any case they are much more than this. They are symbolic parables of God's dealings with His children in every age of human history; they are narratives to which the spiritual experience of saints has set its seal. The phrase 'children of Abraham' tends from the first employment of it in Scripture to acquire a moral and spiritual significance. The great patriarch is *the father of all them that believe*. That the idealized sketch of his life was intended to convey sacred teaching is actually proved by the continuous experience of those who in every age have set their faith and hope on God [1].

On the whole, we shall feel that in frankly recognizing the idealistic element in the Old Testament narratives we are on the way to a more sympathetic and intelligent study of them. For the element is present in other historical books; to some extent it is to be looked for in all. The character of David, for instance, is idealized in the first book of the Chronicles, much as Abraham's figure is in Genesis [2]. Confining our attention, however, to the patriarchs, we may observe that the spirit of due veneration for them was displayed not only in the circumstantial minuteness of the beautiful narratives relating to their career, but in the ascription to them of ancient oracles, like the Blessing of Jacob, which probably had an independent

---

[1] Cp. 1 Pet. i. 21.
[2] On the character of David see Cheyne, *Aids to the Devout Study of Criticism*, part 1. Renan's account of David is greatly impaired by the strong prejudice displayed in it (*Histoire*, &c., bk. ii. chh. 16 foll.).

origin [1]. Thus, in the memory of the nation of which they were the honoured progenitors, the patriarchs veritably survived in such a way that they, being dead, yet continued to speak [2].

Before, however, we leave the subject, it is desirable to suggest an answer to the question whether idealization of history such as we have indicated is morally justifiable. In part the answer has already been given in the consideration that the Bible was intended to teach religion rather than natural knowledge, the ways of God rather than the exact course of history, the needs, aspirations, and capacities of human nature rather than the achievements or sufferings of individual men. But a further suggestion may be advanced. A true justification of the scriptural mode of presenting history lies, we may think, in the fact that the sacred writers are reading the story of human life from a divine point of view. We are told of each stage in creation that, though relatively imperfect, it was good in the sight of God: *God saw that it was good.* On a somewhat similar principle the characters of the patriarchal age and of subsequent periods are delineated not merely from the human, but also from the divine standpoint. We see them in their imperfections, their frailties, their deceits, their deeds of violence, lust or revenge, which do not surprise us if we bear in mind that even the highest level attained by Old Testament morality is comparatively low and defective; but there is another way of estimating human character, which is more true and more God-like. He who discerned the end in the beginning loved even a fallen and alienated world; He beheld it ennobled, transfigured, and glorified; He saw what the universe might ultimately become, *new heavens and a new earth, wherein dwelleth righteousness* [3]. In the same spirit perhaps the inspired writers idealize the characters which they describe, for it is the mark of the spirit of goodness not to impute

---

[1] Ewald, *Revelation and its Record*, p. 323.
[2] Cp. Heb. xi. 4.
[3] 2 Pet. iii. 13.

evil, but to discern in all things the best and highest
that they contain. Indeed, this habit of idealization is
a fundamental trait of the sacred writers both in the
Old and New Testament. How cordially St. Paul
appreciates and makes much of what is good and
promising in the several churches to which he indites
his epistles! He commends their faith, their goodness, their patience, their love; he gives thanks to
God that *in everything* they are *enriched by him, in all
utterance and in all knowledge*; he rejoices over their
election of God[1]; he glories in their constancy; he
recognizes with large-hearted charity each token that
they exhibit of Christian sanctity and grace. Similarly
St. John in each of his messages to the seven churches
begins with praise. And our blessed Lord Himself
ever sets us the example of quickness and readiness
to welcome goodness wherever it is to be found.
'A devil,' it has been said, 'can mark our faults, but it
needs the grace of God to mark the dawn of grace[2].'
When God looks upon us He loves us *non quales
sumus sed quales erimus*; and it is not unfair to suppose
that even this tendency to idealization, which might at
first sight be supposed to impair the strictly historical
value of the early narratives, is after all a token of the
working of the divine Spirit, who alone can penetrate
below the surface of life and discern in each human
soul what it may yet become—what it is on the way
to be. It is not fanciful, but the truest wisdom, to
think loftily of the early stages of a movement which
was destined to culminate in the Incarnation of the
Word. There was an ideal greatness about him who
*rejoiced to see Christ's day; and he saw it, and was
glad*[3]. Poor, base, and low may have seemed the
origins of Hebrew religion; Jacob was as a wandering
Syrian ready to perish in the eyes of Laban, but the
favour, the tenderness, and the gentleness of God
lifted him to greatness. *Hast thou*, says the writer of

---

[1] See 1 Cor. i. 5; 1 Thess: i. 4, &c. [2] Jukes, *op. cit.* p. 9.
[3] John viii. 56.

Job, *eyes of flesh, or seest thou as man seeth? Are thy days as the days of man? are thy years as man's days, that thou enquirest after mine iniquity, and searchest after my sin*[1]*?* Job appeals to his Maker as any man may appeal who is conscious of his frailty, yet is assured of his heavenly vocation, who has been haunted by heavenly visions which he fears to disobey, who has dreamed splendid dreams of the heights to which human nature may attain, and of *the things which God hath prepared for them that love him*[2].

It has seemed desirable to dwell at some length on this point, inasmuch as it is of more importance to recognize the principles which have moulded the structure of the Old Testament narratives, than to determine precisely their historical value, even if we could reasonably hope to do so. What has been said about the patriarchal history practically amounts to this: that in it we possess a general outline of Israel's origins, coloured to a considerable extent by the thoughts and habits of a later period. The writers were evidently penetrated by certain moral and religious ideas; their aim was apparently didactic, and they were influenced by an instinctive tendency to idealize what they described. This peculiarity, while it is very far from depriving the narratives of all historical value, is yet specially calculated to serve the purposes of spiritual edification and *instruction in righteousness*[3]. The historian may complain with Kuenen that the strictly historical kernel which can be safely extracted from such a book as Genesis is vague and more or less indefinite[4]. The fact is that the great figures of the patriarchal period are presented to us in narratives 'of which,' says Prof. G. A. Smith, 'it is simply impossible for us at this time of day to establish the accuracy.' We have simply to accept

---

[1] Job x. 4 foll. [2] 1 Cor. ii. 9. [3] 2 Tim. iii. 16.
[4] See *The Religion of Israel*, vol. i. p. 113. Cp. G. A. Smith, *The Preaching of the Old Testament to the Age*, p. 37. See Note A at the end of the lecture.

the fact that in the present state of our knowledge there are no clear *criteria* by which to distinguish precisely the historical nucleus contained in the patriarchal narratives from the idealized picture. If there is uncertainty on this point we can only conclude that knowledge of the precise details of the history is not of vital importance. But from the standpoint of religion, the book is rich in instruction beyond what even the keenest student can fathom. 'In Genesis,' it has been said, 'is hid all Scripture, as the tree is in the seed[1].' 'The book of Genesis,' says another living writer, 'is the true and original birthplace of all theology. It contains those ideas of God and man, of righteousness and judgment, of responsibility and moral government, of failure and hope, which are presupposed through the rest of the Old Testament, and which prepare the way for the mission of Christ[2].' Such an estimate every Christian who thoughtfully studies the Old Testament will eagerly endorse.

II.

Passing to the period of Mosaism, we touch ground which is acknowledged on all sides to be comparatively solid. Even those critics who regard the records of the entire pre-Mosaic period as legendary, allow that the exodus of Israel from Egypt and the personality of Moses are 'assured historical realities[3].' It is no doubt true that the figure of Moses himself is drawn in the light of a much later age, but that which made him the most conspicuous creative genius of Hebrew history stands out with luminous clearness, namely, the fact that he was a *prophet*, a man conscious of a supernatural call, strengthened and sustained throughout his eventful career by the sense

---

[1] Jukes, *op. cit.* p. 4.
[2] Girdlestone, *The Foundations of the Bible*, p. 155. Cp. Delitzsch, *New Commentary on Genesis*, vol. i. p. 56.
[3] Montefiore, *Hibbert Lectures*, p. 14.

of divine mission. Indeed, since the consolidation of Israel's nationality was in every sense a creative act, it cannot be adequately explained apart from the appearance of a personality like that of Moses[1]. 'Nothing,' says Professor Kittel, 'is less likely to arise spontaneously out of the depths of a people's life than those new creations which make epochs in the history of religion and morals. They slumber there, but they do not come to the surface until a single spirit, of whom they have taken entire possession, finds them in himself, grasps them, understands and proclaims them, and thus becomes the religious and moral hero, the prophet of his people[2].' The prophetic activity of Moses is not the less real because it is rather displayed in action than embodied in writings. The results of his activity, which are plainly visible in the subsequent history, show that his work was a work of God, and he himself a commissioned organ of Jehovah's will[3].

It seems to be most probable that what we call 'Mosaism' had an historical basis in existing religious beliefs, that there already prevailed religious ideas and aspirations to which Moses could appeal, that at least in some inner circle of the Hebrew clans the rudiments of a pure and simple faith had been cherished since patriarchal times. Something, too, may have been owing to the influence of Egyptian culture, with which, according to tradition, Moses was familiar,

---

[1] Bruce, *Apologetics*, p. 197, makes a suggestive remark: 'The creation of Israel, like the creation of the world, may have been a much more complicated process than it appears in the sacred page, and the secular history of the process, if it could be written, might assume a very different appearance in many respects to the biblical, just as the scientific history of the physical creation differs widely from that given in the first chapter of Genesis.'

[2] *History of the Hebrews*, vol. i. p. 240. Observe that Moses is referred to as a 'prophet' in Num. xii. 7; Deut. xviii. 15 foll., xxxiv. 10; Hos. xii. 13. God holds converse with him *as a man speaketh with his friend*, Exod. xxxiii. 11. To him is vouchsafed the manifestation of God's character 'which dominates Israel's history,' Exod. xxxiv. 6-8. (Driver, *Sermons on the O. T.* p. 128.) Cp. Wellhausen, *Prolegomena*, p. 399.

[3] Cp. Riehm, *A Tl. Theologie*, pp. 54–56.

though it is on the whole probable that the influence of Egypt was prejudicial to the comparatively pure faith which the tribes of Israel may be thought to have inherited from their ancestors [1].

Further, there is no reason *a priori* for rejecting the supposition that Moses borrowed from other sources such religious forms or institutions as he judged to be suitable vehicles of the main religious thoughts that formed the basis of his system. Nevertheless, his work was that of an originator. Channing has said that the true task of God's ministers is 'to give vitality to the thought of God.' Such was indeed the aim of Moses. He has been sometimes represented as nothing more than a powerful leader or social reformer; but the history of Hebrew religion shows that he was a prophet indeed. In his proclamation of the truth that Jehovah was Israel's God, and that He was a God of righteousness [2], was contained the expansive germ from which the higher faith of subsequent times was developed.

When we turn to the books of the Pentateuch, in which the historic narratives relating to Mosaism are contained, we notice at once that they do not profess to be complete. The greater part of the history of this period is contained in the priestly document, but the book of Deuteronomy contains a retrospect which is in all probability earlier than the narrative of the priestly writer. It is a striking fact that the Deuteronomic writer is silent in regard to those very subjects which occupy a central place in the priestly writing; for instance, the erection of the tabernacle and the

---

[1] Riehm, p. 53, thinks that the old Semitic worship of Jehovah under the symbol of a bull was revived under Egyptian influence. He also traces to Egypt the worship of satyrs, Lev. xvii. 7 (שְׂעִירִים). Cp. Renan, *Histoire*, &c., bk. i. ch. 11.

[2] Montefiore, *Hibbert Lectures*, p. 48. Cp. p. 55. 'The story of Israel's religion opens with the work of a great personality, who taught his people to worship one God only, a severe but just deity, demanding from the tribes which acknowledged his dominion the practice of the simplest rules of civic morality.'

institution of its worship[1]. But taking the narratives as a whole, it is plain that they do not aim at giving an exhaustive account of the historical facts. The thirty-eight years of wandering in the wilderness are passed over almost in silence, while other incidents, which must have occupied considerable spaces of time, are compressed or grouped together in cameo-like pictures. There are indeed many phenomena in the Pentateuch which justify Kuenen's observation, that 'in the memory of a nation the events of a series of years become compressed into one great fact and are attached to one great name[2].' Nothing indeed can be more natural than that the events of one great crisis in a nation's history should become encircled with a halo of sacred tradition, in which particular incidents recede into the background, and general features and principles of divine action emerge and come to the front. The all-important fact of Jehovah's deliverance and guidance of His chosen people seems to live in the religious consciousness of the Pentateuchal writers, and perhaps somewhat overpowers or dims their interest in historical details.

Let us attempt to indicate briefly the main features of the narrative which deals with the history of the exodus and the wanderings in the wilderness.

1. First, we mark the general tendency of the account, to represent the wonderful deliverance from Egypt as the fundamental fact of Israel's national career. The leading incidents we may regard as practically certain: Israel's flight from Egypt, the passage of the Red Sea, the desert journey, the conflict with Amalek, the delivery of a law at Sinai embodying some definite but rudimentary system of

---

[1] Robertson Smith, *O. T. in J. C.* pp. 391-393.
[2] *The Religion of Israel*, vol. i. p. 135. Observe that this compression is found also in the account of the processes of creation (see Driver, *Sermons on the O. T.* p. 173), and also in such a narrative as that of Joshua x. foll., which 'gathers up all the details of slow conquest and local struggle in one comprehensive picture, with a single hero in the foreground.' See Joshua xi. 18 (*O. T. in J. C.* p. 131).

worship and polity, the long sojourn at Kadesh, the conquest of the region east of Jordan, the occupation and gradual appropriation of the promised land. It is in regard to minor points that the evidence is defective, for the circumstantial and curiously minute sketch of the priestly writer, systematic, detailed, and precise though it be, cannot for reasons already indicated be regarded as constituting an independent historical authority [1]. Thus in regard to the nature of the 'tent of meeting' and its precise position in the camp there is a conflict of evidence, nor is it ever likely to be determined to what extent a sacrificial *cultus* was actually carried on in the wilderness. The outstanding fact, however, of the Mosaic history is contained in a passage which has been called 'the gospel of the exodus.' *Ye have seen what I did unto the Egyptians, and how I bare you on eagles' wings, and brought you unto myself. Now therefore, if ye will obey my voice indeed, and keep my covenant, then ye shall be a peculiar treasure unto me above all people* [2]. The exodus implied first and foremost the exaltation of Israel's God [3]; next, it marked the birth of a nation, and its call to a special position of dependence on its deliverer. *Thus saith the Lord, Israel is my son, even my firstborn* [4]. The new title corresponded to a unique fact, viz. that the Hebrew race was adopted by Jehovah, and brought into a peculiar relationship to Himself. The prophets occasionally describe God as the *creator of Israel* [5], in virtue of those mighty redemptive acts by which Israel was severed from Egypt and made the people of divine election. In this display of condescending grace Israel recognized the God of its fathers as the

---

[1] As instances of P's partiality for definite and precise details of number, measure, and weight, see the description of Noah's ark (Gen. vi. 14 foll.), and such passages as Exod. xxxviii. 24-31, Num. vii and xxxi. See Driver, *Introduction to the Literature of the O. T.* pp. 118-122.
[2] Exod. xix. 4, 5.   [3] Exod. xv. 1, 2.   [4] Exod. iv. 22.
[5] See Isa. xliii. 15.

founder of its nationality[1], and accordingly it is with the exodus that the real history of Israel begins, at least in the view of the earlier prophets[2]. Then for the first time was established that unique relationship between Jehovah and Israel which became the basis of a theocratic polity; nor can we wonder that prophetic and priestly writers of a later period incorporated in the Pentateuchal picture of the Mosaic age an account of those fully-developed theocratic institutions, the germinal origin of which could be traced to Moses himself. For the primitive ordinances established at the period of the exodus, the sacrifice of the Passover with its accessories, the feast of Mazzoth and the sanctification of the firstborn, gradually came to be regarded as symbols of Israel's original consecration to the worship and service of Jehovah. *Observe the month of Abib*, says the writer of Deuteronomy, *and keep the passover unto the Lord thy God: for in the month of Abib the Lord thy God brought thee forth out of Egypt by night. . . . Thou shalt eat no leavened bread with it; seven days shalt thou eat unleavened bread therewith, even the bread of affliction; for thou camest forth out of the land of Egypt in haste: that thou mayest remember the day when thou camest forth out of the land of Egypt all the days of thy life*[3]. To this corresponds a passage in the book of Exodus: *By strength of hand the Lord brought us out from Egypt, from the house of bondage: and it came to pass when Pharaoh would hardly let us go, that the Lord slew all the firstborn in the land of Egypt . . . therefore I sacrifice to the Lord all that openeth the matrix, being males; but all the firstborn*

---

[1] Cp. Amos ii. 9 foll., iii. 1; Hos. ii. 15, xi. 1, xii. 9, 13, xiii. 4 foll.
[2] Meinhold, *Jesus und das A. T.* p. 133, observes that if the story of Genesis is of fundamental importance, it is difficult to explain the fact that the prophets generally regard the exodus as the beginning and foundation of Israel's religion. It is certain that Abraham is very seldom alluded to by pre-exilic prophets (Isa. xxix. 22; Jer. xxxiii. 26. Mic. vii. 20 is not certainly pre-exilic. See Kirkpatrick, *The Doctrine of the Prophets*, p. 230).
[3] Deut. xvi. 1-3.

*of my children I redeem*¹. We know how the events of the exodus lived in the memory of the people. Again and again, in the days of alarm and calamity, the thoughts of the faithful reverted to that signal manifestation of Jehovah's beneficence and might. It was a comprehensive type of all divine salvation; it constituted a sure basis of the loftiest hopes; it rekindled faith even when it seemed to be overwhelmed by the disasters of later history; it was the ground of the most passionate appeals: *Awake, awake, put on strength, O arm of the Lord; awake, as in the ancient days, in the generations of old. Art thou not it that hath cut Rahab in pieces, and pierced the dragon*². *God is my King of old, working salvation in the midst of the earth. Thou didst divide the sea by thy strength: thou brakest the heads of the dragons in the waters*³. *I will meditate of all thy work, and talk of thy doings. Thy way, O God, is in the sanctuary: who is so great a God as our God? Thou art the God that doest wonders: thou hast declared thy strength among the people. Thou hast with thine arm redeemed thy people, the sons of Jacob and Joseph. The waters saw thee, O God, the waters saw thee; they were afraid: the depths also were troubled*⁴. With these inspired outbursts may be classed the wonderful song of Moses, which is inserted in the prophetic narrative of the exodus, and is the most exalted expression of the triumphant feelings aroused by that memorable event⁵. The exodus was indeed a turning-point not merely in the history of the world, but in the development of human faith. It not only gave birth to a nation, but was the starting-point of a higher religion. *Israel saw the mighty act which Jehovah performed upon the Egyptians: and the*

---
¹ Exod. xiii. 14, 15.   ² Isa. li. 9.
³ Ps. lxxiv. 12, 13.   ⁴ Ps. lxxvii. 12 foll.
⁵ The structure of the song is examined by Kittel, *Hist. of the Hebrews*, vol. i. p. 225. He follows Dillmann in distinguishing between a shorter, older form contemporary with the event, and the enlarged form, 'which is a psalm composed according to the rules of art' and belongs to a later period. Cp. Driver, *Introduction to the Literature of the O. T.* p. 27.

people feared Jehovah, and believed in Jehovah, and in Moses his servant ¹.

2. Another principal aim of the Mosaic narratives of the exodus and settlement in Canaan appears to be that of bringing into clear relief the character and requirement of God. The very programme of the new religion is contained in the sentence prefixed to the Decalogue, *I am Jehovah, thy God;* while, as Riehm observes, the ideas of mercy and truth as elements in the character of God seem to dominate the course of the entire narrative ². Certainly the purport of the book of Exodus is on the one hand to extol the patience, longsuffering, and condescension of Jehovah, and on the other to give prominence to His moral requirement. In a later lecture this last point will be more particularly considered. It is only necessary in this place to draw attention to the ethical tendency of Mosaism as illustrated in what is generally reckoned to be the earliest legislation: the Decalogue³ and the so-called 'Book of the Covenant' (Exod. xxi–xxiii). Worthy of notice is the comparative silence of this legislation on points of ritual and ceremonial observance. The characteristic contribution of Moses to the religion of Israel was the teaching embodied in the Decalogue. His aim was to foster a higher morality; 'the distinctive character of the [Mosaic] religion,' says Prof. Robertson Smith, 'appears in the laws directed against polytheism and witchcraft, in the prominence given to righteousness and humanity as the things which are most pleasing to Jehovah and constitute the true significance of such an ordinance as the Sabbath, and, above all, in the clearness with which the law holds forth the truth that Jehovah's goodness to Israel is no mere natural

---

[1] Exod. xiv. 31. Cp. Delitzsch, *O. T. History of Redemption*, § 23.
[2] Riehm, *A Tl. Theologie*, p. 63.
[3] There are difficulties in regard to the 'Ten Words' arising from the fact that 'in ancient Israel there were two opinions as to what those words were' (Robertson Smith, *O. T. in J. C.* p. 335). The question must for the present be waived.

relation, such as binds Moab to Chemosh, that His favour to His people is directed by moral principles and is forfeited by moral iniquity[1].' The chief object, however, of the whole Mosaic narrative seems to be that of emphasizing the significance of the divine self-revelation implied in Israel's deliverance from Egypt. The marvels of the exodus, like some of our Lord's miracles, appear to have been intended to arrest attention, and to rivet Israel's gaze, as it were, upon its divine teacher. *Jehovah alone did lead him, and there was no strange god with him*[2]. We have already noticed that each of the first five commandments of the Decalogue is based on some trait of the divine character. And in the long and pathetic story of Jehovah's forbearance with Israel's stiff-necked perverseness and perpetual backsliding we have a revelation of the divine nature more striking than any mere display of omnipotence could possibly be. *Forty years*, we read, *suffered he their manners*, or, possibly, *bare he them as a nursing father in the wilderness*[3]. Sternness mingled with generosity, righteous indignation controlled by pitying love, patience as of a father with a fractious child—these are traits which lie upon the surface of the narrative. At times Jehovah is represented as weary—as even longing to be released from the burden of Israel's folly, ingratitude, and perverseness[4]. But each fresh rebellion leads to a new manifestation of love. Throughout the narrative 'we behold,' says Dr. Bruce[5], 'a manifestation of all the divine attributes, power, wisdom, patience, faithfulness, unwearied loving care —not a momentary manifestation only, but one extending over a lengthened series of years, supplying material for a history rich in pathetic stirring incident which endures for ages, an imperishable monument to the praise of Israel's God.' Who can fully measure

---

[1] *O. T. in J. C.* p. 344.   [2] Deut. xxxii. 12.   [3] Acts xiii. 18.
[4] See R. W. Dale, *The Ten Commandments*, p. 18.
[5] *The Chief End of Revelation*, p. 108.

the significance of this new and profound idea of God
—an idea which, possibly even in the mind of Moses
himself, was dim and vague, but which to the faith of
his prophetic successors became distinct and clear?
'The significance of that struggle for a new conception
of God,' observes Prof. Kittel, 'can be estimated by
any one who possesses two qualifications. He must
know the illusions and the degrading bondage in
which the people of Israel were held, owing, doubtless,
to their view of God. He must reflect on the religious
usages of western Asia, which deeply wounded man's
moral sense and trampled the dignity of human nature
in the dust: these, with their bewildering orgies, he
must compare with the spirit of the religion of Moses.
Nature-religion, with its tendency to enslave man, to
set at nought his natural freedom and moral dignity,
could not but rob the nations in ever-increasing
measure of their civilization and humanity. By his
religion, Moses won for his people and the world the
road to freedom, human dignity, and the development
of pure humanity [1].'

3. A third aim of the Mosaic narrative, regarded as
a whole, is doubtless to depict an ideal theocracy or
kingdom of God. The conception of a theocracy
may have been only dimly present to the consciousness of the newly formed nation [2], but the essential
elements of such a conception were implicitly contained in the belief that Israel belonged to Jehovah,
and that He was Israel's God. At any rate, in the
view of the Pentateuchal writers, prophetic or priestly,
it is clear that Jehovah is the king of His elect people,
and Moses a human deputy divinely empowered to
act as mediator between Jehovah and His subjects.

[1] *Hist. of the Hebrews*, vol. i. p. 251.
[2] Montefiore, *Hibbert Lectures*, p. 105, seems to speak too strongly
when, following Wellhausen, he asserts that 'the old Israelite has no
knowledge of his nation's peculiar position or destiny. The idea of
a theocracy is wanting.' Riehm's opinion seems the more probable
(*ATl. Theologie*, p. 58): 'Der Grundgedanke des Mosaismus ist nichts
anderes als eine Fortbildung und Näherbestimmung des Bewusstseins der
Patriarchen über ihr *Angehörigkeitsverhältniss* zu dem einen wahren Gott.'

Jehovah is represented as communicating His will through organs appointed by Himself. The ordinances of the Law are treated as His express commands; even the leadership of Israel's armies is ascribed to Him[1]. Indeed, the narratives were, in point of fact, compiled and edited by men to whom the thought of God's immediate sovereignty over His elect people was a self-evident truth, and to whom, consequently, Israel's demand for an earthly king appeared to be a rejection of Jehovah[2]. Certainly this idea seems to pervade the story of the exodus and the description of Moses' legislation. Moses was the vicegerent of Israel's unseen ruler, and accordingly to his express authority are ascribed all the ordinances and institutions in which the truth of Israel's special consecration to Jehovah was visibly embodied.

The question naturally arises how the completed priestly code stands related to the Sinaitic legislation. Roughly speaking, there are upwards of eighty chapters in the Pentateuch comprising the priestly law as it actually existed in a developed and codified form at a period subsequent to the return of the Jews from Babylon. They form the central portion of our present Pentateuch, and the picture they present of Israel's institutions embodies an ideal which was aimed at but not actually attained before the exile. The fundamental thought which inspires the sketch we have already noticed, viz. the idea of Israel's holiness as a consecrated community, in the midst of which Jehovah himself dwells as lawgiver and king. Now all the evidence confirms the supposition, antecedently probable, that the legislation of Moses himself was primitive and simple in its features and confined itself to the regulation of the most essential points, in the matter of *cultus* probably adopting some traditional usages of ancient Semitic worship. The most reasonable view is that in the detailed descriptions of the tabernacle and the sacri-

---

[1] Exod. xiii 17. Cp. Judges v. 23.   [2] 1 Sam. viii. 7.

ficial ordinances contained in the priestly code we have a highly idealized sketch of institutions which probably existed only in a rudimentary form during the wanderings of Israel in the wilderness. Thus, for example, the simple tent of Mosaic days known to the early narratives is represented as an elaborate and costly structure, such as can hardly be supposed to have existed under the difficult circumstances of life in the wilderness [1]. Nevertheless, when all reservations have been made, it cannot be fairly denied that in germ at any rate the idea of a theocracy was Mosaic, and that the first legislation was based on the idea of Jehovah's immediate sovereignty. It is impossible to account satisfactorily for the collapse of Canaanitish civilization before the advance of the invading hosts of Israel, except on the supposition that there was some inspiring idea which animated the nation, welded it into unity, and stimulated it to extraordinary efforts. Such an idea certainly was the kingship of Jehovah; Israel was conscious of being under the immediate rule and guidance of the God who had promised to their fathers the land of Canaan for their inheritance.

4. Once more the typical significance of the Mosaic narratives must not be overlooked. The New Testament writers habitually refer to the actual experiences and characteristic institutions of *the church in the wilderness* [2] as foreshadowing the mysteries of the spiritual life and of the divine kingdom in its widest sense. The general principles of redemption as they are exhibited in the fortunes of the Church and in the experience of its individual members, the great characteristic conceptions of Christianity, the phraseology and imagery of the New Testament—all these are rooted in the Pentateuch.

[1] Kittel, *Hist. of the Hebrews*, vol. i. p. 238. 'The description of P corresponds to the idea which people in later times, influenced probably by what they saw of the continually increasing costliness of their sanctuaries, formed of the sacred desert-tent of the days of Moses.'
[2] Acts vii. 38.

We are in fact justified by the express authority of the New Testament in recognizing the symbolic character of the Pentateuchal history. The narratives, whether prophetic or priestly, come from the hands of men who loved to trace in history the action of eternal principles. Israel's deliverance from servitude, its maintenance in the wilderness and its victory over the hostile powers of heathendom exemplified fixed and constant laws of divine action. It was confidently expected that the future development of the kingdom of God would proceed on lines already laid down, and would be accompanied by conditions closely parallel to those which the nation had experienced in its youth. Moses was regarded as bearing a figurative and predictive relation to a prophet greater than himself, yet to come. Again, the compilers of the priestly law belonged to a period when men were becoming conscious of the sacramental character of the ancient ceremonial worship. They understood, at least in a measure, that the sanctuary and sacrificial system veiled under material forms spiritual mysteries hereafter to be revealed; that outward ceremonies, objects, and acts embodied the thoughts of God concerning salvation and His kingdom. It was, however, only an instructed faith, and a fully developed experience that could discern in the Mosaic system the shadow or outline sketch of heavenly realities, of which the Gospel presents a complete picture[1]. The significance of the Pentateuch for Christians lies in the fact that the fundamental conceptions which pervade each Testament are the same: the redemptive action of Almighty God; the separation from an evil world of a people brought by grace into covenant-relationship with its divine King and consecrated to His service; the foundation of a kingdom of God upon earth; the setting up of His tabernacle among men

---

[1] See Heb. x. 1. Cp. Ambrose *in psalm.* xxxviii. 25: 'Umbra in lege, imago vero in evangelio, veritas in caelestibus.' The quotation is given by Willis, *Worship of the Old Covenant*, p. 14.

and the building of a city which bears the title, *The Lord is there*[1].

Enough has been now said to indicate that in the Pentateuch we are not dealing with history in the ordinary sense of that term, but with an idealized and partly prophetic picture, the principal purpose of which is to convey certain religious thoughts and ideas which beyond doubt formed the permanent basis of Judaism. This is the positive point on which it is needful to insist. The possibility of wide differences of view in regard to the intrinsic character and value of the Pentateuchal narratives must be frankly recognized. It is only necessary to make two concluding observations. First, to question the strict historical accuracy of the Mosaic story involves no denial of its inspiration. Whatever be the nature of the narratives, they have unquestionably been selected by the wisdom of the divine Spirit as the vehicles of spiritual truth best adapted to human needs and capacities. Secondly, there is every reason to suppose that the Pentateuch, whatever be the date of its final compilation, is based on genuine historical traditions and embodies in their developed form very ancient institutions and usages. It seems not improbable that the prophet Ezekiel led the way in reducing to theory and formulating the traditional usage of the pre-exilic sanctuary, and that he thus practically became the founder of a school which devoted itself to the task of codifying the priestly ordinances and regulations[2]. If, however, it is difficult to determine the precise antiquity of particular elements in the Mosaic system of worship, it is possible, under the guidance of the New Testament, to comprehend the typical significance of the system, regarded as a single complex product of a germ planted by the hand of

---

[1] Ezek. xlviii. 35. Cp. Riehm, *Einleitung in das A. T.* vol. i. pp. 362 foll., especially his remark: 'Die in einem Institute verkörperte Idee ist das innere Band zwischen dem Typus und Antitypus.'

[2] Cp. Wellhausen, *Sketch of the History of Israel and Judah*, p. 131; Ryle, *The Canon of the O. T.* p. 72.

Israel's inspired legislator at the very dawn of its history.

III.

In passing to the historical books and prophecies, we enter upon firm historical ground. For there is little reason to doubt that the documents which form the substratum of the books of Samuel and Kings were official notices of political events, and nearly contemporary narratives, some of which may reasonably be supposed to have been written by prophets like Gad, Nathan, Iddo, and others. These books, then, contain very ancient materials, although the framework is unquestionably due to later editors. The main influence that can be detected in the compilation is that of the book of Deuteronomy. Writers of the Deuteronomic school seem to have reduced the books of Judges, Samuel, and Kings to their present form between the death of Josiah and the exile. The books did not, apparently, 'escape further additions and interpretations in the post-exilic period; but their main character, the framework in which the facts are arranged, and the uniform lesson they are made to teach, were the product of the periods immediately before, and either during, or soon after, the exile[1].'

What, then, are the general features of these books? In the first place they are compilations, and in their work the compilers seem to have retained considerable freedom, incorporating their authorities as they stood with but few changes, arranging the material on some plan of their own, and adding comments

---

[1] Montefiore, *Hibbert Lectures*, pp. 231, 232. Cp. Wellhausen, *Prolegomena*, ch. vii. The book of Joshua is not particularly dealt with because it is closely connected both by its subject-matter and its literary structure with the Pentateuch. It describes the closing stage of the movement that began with the exodus. By the Jews, however, the book is classed among the 'former prophets.'

here and there in order to bring out the religious significance of the facts recorded[1]. They would not be at pains to harmonize the style or even the contents of the different documents employed, the truth being, as we have more than once pointed out, that their interest in fact as *mere* fact was quite subordinate to the religious ideas by which they were influenced. And what is true of the compilers is to a great extent true of the original narrators. Their aim was to draw out the moral import of what they related, and in depicting the more prominent figures of their story, they were occasionally apt to ascribe their own beliefs and modes of thought to their hero[2].

Another point that strikes us in reading these books is the uniformity of tone displayed by the compilers. It is evident that they represent the views of a particular prophetic school, possessed by the conviction that the capital offence of Israel throughout the pre-exilic history had been perverted worship of Jehovah and idolatrous worship of other deities. Hence their conception of the past is uniformly pessimistic. The institution of monarchy, which seems at its first foundation to have been hailed with such hope and rejoicing, is in one of the two narratives of Saul's elevation regarded as the result of a disastrous apostasy from Jehovah[3]; and though after the establishment of the kingdom the reign of David for a time actually realized the ideal hopes of the nation, yet the general course of Israel's history is represented by these writers as one long and continuous declension from the religious position which the nation occupied at the death of Moses[4].

---

[1] See 'the methods of oriental historiography,' well described in Prof. Kirkpatrick's *Divine Library of the O. T.* pp. 13–15. He observes that 'this compilatory method of composition brings us into a closer contact with the events and the actors than any other method of historical writing could have done.'

[2] Cp. Cheyne, *Aids to the Devout Study of Criticism*, p. 26.

[3] 1 Sam. viii. 7. Cp. Driver, *Introduction to the O. T.* pp. 165 foll. Renan, *Histoire*, &c., bk. ii. ch. 14.

[4] Montefiore, *op. cit.* pp. 232 foll.

A somewhat closer study will reveal to us a leading tendency in each book, and will show how far the historical element has given way to the didactic purpose of the writer. The book of Judges, which seems to be based on archaic narratives and songs already extant in oral or written form, describes the period of disintegration and comparative anarchy which followed the death of Joshua. There are elements of hope in the story, an upward movement towards the monarchy[1], an occasional outburst of fiery zeal for the honour of Jehovah[2], and a certain pride in adhering to His worship[3]. Nor does it appear that the state of morals was utterly lax. The phenomena are in fact such as might be looked for in a young and robust nationality in 'a dark age of beginnings[4].' But the period was certainly one of great disorganization. The conflicts described are mostly those of individual tribes—a fact which justifies the inference that the Judges were not so much rulers of the whole nation as tribal heroes or captains with local authority[5]: probably some of the judges were holding office simultaneously in their respective tribes. The books of Samuel describe the origin of the two important institutions on which the future progress of the national religion mainly depended. It was the mission of Samuel to revive and reorganize the functions of prophetism, and to inaugurate the monarchy. Both of these institutions served the common purpose of impressing upon the nation the idea of Jehovah's immediate personal sovereignty, and of quickening the consciousness of Israel's ideal calling and destiny. The appointed task of the prophets was that of keeping alive *the light of the Lord*[6] and causing it perpetually to

---

[1] Cp. Wellhausen, *Prolegomena*, p. 235; Bruce, *Apologetics*, p. 227.
[2] Judges v. 13 foll., 23; viii. 4 foll.; xix. 29 foll.; xx. 1; xxi. 10 foll.
[3] Judges xvii. 7 foll.; xviii. 18.
[4] Bruce, *l. c.* Cp. the account in Renan, *Histoire*, &c., bk. ii. ch. 7.
[5] Wellhausen, pp. 233, 413. Cp. Meinhold, *Jesus und das A. T.* p. 36.
[6] Isa. ii. 5.

beam out anew. They were to be in the highest sense 'the watchmen of the theocracy,' 'the conscience of the state,' the occasional organs of divine interposition in the national history. The beginnings of prophetism have been rightly called a 'pentecostal phenomenon' in the Old Testament. Though its origin was rude and chaotic, prophetism was destined to become a dominant factor in the progress of Hebrew religion [1]. The special significance of the monarchy, on the other hand, was that it habituated the nation to the idea of a human deputy or representative sitting upon the throne which properly belonged to Jehovah Himself [2]. Its institution was the starting-point of the Messianic expectation in its stricter sense. And there are indications that the pessimistic view of the monarchy was not commonly held before the exile. It is neither consistent, strictly speaking, with the solemn significance attached to David's reign, nor with the glowing language of the prophets, whose ideal hopes centred in a prince belonging to David's house [3].

The books of Kings trace the fortunes of the kingdom down to the period of its dissolution, a noticeable feature of the record being the prominence assigned to prophets, of whom Elijah and Elisha are the chief. Where the historical narratives become fragmentary or defective, we are able to supplement them by means of the books of contemporary prophets. The general impression left by the story of the kingdom is one of ever-deepening gloom. The nation, together with its kings, continues to move along a downward path; the

---

[1] See Delitzsch, *O. T. History of Redemption*, § 35.
[2] 1 Chron. xxviii. 5; xxix. 23. Cp. Schultz, *O. T. Theology*, i. 169.
[3] See Wellhausen, *Prolegomena*, pp. 253, 254. Riehm observes in *A Tl. Theologie*, p. 253: 'Nach dem älteren, dem nationalen Interesse mehr Rechnung tragenden Bericht (1 Sam. ix–x. 16) erscheint das Königtum schon als eine *gottgewollte*, die Freiheit, Selbständigkeit und Macht des Gottesvolkes bezweckende (1 Sam. ix. 16), den theokratischen Organismus konsolidierende und krönende Institution.' The same general tone of comment is found in Gen. xvii. 6, 16; xxxv. 11, and in the prophecy of Balaam (Num. xxiv. 7, 17).

heavy task of the prophets is to announce that the theocracy in its existing state is inevitably doomed. Such is the character, briefly described, of the writings included in 'former prophets.'

Of the later books, such as the Chronicles, I need here say very little. No one would place this work on a level with the original sources from which it derives its material[1]. The peculiarity of the chronicler is his intense interest in the sacred forms of Jewish religion as they existed during the period of the second temple. His work has been well described as 'a great historical theodicy ... intended to further and to strengthen a religious ideal as it had shaped itself in the author's mind[2].' The value of the work lies chiefly in its faithful portraiture of a prevalent mood, or temper of mind, which marked the closing centuries of Israel's history[3]. Occasionally no doubt the writer preserves information drawn from trustworthy ancient sources. But in one or two significant allusions to a *Midrash*[4], the chronicler seems to indicate the standpoint and character of his own work, which is to be regarded as a specimen of *Haggadah*, i.e. an independent and imaginative handling of historic tradition for purposes of popular edification. It is enough to mention by way of illustration the writer's transformation of David into a levitical saint, and his tendency to judge the character of each king of Judah by the standard of devotion to the levitical *cultus* and ceremonial law. What has been said of the books of Chronicles applies in some measure to those of Ezra and Nehemiah, since these works, which in the Jewish canon form a single book, were apparently compiled

---

[1] 'There is an end to historical study if we accept the later account against the earlier' (Robertson Smith, *O. T. in J. C.* lect. v). The Chronicles are minutely investigated by Wellhausen, *Prolegomena*, ch. vi, and Kuenen, *Religion of Israel*, ch. x. See also Kittel, *Hist. of the Hebrews*, ii. 229 foll.

[2] Montefiore, *Hibbert Lectures*, p. 448.

[3] Schultz, *O. T. Theology*, i. 407; Kuenen, *l.c.* The date of the books of Chronicles is probably between 300 and 250 B.C.

[4] 2 Chron. xiii. 22; xxiv. 27. Cp. Wellhausen, *Prolegomena*, p. 227. Driver, *Introduction*, &c., pp. 497, 506 foll.

by the author of the Chronicles[1]. Contemporary documents no doubt form the basis of each, but their historical value is somewhat impaired by their incompleteness and by the lateness of their compilation. It is not necessary, however, to consider these books particularly, especially in view of the fact that they find a place not among the historians in the 'former prophets,' but in the Hagiographa[2]. With regard to the three last-mentioned books, our only concern is to disclaim for them a character which their very position in the canon seems to contradict[3].

We are now free to reconsider the historical books, properly so called, the books of Judges, Samuel, and Kings, with a view to ascertaining their true importance and value.

We perhaps find a clue to the real character of these books in the significant circumstance that tradition ascribed the authorship of them to prophets. Wellhausen questions the opinion that the Hebrew people owed its historical annals to the labours of the prophets[4]. But he allows that they 'shed upon the tradition their peculiar light,' and 'infused into it their own spirit.' In any case these books are clearly not to be regarded as history in the narrow sense of mere chronicles or annals. Their historical importance is undeniably great; taken in conjunction with the writings of contemporary prophets, where these are available, and with the evidence of inscriptions, they enable us to construct a fairly complete and trustworthy account of the actual course of events during the period they cover. But the point of chief importance is that their very title, 'former prophets,'

---

[1] Robertson Smith thinks the Chronicles originally formed one book with Ezra and Nehemiah (*O. T. in J. C.* p. 182). Cp. Ryle, *Canon of the O. T.* p. 134.

[2] The same remark applies to the book of Esther, the historical value of which is a matter of dispute. See Driver, *op. cit.* p. 452. It was with some difficulty admitted to the canon (Robertson Smith, *O. T. in J. C.* pp. 183 foll.).

[3] Cp. Ryle, *Canon of the O. T.* pp. 139-141.

[4] *Prolegomena*, p. 293.

exempts them from the rigid application of ordinary historical canons. They contain history and something more. They record events in the light of a known purpose of God, and consequently do not hesitate to interpret what they relate, in order to exhibit the leading principles of the divine government, and the laws which control the development of events [1]. Accordingly our task is to estimate the truth and validity of the theory which guides the sacred historians in their selection of incidents, and in their comments upon character and upon matters of fact [2].

Now the leading ideas which constitute the prophetic theory of Israel's history, and which give a characteristic complexion to the historical books, would seem to be mainly three: (1) the reality and perpetuity of Jehovah's redemptive grace; (2) the idea that Israel's election implied obligations which the nation constantly failed to discharge; (3) the uniformity of method exhibited in divine deliverances.

1. One leading idea of the narratives is the reality of divine grace. The foreground of the picture is occupied by self-revelations of Jehovah in act or prophecy: displays of power and compassion in which His undeserved favour towards Israel is manifested.

[1] Riehm, *A Tl. Theologie*, pp. 209 foll.: 'DerProphet hat die Verhältnisse und Ereignisse seiner Zeit in das Licht des göttlichen Ratschlusses zu stellen, und so über Bedeutung und Zweck der göttlichen Führungen Aufschluss zu geben. Überhaupt ist er Interpret dessen was Gott in der thatsächlichen Sprache der Geschichte zu seinem Volke redet, weshalb auch die Geschichtschreibung zu den prophetischen Berufsaufgaben gehört.'

[2] Bruce, *Apologetics*, p. 197. The function of the prophetic writers was 'not to narrate facts, but to teach the right point of view for reading truly the religious significance of Israel's whole history.' Cp. Kittel, *Hist. of the Hebrews*, vol. ii. p. 5: 'We recognize [in the historical books] the historical standards of men who had absorbed the ideas of the prophets, and who regarded the national past from a purified point of view in consequence of Israel's calamity. It is not so much history as a philosophy of history. It is elucidation, estimation, adjustment of facts *from the standpoint of subsequent knowledge of the consequences and goal of the historical development*, rather than simple narration of the course of the events themselves; a history that is more satisfactory as a means of religious and moral improvement, than as supplying historical knowledge about the original course of events.' See also Kuenen, *Hibbert Lectures*, pp. 72 foll.

The thought of divine intervention on Israel's behalf is evidently uppermost in the minds of the historians. It forms the keynote of those summary reviews of the history which meet us at different points in the narrative[1]. The most conspicuous feature of the past had been the display of divine lovingkindness and forbearance. It had been signally manifested in the deliverance from Egypt, in the protection and sustenance of the people during the long years of pilgrimage in the wilderness, in the amazing conquests both on the east and west of Jordan, and in the raising up of strong and heroic leaders in times of national pressure and distress.

2. But, secondly, in close connexion with repeated declarations of Jehovah's grace and longsuffering, we find descriptions of critical moments at which Israel's own relation to God is determined or manifested. The Old Testament history is remarkable in this respect especially—that in the main it is the record of a series of crises. Long periods are passed over in silence, e.g. the thirty-eight years of wilderness life, the seventy years of exile. Between the death of Joshua and the appearance of Samuel a period of considerable length, possibly nearly three centuries, elapsed; yet how brief and compressed is the record of an age in regard to which Kuenen declares that it 'is of the highest importance for Israel's entire development[2].' How much that might have filled the pages of a modern manual of history do the biblical writers ignore: the slow process by which the tribes of Israel passed from the rough habits of nomadic life to the settled ways of agriculturalists, the rise and growth of the trading instinct through intercourse with the cities of Phoenicia, the religious syncretism which resulted from Israel's self-identification with the conquered territory[3]. How much that might absorb the

---

[1] Judges ii. 6 foll., iii. 6 foll.; 1 Sam. xii. 7 foll.; 2 Kings xvii. 7-23, 34-41.
[2] *The Religion of Israel*, vol. i. p. 143.
[3] Cp. Wellhausen, *Sketch of the History of Israel and Judah*, p. 36; cp. Kittel, *op. cit.* vol. ii. pp. 93 foll.; G. A. Smith, *Hist. Geog. of the Holy Land*, pp. 88 foll., and 111.

attention of a student, or kindle a poet's imagination[1], is passed over. The record is essentially a religious history, of which the gist is practically this : that Israel as a nation had been peculiarly favoured by God, that the calamities and reverses which followed the settlement in Canaan were due to national shortcoming and sin, that in the sorest straits deliverance came through some human instrument specially raised up by Jehovah, and that, finally, popular expectation was directed towards the southern tribe of Judah, as if the imperative need of a stable monarchy was likely to be supplied from that quarter[2]. It may be granted that the picture of this period is somewhat highly coloured, for Israel's shortcomings scarcely seem on a superficial survey to have amounted to a formal or visible apostasy from Jehovah again and again repeated, as the Deuteronomistic passages in the book of Judges apparently suggest[3]. But at least the general fact of unfaithfulness to a recognized standard of worship and morals is clear, and it is judged from the standpoint of Him whose thoughts are higher than our thoughts. The pure worship of Jehovah was evidently hindered or tainted by the spirit of religious syncretism, i. e. the corruption of the Mosaic *cultus* by the admixture of usages and symbols borrowed from the nature-worship of Canaan[4]. The manifest elements of retrogression which appeared in the period of the Judges are regarded by the Deuteronomic school as constituting

[1] One naturally thinks of Mr. Keble's beautiful lines in *The Christian Year*, poem for the third Sunday in Lent.
[2] Observe that the book of Judges begins with an oracle implying the promise of victory to Judah, *Judah shall go up* (i. 2), and closes with narratives connected with Bethlehem Judah, designed apparently to illustrate the remark, *In those days there was no king in Israel* (xxi. 25). The book of Ruth, which is an idyll of Bethlehem and gives the ancestry of the first true king, forms an appendix to the book of Judges. Cp. Riehm, *Einleitung in das A. T.* vol. i. p. 473 ; Delitzsch, *O. T. History of Redemption*, § 33.
[3] Judges ii. 11 foll., iii. 5 foll., viii. 33, x. 6 foll. Cp. Kittel, vol. ii. p. 97. It is significant that in the *résumé* of Israel's history contained in Neh. ix. 7 foll. the same salient features appear, the faithfulness of God and the faithlessness of His people. See Hunter, *After the Exile*, part ii, pp. 201 foll.
[4] Cp. Oehler, *Theol. of the O. T.* §§ 158, 159 ; Kittel, vol. ii. p. 98.

formal apostasy to heathen gods; and it may be contended that, from an idealistic and prophetic point of view, the representation corresponds with the facts. Israel was during this period falling short of better knowledge; from the earliest times the spirit of unfaithfulness to the obligations implied in Israel's special relationship to God did manifest itself in the national life. In a word, the picture is dark and sombre, but we have every reason to suppose that in essential features it is correct. If, as we have no reason to doubt, Israel recognized in the events of the exodus its special vocation to be the people of Jehovah, if this had been the burden of Moses' teaching, the point of view from which the compilers of the historical books contemplate the course of events is true; and it may be remarked that it is common to these writers with the great prophets of the eighth and following centuries, notably Amos, Hosea, and Jeremiah [1]. The same general line of thought applies to the view which the historical writers take of the schismatic *cultus* established in the northern kingdom by Jeroboam. The theory of the writers and of the prophets is that the pure and imageless worship of Jehovah inculcated by Moses has in the calf-worship sunk back to the level of a heathen *cultus*. That it represented a reactionary movement can scarcely be doubted, and it is equally probable that the relative purity of religious *praxis* in Judah was due to the persistency with which the prophets represented the northern *cultus* in its true character [2].

3. A third feature of the historical books is that they dwell with peculiar interest upon the method of the divine deliverances. The intention of the narratives does not seem to be that of glorifying the heroic figures of old time, but rather that of illustrating the principles on which Jehovah acts in His work of salvation. There is little or no attempt to idealize the

---

[1] See Robertson, *The Early Religion of Israel* (Baird Lecture for 1889), ch. v.
[2] Cp. Riehm, *A Tl. Theologie*, p. 195.

character of the Judges, or of Samuel, or even of prophets like Elijah. The period of the Judges was no doubt 'an age of contradictions [1],' like other periods of religious transition which are apt to witness a certain relaxation of moral principles and disintegration of beliefs; and the figures that appear in the forefront of the history reflect the tendencies of the time: its hold upon certain fundamental religious truths and its laxity in religious practice, its capacity for wild moral excesses combined with 'a certain robustness of conscience [2].' In this point the narratives are life-like and consistent, but the main truths which the historians bring into prominence are—first, that the saviours sent by Jehovah are men directly empowered by His Spirit; secondly, that it is His habit to select lowly and despised instruments in the execution of His redemptive purpose. Thus the exploit of Gideon is always regarded in the Old Testament as a typical deliverance; *the day of Midian* becomes indeed a kind of proverbial expression in later prophecy [3]. The choice of Saul, from *the least of all the families of the smallest of the tribes of Israel* [4], is another illustration of the same principle, while the career of David derives its special significance from the lowliness of his origin. *He chose David also his servant, and took him away from the sheepfolds. As he was following the ewes great with young ones he took him: that he might feed Jacob his people, and Israel his inheritance* [5].

In their conception, then, of the period embraced in the historical books, the writers cannot be fairly regarded as mistaken. In its estimate of the pre-prophetic period modern criticism does not always make due allowance for the factor which imparted to Israel's history, throughout its course, a unique significance—the factor which we call 'Inspiration.' The 'Song of Deborah,' for example, which seems to be contemporary with the

[1] Schultz, *O. T. Theology*, i. 150.
[2] Bruce, *Apologetics*, p. 227. The book of Ruth forms a valuable counterpart to the stormy scenes of Judges.
[3] Judges vi. 15; vii. 2. Cp. Isa. ix. 4 foll.; x. 26; Ps. lxxxiii. 10 foll.
[4] 1 Sam. ix. 21.   [5] Ps. lxxviii. 70, 71.

events described in it, clearly proves that the age of the Judges was not merely one of rude prowess and warlike adventure, but that, at least among the leaders of the nation, there existed conceptions of Jehovah which could not fail to be a motive force in religious development, and a certain sense of consecration which inspired conspicuous acts of heroic valour. The action of the Spirit of God upon men was a fact which alone sufficed to explain the greatness of their achievements [1]. It was a power very dimly understood, but recognized as working in and through human instruments on behalf of God's purpose of salvation [2]. This continuous operation of the divine Spirit forms part of that ideal element in Israel's history which is plainly reflected in the prophetic narratives. Moreover, supposed inconsistencies are softened or removed if we remember to draw necessary distinctions between the religious leaders of Israel and the mass of the people; between the fundamental Mosaic beliefs cherished in religious centres like Shiloh, and the general level of culture, morality, and worship exhibited by the nation as a whole [3].

On a survey of the ground we have traversed, it appears that there are good reasons for believing that the inspired writers give a presentation of the facts which is not primarily historical, but prophetic, their

---

[1] Cp. Judges iii. 10; vi. 34; xi. 29; xiii. 25; xiv. 6, 19; xv. 14; 1 Sam. x. 6, 10; xvi. 13.

[2] Cp. Schultz, vol. ii. pp. 204 foll.; Robertson, *op. cit.* pp. 118 foll.

[3] Some such distinction is recognized as 'a fair inference from the Song of Deborah' by Cheyne, *Aids to the Devout Study of Criticism*, p. 31. Cp. Driver, *Serm. on the O. T.* p. 138: 'Throughout their history the people are represented as needing to be taught by others, as declining from truth by which they ought to have been guided, as falling short of the ideal propounded to them. The natural tendencies of the nation did not move in the direction of spiritual religion. There is no ground to suppose that, apart from the special illumination vouchsafed to the great teachers who originated or sustained the principles of its faith, the religious history of Israel would have differed materially from that of the kindred nations by which it was surrounded.' There were, in point of fact, repeated occasions when the Israel of the Spirit found its almost solitary representative in a single prophet.

main design being that of religious edification. It
follows that we can await with equanimity the verdict
of criticism in regard to the exact historical worth of
the narrative. That there is a great regard for certain
outstanding facts of the history is unquestionable, but
the facts are often coloured by high imaginative power,
and are estimated according to moral significance. In
regard to minor details there is ample room for diversity of opinion. To take two passing illustrations. The
religious lessons of Samson's history are not materially
affected by any particular view respecting the precise
character of the narrative which describes his career [1].
The portrait of David is not the less a treasure for
all time because to a great extent it is idealized by
devout writers of a later age [2]. The important question is whether, in their interpretation of Israel's
history, the prophetic writers of the Old Testament
are fundamentally wrong. We have found reasons
for supposing that in its general point of view 'the
prophetic philosophy of history' is true, and we may
accept the cautious summary of Prof. Robertson as
fairly stating our conclusions. 'The great events,'
he says, 'of Israel's history, the turning-points, the
points determinative of the whole life and history, are
attested by the nation at the earliest time at which we
are enabled to look for materials on which an opinion
can be based. No reason can be given for the
invention of them just at this time, or for the significance which the prophets assign to them. It may be
that a fond memory invested with a halo of glory the
great fathers of the race; it may also be that a simple
piety saw wonders where a modern age would see

---

[1] As is well known, there is a view that the story of Samson originates
in a solar myth (שמשון='Sun-man.' See Kuenen, *Religion of Israel*
[Eng. Tr.], vol. i. p. 307). It is far more probable that Samson was an actual
hero of the tribe of Dan, around whose name a certain 'mushroom-
growth of legend' gradually gathered, intermingled possibly with some
foreign elements. See Kittel, *Hist. of the Hebrews*, vol. ii. pp. 91, 92.

[2] See Cheyne, *Aids to the Devout Study of Criticism*, part i, on the
David-narratives.

none. Yet the individuality of the characters is not destroyed, nor are the sequence of events and the delineations of character shown to be the work of a fitful and unbridled imagination¹.'

It is, on the whole, sufficiently clear that the aim of the historical writers of the Old Testament was to bring out the religious significance of Israel's history. They interpret events in accordance with their steadfast belief in Jehovah's original election of Israel. This idea of election was one of which the nation as a whole probably became conscious very gradually. But it is reasonable to suppose that even in the earliest period there were men of prophetic spirit who discerned the drift and tendency of God's dealings with their race. An English historian has pointed out the effect on our nation of the destruction of the Armada. 'The pride of the conquerors,' says Mr. Green, 'was hushed before their sense of a mighty deliverance. . . The victory over the Armada, the deliverance from Spain, the rolling away of the terror which had hung like a cloud over the hopes of the new people, was like a passing from death unto life².' It is not too much to claim that such an event as the exodus, impressed as it had been on the national memory, profoundly affected the point of view from which the whole subsequent history was studied. Here, I think, we have the very heart of the matter. Some critics think that the general scheme of biblical history is an after-thought leading to 'a systematic representation of earlier events in the light of much later times³'; but the point to be observed is that the early history itself suggested the ideas by which all the subsequent development was interpreted. The Hebrew mind was not what the modern mind sometimes is, intensely matter of fact, and consequently it did not set the

---

[1] *The Early Religion of Israel*, p. 135. It is worth while drawing special attention to the retrospect of Israel's history in the book of Judith (ch. v. 6-19) as a main outline of historical facts.
[2] *History of the English People*, vol. ii. pp. 446-447.
[3] See Robertson, *op. cit.* p. 30.

same exaggerated store on mere outward fact as if it were synonymous with the essential truth of things. In his *Studies in Judaism*, Mr. Schechter makes the suggestive remark that Judaism ever 'bowed before truth, but it had never made a covenant with facts only because they were facts. History had to be remade and to sanctify itself before it found its way into its sacred annals[1].' The Jew looked at historical events as manifestations of that which he deemed to be of infinitely higher interest, viz. the purposes and character of God. And while we may admit the defectiveness of the historical writings if judged by modern standards, it is a fair question whether this point of view was that of the sacred writers themselves, and whether it is of the supreme importance which the scientifically trained mind is apt to assume.

The fact is that these narratives which historical criticism analyzes so minutely are lifted by the touch of divine insight displayed in them to a level higher than that on which the scientific faculty moves. The Old Testament records the history of the people of God as it unfolds itself before the eyes of Him who sits upon the throne of heaven judging the deeds and lives of men *according to truth*[2]. We who believe that Scripture is divine as well as human are prepared to find anticipated in it that awful reversal of human judgment and of the earthly estimate of things for which we look hereafter *in the day when God shall judge the secrets of men by Jesus Christ*[3].

[1] *Introd.* p. xxv. Prof. Ramsay, in his striking vindication of St. Luke's genius as an historian, observes that 'Historical truth implies not merely truth in each detail, but also truth in the general effect, and that kind of truth cannot be attained without selection, grouping, and idealization' (*St. Paul the traveller and the Roman citizen*, p. 4). See also Bruce, *With open face*, ch. iii. ('The idealized picture of Luke').

[2] Rom. ii. 2.

[3] Rom. ii. 16. See Mozley's sermon on 'The reversal of human judgment' (*University Sermons*, no. iv). Bp. Wordsworth makes a suggestive remark in reference to the thirty-eight years of Israel's wandering in the wilderness: 'We know that the people existed.... They themselves have no history. Their names are written in water; they have no place in the annals of heaven' (*The Holy Bible with commentary*, Introd. to Genesis and Exodus, p. xxxi).

NOTE A.

ON the patriarchal narratives Prof. G. A. Smith says (*op. cit.* p. 49), 'If we will go to the characters of the O. T. as they are, and treat them, not as our dead prey, but as our masters and brothers, whom it is our duty to study with patience and meekness, there is almost no end to the real benefit they shall do us. The careful study of the original narrative, the study of the history of the times, the study of the contemporary monuments, which of late are being discovered in such large numbers, reveal to us that these characters are neither the lay figures nor the mere symbols of doctrine which they are often represented to be by a certain kind of preaching, nor, on the other hand, can they be only mythical heroes—incarnations of a tribe or reflections of natural phenomena—to which some mistaken schools of criticism think to reduce them. There is a vividness, a moral reality, about nearly all of them; and although they rise amid circumstances that we cannot always explain, and are sometimes surrounded by miracles to which our conscience does not always respond—through all this they stalk unhindered, real characters with life and way upon them.' A reader of Renan's *Histoire du peuple d'Israël*, bk. i, will, I think, derive from it a very strong impression of the general truth of the patriarchal story. See, however, the temperate remarks of Dillmann, *Commentary on Genesis* [Eng. Tr.], vol. ii. pp. 1 foll.

LECTURE IV

And God spake all these words, saying, I am the Lord thy God, which have brought thee out of the land of Egypt, out of the house of bondage. Thou shalt have no other gods before me.—Exod. xx. 1 foll.

WE have considered the Old Testament in its historical aspect as the record of a divine movement towards the human race, which formed the starting-point of a higher religion; and we have attempted to estimate the character and value of this record, regarded as a collection of historical documents. It is now our task to survey the Old Testament as the account of a progressive self-revelation of God.

The writer of the Epistle to the Hebrews opens his letter with the words θεὸς ὁ λαλήσας, and it may be observed how closely such an exordium corresponds with the apparent object of the writer in keeping himself anonymous. To this great Christian apologist God is the one speaker in revelation. Human agency falls entirely into the background. Throughout redemptive history a single voice, the voice of God, was making itself heard, speaking by the prophets *in divers portions and in divers manners;* and the highest function of the Scriptures, whether of the Old or New Testament, is to transmit from age to age the record of that continuous utterance. *God spake.* Revelation had its several parts, stages, chapters or acts. The whole could only be judged retrospectively in the light of the final result. The key to the meaning of the voice, which spake to the fathers by the prophets, was the Word made flesh. It was the divine message to

M

man contained in the life and labours, the death and glorification, of Jesus Christ, that illuminated and interpreted the method of divine action in the past. The Incarnation enables us to distinguish what is fragmentary and provisional in revelation from what is complete and final. The *divers modes* of divine self-communication were adapted to the existing needs and capacities of human nature at each particular stage of its development. In visions and dreams, in types and symbols, in precepts and ordinances, in voices and prophecies, in the unmistakeable language of outward fact and in secret communications to elect souls, *God spake* to mankind. Revelation is one because its Author is one, and we approach the Scriptures with this end in view above all others—that we may know God: what He is in Himself, what He has wrought in history, what are His thoughts for human nature, and what His purposes for the universe. In Scripture the word of God comes to us through the medium of human language; but it is the very mind of God which unveils itself therein, teaching us how to live according to His will, and revealing to us what in His eternal being and character He is.

In this lecture I wish to consider, first, the progressiveness of the divine self-revelation, and secondly, its content. We must glance at the spiritual education of man described in the Old Testament, and we must examine the import of the successive names or designations by which Almighty God condescended to make Himself known to His creatures.

I.

The idea of progressive revelation has profoundly influenced all modern attempts to reconstruct the history of Hebrew religion [1]. It has been the legitimate and necessary outcome of applying to the Old Testament those historical or comparative methods of

---

[1] Cp. Oettli, *Der gegenwärtige Kampf*, &c., p. 11.

study which have proved so fruitful in other fields of knowledge and were themselves suggested, or at least encouraged, by the recognition of the evolutionary principle in nature. The modern habit of mind is to study institutions, social phenomena, opinions, literature, creeds, in the light of their development. We delight in the observation of growth or process, and there is perhaps no department in which study based upon this method has been more serviceable than in that of Christian apologetics. It has assisted us to estimate aright the inevitable defects of early morality and religion. It has enabled us to form a true judgment of the divine dealings with mankind during the primitive stages of its spiritual development. It has, we may say with reverence, vindicated the character of Almighty God by imparting the necessary point of view from which His recorded commands, requirements, and modes of action should be regarded. It has opened our eyes to the infinite wisdom, tenderness, and patience of the actual course which redemptive love has pursued. Indeed, the contemplation of the patience exhibited in the moral government and education of the world may, in some cases, have led thinkers to qualify or correct their conception of the laws which guide the operations of nature itself. They have learned that the perplexing slowness and apparent imperfection of physical processes corresponds to the comprehensiveness of the divine plan for the universe[1]. Further, the divine character revealed in Jesus Christ prepares us to recognize the principle of accommodation in the Old Testament. The direction of the movement therein described is towards a liberation of human nature from the shackles of a rudimentary state. There was evidently a law of progress at work in the Mosaic system; some element which exerted a steady and continuous upward pressure. At the same time there was a gradual extrication of eternal principles from their local, material, and temporary embodiment,

---

[1] See a striking passage in Flint's *Theism*, pp. 258 foll.

and to this process no doubt the teaching of the prophets mainly contributed. It has indeed been maintained that the chief ethical and religious ideas of Judaism were practically the creation of the prophets, but there are ample indications that their task was rather that of bringing to light principles which, in a germinal form at least, had been asserted by Moses himself; and that the foundations of Hebrew religion had already been deeply laid in the days of the nation's youth [1]. It was indisputably the preaching of the prophets that brought home to Israel's consciousness the moral conditions attaching to its privileged position; but from the first the nation had been instructed that its special relationship to Jehovah, the holy God of redemption, involved a call to separation from the sins and pollutions of Semitic heathenism. Granted that the nature and meaning of its vocation was for centuries very imperfectly realized by the Hebrew people, it is at least abundantly evident that the religion of the Old Testament originated in the fact of an election—that is, in a special consecration of Israel to the service of its Redeemer. And the enduring value of Israel's religious history lies to a great extent in this—that it expands and enriches our whole conception of deity. For it bears witness to the operation of an omnipotent Being who stoops from His throne to become the educator of man, and who is guided in His dealings with our race not merely by a fixed purpose of love, but by a perfect insight into human limitations. In His Son God has explicitly revealed the principle which had all along determined the method of His self-manifestation. We are told that the Saviour of men *spake the word unto them as they were able to hear it* [2]. And while the advance of knowledge has filled these words with

---

[1] Cp. König, *The Religious History of Israel*, ch. xi.
[2] Mark iv. 33; cp. Isa. xxviii. 10. Oettli, *op. cit.* p. 19, remarks: 'Im Lichte der Offenbarung sich uns die Entwicklung nunmehr als Erziehung darstellt.'

deeper significance in proportion as it has taught us to take more sober views of human nature and its capacities, practical experience has vindicated the intrinsic reasonableness of the wearisome tardiness which has marked the onward progress of revelation. 'Grace submitting to delay,' it has been beautifully said, 'is only love consenting to be guided by wisdom[1].' The protracted discipline to which the chosen people of God was subjected, was the one and only means, so far as we have faculties for judging, by which the blessings of a higher religion could have been in the long run secured for mankind at large.

We proceed, then, to illustrate the progressive character of the Old Testament religion; but it will not be superfluous in passing to remind ourselves that Christian criticism is distinguished from purely naturalistic by its belief in a supernatural revelation. We speak indeed of the 'progressive development' of religious ideas. It must not, however, be forgotten that the Old Testament exhibits not merely an inevitable evolution of human thought, but a progressive self-manifestation of God. Israel's religion is a religion not of thinkers but of prophets, whose characteristic formula is *Thus saith the Lord*. It presupposes the immanence of God in history and the reality of His self-communications. With this prefatory remark we enter upon our subject, and we may begin by directing attention at once to the beneficent moral purpose which lies upon the very surface of the Old Testament dispensation. The goal of the entire redemptive movement was an ethical one, the salvation and perfecting of human nature. Thus in judging of any particular stage of Israel's religious or moral attainment, we are bound to take into account the dominating tendency of the entire Old Testament. The observation of tendencies is, as Bishop Butler reminds us, a true source of knowledge[2]. It gives us

---
[1] A. B. Bruce, *The Chief End of Revelation*, p. 112.
[2] See *The Analogy*, Part I, ch. iii.

a clue to the existence of rational purpose in movements which at first sight perplex the mind by their unaccountable anomalies.

Accordingly it is our duty to estimate the character and object of Israel's spiritual education in the light of its final stage. And if the distinctive element in the religion of Christ is 'inwardness[1],' there can be no question that the conspicuous feature of the old dispensation is that it uniformly exhibits a principle of progress, from outward to inward, from legal status to ethical attainment, from external restraints to internal principles, from law to love. The regulation of conduct precedes the cultivation of religious affections; active conformity to a code or system comes before renewal of heart; the sign or symbol prepares the way for what is real and essential; the material and physical for the spiritual and moral. No ancient writer, it may be remarked, has a clearer conception of the educational significance of the Old Testament history than Irenaeus. 'God,' he says in one memorable passage, 'was all along instructing the people which so readily turned back to its idols, educating them by repeated admonitions to persevere and to serve God, calling them by means of things secondary to things primary—that is, by means of things typical to things real, things temporal to things eternal, things carnal to things spiritual, things earthly to things celestial[2].'

Thus, to take the sphere of worship, we must begin by recalling to mind the usual characteristics of early religion. 'Ritual and practical usage,' says Prof. Robertson Smith, 'were, strictly speaking, the sum total of ancient religions. Religion in primitive times was not a system of belief with practical applications; it was a body of fixed traditional practices to which every member of society conformed as a matter of course... Practice preceded doctrinal theory[3].'

---

[1] Aug. *de nat. et grat.* lxxii : 'Facere est iustitiam in vero Dei cultu cum interno concupiscentiae malo interna conflictatione pugnare.'
[2] *Haer.* iv. 14, § 3.
[3] *The Religion of the Semites*, p. 21.

Now the distinctive ordinances of the Hebrew *cultus* were ascribed to Moses, and were usually sanctioned by the formula, *Jehovah spake unto Moses*. The study of comparative religion, however, renders it practically certain that the primitive lawgiver selected from an existing body of practices those which might best promote the purpose of moral cultivation. It will probably never be clearly ascertained what usages were thus inherited, and what were newly instituted by Moses himself; what is plain, however, is the principle which guided the organization of Mosaic religion. Whatever traditional customs, institutions, or ideas peculiar to the Semitic race Moses adopted or retained, they were, under divine guidance, so regulated and purified as to become disciplinary agents in the evolution of a higher type of spiritual and moral life; they were consecrated to the service of a purer faith, and were made the instruments of a purpose of grace. As Riehm observes, 'What the Old Testament religion has in common with the other religions of antiquity is to be regarded as permitted by God, and as having a basis in the divine educational purpose' for mankind. Restriction, however, seems to be more characteristic of Mosaism than comprehensiveness. Indeed, the earliest legislation confines itself mainly to prohibition. It rather regulates existing institutions than adds to them, but its dominating tendency is manifest. It 'ever aims at bringing popular custom into conformity with the principles of equity, generosity, and truth [1].' Thus, for example, the rite of circumcision was not set aside, but was retained, and hallowed as a token of the new relationship established between God and man at the exodus. Though its actual origin and purpose is somewhat obscure, there is no doubt that the practice was customary in other Semitic tribes [2]. Apparently it was known to the Hebrews in patriarchal times, and was

---

[1] Schultz, *O. T. Theology*, vol. ii. p. 62.
[2] Cp. Riehm, *ATl. Theologie*, p. 51; Robertson Smith, *Religion of the Semites*, pp. 309, 310; Renan, *Histoire du peuple d'Israël*, bk. i, ch. 9.

then adopted as a seal and condition of admission to religious privileges. Under the influence of Moses it firmly established itself in the national religion of Israel; and the moral effect of the practice may be inferred from the fact that in course of time the word 'circumcised' became equivalent to 'consecrated,' and could be indifferently applied to the heart, the ears, and the lips [1]. No circumstance could more aptly illustrate the aim and tendency of Mosaic institutions. So, again, the tribal customs connected with slavery, retaliation, the observance of the seventh day, the payment of tithes, divorce, marriage with a brother's wife, and even polygamy, were probably recognized by Moses. Some of these institutions were tolerated in view of the hardness of the people's hearts; others were so regulated and restricted as to become effective *media* in Israel's moral improvement — *media* full of religious significance, and pointing beyond themselves to a spiritual counterpart of all that was as yet purely material and external.

The system of sacrifice itself is a striking illustration of divine accommodation to immature ideas. It is apparently recognized in the Old Testament as a natural means of approach to God [2]. Man's instinctive way of rendering homage to God and appeasing his own consciousness of guilt was incorporated in the practical system of Mosaism, and the very fact that the institution was divinely sanctioned raised it to a new level of importance. Israel's sacrificial worship tended to become an elaborate and comprehensive system of spiritual instruction, awakening aspirations which no material oblations could ultimately satisfy. It was, however, at a mature stage of Hebrew civilization, in dark days

---

[1] Lev. xix. 23, xxvi. 14; Exod. vi. 12, 30; Deut. x. 16, xxx. 6; Jer. vi. 10, ix. 25, &c.

[2] Lev. xvii. 11: 'The life of the flesh is in the blood: and I have given it to you upon the altar to make an atonement for your souls.' This passage implies that what Jehovah accepts and blesses is in a true sense His *gift* to man.

of national decline, that the spiritual truths symbolized by sacrifice were brought into prominence [1]. Hebrew faith then at length perceived that sacrifice was a means and not an end; that it had a value only in so far as it represented an inward act of self-oblation to Jehovah. On the other hand, it came to be recognized that where a man's heart was true, external offerings might be acceptable to God as proof of his devotion. It is the broken-hearted penitent who, after declaring that the only true sacrifice is a contrite heart, utters the fervent vow, *Then shalt thou be pleased with the sacrifices of righteousness, with the burnt-offerings and oblations: then shall they offer young bullocks upon thine altar* [2].

A true revelation, then, of God's character is involved in the very fact that He sanctioned sacrificial worship and such other primitive customs as found a place in the system of Moses. It may indeed be questioned how far Israel in Egypt is correctly represented as a sunken and barbarous race [3]. Oehler points out that in the Pentateuch the Israelites appear to be rather an unmanageable than an uncultivated people. In any case, however, a prolonged and carefully graduated discipline was needed to lift them above the degraded nature-worship towards which, when left to themselves, they habitually gravitated, and it is analogous to the ordinary method of God's providential government that He should condescend to use existing customs and institutions; that He should even for a while bear with very crude and imperfect conceptions of His own nature and character. This is the significance of the fact that the Pentateuch repeatedly dwells upon the low standard actually exhibited by the people in early times. Indeed, one object of the prophetic book of

---

[1] Cp. Ps. l. 8 foll., li. 15 foll.; Amos v. 24; Hos. vi. 6; Isa. i. 16 foll.; Jer. vii. 21 foll.
[2] Ps. li. 19.
[3] See Renan, *Histoire du peuple d'Israël*, bk. i, ch. 11; Edersheim, *Warburton Lectures*, pp. 233 foll.; Robertson, *The Early Religion of Israel*, note xxiv; Oehler, *Theology of the O. T.* § 26, note 3.

Deuteronomy is to 'dissuade' the people 'from the opinion of their own righteousness by rehearsing their several rebellions[1].' *Understand therefore,* says the writer, *that the Lord thy God giveth thee not this good land to possess it for thy righteousness; for thou art a stiffnecked people. Remember, and forget not, how thou provokedst the Lord thy God to wrath in the wilderness: from the day that thou didst depart out of the land of Egypt, until ye came unto this place, ye have been rebellious against the Lord*[2]. It is worthy of God that He should deign to be the educator of His people. The mere recognition or toleration of what is rude and morally defective reveals a deity not only righteous and just, but patient, wise, and loving. In the simple precepts delivered to an untutored race, in the directions that were adapted to the circumstances of a primitive age, 'we can recognize,' it has been said, 'the beating heart of the living God[3].'

When we turn from the sphere of religious observance to that of ethical ideas, we see at once how progress depended upon the existence of some well-defined, though simple, conception of the divine character. Nothing short of a belief in the living God was capable of giving impulse and direction to the movement towards a higher standard. In its fundamental idea of Jehovah's character lies the secret of Israel's moral superiority to the surrounding heathen. The ethics of Mosaism are in fact rooted in its theology, just as its theology is based on the historic fact of the exodus from Egypt. *I am Jehovah thy God, that brought thee out of the land of Egypt, out of the house of bondage.* As a consequence of its deliverance, Israel entered into definite relationship with a Being personal and moral, a Being not merely possessed of invincible might, but manifesting Himself as righteous; for the overthrow of Egyptian power was a triumph both of grace aiding the weak, and of right-

---

[1] Deut. ix (heading in A. V.). [2] Deut. ix. 6, 7.
[3] Oettli, *op. cit.* p. 20.

eousness punishing the oppressor. Thus an ethical conception of deity formed the starting-point of Israel's religion. Holiness was declared to be at once the rule of divine action and a law for human conduct[1]. It would be misleading to speak of Mosaism as if it embraced a formal system of ethics. It did, however, prepare the way for a system by a gradual, but in the long run effectual, elucidation of two ideas which a religious system of morals seems to presuppose: first, the idea of holiness; secondly, the idea of the worth and dignity of personality.

In a former lecture we have noticed how the idea of holiness was transferred in process of time from the sphere of ritual to that of ethics; how the notion of religious separation gradually passed into that of moral sanctity. The point, however, to be observed here is that the deeper sense of the word 'holiness' was suggested at the very starting-point of Israel's career. The proof of this statement lies in the general characteristics of the earliest legislation. On the one hand, there is a comparative silence in regard to points of ritual. Certainly the Mosaic *cultus* was for a long period merely 'an affair of practice and tradition, resting on knowledge that belonged to the priestly guild[2].' It does not appear to have been reduced to theory or formally codified at the time of the exodus. The positive ordinances that relate to worship in the 'Book of the Covenant' are of the most simple and primitive character. There is only one direction that touches upon ceremonial purity, viz. a precept to abstain from the flesh of animals torn by wild beasts[3]. There are also injunctions bearing upon the erection of altars, the offering of firstfruits, and the observance of three stated feasts connected with the ordinary conditions of agricultural life. All the other

---

[1] Cp. W. S. Bruce, *Ethics of the O. T.* ch. iii.
[2] Robertson Smith, *O. T. in J. C.* p. 332.
[3] Exod. xxii. 31. Cp. xx. 24, xxii. 29, xxiii. 14 foll. Observe two points of sacrificial ritual in xxiii. 18. Cp. Driver, *Introduction to the Literature of the O. T.* pp. 33 foll.

precepts of the first legislation are social and ethical; they regulate the transactions of man with his fellow; they provide for the due punishment of injuries inflicted upon a fellow Israelite either unwittingly or with malicious intent; they define the elementary rights of the slave and they enjoin certain minor duties of humanity. The crimes restrained are such as would be common in a rude and semi-civilized community. What is most striking, however, is the constant reference made to the divine authority behind the law. If the widow or fatherless child is afflicted, Jehovah *will hear their cry*, and His *wrath shall wax hot*[1]. Jehovah himself watches, as it were, over the administration of justice and guards the interests of the helpless and friendless. Indeed, the distinctive peculiarity of the legislation is the prominence assigned to righteousness and humanity. Its effect could not fail to be that of deepening the sense of Jehovah's chief requirement, or, in other words, elucidating the notion of His holiness.

The Decalogue is especially significant in this connexion, for in it we may confidently believe that we have an original monument of Mosaism. It is indisputable that 'the ten words' are an index to the character of Moses' work in so far as they place morality in the forefront of Israel's religion, and form a commentary on the meaning of the 'holiness' ascribed to the God of redemption. I am aware of the view advanced by some eminent critics that the Decalogue, even in its original form, cannot be ascribed to Moses[2]. Moreover, as is well known, there is a so-called second Decalogue contained in Exod. xxxiv. 10–28[3], which is one of the puzzles of

---

[1] Exod. xxii. 24.
[2] See e.g. Cornill, *Der Israelitische Prophetismus*, 17; Wellhausen, *Sketch*, &c., p. 21; Montefiore, *Hibbert Lectures*, appendix i. (p. 553). There is, of course, an important revelation of Jehovah's character in the sanctions attached to the first four 'words'; but on this point it would be unwise to insist, inasmuch as these sanctions appear to belong to a later age than the Decalogue itself.
[3] Robertson Smith, *O. T. in J. C.* p. 335; Driver, *op. cit.* p. 37.

criticism. But we seem to be justified in adhering to the traditional view of the Decalogue chiefly on the ground that it is intrinsically credible. It is consistent with all that we know of Israel's subsequent history, and it would be impossible to explain satisfactorily the vitality and vigour displayed in the conquest of Canaan without the supposition that the long observance of some primary laws of moral conduct had moulded the character of the nation and consolidated its strength [1]. On the other hand, it is scarcely conceivable that the prophets were the first ethical teachers of Israel. It has been justly pointed out that 'the more the pre-prophetic religion is depreciated, the more difficult it will be to account for its sudden rise to the level in which we find it in the earliest writing prophets [2].' The prophets never claim the position of pioneers in religion; they regard themselves as restorers of a moral and religious ideal which had been set before the people at the very outset of its history [3]. Their language implies that Mosaism was pre-eminently an ethical religion ; that, in fact, it had laid the foundations of Israel's polity in a lofty conception of God, and in the exaltation of righteousness as the essential element in true and acceptable worship. Certainly this view harmonizes with the fact that the Old Testament uniformly ascribes to Moses a prophetic character.

The notion of holiness, then, was closely associated with morality in the Sinaitic legislation, and each fresh disclosure of Jehovah's character contributed something to the education of conscience and developed more profound conceptions of human duty. In this progressive movement the book of Deutero-

---

[1] Prof. Kamphausen, quoted by Montefiore (*Hibbert Lectures*, p. 47), says: 'I recognize in the fact that the small number of the Israelites was not absorbed by the Canaanites, who were by far their superiors in all matters of external culture, a convincing proof of the ethical power of the Yahvistic religion.'
[2] Robertson, *The Early Religion of Israel*, p. 264.
[3] Cp. König, *Religious History of Israel*, p. 25.

nomy may be said to play a decisive part[1]. The didactic recapitulation of the history and legislation, which is characteristic of this book, was apparently intended to serve the purpose of deepening the religious life of Israel by bringing out the spiritual significance of its past experience. It is the spirit of the prophets which gives to Deuteronomy its peculiar tone and impress. In teaching that the service of Jehovah demands not formal compliance with the external precepts of the law, but an inward devotion of heart and will, the book bears eloquent testimony to the true genius and character of Mosaism. It evidently presupposes the existence of a well-understood moral code reaching back to the very commencement of Israel's national life. And if it is urged that the low moral condition of the people during the wanderings contradicts the idea that Moses instituted a pure and imageless worship of the true God, it may be rejoined that the practical failure of the prophets to win the mass of the people to a higher standard of morals and worship proves the possibility at least of an analogous condition of things in the time of Moses himself. Wellhausen and others question the authenticity of the second commandment on the express ground that its observance was virtually unknown throughout the older period of the history. 'Could Moses,' it is asked, 'have forbidden image-worship, when we know that the representation of Jehovah under the form of a bull was a common and scarcely reprehended custom down to the age of Amos[2]?' Now the analogy of later history renders it perfectly credible that a spiritual worship of Jehovah was enjoined as an ideal by Moses, but that it did not prevent an occasional or even constant declension of the people to a lower standard. This account of the matter is more simple than the supposition that the second commandment is a late insertion into an earlier form of

---

[1] Cp. W. S. Bruce, *The Ethics of the O. T.* pp. 224 foll.
[2] Montefiore, *Hibbert Lectures*, appendix i.

the Decalogue[1]; moreover, it is consistent with the fact, pointed out by M. Renan, that nomadic religion is as a rule simple in character, and that the primitive Semites had little liking for figured presentments of the deity[2]. Neither theory, however, vitally affects the main point on which I have been insisting, namely, the distinctively ethical character of Mosaism. The basis of righteousness was laid in simple precepts designed to protect life, property, chastity, and the reverence due to parents[3]. The holiness of Jehovah was in process of time seen to consist in His utter abhorrence of inhuman and unrighteous conduct; and in the ethical connotation imparted to the notion of holiness lies the characteristic contribution of Mosaic religion to the advancement of ethical theory and practice.

There was another idea which needed development before morality could become in any sense systematic: the idea, namely, of the worth, dignity, and rights of personality.

In the early stages of Hebrew civilization, religion appears to accommodate itself to a defective or even debased notion of human individuality. This statement may be justified by such incidents as the destruction of Achan's household, the doom of Dathan and Abiram with their company, and the slaughter of the Canaanites whom Israel dispossessed of their land. An attentive reader of the Old Testament, however,

---

[1] Cp. Bruce, *Apologetics*, p. 212. Kittel, *Hist. of the Hebrews*, vol. i. p. 235, takes a mediating view. 'Neither the Decalogue nor the Book of the Covenant in their present form can be directly Mosaic. Criticism must be allowed a free hand in separating the later additions and enlargements, which here also are quite intelligible. When this is done, the original kernel, both of the one document and of the other, must remain. Their Mosaic origin is witnessed to in a manner which deserves the fullest credence: the infrequency with which such witness is borne; the contents, as well as the concise and lapidary style, of these two fundamental laws; the history of the circumstances amidst which we have shown they originated;—are sufficient proofs.'

[2] *Histoire du peuple d'Israël*, bk. i, ch. 4 init.

[3] It is significant that in referring to 'the commandments' our Lord does not mention the first, second, third, or fourth (Mark x. 19; cp. Matt. xix. 16 foll., Luke xviii. 18 foll.).

will observe that the foundations of a true conception of personality are being laid even at a period when the existence of individual rights seems to be totally ignored. The germ of a doctrine of human individuality is perhaps to be traced in the rite of circumcision, which was extended to children and even to the servants of a Hebrew household. Further, we may point to all primitive enactments which limited the arbitrary power of those who owned slaves [1], or enjoined simple duties of charity and humanity [2]. Nor must we overlook the influence of those sacred traditions which witnessed to a divine tenderness for the humble and lonely soul, the story of Hagar, for example, whom the angel of the Lord 'found' by a fountain of water in the wilderness of Shur and addressed by name: *Hagar, Sarai's maid, whence camest thou? and whither wilt thou go* [3] *?* These considerations show that the Law in its earliest stages implicitly recognized that very truth of man's relationship to God and to his fellow which ultimately led to the recognition of his own personal rights as an individual [4]. By way of illustrating this point, we may notice the practice of human sacrifice and the divine injunction to slaughter the Canaanites.

In regard to human sacrifice we may at once set aside the notion of an original connexion between the worship of Moloch and the service of Jehovah, which some critics base, somewhat fancifully, on the description of Jehovah as 'fire [5].' Nevertheless, it is clear that the primitive Semites regarded human life—the life, for instance, of a fellow-tribesman—as a thing of unique sanctity, and therefore likely to be specially efficacious when employed as

---

[1] Exod. xxi. 20; Deut. xxi. 10 foll.
[2] See Exod. chh. xxi-xxiii; Deut. chh. xx, xxii, xxiv, xxv.
[3] Gen. xvi. 8; cp. xxi. 17.
[4] Cp. Mozley, *Ruling Ideas in Early Ages*, p. 235.
[5] See König, *The Religion of Israel*, ch. ix; Robertson, *Early Religion of Israel*, ch. x. On human sacrifice in Israel see Schultz, *O. T. Theology*, vol. i. p. 191; Dillmann on *Genesis* xxii; Kamphausen, *Das Verhältnis des Menschenopfers zur Isr. Religion*, &c.

a medium of atonement. This will account for the occasional tendency of Israel to relapse into the barbarous customs of heathen worship. The primitive notion that God might claim for Himself a human life as man's most acceptable offering, probably lingered long in the popular mind. The idea, indeed, contained an element of nobility and truth which the religion of Jehovah was destined to extricate and purify. We naturally think in this connexion of the offering of Isaac by Abraham described in the twenty-second chapter of Genesis. What, then, is the purport of this narrative? The point of it appears to depend on the 'prevailing low theology of sacrifice,' in which for the moment Jehovah seems to acquiesce [1]. The injunction to sacrifice a human victim to Jehovah was in accordance with the ideas common to Abraham's race and the age in which he lived [2]. There was nothing in the spirit of his time that would necessarily deter the patriarch from executing it. Further, the passage in question supplies an explanation of the fact, that at a comparatively early stage in its history the Hebrew people was distinguished from its heathen neighbours by the disuse of human sacrifice [3]. God dealt with the custom pedagogically, and in a manner analogous to His action in other departments of man's moral education. The element of good which lies at the root of human sacrifice was enforced—viz. the principle that man is bound to devote to God his best and choicest gift. It was this element which made Abraham's act not only morally glorious, but typical of the perfect 'sacrifice, oblation, and satisfaction' which was consummated on Calvary. The subsequent effect of the tradition embodied in this narrative was twofold. On the one hand, the practice of human sacrifice came to be regarded with horror as

---

[1] Cp. Newman Smyth, *Old Faiths in New Lights*, pp. 84-90.
[2] Cp. Renan, *Histoire du peuple d'Israël*, bk. i. ch. 9 [Eng. Tr. p. 102].
[3] Robertson, *Early Religion of Israel*, p. 254. Cp. Fairbairn, *Religion in History and in Modern Life*, lect. ii. p. 129.

a shocking relapse into heathen atrocities; on the other, there arose a more profound conception of Jehovah's requirement: He was a God 'who did not delight in destroying life, but in saving and sanctifying it[1]'; and the oblation in which alone He could delight was the free-will offering of a perfect human obedience. Thus the divine Educator practically succeeded in destroying the fatal errors, and saving the vital truth, of sacrifice[2]. He accepts the best that primitive man can offer, and, as Dr. Mozley observes, directs his 'earlier ideas and modes of thinking towards such great moral achievements as are able to be founded upon them[3].'

So much may be said from an apologetic point of view in regard to Genesis xxii. The bearing of the narrative, however, upon our present subject lies in its contribution to the idea of the worth of personality, and in its restriction of absolute paternal rights. It inculcates the lesson that 'parents have only such rights over their children as are consistent with the acknowledgment of God's higher right of property[4].'

This last point leads naturally to the consideration of the divine injunction to exterminate the inhabitants of Canaan. Various attempts have been made to explain, or mitigate, a sentence of destruction which at first sight seems so inconsistent with the very features of Jehovah's character which the deliverance of Israel from Egypt had manifested[5]. As in the matter of human sacrifice, so in this case it might be said that God appears to acquiesce in a view of human life which knows nothing of individual responsibility.

---

[1] Robertson, *Early Religion of Israel*, p. 255.
[2] Newman Smyth, *op. cit.* p. 89. Cp. Oehler, *Theol. of the O. T.* § 23. On the sacrifice of Jephthah's daughter see Schultz, vol. i. p. 191; Robertson, *Early Religion of Israel*, p. 255.
[3] Mozley, *Ruling Ideas in Early Ages*, p. 55.
[4] Oehler, § 105. He observes that the same principle appears in the ordinances relating to the redemption of firstborn sons, representing perhaps the whole family (Exod. xiii. 13).
[5] See W. S. Bruce, *The Ethics of the O. T.* pp. 259 foll.; Mozley, *Ruling Ideas*, &c., lect. iv.

But the judicial extirpation of the Canaanites may rather be regarded as a proof that the interests of man's moral progress occasionally demand the employment of stern and relentless methods. The Old Testament itself indicates the real ground of the transaction when it insists that the inhabitants of the land had already been long spared in spite of their abominations, and that the cup of their iniquities was now full[1]. Herein consists the moral impressiveness of the tragic doom that overtook the Canaanites— a doom delayed for centuries, but at length descending upon the guilty with appalling severity. The whole proceeding enters as a wholesome element into the moral education of Israel and of the world. It had at least the effect of signalizing the divine abhorrence of portentous sensuality. It was an act characteristic of that Power which throughout human history 'makes for righteousness[2],' and sweeps away degenerate races in order to make way for such as are fresh and vigorous. 'Here is no partiality,' says Dr. Bruce, 'of a merely national God befriending His worshippers at the expense of others without regard to justice ; here rather is a Power making for righteousness and against iniquity; yea, a Power acting with a beneficent regard to the good of humanity, burying a putrefying carcase out of sight lest it should taint the air[3].' After all, the Canaanite nations were put under the ban, 'not for false belief, but for vile actions[4],' a significant circumstance which plainly implies that in the execution of His righteous purpose Almighty God is guided by one supreme aim, namely, the elevation of human character. If Israel was duly to discharge its mission, and to become the vehicle to mankind of a purer religion and a loftier morality, it was necessary, humanly speaking, that

---

[1] Lev. xviii. 27 foll.; Deut. xii. 31. Cp. Gen. xv. 16.
[2] See Oehler, § 32, note 3.
[3] *Chief End of Revelation*, pp. 140 foll.
[4] Westcott, *Epistle to the Hebrews*, p. 139.

a signal manifestation should be made, at the very outset of its history, of the divine hostility to sin. It is to be observed, finally, that Israel itself is threatened with a similar judgment in the event of its yielding to the depraved rites or practices of heathendom [1]. These considerations at least suggest that the idea of individuality is one for which a moral basis is required. The interests of morality may well have demanded an inexorably severe treatment of an evil which might have fatally thwarted God's beneficent purpose for mankind at the very outset. It was more important that a people, destined to be the missionary of the world, should have a just conception of the meaning of divine holiness, than that it should learn the duty of respect for individual rights. The sense of national consecration was utilized as a factor in the development of morality, but it naturally preceded by a long interval the idea of *personal* sanctification.

With these few illustrations of the progressiveness of Israel's ethical education I must be content. The caution however may be repeated, that it is inconsistent with all sound historical principles to pronounce a verdict upon the morality of the old dispensation apart from due consideration of its uniform tendency, and of the purpose by which it was manifestly inspired and guided [2].

---

[1] Deut. viii. 19, 20; xiii. 12 foll.; Josh. xxiii. 15 foll.

[2] Cp. Mozley, *Ruling Ideas in Early Ages*, p. 238: 'When you talk of the imperfect and mistaken morality of the Old Testament dispensation, ask yourself, to begin with, what you mean, and what you intend to assert by the expression. Do you mean to assert that the written law was imperfect? If that is all, you state what is simply a fact; but this does not touch the morality of the Lawgiver, because He is abundantly fortified by the defence that He could give no higher at the time to an unenlightened people. Do you mean to assert that the scope and design was imperfectly moral? In that case you are contradicted by the whole course of history. ... You blame in the Old Testament dispensation, i.e. in its Author, what? The moral standard He *permits*? It is the highest man can then receive. The moral standard He *desires*? He desires a perfect moral standard, and ultimately establishes it.'

II.

Hitherto we have been engaged in considering the progressive character of revelation, and the light which the history of Israel's moral development throws upon the nature and attributes of God. The prophets and psalmists are fully alive to the inner significance of the divine dealings with Israel, and they delight to describe in homely and tender imagery the relationship of love which bound Jehovah to His people. They conceive of Him as guiding Israel's footsteps with a father's compassion, and feeding His people with a shepherd's watchful care. *Thou hast seen,* says the writer of Deuteronomy, *how that the Lord thy God bare thee, as a man doth bear his son, in all the way that ye went, until ye came into this place* [1]. *As for his own people,* sings the psalmist, *he led them forth like sheep, and carried them in the wilderness like a flock* [2]. *In all their affliction,* says a prophet, *he was afflicted, and the angel of his presence saved them; in his love and in his pity he redeemed them; and he bare them, and carried them all the days of old* [3]. Such passages have a religious importance apart from their literary beauty. The psalmists and prophets look back upon the chequered history of God's relationship to Israel with the eyes of love. In the stern but merciful discipline of the wilderness, in the intervention of almighty power, in the miracles of redeeming and sustaining grace, they discern the unwearied faithfulness and tenderness of a self-revealing deity. Their chief interest is to trace at every stage or crisis of national development the handiwork of God; they dwell upon all situations or incidents that illustrate the attributes of God and the methods of His action. History, in a word, is to the prophets and saints of old the continuous self-manifestation of a person, the gradual disclosure of the ineffable Name.

---

[1] Deut. i. 31; cp. Hos. xi. 1.   [2] Ps. lxxviii. 53.   [3] Isa. lxiii. 9.

The 'Name' of God signifies that which may be known of Him, or rather that which He has made known of Himself to man. It does not represent the divine essence in itself, but such a manifestation of it as human faculties can apprehend. In short, the Name of God is His character as He would have it acknowledged and held in honour by man. It is that which in the life of His beloved Son was finally manifested, and the successive declarations of the divine Name may be said to mark in broad outline different stages of revelation. The conception of deity becomes more definite and clear in proportion as redemptive history advances.

Now speaking broadly, there appears to be a gradual transition from general designations of the divine nature to specific and full statements of character. The ancient Hebrews started from some indeterminate conception of God common to the whole Semitic race, and were led on by slow degrees to a living apprehension of the being whom they worshipped. There was a relative purity and spirituality in the most ancient Semitic ideas of deity which distinguished them from those of Aryan peoples. This might be inferred from the different titles of Semitic deities: thus *El* signifies 'strong one'; *Bel* or *Baal,* 'owner'; *Adonis,* 'lord'; *Moloch,* 'king'; *Rimmon,* probably 'thunderer[1].' The fact is one which confirms the impression that Israel had antecedent aptitude for becoming the vehicle of the true religion to the world. The Hebrew started fairly; he had not utterly confounded God with nature. And thus from a feeling of vague dependence and fear he was led onward and upward towards the perception of a personality to whom he could stand in a moral relationship of devotion, trust, and love. He outgrew the stage in which the thought of deity merely inspired

---

[1] Riehm, *A Tl. Theologie*, pp. 46, 47. Riehm observes that among the Semites 'die Gottheit wird nicht so tief, wie bei den Ariern, in die Natur und das Naturleben herabgezogen.'

awe, and finally attained that in which the very mention of God was a joy, the very thought of Him a refuge and a solace. It is a wonderful ascent in religious experience, the successive moments of which seem to be indicated in the different designations of God contained in the Old Testament.

The names of God must first be briefly considered with reference to their meaning and origin. We have, first, a group of general names, of which the most common are *'El, 'Eloah, 'Elohim,* and *'El 'Elyon.* The name *'Elohim* has been thought to point to the polytheistic idiom of the early Semites; but, as is well known, when applied to the God of Israel it denotes the one and only God, and is used with a singular verb [1]. The name may perhaps be traced to a time when it was commonly believed that there were supernatural beings infesting certain localities, and vaguely supposed to be hostile to men. 'If,' says Prof. Robertson Smith, ' the *'Elohim* of a place meant originally all its sacred denizens . . . the transition to the use of the plural in a singular sense would follow naturally as soon as this indeterminate conception gave way to the conception of an individual god of the sanctuary [2].' It should be borne in mind that the word is by no means exclusively applied to God. It is occasionally applied to a person who is regarded as the mouthpiece of a divine sentence, for instance to a judge or to a civil magistrate. Moreover, *'Elohim* is commonly used, not only of the false deities of alien nations, but also of a class of beings, *Sons of 'Elohim*, who possess supernatural powers, and belong to an invisible and spiritual order. When applied to the God of Israel, the plural *'Elohim* is best described as intensive, expressing the notion of 'fullness'—plenitude of superhuman might, or, as others prefer to explain,

[1] See Schultz, i. 121 ; ii. 126 foll.
[2] *Religion of the Semites*, p. 150. Cf. Renan, *Histoire du peuple d'Israël*, bk. i. ch. 3 [Eng. Tr. pp. 25, 26].

of that which inspires awe[1]. In any case it implies a being who claims the submission and adoration of men; and it may fairly be maintained that the word, especially when united to a singular verb, indicates that all divine powers are, as it were, concentrated in one personal being[2]; indeed, the phrase may be thought to have possessed dogmatic value as combating the notion of an abstract and sterile monotheism.

Akin to *'Elohim* may be the name *'El*, which is sometimes found in poetry, but scarcely ever in prose. The root-meaning of the word is apparently 'the strong one,' and the fact of its appearing in old proper names, e. g. Methusael, Ishmael, or Bethel, points to its being the most primitive Hebrew designation of God[3]. With respect to the name *'Eloah*, the singular of *'Elohim*, some scholars hold that it corresponds to *'El* as a subjective to an objective designation: *'El*, the absolutely strong one, being regarded by man as *'Eloah*, the object of man's dread[4]. Finally, the phrase *'El 'Elyon*, 'Most High God'—a title which has Phoenician affinities[5]—implies the relative transcendence or elevation of the Deity, and it has been surmised that the use of this name in the passage relating to Melchizedek (Gen. xiv. 18) points to the early existence of an ancient monolatrous worship on Canaanite soil[6].

Next to these general names comes the title which

---

[1] See Riehm, *op. cit.* pp. 48, 49. Riehm questions the correctness of the opinion that *Elohim* had originally the notion of plurality. He thinks that, like other words, e. g. שׁמים and מים, it might simply imply extension, mass, or fullness. Darmesteter makes a similar remark: 'Le pluriel *Elohim* construit avec un verbe au singulier est un fait de grammaire et non de psychologie religieuse, et ne prouve guère plus la multiplicité primitive du dieu que *Nous* et *Notre Majesté* ne prouvent la multiplicité des majestés humaines; bref, *Elohim* est *un* de naissance autant que *Jahvé*' (*Les Prophètes d'Israël*, p. 215).
[2] See Robertson, *Early Religion of Israel*, note xv (p. 502). Cp. 1 Cor. viii. 5, 6.
[3] Renan points out the religious significance of this fact, as attesting the relative purity of the Hebrew conceptions of deity (*op. cit.* bk. i. ch. 8 init.).
[4] Oehler, § 36. Cp. Riehm, p. 49.   [5] Schultz, ii. 130.
[6] Oehler, § 23, note 8. Cp. Westcott on Heb. vii. 1.

is characteristic of the patriarchal period, *El Shaddai*[1]. There can be no question that the general import of the name is correctly given in the usual English equivalent, 'God Almighty.' The idea conveyed by it is that of absolute control over the forces of nature and the course of history. Abraham, as the recipient of Jehovah's gracious promises, may lean confidently on Him, with full assurance that *what he hath promised he is able also to perform*[2]; He is unfettered either by human perversity, or by the fixity of physical laws. The appearance of this designation of God marks a significant advance in religious ideas. It seems to imply the drawing of a conscious distinction between the one true omnipotent God and the powerless deities of heathendom. It corresponds to the simplicity and relative purity of patriarchal faith and worship when compared with the debased nature-religion of the Canaanites.

Specially distinctive of the Mosaic period is the title which is peculiarly *the Name*[3] of revelation, *Jahveh*. Into the disputed history and origin of the word there is no occasion to enter minutely. It may suffice to say briefly that it appears to be a genuine Hebrew formation, directly connected with the third person singular imperfect of a verb[4]. But it is still a matter of some uncertainty what was the precise significance of the original verbal stem; whether the form is a *Qal* or a *Hiphil*; and therefore whether the word itself means 'the living one' or 'he who causes to be,' 'the Creator.' It is noteworthy, however, that names derived from the imperfect tense—such names, for instance, as *Jacob* or *Israel*—seem generally, like Latin formations ending in *-tor*, to indicate a constant quality in the object of which they are predicated. There is sufficient reason on the whole for accepting

---

[1] Exod. vi. 3. Observe this is according to P.   [2] Rom. iv. 21.
[3] Lev. xxiv. 11: הַשֵּׁם, LXX. τὸ ὄνομα.
[4] For various accounts of the derivation see Riehm, p. 59; Robertson, *Early Religion of Israel*, pp. 268 foll.; Renan, *Histoire du peuple d'Israël*, bk. i, ch. 6; *Studia Biblica*, vol. i. pp. 11 foll.

the view that the word means 'he who will be.' There is an inevitable vagueness in the phrase, but, as Prof. Robertson Smith explains, it implies that 'no words can sum up all that Jehovah will be to His people[1].' It essentially conveys the notion of a living and active moral personality. Jehovah is a personal being possessed of definite will and character; free to intervene in the course of events, and to enter into a relationship of grace with His creatures; faithful to His own nature, persistent and self-consistent, an object, therefore, on which human hopes may securely rest; a being moreover who, because He truly *is*, is therefore holy, for evil is only the negation of true being. *Id malum est*, says Augustine, *deficere ab essentia et ad id tendere ut non sit*[2].

There remain two Hebrew titles of deity, *Adonai* and *Jahveh Tsebaoth*, 'Jehovah of hosts,' of which the latter only needs a word of explanation at this point. The name first appears in the narrative of the books of Samuel, a circumstance which suggests that it was commonly associated with the early fortunes of the monarchy. The original sense and application of the name is disputed, but most probably its earliest application was to the armies of Israel itself, which were habitually regarded as the hosts of Jehovah, marching under Him as their captain and waging war in His name[3]. According to this view the title naturally occurs in the early historical books, having been suggested by the warlike experiences of the exodus and the entry into Canaan.

Before we consider the relation in which these various names of God stand to one another, and the special importance of each in the history of revelation, let us pause to notice the general conception of revelation which they imply.

---

[1] *Prophets of Israel*, lect. ii, note 10. Cp. Robertson, *Early Religion of Israel*, p. 286.
[2] *de mor. Manich.* ii. §§ 2, 3. Cp. *Conf.* vii. 12; Ath. *c. Gent.* iv, vi.
[3] Cp. Exod. vii. 4, xii. 41; Num. xxi. 14; 1 Sam. xvii. 45. Cp. Robertson, *Early Religion of Israel*, note 16, p. 503.

In the first place, the Old Testament witnesses to an implicit belief that God approaches man independently of man's efforts to find God. The Hebrew idea of God was simple and concrete. The Jew instinctively thought of Jehovah as a personal being, and therefore capable of making communications to man. A single expression marks the gulf that parts the ancient from the modern habit of mind. The Hebrew prophet speaks of 'seeking God,' not of 'seeking after truth.' God is already for him an existing personal being, *the high and lofty one that inhabiteth eternity, whose name is holy*[1], but who has revealed to man the conditions of entering into communion with Himself. In a word, the religion of the Old Testament has rather a prophetic than a philosophic character. It is presupposed that God can and does speak to man in language that he is capable of comprehending: dreams, visions, oracles, theophanies, angelic communications, prophetic messages—these are the usual *media* of communication between God and His creatures, and they all point onwards to the possibility of that immediate converse between the human spirit and the Spirit of God, which is the goal and crowning-point of revelation. The childlike narratives of the early history represent Jehovah as holding intercourse with His elect, talking with them *as a man speaketh unto his friend*[2]. In proportion as the idea of deity becomes more developed this kind of language disappears. The distance is not widened between the Creator and His creatures, but the mode of His communication with them is more spiritually conceived. Throughout the Old Testament, however, there is no change in the general idea of divine revelation, namely, that a self-acquired knowledge of deity is impossible for man, that the first approach must be made by God Himself, that so much only can be known of Him as He is willing to manifest from time to time in the course of history.

[1] Isa. lvii. 15.   [2] Exod. xxxiii. 11.

That Jehovah, then, is a being who communicates with man is, for the Hebrew, an instinctively drawn inference from the belief in the divine personality. That God should enter into close relationships with men, that He should intimately associate Himself with their tribal and family life, with their traditional customs of worship, with their joys and sorrows, their migrations and feuds—this was an integral element in early Semitic belief. Not less habitual was the ascription to deity of a readiness to intervene with counsel in difficulty, or with an authoritative sentence in matters of dispute. There was something in this habit of mind which manifestly fitted the Semitic race to be the vehicle of divine revelation to mankind. The desire to know God and to hold fellowship with Him was a natural basis on which the fabric of revealed religion could be built up. Imbued with the sense of a close antecedent relation to God, determining his tribal status and his social duties, the primitive Semite displayed an habitual inclination to explore the purposes and to ascertain the will of the powerful being to whom he felt himself so closely bound and so irresistibly attracted. Hence doubtless it is that soothsaying and prophecy, whether in its lower or higher forms, are so constant a phenomenon in Semitic religion [1]. It seemed entirely natural that the deity should converse with man, that He should employ human organs in the declaration of His will, that by secret communications of His Spirit He should impart that knowledge of His nature and requirement which constitutes the true life of man.

On the other hand, the Old Testament teaches that the faculty which apprehends the divine communications is moral rather than intellectual. What differentiates Hebrew prophecy from heathen mantic is not only its actual content, but the moral conditions which it presupposes. The power of prophecy implies as its basis the life of friendship with God, and friend-

[1] Riehm, *ATl. Theologie*, p. 46.

ship can only exist where there is likeness in character and aim. The religion of Israel tends ever more completely to exclude the ethnic notion of inspiration divorced from morality. Spiritual insight is the outcome of the fear of God—a fear which is no mere slavish emotion of abject dependence or terror, but a principle of practical wisdom [1] and a faculty of spiritual perception, discerning in all things the divine purpose and in all action guided by the divine will [2]. Such fear involves the renunciation of self-conceit. *Lean not*, says the Hebrew sage, *unto thine own understanding. Be not wise in thine own eyes* [3]. And Jeremiah insists even more emphatically. *Let not the wise man glory in his wisdom,... but let him that glorieth glory in this, that he understandeth and knoweth me, that I am the Lord which exercise lovingkindness, judgment, and righteousness in the earth* [4]. Thus the inspired wisdom of the Old Testament anticipates the teaching of the New, in laying down two main conditions under which alone a true knowledge of God is possible for man. First, human faculties cannot reach a deity who hides himself; religion, the life of friendship between the human heart and God, is impossible except on the basis of a divine self-communication. And, secondly, the capacity to know God is a moral quality; inspiration and revelation are the correlative aspects of a moral relationship subsisting between God and man, God making His communications to a being whose power of response primarily depends on the condition of his heart and will, on the degree of his moral sympathy with his holy Creator.

We may now consider somewhat more in detail the revelation of God in which the several names above mentioned seem to mark distinct and definite stages.

The general names, *'El, 'Elohim, 'Eloah, 'El 'Elyon*, which were apparently common among the Semitic

---

[1] Cp. Prov. ix. 10.   See Oehler, § 240.
[2] Cp. Prov. iii. 6.   [3] Prov. iii. 5, 7.   [4] Jer. ix. 23, 24.

tribes, correspond to that vague and undefined conception of deity which would be natural at a primitive stage of civilization. *'Elohim* is a power who transcends nature and man, who is elevated above the limitations of the visible universe. The title seems to concentrate in a single term all that may be known of God by contemplation of the universe, regarded as His handiwork [1]. *'Elohim* is the Creator manifesting His wisdom and omnipotence in all the varied processes of nature which at the same time He transcends. From the first, the use of the name in Hebrew religion served to exclude pantheistic conceptions of deity. The notion of transcendence, however, came to be more distinctly conveyed by the rare *'El 'Elyon*, 'God Most High,' a name which distinguishes the one true God from other conceivable *'Elohim*. Speaking generally, this entire group of terms may be described as universalistic in their connotation. They indicate the relation of God to all that He has made, as its creator and sustainer. Thus when creatures other than man are represented as speaking, they employ the term *'Elohim* [2]. Again, it has been observed by scholars that *'Elohim*, as the title of God most frequently employed in post-exilic days, is a symbol of the increasingly spiritual and transcendental conceptions of God which the teaching of later prophecy displays [3]. The tendency of religion at this period was to exalt the deity to a point where He stood far removed from contact with the world, and consequently to describe Him in abstract and general terms. 'The names *God of heaven, Most High God* begin to be used, and

---

[1] Cp. Rom. i. 19. [2] e. g. Judges ix. 9.
[3] Renan strangely regards the name *Jahveh* as representing a lower stage of faith than *Elohim*. 'The religious progress of Israel will be found to consist in reverting from Jahveh to Elohim, ... in stripping him of his personal attributes and leaving him only the abstract existence of Elohim' (*Histoire du peuple d'Israël*, bk. i. ch. 6). 'The history of Israel,' he says elsewhere (bk. ii, ch. 5), 'was an effort continued through long ages to shake off the false god Jahveh, and to return to the primitive Elohim.'

are even put into heathen mouths¹.' The covenant-name *Jehovah* is withdrawn, as if a reluctance had gradually arisen to name the living God, or perhaps a vague dread of dishonouring His awful majesty². But a providential purpose may be discerned in what might at first sight seem to be a retrogression. The revival of these primitive titles '*Elohim* and '*El 'Elyon* has a theological significance in so far as they bear witness to a redemptive purpose of God extending beyond the pale of His covenant with Israel. In the third book of the psalter, for example, the use of the word '*Elohim* was perhaps designed by the compiler to counteract the exclusive temper, which was Israel's peculiar danger in the age subsequent to the return from Babylon. A good instance of the same point is furnished by the book of Ecclesiastes. Here '*Elohim* is the solitary title of deity employed; and the divine nature is described in such general terms as might awaken a response in the heathen conscience. While '*Elohim* testifies to the providential regard of the God of Israel for the Gentile world, the names 'Creator' and 'Judge' would suggest a character and function already ascribed to deity by the higher spirits of heathendom. The name '*Elohim*, corresponding to the Greek title τὸ θεῖον, would constitute one of those links between the religion of Israel and the higher thought of the Hellenic world on which the future spread of Christianity so largely depended. Indeed, in the system of Philo the later Jewish mode of conceiving the deity easily coalesces with the transcendental tendencies of Platonism.

The name '*El Shaddai*', 'God Almighty,' is represented by the priestly document in the Pentateuch as characteristic of the first stage in redemptive history³.

---

[1] See Neh. ix. 32 foll.; Ezra i. 2; 2 Chron. xxxvi. 23 (Schultz, vol. ii. p. 114).

[2] To blaspheme *the Name* was to blaspheme God as He had revealed Himself through Moses to His people. See Lev. xxiv. 11, 16.

[3] Gen. xvii. 1, xxviii. 3, xxxv. 11; Exod. vi. 3. The name *Shaddai* is also characteristic of the book of Job. See Driver on *Joel*, p. 81.

It denotes a divine power to control or overrule nature in the interests of a providential purpose. It is 'El Shaddai who makes childless Abraham the father of many nations, and supports him in his loneliness among the heathen. The expression obviously marks an advance beyond the notion that the deity is merely strong or powerful ('El), for it suggested the higher moral attributes of God to which His omnipotence is subject. 'El Shaddai was a name that prepared the way for the notion of grace. 'Grace,' observes Delitzsch, 'always raises itself on the foundation of the natural after it has destroyed it; thus the body of Abraham must become *as good as dead* before he could become the father of the son of promise[1].' It is an instructive circumstance that in the hymn of the blessed Virgin the thought contained in 'El Shaddai recurs. *He that is mighty* (ὁ δυνατός) *hath done to me great things, and holy is his name*[2]. Finally, while the title lifts the conception of God high above old polytheistic associations, it also confirms the tradition that the foundations of the true religion had already been securely laid in the pre-Mosaic period. 'El Shaddai had manifested Himself in the separation of Abraham from the falsities of encompassing idolatry, in the guidance and protection vouchsafed to him during a long and chequered career, in the gift of a son when the patriarch was far advanced in years, in the gracious promises made to him and to his seed. And all these blessings were tokens not only of God's favour, but also of His all-sufficing power.

There is another title of God which we are justified in considering at this point, inasmuch as it represents the subjective aspect of the truth implied in 'El Shaddai, I mean the name 'Adonai, 'My lord.' This name appears to express the temper of trustful dependence; the consciousness of being linked to God by a tie which constitutes a continual claim on the

---

[1] *Old Test. History of Redemption*, § 16. Cp. Rom. iv. 19; Heb. xi. 12.
[2] St. Luke i. 49.

divine bounty and protection. The term 'Lord' (*Adon*) is specially used in connexion with two kinds of relationship: that of wife to husband, and that of servant to master[1]. It is not uncommon in prophecy[2]. There are some indications that in the pre-prophetic period the term *Baal*, 'Master,' 'Owner,' or 'Lord,' was occasionally used in the same connexion, but it was naturally repudiated when the worship of Jehovah under this title had become merged in the local cults of the Canaanitish *Baalim*[3]. The name *'Adonai* implies that man's relationship to God is one of loving trust rather than of fear. In it, says a recent writer, ' was couched a strong ethical motive, which becomes influential in Christian ethics, being accentuated especially in the Pauline theology;... the Old Testament saint delighted to call God by the name that helped him to realize that he was both the subject and the property of his Lord[4].'

We now pass to the most important and distinctive designation of God in the Old Testament. The name *Jehovah* (*Jahveh*) may be considered in itself and in its relation to the names of deity already discussed. The title connotes primarily that which differentiates the nature of God from the changeableness and dependence of created being. Jehovah is absolutely self-subsistent and independent. With Him is the fountain of life; He *has life in Himself*. Further, the name points to the future. Jehovah is one whose intercourse with the human race is continuous, living, and progressive. He is a personal being who in free self-determination can manifest Himself to man according as His purpose may require, whether in a moral law, or in deeds of power, or in acts of forgiveness and beneficence. Thus,

---

[1] Cp. Jukes, *The Names of God*, pp. 114 foll.
[2] אדני Isa. vi. 1, xxi. 16, xxix. 13. האדון Isa. x. 16, 33, &c. Cp. Schultz, ii. 129.
[3] Cp. Hos. ii. 8, 13; and see Robertson Smith, *Religion of the Semites*, p. 95; and Robertson, *Early Religion of Israel*, pp. 171–173.
[4] W. S. Bruce, *Ethics of the O. T.* p. 44.

O

when contrasted with '*Elohim*, the title signifies a being who continuously unveils Himself in history, as opposed to a supra-mundane power once for all manifested in nature; on the other hand, the title supplements the thought of omnipotent power (*'El Shaddai*) by that of covenantal love. The notion of grace from the first qualifies the attributes of a merely national deity. The appellations which the heathen gave to their deities, *Baal*, *Milcom*, and the like, point to little more than a relationship of abject dependence. The title *Jehovah*, on the contrary, implies that God's dealings with His people are not those of mere arbitrary sovereignty, but those of covenantal love[1].

And at this point let us observe the special significance of the fact that it is in connexion with this name that anthropomorphic expressions are most frequently employed. The personality of God is emphasized by phrases borrowed from the common actions and bodily motions of men. We hear of the 'mouth' of Jehovah speaking, the 'hand' of Jehovah being outstretched, the 'voice' of Jehovah shaking the wilderness, the 'eyes' of Jehovah running to and fro through the whole earth. 'The Old Testament writers,' says Schultz, 'speak like materialists, simply because they have not yet clearly apprehended the distinction between spirit and matter[2].' What they are concerned to maintain is something more important for religion than any philosophical or speculative conception of Godhead, namely, the truth that the Creator is a living person who thinks, purposes, wills, and chooses[3]. They

---

[1] Kittel, *Hist. of the Hebrews*, vol. i. p. 246. Renan, *Histoire du peuple d'Israël*, bk. i, ch. 3, remarks that 'religious abjection was repulsive' to the primitive Semites 'and this fine feeling afterwards brought its reward.'
[2] *O. T. Theol.* ii. 107.
[3] Riehm, *ATl. Theologie*, p. 61 : 'Dass nun Jahve *Personenname* des Gottes Israels ist und die Vorstellung Gottes als eines freien, selbstbewussten und sich selbst bestimmenden *Ichs* mit ihm sich verknüpft, dafür ist ein augenfälliges Zeugniss, dass mit diesem Gottesnamen in der Regel die Anthropomorphismen und Anthropopathismen ... verbunden sind, während sich *Elohim* in solcher Verbindung selten findet.' Origen defends the anthropopathic language of Scripture against Celsus as illustrating the divine condescension. See *c. Cels.* iv. 71 : 'As

interpret deity by the highest category within their reach, and though their phraseology is sometimes incongruous, it is perfectly consistent with their purely religious aim and interest. It is, moreover, significant that precisely in those later passages of the Old Testament which insist most impressively upon the divine transcendence and freedom from the limitations of creaturely existence, we find the most unrestricted use of anthropomorphic language. In no other way could the fundamental postulate of Hebrew religion, the personality of God, be clearly enforced; while from the Christian standpoint the habitual employment of such phraseology may be regarded as an element in the educational process by which humanity was being prepared for the advent of the Word made flesh.

The name *Jehovah*, then, embraces all that God has made known of Himself in His successive dealings with His chosen people; the content of it, so to speak, is unfolded by the advancing experience of the faithful. Thus it happens that the compilers of the records of revelation occasionally seem to make a point of identifying Jehovah with other manifestations of the divine Being. In the phrase *Jehovah Elohim*, which is characteristic of a small section of the Pentateuch[1], and is frequently employed by Ezekiel, Jehovah is identified with the Creator of the universe; in the expression *Jehovah God most high*[2], Jehovah is acknowledged to be supreme in majesty and in His claim to Israel's homage and adoration. To Hagar,

---

we ourselves when talking with very young children do not aim at exerting our own power of eloquence, but, adapting ourselves to the weakness of our charge, both say and do those things which may appear to us useful for the correction and improvement of the children as children; so the Word of God appears to have dealt with the history, making the capacity of the hearers, and the benefit which they were to receive, the standard of the appropriateness of its announcements [respecting God].' In *de Orat.* xxiii. he says that the passages which ascribe corporeal acts or conditions to deity μεταληπτέον πρεπόντως ταῖς μεγάλαις καὶ πνευματικαῖς ἐννοίαις περὶ θεοῦ. Cp. Novatian, *de Trin.* vi-ix.

[1] Gen. ii. and iii.; Exod. ix. 30.   [2] Gen. xiv. 22.

Abraham's bondmaid, Jehovah manifests Himself as *the living one who seeth*[1]. This wonderful expression is one which makes us pause. *The living one!*[2] the home and source of life, the being whose will is that all His creatures should share in His inexhaustible fullness of life, who is utterly separated from all that is dead, or formal, or mechanical, or unspiritual[3]. Such passages as Psalm cxv, or Isaiah xliv, develope in detail the thought of the measureless interval that parts Jehovah from idols, *the work of men's hands*. Nor is Jehovah only a living person; He is *'El 'Olam*[4], 'the everlasting God,' unchangeable in character, persistently fulfilling His purpose of grace throughout age-long dispensations of mercy and power. It corresponds with the thought of the continuity of Jehovah's work that He is described by titles which define His special relation to the elect people. He is the *God of Shem, God of the Hebrews, God of the fathers, God of Abraham, Isaac, and Jacob*—phrases which seem to imply that the worship of Jehovah was already traditional before the time of Moses. Nor must we overlook the expression which is the very charter of the Mosaic religion, *Jehovah the God of Israel*. The more developed form of this last title, *the Holy One of Israel*, has special importance as marking a stage in the evolution of Israel's faith into a universal religion, a moment of transition when the idea of Jehovah's uniqueness as the object of Israel's devotion passes into that of His moral perfection as revealed in the Law and in the work of grace. First employed, as it would seem, by Isaiah, the name gathers up all that Israel might have learned touching the character of

---

[1] Gen. xvi. 13, 14.
[2] Cp. Josh. iii. 10; 1 Sam. xvii. 26, 36; Deut. iv. 28; v. 26; Ps. xxxvi. 9; xlii. 2, 8; Jer. ii. 13; x. 10, &c. Cp. the phrase *The Lord liveth*.
[3] Contrast the frequent phrase applied to idols, אלילים. Lev. xix. 4; Ps. xcvii. 7; Isa. ii. 18, 20; x. 10; xix. 1, 3; Ezek. xxx. 13. Cp. Ps. cvi. 28.
[4] Gen. xxi. 33. Cp. Jukes, *Names of God*, pp. 138-141. See also Ps. xc. 2; 1 Tim. i. 17.

Jehovah in the pre-prophetic period: His love in separating unto Himself a peculiar people, His moral requirement revealed in the Law, His abhorrence of ceremonial worship divorced from righteous conduct. When it was first proclaimed, the name served a double purpose: it was intended at once to alarm and to console. Jehovah's holiness was a principle which must assert itself at once in the chastisement of Israel's sins, and in the overthrow of their oppressors [1].

The above illustrations sufficiently prove that in the view of the Old Testament writers Jehovah can only be fully apprehended, under a large diversity of names or attributes; and it has been truly remarked that this very fact implies that Jewish monotheism is not of a bare and merely abstract character, like the doctrine of Islam. 'The idea of God is not a bare unit'; the divine nature 'involves diversity as well as unity[2]'; and from the idea of a diversity of external relationships, a short step leads to the conception of a being who possesses in the fullness of His own self-sufficing life internal relationship of love.

There appear to be successive stages discernible in the manifestation of Jehovah's attributes. As we have already seen, He is revealed first as 'holy,' that is, absolutely 'separate' from the world; and by His gracious severance of Israel from Egypt He consecrates to Himself a people to share His holiness. *Ye shall be holy unto me: for I the Lord am holy, and have severed you from other people, that ye should be mine* [3]. Under the discipline of the Law, which awakened and educated the sense of moral shortcoming, the prophetic spirit in Israel gradually elucidated the ethical meaning of holiness as involving separation from sin. But already, at an early point in the history, an explicit manifestation of Jehovah's character was elicited by the very fact of Israel's unfaithfulness. It

---

[1] Cp. Kirkpatrick, *The Doctrine of the Prophets*, pp. 175 foll.
[2] Caird, *The Philosophy of Religion*, p. 312. [3] Lev. xx. 26.

should be noticed that the wonderful declaration of the Name of Jehovah recorded in Exod. xxxiv, stands in close connexion with the account of Israel's first signal act of apostasy, the making of the golden calf. The exact nature and degree of the nation's guilt in this matter is not a point which concerns us here. It is sufficiently evident that the compiler of the narrative intended to suggest a close connexion between Israel's guilt and the self-revelation of God which was occasioned by it. Let us devote a few minutes' attention to the great passage in question. *Jehovah,* we read, *passed by before him, and proclaimed, Jehovah, Jehovah Elohim, merciful and gracious, longsuffering, and abundant in goodness and truth, keeping mercy for thousands, forgiving iniquity and transgression and sin, and that will by no means clear the guilty; visiting the iniquity of the fathers upon the children, and upon the children's children, unto the third and to the fourth generation* [1].

Here are described two sides of the divine character, which may be said to constitute two permanent and complementary elements in the Old Testament conception of God. On the one hand, the passage ascribes to Jehovah the attribute of truth or righteousness; on the other, that of kindness or grace [2].

1. First, then, Jehovah is righteous and true [3]. These two attributes, if not precisely synonymous, do at least mutually explain each other. The attribute of 'righteousness' denotes the moral exactitude with which Jehovah necessarily acts and judges. He deals with men by rule and measure—by the standard of His own moral perfection. He requites them according to their deeds; He fulfils His purposes in perfect accordance with His threats and promises; He is ever mindful of that which He has pledged Himself to perform, ever true to the character which He has already

---

[1] Exod. xxxiv. 6, 7.
[2] 'Die beiden entgegengesetzten Pole des Wesens Gottes.' (Riehm, p. 62.)
[3] On צדיק, צדקה, see Schultz, ii. 152; Gesenius, *Lexicon*, s. v.

made known. The word 'truth¹' or 'faithfulness' answers to 'righteousness' as subjective to objective, implying the fidelity, stability, dependableness of the divine character. In Jehovah man finds that on which he may lean with confidence, security, and hope. Faithfulness is, in fact, an attribute of God before it is an element in true human goodness; and there is no attribute of God more frequently alluded to and more trustfully appealed to, throughout the records of Israel's troubled history, than this of the divine faithfulness. It finds expression in such ancient designations of God as *the Rock* ². In a world of movement and change, as contrasted with the transitoriness and mutability of man, the divine character is fixed, permanent, and changeless. It is poetically likened to those immense landmarks in nature which endure when countless generations of men are no more. *Thy righteousness*, cries the psalmist, *is like the mountains of God*³. Nay, *Before the mountains were brought forth, or ever the earth and the world were made, thou art God from everlasting and world without end*. Thus the persistence and self-consistency of Jehovah is regarded in a moral light as the necessary condition of His moral government, and as the stable foundation of the divine kingdom.

2. On the other hand, God is gracious and merciful, full of lovingkindness and of pity for the penitent, the suffering, the oppressed. It is this side of the divine character which manifests itself on the occasion of Israel's wilful apostasy. It is the deepest and most enduring element in Jehovah's nature⁴. The most expressive term denoting this attribute is *cheṣed*, 'grace' or 'lovingkindness,' which, though frequently applied to man, belongs primarily to Jehovah ⁵. One of the

¹ אמת, אמונה. Cp. Schultz, ii. 156.
² צור. See especially Deut. xxxii. 4; cp. Num. i. 5, 6, 10; iii. 35.
³ Ps. xxxvi. 6. Cp. xc. 2.
⁴ Cp. Robertson, *Early Religion of Israel*, pp. 323 foll.; Schultz, ii. 159.
⁵ As applied to man, חסד means (1) the piety or covenant-love of Israel towards Jehovah, (2) brotherly kindness between man and man.

first of the eighth-century prophets, Hosea, conceives of Israel's entire history as a love-story. The only metaphor which can express the tenderness of Jehovah's dealings with His wayward people is borrowed from the marriage-tie. God's love for Israel has been like that of a husband for the erring wife of his youth. But the conception of the divine lovingkindness was broadened by experience. It came to be understood that the attribute was proper to Jehovah, not merely as Israel's God, but as Creator. The glory and beauty of creation, the providential care displayed towards even the lowest creatures, testified to the creative goodness and compassion of God; in the book of Jonah the divine pity is extended even to the heathen world, which Israel held in such abhorrence. Indeed, as Israel's religious consciousness developed, it came to be understood that the most fundamental and far-reaching attribute in the character of Jehovah was lovingkindness. This seems to be clearly proved by the frequency with which the great passage in Exodus is alluded to in other books of the Old Testament. Three of the minor prophets, Jonah, Micah, and Nahum, are linked together by their common interest in it[1]; and in such a psalm as the hundred and third, its characteristic teaching is beautifully and richly expanded.

It is a direct consequence of Jehovah's love that He is also represented as jealous[2]. Jealousy in God is the zeal of outraged love. In the Mosaic period we cannot but recognize the imperfectly moral conception formed of Jehovah's character. The wrathful and fiery elements of the divine nature are regarded as the most prominent. The anger of Jehovah is kindled by any infringement of covenant-conditions; it blazes forth with sudden vehemence at the least outrage done to His honour[3]. It has even been maintained

---

[1] See Jonah iv. 2; Mic. vii. 18; Nahum i. 3. Cp. Riehm, p. 63.
[2] אל קנא. Num. xxv. 11; Deut. iv. 24; v. 9; vi. 15, &c.
[3] Cp. Montefiore, *Hibbert Lectures*, pp. 38, 39; and see Robertson

that the conception of Jehovah marks a retrograde step in the evolution of the doctrine of God; that the patriarchal *Elohim* is a more benevolent being than the *Jehovah* of Moses and the prophets [1].

It may be replied, however, that the primitive idea of Jehovah's wrath as roused by even the slightest disregard of His holiness, marks a necessary stage in the education of the human conscience; it is the first step towards the development of the sense of sin. To the prophets the anger of Jehovah means His essential hostility to moral evil; they do not think of it as lightly or quickly aroused: they point to *a day of vengeance* in the future, when the long-delayed judgment of God upon human sin will be manifested [2]. But the distinctive point of the prophetic teaching is that it connects the wrath of Jehovah with the thought of His covenant-love. There are two things by which that wrath is specially provoked: the faithlessness or apostasy of His chosen people, and outrage done to them by others. Thus the metaphor of a marriage-bond subsisting between Jehovah and His people moralizes the older view of the divine wrath. While the prophets denounced the popular delusion of their time, that in any event, and apart from ethical conditions, Jehovah was bound to be on Israel's side, they ascribed to Him a love for Israel that did not exclude, but rather demanded, the occasional display of His holy indignation. While, however, earlier prophets dwell chiefly on the thought of divine jealousy as provoked by Israel's sin, Ezekiel and Zechariah generally regard it as a vindication of Jehovah's personal honour and holiness, which is bound up with Israel's fortunes. Jehovah's anger is righteous jealousy on behalf of those whom He has received into covenant union with Himself. Whoso-

Smith, *Religion of the Semites*, p. 147; Robertson, *Early Religion of Israel*, p. 298.
[1] See Darmesteter, *Les Prophètes d'Israël*, p. 213; Renan, *Histoire du peuple d'Israël*, bk. i. ch. 13.
[2] Cp. Isa. xxxiv. 8; lxi. 2; lxiii. 4; Ps. xciv. 1.

ever touches them *touches the apple of his eye*[1]. His holiness has been profaned by the exile of His people; He has been reproached as though He were unable or unwilling to protect His chosen. But he has *pity for His holy name*, and accordingly He promises to deliver Israel from captivity, and so to *sanctify His great name, which was profaned among the heathen*[2]. Thus since lovingkindness is the dominant element in the being of God, the manifestation of His indignation against Israel's sin is only a transient stage in His dealings with His chosen. In wrath Jehovah remembers His mercy. *For a small moment have I forsaken thee; but with great mercies will I gather thee. In a little wrath I hid my face from thee for a moment; but with everlasting kindness will I have mercy on thee, saith the Lord thy redeemer*[3].

We have now considered the two complementary sides or aspects of Jehovah's revealed character. How deeply they enter into the theology of the Old Testament may be gathered from the fact that the divine 'kindness' and 'truth' are habitually co-ordinated in Israel's hymns of praise and in prophetic visions of the future. The short Psalm cxvii, for example, has been said to embody 'the essence of all Messianic psalms.' *O praise the Lord, all ye heathen: praise him, all ye nations. For his merciful kindness is ever more and more towards us: and the truth of the Lord endureth for ever*[4]. And we may observe that in the 'truth' and 'kindness' of the Old Testament conception of Jehovah is contained a pledge and

---

[1] Zech. ii. 8. Cp. Deut. xxxii. 21, 22, 36. The phrase 'to be jealous for' is apparently first used in the prophetic period; see Zech. i. 14, viii. 2.

[2] Ezek. xxxvi. 21-24. See Kirkpatrick, *The Doctrine of the Prophets*, pp. 339, 340.

[3] Isa. liv. 7, 8.

[4] Cp. Pss. xl. 10 foll.; lxi. 7; lxxxv. 10; lxxxix. passim; cxv. 1, &c. See the combination of ἔλεος and ἀλήθεια in Rom. xv. 8, 9. Obs. The abbreviated form *Jah* expresses in a concentrated form all essential elements of Jehovah's revealed character. It is found in Exod. xv. 2; Ps. lxviii. 4; Isa. xii. 2, and especially in the Hallelu-jah.

prophecy of One in whom should be manifested the fullness of *grace and truth*[1]; who should be at once the author of a perfect redemption and of a final revelation: manifesting God as love and as light.

There is yet one more title of God peculiar to the Old Testament which needs some notice, viz. *Jehovah Tsebaoth*. This name seems to have arisen as the result of prolonged national experience, since it commemorates the visible proofs which Jehovah had given of His presence with the armies of Israel. The title, so far as we can judge, was specially prominent during the period of the monarchy, the victories of Israel's kings over the heathen being looked upon as pledges of Jehovah's sovereignty over a hostile world. It was 'a name of memories and triumphs,' and perhaps came to be regarded as that title of Israel's God to which a ruined state or church might most fittingly appeal in times of national distress. The frequency of its occurrence in the writings of Isaiah, and in the books of the three post-exilic minor prophets, is significant. There are, however, clear tokens of expansion in the use of the name *Jehovah Tsebaoth*; for while in the early historical books it has military and national associations, in the prophets it includes the hosts of heaven, the stars and angels, as well as the armies of Israel[2]. The post-exilic use of the title accordingly marks a striking advance. 'The old popular notion,' says Prof. Cheyne, 'of a territorial and local deity had faded away, and the traditional names of God had received an ampler meaning. Jehovah was not merely *the God of the armies of Israel*, but the God of all the hosts of heaven ... and of all the forces of nature.' Thus, in such a psalm as the twenty-fourth, the psalmist 'is really thinking of the triumph of the omnipotent God in His holy

---

[1] John i. 14.
[2] See Robertson, *Early Religion of Israel*, note xvi (p. 583); König, *The Religion of Israel*, pp. 89 foll.

temple. *Who is this King of glory? Jehovah of hosts, he is the King of glory*[1].

Within the Old Testament itself we find a distinct approach to the doctrine of the divine fatherhood. As applied to God the term '*Father*' quickly loses any physical associations that may have originally attached to it, and comes to denote the relationship of 'love and moral communion in which Jehovah has placed Israel.' God is the 'Father' or 'Creator' of Israel in the sense that by divine acts of power and grace He brought the nation into special relation to Himself[2]; or it is used with a personal reference to the theocratic king, who was the official representative of the people and inherited the promises originally vouchsafed to David and his house. It seems to be a title suggestive of the close and continuous relationship in which Jehovah had stood to Israel; it would recall memories of divine protection, help, and guidance, and of the condescension manifested in Israel's prolonged spiritual education[3]. In the later Judaism we mark an advance: God is conceived as a pitying Father, whose compassion extends to those that fear Him. *Yea, like as a father pitieth his own children, even so is Jehovah merciful unto them that fear him*[4]. Yes; but only to those who fear Him. The limitation is characteristic. Judaism recognizes indeed that God, the Father of Israel as a nation, is also the Father of Israel's faithful sons. The pious Israelite rejoiced in the sense of divine favour. 'He was gladly conscious,' says Mr. Montefiore, 'that God was cognizant of all, and cared not only for His people in the mass, but for every unit of which it was composed[5].' But outside the pale of love were the godless

---

[1] *Aids to the Devout Study of Criticism*, pp. 284, 285.
[2] Cp. Exod. iv. 22; Deut. xxxii. 6; xiv. 2; Hos. xi. 1.
[3] Cp. Riehm, *ATl. Theologie*, p. 227. Observe the title 'son' used of Israel (Deut. viii. 5; xiv. 1; Mal. i. 6; Jer. iii. 19; xxxi. 10; Isa. i. 4; xxx. 1, 9) implies corresponding national obligations. The individual Israelite could not appropriate the name for himself.
[4] Ps. ciii. 13.
[5] *Hibbert Lectures*, p. 463; cp. pp. 539 foll.

members of the nation itself and the heathen world in general. It was only through the revelation of the incarnate Son that men could be brought to apprehend the universality of the divine Fatherhood[1]. As Tertullian tersely remarks, *Nobis [nomen Dei] revelatum est in Filio.* In concluding this lecture, let us acknowledge the debt which theology owes to the evolutionary conception of Israel's history and theology. It seems to be the object of writers like König to minimize, or even to question altogether, this conception. But all analogy forbids us to suppose that the religion of Israel was revealed in its completeness from the very first. The metaphors by which in the Old Testament God's relationship to Israel is described point to a very different conclusion, suggesting a view of the divine action which is at once supremely worthy of God and consistent with all that we know of His methods and character. Historical science professes to trace the process of revelation, and its account in the main we can scarcely hesitate to accept. The tribal God becomes the God of a nation, and finally the God of the universe. Each advance in man's moral receptivity renders possible a further disclosure of the divine nature. All that is debased, crude, limited, or ethically defective in the earliest Semitic ideas of deity gradually falls away, until in the fullness of time man is enabled to recognize *the glory of God*, His essential character, His eternal attributes, *in the face of Jesus Christ*[2]. Thus we find that critical science does, after all, vindicate for Jesus Christ the position which He claims for Himself. He came to crown a long ascent, to fulfil anticipations which His own Spirit had inspired. In the Old Testament the record of the divine preparation for His coming lies before us. It describes the different stages in the progressive manifestation of God; it exhibits the actual and living

---

[1] Cp. Westcott, *The Historic Faith*, p. 35. Cp. Tert. *de orat.* iii.
[2] 2 Cor. iv. 6. Cp. Meinhold, *Jesus und das A. T.* p. 139.

operation of those divine attributes which are now, as
ever, the hope, the support, and the solace of the
individual soul. A gifted French writer has spoken
mournfully of 'a cry which fills our age—the cry of the
orphan who no longer possesses a Father in heaven to
speak to him and guide him. It rings from one end of
the century to the other; it makes itself heard beneath
the tumult of wars and revolutions, the triumphant
declarations of science, the sarcasms of egotism and
scepticism, the ceaseless murmur of life as it passes on
its course [1].' Nay, the truth of the divine Fatherhood
is not lost. It is overclouded indeed and obscured by
the apparent rigour of Nature, by the discoveries of
science, by the appalling catastrophes which sometimes
overwhelm us with the sense of our frailty, our
ignorance, our helplessness. Nevertheless in God,
God Almighty, the Lord Jehovah, the Father revealed
in the passion and resurrection of Jesus, the Father
who watches over even the least of His children with
wise providence, with discriminating tenderness, the
burdened and perplexed heart of man may find refuge
and rest. For the divine self-manifestation, even if it
fails to satisfy all our questionings, is at least co-
extensive with our needs. Blessed indeed is he to
whom, as to Moses, the unfolding of the ineffable
Name is a fact of personal experience; whose ear has
caught amid the tumults and distractions of time the
accents of the eternal voice whispering to the soul,
*I will make all my goodness pass before thee, and
I will proclaim the name of the Lord before thee; and
will be gracious to whom I will be gracious, and will
show mercy on whom I will show mercy* [2].

[1] Darmesteter, *Les Prophètes d'Israël*, pref. p. iii.
[2] Exod. xxxiii. 19.

LECTURE V

Gather my saints together unto me; those that have made a covenant with me by sacrifice.—Ps. l, 5.

BOTH in this psalm, and in some passages that might be quoted from the prophets, we observe how the devout Israelite gradually awoke to a consciousness of those spiritual realities which were symbolized by the external institutions of his religion. The fiftieth psalm, and perhaps the fortieth and fifty-first, seem to mark a new stage in the development of inward religion, when the practice of the sacrificial system had already ceased in great measure to satisfy the moral needs of men, and had driven them to reflect upon the spiritual truths which the system was intended to foreshadow[1]. A bond such as that which the Israelite believed to exist between his people and Jehovah could be no merely external link of connexion. It was the token of a special relationship between personal and moral beings, implying on one side an act of condescending grace, on the other certain ethical and spiritual obligations. And when the Pentateuch finally attained its present form, the relation between Jehovah and Israel was universally conceived as based upon an original covenant. The deliverance which had resulted in the formation of Israel's nationality was regarded as an act of grace by which the new relationship was established. The covenant was ratified by a sacrifice of victims and by the ceremonial sprinkling of blood. The people on their part accepted the proffered con-

---

[1] Cp. Cheyne, *Aids to the Devout Study of Criticism*, pp. 194 foll.; Westcott, *Ep. to the Hebrews*, p. 225.

ditions: *all that the Lord hath said will we do and be obedient*; and when the solemn formalities were finally completed, chosen representatives of the nation—Moses, Aaron and his two sons, together with seventy of the elders of Israel—were admitted to a mysterious communion with Deity; they were called to participate in the feast and the vision which were, so to speak, a foretaste of the entrancing delights of the divine kingdom [1]. Thus at the very outset of its national history Israel was subjected to a law of obedience as the indispensable condition of fulfilling its high destiny. It was taught that covenantal union with God demanded a special character in man. The principle was for ever established that the great link between God and humanity is the moral law. The Mosaic Law thus retains an essential significance for mankind in virtue of the fundamental idea which it embodies. We may study the Pentateuch with a keen historical or archaeological interest, but critical investigations must never blind us to the fact that the Law witnesses mainly to a spiritual truth, viz. that in the life of fellowship between God and man, moral obligation is the master fact. The central principle of the entire levitical system is comprehended in the words, *Ye shall be holy, for I the Lord your God am holy* [2].

At the same time, no one, I think, can read the twenty-fourth chapter of Exodus without a very strong impression of its idealistic character. There are few passages in the Old Testament so mysterious, so sublime, so prophetic. The bare mention of a solemn slaughter of sacrificial victims and of a meal symbolizing covenant fellowship does not carry us beyond the limits of ordinary historical fact. But the description of the mysterious vision of God and of the feast in His presence can only be a mode of symbolical representation, foreshadowing a future spiritual consummation, recorded for our admonition who look and wait for a time when *his servants shall serve him and shall*

---

[1] Exod. xxiv. Cp. Jer. vii. 21 foll.   [2] Lev. xix. 2; cp. xi. 44; xx. 7.

see his face; when they that are called shall sit down at *the marriage supper of the Lamb*[1].

In the present lecture it is proposed to consider (1) the idea of covenant relationship in general; (2) the requirement which this relationship involved; (3) the institutions in which the spiritual truths underlying it found a typical outward embodiment; (4) the fulfilment of the levitical types in Jesus Christ.

I.

For our present purpose, which is theological rather than historical, the questions that have been raised respecting the antiquity of the covenantal idea in Israel's religion are comparatively unimportant. There can be no doubt that the Hebrew tradition of an actual covenant concluded at Sinai between God and Israel is constant and unanimous, nor does there seem to be any convincing reason for setting it aside in favour of the idea that the word 'covenant' in this connexion represents only a later mode of conceiving the Sinaitic revelation. Certainly the thought of Israel's covenant *status* is very prominent in the mind of the author of the priestly document in the Pentateuch. This narrative, which forms the framework of the whole, carries back the tradition of a divinely instituted covenant into the dim prehistoric past. It even regards the relationship of God to the patriarchs as based in each case upon a formal covenant. Three such compacts are in fact mentioned: the first covenant with Noah, the second with Abraham, the third with the newly-formed nation of Israel. In each case there is a distinctive sign. The Noachic covenant is attested by the bow in the cloud; the covenant with Abraham is sealed by the rite of circumcision; the covenant with Israel by the sprinkling of sacrificial blood. Moreover,

---

[1] Rev. xxii. 3, 4; xix. 9.

each covenant had its characteristic obligation, each its accompanying revelation of grace[1]. It is, in short, evident that the covenantal idea was dominant at the period when the Pentateuch was compiled, but there seems to be no sufficient ground for supposing that it was unknown in pre-prophetic times. For our present purpose, however, it is immaterial whether the traditional view is correct, or whether Wellhausen, Stade and others are justified in asserting that the relation between Jehovah and Israel was only thus conceived first in the prophetic period[2]. We are concerned with the total result, as embodied in the Pentateuch, of an historical movement which began with the exodus. It will be generally admitted that, after the exodus, Jehovah instituted between Himself and Israel a special relationship of grace, and that the historical severance from Egypt which constituted Israel the *peculiar people* of Jehovah[3], was intended to symbolize an inward separation from the idolatries and immoralities of the heathen world. The question, however, respecting the mode under which this unique connexion between God and Israel was conceived is, I repeat, one of secondary importance. Hosea, although he uses the word ברית in more than one passage[4], speaks of the relationship under the metaphor of a marriage; while occasionally, like Isaiah, he represents it as an act of divine adoption whereby Israel as a nation became the son of Jehovah[5]. Amos, without employing the *term* 'covenant' in its theological sense, gives prominence to the *idea*, in so far as he emphasizes the moral obligations which the connexion between Jehovah and Israel involved. The same conception was probably emphasized by the reformation which followed the publication of the

---

[1] Cp. Gen. ix. 1-17; xvii. 1-14; Exod. xxiv. 3-8; xxxi. 13-17.
[2] Wellhausen, *Prolegomiena*, 417 foll. Cp. Montefiore, *Hibbert Lectures*, pp. 124 foll. See on the other side, König, *Religion of Israel*, ch. x; Robertson, *Early Religion of Israel*, note xxii, &c.
[3] עַם סְגֻלָּה Exod. xix. 5. Cp. Num. xxiii. 9.
[4] Hos. vi. 7; viii. 1.   [5] Hos. xi. 1; Isa. i. 2; cp. Exod. iv. 22.

Deuteronomic law in the reign of Josiah. There is at any rate no difficulty in accounting for the influence of the idea on the thought of Jeremiah, Ezekiel, and the later Isaiah, and we may reasonably suppose that the exile tended to popularize the conception, and to foster the belief that the continuance of Israel's covenant *status* depended upon the strict maintenance of 'holiness' with all that this might imply.

Such in brief outline is the history, so far as it can be certainly traced, of the idea of a covenant between Jehovah and Israel. The attempt, however, to ascribe its origination to the prophets of the eighth century seems to be based on inconclusive arguments. There is good reason to suppose that the idea had its foundation in pre-prophetic times, for the prophets 'plainly do not regard the conception as an innovation,' and it harmonizes entirely with the distinctively ethical character of Mosaism. Further, the thought constantly recurs that even the legal covenant is essentially a work of grace, prepared for in patriarchal times by a covenant of promise [1]. The initiative comes from Jehovah, who necessarily appoints the conditions upon the observance of which the maintenance of covenant union depends. It is a 'disposition' (διαθήκη) rather than an 'agreement' or contract between two equal parties (συνθήκη); and its basis is purely moral [2]. According to the prophetic survey of the national history which we find in the book of Deuteronomy, the covenant requirement was wholly contained in the Decalogue: *These words the Lord spake unto all your assembly in the mount out of the midst of the fire, of the cloud, and of the thick*

---

[1] Cp. Lev. xxvi. 42; Deut. iv. 31.
[2] Oehler in Herzog, *Real-Encyklopädie* s.v. 'Testament': 'Unterscheidet sich διαθήκη von συνθήκη dadurch, dass bei jener kein rein wechselseitiges Verhältniss stattfindet, sondern von einem der beiden Paciscenten, als dem διαθέμενος, die Initiative und die Feststellung der Vertragsbedingungen ausgeht.' Riehm points out that in this use of διαθήκη is involved the possibility of a transition from the thought of a 'covenant' to that of a 'testament' (*Handwörterbuch des Bibl. Altertums*, s.v. 'Bund').

darkness, with a great voice, and he added no more[1]. The prophetic view manifestly was that the moral element in the Mosaic system was predominant if not exclusive; that the Decalogue, not the ritual law, was its peculiar characteristic. It was in fact the work of Moses to teach Israel two things : first, the significance of the revelation of God's nature and character implied in the events of the exodus; secondly, the truth that the vocation to be Jehovah's people involved a higher and purer morality. It has been justly said that Moses' work as the originator of a higher religion bears the impress of 'a simplicity analogous to the simplicity of Christ[2].' The later prophets recognized that they were called to be continuators of his mission, and in looking back on the forces which had moulded Israel's history, they discerned in the moral law the distinctive feature of the covenant. They strenuously endeavoured to reinstate this law in its original position, and to vindicate its supremacy by applying it as a standard of measurement to the social and political conditions of their age.

But behind the fact of human obligation lay the mystery of redemptive love, deigning to enter into relationship with man. It was this high relationship that was conceived as a covenant, implying as it did both the dignity of human nature and the condescending grace of God. It was in fact such a contract as can only subsist between beings who are united by a pre-existing kinship of nature. Indeed the covenantal idea is most aptly illustrated by actual examples of primitive contracts between man and man. In its essence a covenant did not materially differ from an oath; both were generally accompanied by symbolic ceremonies[3]; both imposed mutual obligations

---

[1] Deut. v. 22 ; cp. Jer. vii. 22.   [2] Bruce, *Apologetics*, p. 222.
[3] On the phrase כרת ברית see Driver on the *Book of Deuteronomy*, iv. 13; Delitzsch, *New Commentary on Genesis*, vol. ii. pp. 13, 14. On the relation between a covenant and an oath see R. Kraetzschmar, *Die Bundesvorstellung im A. T.* (1. Teil), pp. 15, 16.

of service. It was a covenant that linked together in perpetuity friends like Jonathan and David[1]; a covenant that secured a man's fidelity to his betrothed[2]. The prophets were the successive witnesses of the act of divine grace by which the life of divine fellowship and covenant consecration had been initiated. But the Mosaic covenant did but indicate in a rudimentary fashion the true consummation to which the deliverance from Egypt pointed, namely the life of personal friendship between God and man. God reveals Himself in the Decalogue as educating man for that life; to use the striking phrase of Irenaeus, He is seen *praestruens hominem per decalogum in suam amicitiam*[3].

II.

It was then the moral requirement involved in the covenant which formed the basis and distinctive mark of Israel's religion. He who made Himself known to the people in acts of grace and power demanded of them a life conformed to His own character. He required not merely the ordinary expressions of religious homage, but a higher morality, justice, humanity, mercy, and good faith. In other words, at Sinai were laid down the great ethical principles which afterwards became the standard of prophetic religion, and within the lines of which all subsequent *Torah*, all prophetic or priestly instruction, was bound to move[4]. The *knowledge of God*[5] mentioned by Hosea may certainly have embraced legal, civil, and ceremonial decisions,

---

[1] 1 Sam. xviii. 3; xx. 8, 16, 42; xxiii. 18. Cp. Kraetzschmar, p. 20.
[2] Ezek. xvi. 8.   [3] Iren. *Haer.* iv. 16. 3.
[4] Robertson Smith, *O. T. in J. C.* p. 305. Montefiore, *op. cit.* p. 45, says: 'The *Torah*—or teaching—of the priests, half-judicial, half-pedagogic, was a deep moral influence.... There is good reason to suppose that this priestly *Torah* is the one religious institution which can be correctly attributed to Moses. If that be so, then not only did the pre-prophetic religion itself include an important ethical element, but this very element was part and parcel of the original Mosaic teaching,' &c. See generally Wellhausen, *Prolegomena*, ch. x.
[5] Hos. vi. 6.

but, says Wellhausen, 'since its practical issue is that God requires of man righteousness, faithfulness and good-will, it is fundamentally and essentially morality, though morality at that time addressed its demands less to the conscience than to society [1].' Indeed, the practical prominence of social righteousness in the Law, which finds comprehensive expression in the sentence *Thou shalt love thy neighbour as thyself* [2], constitutes a link between 'the prophets and the legalists of Israel, and anticipates with whatever limitations the teaching of the Gospel. It is true that in the development of Hebrew morality there seem to be occasional moments of retrogression. For instance, the intense hatred of foreigners and the exaggerated spirit of nationalism does not appear to have prevailed to the same extent in the pre-exilic period as in subsequent times. The older legislation appears in some respects to breathe a higher spirit than the later; and a similar contrast may be traced between the earlier and the later prophecy, between the universalistic utterances of an Isaiah and the tone of such books as those of Daniel, the Chronicles, Ezra and Nehemiah [3]. The fact is that different elements in the religious character became prominent in different ages, nor was the spirit of any particular period strictly uniform or consistent. In the post-exilic period, for example, the germs are discernible of the temper which gradually developed into Pharisaism, the anxious and scrupulous spirit which aimed at strict legal obedience and careful conformity to a code of minute external ordinances. But at the same time this very period awakened the spiritual joy, fervour, and devotion, the filial delight in God and in His worship, which is reflected in the Psalter. It produced also a type of teaching which laid stress on charity to those in need, and on 'the doing of kindnesses' as the chief of human duties [4].

---
[1] *Prolegomena*, p. 395.
[2] Lev. xix. 17.   [3] See Schultz, *O. T. Theology*, vol. ii. p. 61 foll.
[4] See Schechter, *Studies in Judaism*, no. ix, and Montefiore's *Hibbert Lectures*, no. ix, on ' The Law and its Influence.'

The mature fruit of the Law only appeared in an age of violent contrasts, the character of which we are sometimes apt to misconceive. Legalism had its beautiful and beneficent, as well as its baneful and harsh consequences. But if it be true of later Judaism that 'morality penetrated through Jewish society and was a potent link or bridge between class and class[1],' we must trace this result far back to the character once for all impressed on Hebrew religion by Moses, whose 'great merit,' says Kuenen, 'lies in the fact of his connexion of the religious idea with the moral life[2].'

It seems natural at this point to consider somewhat more in detail the *ten words of the covenant*[3], in which the will of God for His elect people finds its most simple and universal expression. The Decalogue indeed has been proved by experience to be a comprehensive summary of human duty. It defines in broad outlines the conditions of a right relation to God and to all that He has made[4].

But first a word is necessary on the question of the antiquity of the Decalogue. We have already noticed that its Mosaic authorship has been questioned mainly on two grounds: first, the uncertainty as to the precise contents of the ten words alluded to in Exodus xxxiv. 27, 28; secondly, the fact that the second commandment seems to be practically unknown until the time of Hezekiah's reformation, when the long-established

---

[1] Montefiore, p. 547. [2] *Religion of Israel*, i. p. 282.
[3] Exod. xxxiv. 28. Cp. Deut. iv. 13; x. 14. In some passages (e. g. Exod. xxv. 16, 21) the Decalogue is called 'the testimony,' (העדות) i. e. the declaration of Jehovah's will. So the ark which contained the tables of stone is called 'The ark of Jehovah's covenant' (Deut. x. 8).
[4] Iren. *Haer.* iv. 15. 1: 'Nam Deus primo quidem per naturalia praecepta quae ab initio infixa dedit hominibus admonens eos, id est per decalogum, nihil plus ab eis exquisivit.' Ibid. 16. 3 : 'Similiter permanent apud nos, extensionem et augmentum sed non dissolutionem accipientia per carnalem Ejus adventum.' Cp. T. Aquin. *Summa Theologiae*, i. ii^{ae}. qu. 100, art. 3: 'Omnia praecepta [moralia] legis sunt quaedam partes praeceptorum decalogi.' See also Riehm, *ATl. Theologie*, § 14; Schultz, *O. T. Theology*, ii. 46 foll.; W. S. Bruce, *The Ethics of the O. T.* ch. vi.

cult of the brazen serpent was finally abolished. There are other more subjective arguments alleged: e. g. that the monotheistic idea embodied in the code is too pronounced to be considered primitive, and that the universality of its moral teaching is incompatible with the notion of an early date [1]. Into the merits of this contention I do not propose to enter at length. It may be observed, however, that even those who abandon the Mosaic authorship of the Decalogue assign to its substance a very high antiquity, and agree in holding that the main element in the teaching of Moses was ethical. In other words, it is generally admitted that the morality of the Decalogue was a factor in Israel's religion from the first. At most the Mosaic origin of one particular commandment is questioned [2]. It seems to me then that the traditional view, even if it has to be slightly modified, is essentially justifiable. Since, however, our present concern is not so much with historical and critical questions as with the moral and spiritual use of the Old Testament, there is the less need to go behind the ordinary belief respecting the origin of the Decalogue. We have simply to review its intrinsic character and importance viewed as the charter, so to speak, of Old Testament religion. The ten commandments fall most naturally into two pentads [3], the fifth in each case having a close connexion with the four preceding 'words.' The first table regulates those duties which result from the spiritual relationship to his Creator into which man finds himself called. The first 'word' warns Israel to be faithful and loyal in the service of its Redeemer, and to regard

---

[1] See Wellhausen's *Sketch of the History of Israel and Judah*, p. 21, and Montefiore, *Hibbert Lectures*, Appendix, pp. 553 foll. Delitzsch, *New Commentary on Genesis*, vol. i. pp. 29 foll., touches briefly on the subject.

[2] Kuenen accepts the Mosaic authorship of the Decalogue, regarding Exod. xx. 2 as the 'first word' and xx. 4–6 as a later expansion of the 'second word' (xx. 3). (*Religion of Israel*, ch. v [E. T. vol. i. pp. 285 foll.].)

[3] This method of division which is adopted by Philo and Josephus is commended by Rom. xiii. 9, and by the fact that the first five 'words' are enforced by reasons.

Him for all purposes of worship as the one and only God[1]. The second directs that the worship paid to God shall be in accordance with His true character; it prohibits the deification of nature, or such sensualism as would entangle the Creator in mundane conditions. Especially noticeable is the revelation of God as jealous. Ewald remarks that heathenism drew a distinction between the loving and the avenging deity. Whereas Aeschylus, for example, believes in two orders of gods—the powers of vengeance and those which make for mercy, the Old Testament leads us to conceive the jealousy of Jehovah as the heat of outraged goodness and love. The third 'word' teaches the holiness of God as revealed to Israel. His name, that is the expression of His revealed character, is to be held in honour, and not to be used lightly, falsely, or without just occasion. The fourth 'word' by its injunction to 'remember' indicates that Israel already inherited a tradition in regard to the observance of the seventh day. But the command to sanctify the day is characteristic. It lifts an ancient Semitic custom to a new dignity, consecrating it to be a symbol of covenant union between Jehovah and Israel[2]. The commandment in effect lays the foundation of all Israel's ordinances of worship. At the same time it provides for the due recreation of that human nature which by creative right belongs to God and is destined for communion with Him. The fifth commandment closing the series gives a religious sanction to family relationship. It implies that the authority of parents is a counterpart of the divine authority. Reverence for an earthly father or mother is a special form of the fear of God[3]. In later legislation the commandment appears to be extended so as to include what we may call spiritual parentage: special precepts enjoin the duty of respect towards old age, and reverence towards magis-

---

[1] Riehm, *A Tl. Theologie*, p. 83: 'Tritt JHVH nur als Nationalgott Israels den Göttern andrer Völker gegenüber mit dem Ausspruch, dass Israel ihn ausschliesslich verehre.'
[2] Cp. Meinhold, *Jesus und das A. T.* p. 71.
[3] Cp. Lev. xix. 3 and 32.

trates and rulers[1], who share the honour due to Him in whose stead they administer justice. Thus the whole social order is securely based on the regulation of family life, and the institutions of government are invested with a sacrosanct character.

The second table deals with duties towards fellow-men, and 'gives to social ethics the sanction of religion[2]': it enjoins respect for the life and property of others, and guards the sacredness of the marriage bond. The ninth commandment probably implies not the duty of truthfulness and integrity in general, so much as that of abstinence from any false oath or declaration which might involve detriment to a neighbour's life or property. The concluding 'word' embodies the principle which was destined to be expanded in the New Testament: the close connexion between act and thought. 'The revealed law,' says Oehler, 'here undertakes the functions of conscience. . . . By bringing man to a consciousness of the essential nature of a higher divine righteousness the Law roused the conscience from its slumber, taught the knowledge of evil as sin, and so awoke the need of reconciliation with God[3].' The tenth commandment virtually anticipates that 'inwardness' which specially characterizes the morality of the New Testament, and it is instructive to remember the function which it discharged in the moral education of St. Paul: *I had not known sin but by the law: for I had not known lust except the law had said, Thou shalt not covet*[4].

Some general observations may be made touching the character of the Decalogue and the relation in which it stands to the rest of the Mosaic legislation.

---

[1] Prophets are hailed as 'father,' Judges v. 7; 2 Kings ii. 12; xiii. 14. Cp. Ps. xxxiv. 11. Rulers have the same title; Gen. xlv. 8. Cp. Lev. xix. 32, and Exod. xxii. 28; Ps. lxxxii. 6. In the N. T. cp. Rom. xiii. 1–7.
[2] W. S. Bruce, *op. cit.* p. 136.
[3] *Theol. of the O. T.* vol. i. p. 266. Cp. R. W. Dale, *The Ten Commandments*, p. 241. Obs. Some suppose that 'coveting' implies an actual attempt to get possession by fraud or force or false pretence of another's property. See e. g. Schultz, ii. 52, and cp. Mark x. 19, μὴ ἀποστερήσῃς.
[4] Rom. vii. 7.

1. First we notice that the Decalogue makes religion the foundation of all personal morality and social duty or right. Human duty is here based on the revelation of God's character. The first table recalls to Israel's recollection the redemptive grace which as a nation it had actually experienced. The gracious acts of Jehovah are set forth partly as an incentive to gratitude, partly as a motive to obedience. The prophetic writer of Deuteronomy dwells on the essential unity of the moral law viewed as a law of love: *And now, Israel, what doth the Lord thy God require of thee but to fear the Lord thy God, to walk in all his ways, and to love him, and to serve the Lord thy God with all thy heart and with all thy soul*[1]? This is the point at which Hebrew and Christian ethics practically meet each other. Augustine remarks that the most pregnant and obvious distinction between the two Testaments lies in the fact that the one inculcates fear, the other love; the one points men to a schoolmaster whom they are to fear, the other to a master whom they may love[2]. He is thinking of the prohibitory form of the Decalogue, which of course corresponds to its paedagogic function as part of a primary course of instruction. The will of God, before it can educate that of man, necessarily comes into collision with his natural propensity to evil. There was indeed a law written on the heart of man, but all moral education must begin with definite restriction of undisciplined desire. Augustine, however, seems to overlook for the moment a feature in the Decalogue which lifts it, so to speak, to the New Testament level. The appeal of love lies behind the command to obey. *I am the Lord thy God, which have brought thee out of the land of Egypt, out of the house of bondage.* Jehovah introduces His law by a declaration of His saving

---

[1] Deut. x. 12; cp. vi. 5 foll.
[2] Exod. xx. 2. See Aug. *c. Adimant. Manich. discip.* i. 17; cp. *de util. cred.* 3: 'Ille igitur paedagogum dedit hominibus quem timerent, qui magistrum postea quem diligerent.'

grace, of the compassion which makes so great a claim on the affections and wills of the redeemed. Thus the vital and informing principle of the obedience enjoined in both Old and New Testaments is one: *Thou shalt love the Lord thy God.* The book of Deuteronomy, while it lays much stress upon the spirit of love and loyalty in which the law is to be ideally fulfilled, appears in two points especially to anticipate the teaching of the New Testament: it makes religion consist in devotion of heart[1], and it points to the sphere of moral duty as one near and accessible to all: *The word is very nigh unto thee, in thy mouth and in thy heart, that thou mayest do it.* It has been remarked that the teaching of Deuteronomy is most closely akin to that of Hosea[2]. Certainly in the simplicity of its view of religion, in the conception that the service of God fundamentally consists in a life of active love, Deuteronomy brings us to the very threshold of the Gospel[3]. The history of subsequent prophetic activity shows how immense was the influence of this book in fixing a standard not only of external observance by which the actions of men were to be judged, but also of inward devotion towards which individual souls might aspire. The secret, however, of the appealing beauty that pervades the book lies in its prophetic insistence upon the electing love which lay behind the covenant and its legislation[4].

2. Another striking feature of the Decalogue is the absence of any directions bearing upon worship[5]. Only one commandment, the fourth, provides for

---

[1] See Deut. vi. 2, 5; x. 12, 16; xi. 1, 13, 22; xiii. 4; xix. 9. For the characteristic thought of 'circumcision of heart' (x. 16) cp. Jer. iv. 4; Ezek. xliv. 7, 9. See also Riehm, *A Tl. Theologie*, p. 239.

[2] Montefiore, *Hibbert Lectures*, p. 184.

[3] Cp. Hieron. *ep. ad Paulinum*, 9: 'Deuteronomium secunda lex, et Evangelicae legis praefiguratio; nonne sic ea habet quae priora sunt, ut tamen nova sint omnia de veteribus?'

[4] Cp. Deut. vii. 7 foll.

[5] Riehm, *op. cit.* p. 74: 'Keine Opfer, keine Gaben, überhaupt keine bestimmten äusserlichen Kultushandlungen werden im Grundgesetz des Gottesreiches gefordert, sondern nur die ... thatsächliche Anerkennung der Heiligkeit des JHVH angehörigen Tages.'

a positive religious observance. The second 'word' indeed regulates the general character of the national *cultus*. The true worship of God is to be not only monolatrous, but imageless [1]. We have seen that the question has been raised, when this principle was first explicitly affirmed. The choice lies between the supposition that material representations of Jehovah were forbidden by Moses, though the prohibition was to a great extent forgotten or ignored for centuries; and the view that the commandment was first inserted in the Decalogue at the time when the prophets began to protest against the use of images in worship. In favour of the first supposition is the fact that at the official centres of worship like Shiloh, and afterwards Jerusalem, the use of images seems to have been unknown; and it is also certain that the prophets of the eighth century, who believed themselves to be the true exponents of Mosaism, regarded the bull-worship of the northern kingdom as a danger and a snare to Israel, if not an actual form of apostasy from Jehovah [2]. We must not, however, insist too strongly on the significance of these facts. It is enough that the prophets bear witness to the essential characteristics of the Mosaic legislation: first, in their silence as to questions of ritual—a silence which reflects the negative attitude of the ten commandments; secondly, in their positive insistence on social and personal righteousness as Jehovah's sole requirement. Their attitude towards ritual and sacrifice, to say nothing of such explicit statements as that of Jeremiah vii. 22, incontestably

---

[1] Montefiore, p. 127. Renan points out that the nomadic Semite was distinctly lacking in a taste for the plastic arts, and was if anything averse by temperament to the use of images in worship (*Histoire du peuple d'Israël*, bk. i. ch. 4 *init.*). This fact seems to add credibility to the traditional view of the second commandment.

[2] See Montefiore, p. 128. Amos alludes only once, and with indignant contempt, to the bulls of Samaria (viii. 14). But Hosea's attitude is one of strong antagonism. 'He does not hesitate to call the idols of the national god *Baalim*, and the service thus rendered to Yahveh *Baal*-service.' Cp. ii. 13–16; iii. 1; xiii. 2; xiv. 3. On the difference between the attitude of Hosea and that of Amos, see Robertson Smith, *Prophets of Israel*, pp. 176 foll.

proves that the Mosaic *Torah* was not mainly concerned with matters of *cultus*. Certainly the legal and ritual *Torah* of the priests was traced to Moses, but so also was the *Torah* or word of the prophets—that very word which habitually subordinated ritual observance to the fulfilment of moral duty. This original supremacy of the ethical element in Mosaism corresponds to the conclusion arrived at by criticism that the discipline of the ceremonial law was subsequent to the work of the prophets; that the high development of ritual is characteristic of a totally different and comparatively late stage in Israel's history.

3. One more point may be noticed, namely, that the positive institutions and observances of Hebrew religion gradually came to be regarded in the light of Moses' ethical teaching, as moral symbols, expressive of a spiritual *status* and vocation; and as outward emblems of the holiness that became *a kingdom of priests*. Thus the rite of circumcision, which in Egypt was apparently confined to the priesthood, was looked upon as a token of the purity of life to which every Israelite was called. The ordinance of the Passover again, participation in which was enjoined under pain of extirpation in case of neglect, symbolized the sacerdotal *status* of the nation. It was a yearly memorial of the deliverance which had made Israel a people holy to Jehovah, a yearly renewal of the covenant, a yearly reconsecration of individual Israelites. Each household in which the sacred meal was solemnized was thereby constituted a sanctuary, and each family a priestly company[1]. The readmission of the healed leper to his forfeited privileges was accompanied by ceremonies similar to those observed in the consecration of priests[2]. The same idea was implied in the sanctification of the firstborn, which represented the

---

[1] Cp. Riehm, *A Tl. Theologie*, § 26.
[2] Riehm, loc. cit. Cp. Lev. xiv. 14 foll. with Exod. xxix. 20, Lev. viii. 24.

vocation of the entire people to Jehovah's special service[1].

Even when these rudimentary institutions had been developed into an elaborate ceremonial law, yet the prophetic element derived from the Mosaic covenant would make the levitical code a real aid to the religious life. Its ordinances concerning sabbaths, festivals and fasts, its ideal agrarian regulations, even its careful dietary and distinction between clean and unclean— must have tended 'to give a certain dignity and sanctity to life[2],' and to foster true thoughts in regard to the worth of time, the responsibilities of property, and the solemnity of everyday acts and occupations when carried on under the consciousness of the divine presence. Even in such a book as Chronicles, which is entirely pervaded by the levitical spirit, we find occasionally the prayer for inward devotion, for *a perfect heart and a willing mind*[3], as if this after all was the one thing needful for acceptance with God. So in the ceremonial law, as in the law of worship presently to be considered, we miss the inspiring and informing element if we overlook the result towards which it tended, and which in part it successfully achieved. For the ceremonial observances of the ancient law had a spiritual aim. They were intended to result, says a recent writer, 'in *clean hands and a pure heart*, in a conduct characterized by separation from sin and devotion to the cause of righteousness[4].' Indeed, as Origen observes, there are evangelical elements even in the law: *Sic ergo invenitur et Evangelii virtus in lege, et fundamento legis subnixa intelliguntur evangelia*[5].

---

[1] Exod. xiii. 1 foll. Cp. Num. viii. 16 foll.
[2] Cp. Montefiore, *op. cit.* p. 511. See also a striking passage in Dr. Fairbairn's *Religion in History and in Modern Life*, lect. ii. pp. 127 foll.
[3] 1 Chron. xxviii. 9; cp. xxix. 18, 19; 2 Chron. xvi. 9, &c. (Montefiore, p. 483).
[4] W. S. Bruce, *Ethics of the O. T.* p. 210.
[5] *in Num. hom.* ix. 4. On the application of the Decalogue to Christian conduct, see Gore, *The Sermon on the Mount*, Appendix ii.

III.

There are two institutions minutely described in the Pentateuch which specially presuppose and embody the idea of covenant fellowship—the sanctuary and the sacrifices. Mosaism is throughout a religion of symbolism. Its characteristic institutions give concrete expression to a very vivid and spiritual faith. For we must remember that, in their developed form, the Pentateuchal ordinances do not merely prefigure and typify spiritual realities, but actually give material form to spiritual ideas. There lies behind them the prophetic conception of a holy people, in whose midst the God of holiness Himself has deigned to make His abode. Hence that typical character which belongs to Jewish institutions; they give substance to essential verities of catholic and spiritual religion, and they foreshadow in visible objects and in external ceremonies a consummation towards which Hebrew religion was ever tending [1]. In the Christian dispensation all things are made new. *The tabernacle of God is with men, and he will dwell with them and will be their God* [2]. Yes; but we must not forget that this great thought penetrated the prophet whose influence is most decidedly impressed on the entire sacrificial system. Modern criticism has enabled us to understand the historical place and significance of the ritual code or *Torah* which closes the book of Ezekiel—a passage which has even been described as 'the key of the Old Testament [3].' Ezekiel's plan is partly ideal, partly allegorical, partly based on old priestly usage, re-

---

[1] Aug. *c. Faust. Manich.* vi. 9 : 'Illud enim erat tempus significandi, hoc manifestandi. Ergo ipsa scriptura, quae tunc fuit exactrix operum significantium, nunc testis est rerum significatarum, et quae tunc observabatur ad praenuntiationem, nunc recitatur ad confirmationem.'

[2] Rev. xxi. 3. Cp. Ezek. xxxvii. 27.

[3] Orth ap. Wellhausen, *Prolegomena*, p. 421. On Ezekiel's draft sketch, see Robertson Smith, *O. T. in J. C.* pp. 376 foll.; Montefiore, *Hibbert Lectures*, p. 255.

modelled in accordance with the idea of Jehovah's holiness. Probably in great measure it shaped the post-exilic organization of the priesthood, and the sacrificial worship of the second temple. But the dominating idea of the entire sketch is one which the Incarnation alone was destined to verify; it is indicated in the closing words of Ezekiel's prophecy: *The name of the city from that day shall be, The Lord is there* [1]. This indeed may be said to be the Messianic ideal of the priesthood: the enthronement and permanent presence of Jehovah in the midst of His people. The sanctuary and worship of Israel may or may not have been institutions actually realized in detail; but in any case the description of them has a providential and didactic purpose. We are warranted not only by New Testament references, but by our knowledge of the motive which dictated the elaborate description of the sanctuary, in believing that it was expressly intended to embody certain characteristic ideas of Judaism, and to symbolize religious truths [2]. From this point of view it makes no material difference whether the sketch is strictly faithful to historical fact, or whether it is a partially ideal creation. In either case the religious *idea* is present, and this to a Christian reader of the Old Testament is the point of paramount interest.

It follows from what has been said that the symbolical interpretation of the tabernacle and its services, which we find in the New Testament, especially in the Epistle to the Hebrews, has a foundation in reason and in spiritual fact. There is a sense in which, as Origen boldly says, the Law is 'always new [3].' It interprets

---

[1] Ezek. xlviii. 35. Cp. Darmesteter, *Les Prophètes d'Israël*, p. 108.
[2] Wellhausen, *Prolegomena*, p. 81, says: 'The spiritualization of the worship is seen in the Priestly code as advancing *pari passu* with its centralization. It receives, so to speak, an *abstract* religious character.'
[3] Orig. *in Num. hom.* ix. 4: 'Nobis autem qui eam [legem] spiritaliter et evangelico sensu intelligimus et exponimus, semper nova est, et utrumque nobis novum testamentum est, non temporis novitate sed intelligentiae novitate.' Cp. Aug. *de util. cred.* 9: 'Evacuatur namque in Christo non vetus testamentum sed velamen eius, ut per Christum

to us our own faith, and Christian experience has proved that a close study of the ancient sanctuary and its worship not only gives the clue to the meaning of New Testament thoughts and expressions, but also enlarges our comprehension of the general principles of divine revelation. This will become more apparent in the sequel.

It has, however, already been pointed out that critics appear to be justified in maintaining that the description of the tabernacle in the book of Exodus is very highly idealized. There is no sufficient ground for questioning the existence of a simple tent in the earliest Mosaic period, which formed a shelter for the ark, and stood without the camp in accordance with ordinary Semitic usage. But what is called in question by criticism is the existence in the wilderness, among tribes living under nomad conditions, of a splendid, costly, and elaborate structure, 'wrought in the most advanced style of oriental art[1].' Apart from the character of the building, there is the serious difficulty that Hebrew tradition appears to know practically nothing of such a shrine in pre-exilic days[2]. It knows something of the ark and of a central sanctuary at Shiloh, but of the sumptuous tabernacle *described in the book of Exodus* it makes no mention. A Christian apologist can afford to admit that the elaborate description of the tabernacle is to be regarded as a product of religious idealism, working upon an historical basis, and that the sketch as a whole is largely coloured by reminiscences or traditions of the splendid temple of Solomon. A prophetic idea underlies the picture, namely, that the unity of God implies unity and centralization of *cultus*. 'The tabernacle,' says Wellhausen, 'is not narrative merely, but, like all the

---

intelligatur et quasi denudetur quod sine Christo obscurum atque adopertum est.'

[1] Wellhausen, *Prolegomena*, p. 39.
[2] The writer of Chronicles assumes the existence of the tabernacle in Canaan before the building of the temple, but his evidence does not outweigh, for obvious reasons, the silence of the earlier books.

narratives [in Exodus], law as well; it expresses the legal unity of the worship as an historical fact, which, from the very beginning, ever since the exodus, has held good in Israel. One God, one sanctuary, that is the idea[1].' But there is no reason for questioning the fact that in a rudimentary form suited to the conditions of wilderness life, a simple *tent of meeting* was constructed by Moses as the place of Jehovah's abode. We might infer this not only from considerations of *a priori* probability and from the express testimony of tradition, but also from the very structure of the more elaborate sanctuary, which in its arrangements appears to be modelled on the ancient shepherd's tent, with its open court, its large outer apartment, and its private sanctum[2]. Moreover, as Riehm points out, the ancient law of Leviticus xvii. implies the existence of a simple Mosaic tent, which had essentially the very significance afterwards attributed to the ideal structure of the priestly document[3].

From the symbolic sanctuary we turn to the institution of sacrifice, which in the Pentateuch is ordered and regulated as a legitimate and recognized mode of approach to God: of either entering into covenant relationship with Him, or restoring it when interrupted.

The levitical sacrifices demand special attention in so far as a vital connexion is assumed in Scripture to exist between the death of a sacrificial victim and the inauguration or renewal of a covenant. This connexion is evidently regarded as axiomatic and self-evident in the Epistle to the Hebrews[4], and it seems to underlie the solemn words in which our Lord Himself institutes the perpetual memorial of His sacred passion. The New Covenant had been foreshadowed in the Old, and had been expressly predicted

---

[1] See *Prolegomena*, pp. 34-50.
[2] Schultz, *O. T. Theology*, i. p. 351.
[3] *A Tl. Theologie*, p. 79. Even Renan allows the existence of such a tent. 'But this,' he says, 'was only a germ' (*Histoire du peuple d'Israël*, bk. i. ch. 15 *s. fin.*).
[4] Heb. ix. 17.

by Jeremiah [1]. It was a *better covenant* both in what it promised and what it ordained; but it was better chiefly in respect of the dignity and preciousness of the sacrifice on which it rested. Each covenant was inaugurated with bloodshedding [2], but the ancient slaughter of victims was the symbol of a spiritual self-oblation of infinite worth—a self-oblation which in itself changed the relationship between man and God, and became the foundation of a covenant union permanent and complete. The sacrifice of Jesus Christ comprehends all the moral elements which the Hebrew *cultus* strove to express in a material and symbolic form. It includes that consecration of life, that dedication of will, that devotion of heart which the notion of a 'covenant' between the All-Holy and His creatures necessarily implies. Thus in studying Israel's sacrificial worship we ascertain the spiritual conditions involved in man's communion with his Creator.

Now speaking generally, the purpose of the *cultus* was at once disciplinary and didactic. On the one hand, the sacrificial worship was intended to develope and deepen the consciousness of sin, to make the thought of Jehovah's holiness and of His separation from the creature a practical power in human life. On the other hand, it was intended to awaken and train religious affections: the spirit of dependence and holy fear, the temper of trust, devotion, self-surrender, thankfulness, love, and the longing for divine grace. Thus though the post-exilic elaboration of sacrificial ritual seems at first sight retrogressive and reactionary, yet it was inspired by an ethical and spiritual motive. It was not a reversion to heathenism, with its purely external conception of religious obligation. It was not intended to place ritual on a level with morality, as if both were equally acceptable to God. It was the

---

[1] Jer. xxxi. 31 foll. Cp. Heb. viii. 8 foll. See also Matt. xxvi. 28 and Luke xxii. 20.
[2] Heb. ix. 18.

outcome of a penitent sense of national unfaithfulness to Jehovah in the past, and of a genuine desire to provide safeguards against future apostasy, or negligence in His service. The *cultus* was doubtless regarded by its authors 'as a very important means towards the great end of keeping the people of Israel faithful in heart and life to God [1].'

Before we consider the sacrifices in detail, however, it will be advisable to make four preliminary observations.

1. The institutions of sacrifice described in the Pentateuch are based on pre-existing customs. It has been observed that the origin and *rationale* of sacrifice are nowhere explained in the Old Testament. 'That sacrifice is an essential part of religion is taken for granted [2].' The ritual of the second temple was based on immemorial usage and tradition. In numerous details it illustrates the affinity of Hebrew institutions to those of the Semitic race generally. Consequently much light has been thrown upon the origin and meaning of Mosaic institutions of worship by inquiry into the customs of Semitic paganism. Distinctive, however, of Israel's religion is the tendency visible from the first to moralize the *cultus*, and to reduce its significance as a mere *opus operatum* by insistence on Jehovah's ethical requirement. So far as we can gather, Moses seems to have contented himself with a minimum of ritual legislation, and we may suppose that such ceremonial traditions as were allowed or instituted by Moses himself were cherished and observed in pre-prophetic days by the priesthood at the sanctuary of Shiloh. The codification and further development of sacrificial usage may well have begun at the period when Jerusalem, in consequence of the building of Solomon's temple, became the religious centre of the kingdom. 'The priesthood,' says Riehm, 'as the guardians of the Mosaic

---

[1] Bruce, *Apologetics*, p. 265.
[2] Robertson Smith, *Religion of the Semites*, p. 3.

traditions, traced back the entire contents of the priestly law to Moses, but historically this is only true of the spirit that dominates the whole system and of its main outlines [1].' By the 'spirit of the whole system' we may understand the desire to keep alive in Israel the spirit of loyalty to Jehovah's covenant. Characteristic of Mosaism is the Decalogue: of post-exilic Judaism, the sacrificial system; but the motive underlying the legislation of Moses and of Ezra is practically the same—a desire to secure Israel's faithfulness to the divine covenant [2].

2. We are struck by the attitude of the prophets towards sacrifice. Some of them appear to represent it as a concession to spiritual immaturity; all of them speak of it as wholly subordinate in importance to moral obedience. Such is the force of the celebrated passage, Jeremiah vii. 22 [3]. Later prophecy seems to regard sacrifice as the appropriate symbol of a perfect devotion to God; it values the levitical worship not indeed for itself but for that which it signifies, namely the entire consecration of life to God [4]. Ezekiel in the last nine chapters of his book appears at first sight to co-ordinate ritual worship with morality, but such is not the tendency of his prophecy surveyed as a whole. Legalistic as is the habit of Ezekiel's mind, we must remember that he is pre-eminently the teacher of personal religion and individual responsibility, while in his early chapters the *statutes and judgments* which he proclaims are exclusively moral [5]. On the whole, then, it would appear that the prophets were comparatively indifferent to the actual details of the *cultus*. Their polemical statements prove little as to the Mosaic

---

[1] Riehm, *ATl. Theologie*, p. 81. Bruce, *Apologetics*, p. 221, refers to this passage, and observes that the religious customs were 'ascribed to Moses not so much as author, but rather as authority.'
[2] Cp. Bruce, p. 219.
[3] Cp. Amos v. 25, and see Iren. *Haer.* iv, 17. 3: 'Non enim principaliter haec [sacrificia], sed secundum consequentiam ... habuit populus.' (See the whole passage.)
[4] See Isa. lxvi. 20 foll.; Zech. xiv. 16 foll.; Mal. iii. 4.
[5] See Montefiore, *Hibbert Lectures*, p. 257. Cp. Ezek. xviii.

origin or precise character of the contemporary worship; what they denounce is the immorality and profligacy which had come to be associated with the popular worship, and the hypocrisy which imagined that effusive religiosity was a kind of compensation for unrighteous conduct.

3. The question has also been raised by criticism how far the levitical system was ever actually in operation. The sacrificial usage codified in the Pentateuch represents what was at least intended to be observed in the post-exilic temple. It is evidently a highly complex and artificial system, the product of a reforming movement, which attempted to restore and develope ritual *praxis* on the lines of ancient tradition [1]. The peculiar form of the ceremonial prescribed in Leviticus is determined partly by the antiquarian tendency of the time, partly by the desire to give an adequate symbolic expression to a deepened spiritual experience. There is indeed every reason to suppose that the system existed in germ even at the earliest period of Israel's national history [2]; in outline it is represented in the ceremonies connected with the consecration of the priests, which probably represent a very ancient tradition. But in any case, whatever may have been the extent to which the sacrificial system was practically observed before the exile, it derived new significance from the Deuteronomic law of the one sanctuary. In ancient Israel sacrificial feasts were freely celebrated at local sanctuaries: but with the concentration of religion at one central shrine, sacrifice, though it ceased to be the most vital element in popular worship, acquired special dignity and importance as a representative national service. It virtually served the purpose of an objectlesson to Israel during the period when prophecy was

[1] Schultz, *O. T. Theology*, vol. i. p. 373; Robertson Smith, *Religion of the Semites*, pp. 198 foll.; *O. T. in J. C.*, lect. xi.
[2] Edersheim, *Warburton Lectures*, p. 239, declares that the non-observance of the system in the wilderness was 'unquestionably a necessity imposed by the times.' Cp. Wellhausen, *Prolegomena*, p. 412.

silent. It put an end once for all to the practical
heathenism against which the pre-exilic prophets had
preached without avail; and it embodied in visible
form prophetic teachings in regard to the nature and
character of God, and the conditions of covenantal
fellowship with Him. It is clear that the critical
analysis of the Pentateuch relieves us of a difficulty.
Had the sacrificial ritual been certainly prescribed in
its present form by Moses we should have had to
explain the fact that an elaborate system solemnly
established under divine sanctions of the most stringent
kind was practically ignored for centuries, and failed
in great measure to effect its object, namely the
restraint of the people from idolatry and apostasy [1].
On the other hand, if we accept the modern theory,
the facts to be explained fall into their true place.

4. Lastly, it is noticeable that the chief feature
distinctive of the levitical ritual is the development
of piacular sacrifice. The simplicity and joyousness
of primitive worship, reflecting to a great extent the
conditions of an early age and the placid happiness of
agricultural life, found appropriate expression in rites
and festivals connected with the changing seasons of
the year. But a religion of this type could not with-
stand the strain of prolonged disaster and adversity.
Accordingly in the seventh century B.C. we find the
development in Palestine of a more sombre species of
worship, under the pressure of accumulated national
calamities which appeared to betoken the abiding
displeasure of the deity, and awakened a new consciousness of guilt [2]. Thus the idea of the expiation
of sin gradually tended to displace or modify the
primitive conception of sacrifice as the creation or
renewal of a life-bond between the deity and His
worshippers [3]. The levitical sin-offering is in all

---

[1] Cp. Robertson Smith, *O. T. in J. C.* pp. 315 foll., 377. Cp. Ezek.
xliii. 7; xliv. 6 foll.
[2] Cp. Robertson Smith, *Religion of the Semites*, pp. 240, 374; *O. T. in
J. C.* p 380; Riehm, *Einleitung in das A. T.* vol. i. p. 351; Schultz, ii. p. 176.
[3] Robertson Smith, *Religion of the Semites*, pp. 330, 333.

essential features 'identical with the ancient sacrament of communion in a sacred life¹'; but the men of a later age were led to invest the ancient form of sacrifice with a new significance, in proportion as they came to realize more profoundly the inviolable holiness of Jehovah, the sinfulness of man, and the consequent need of priestly mediation.

The sin-offering then is an institution distinctive of the Hebrew *cultus*, but in other points there is close affinity between the sacrifices of Israel and those of other Semitic tribes. The true ideas latent in ethnic sacrifice appear in a purified and developed form in the levitical system: for instance, the conception of the sacrificial meal as a feast of communion with deity, and a means of participation in the sacred life of a victim. Again, the primitive idea that the offering is a tribute to the divine King or a meal conveyed to Him, underlies such phrases as 'the bread' or 'food of Jehovah².' The last-mentioned idea, however, is carefully guarded by the doctrine that God has no need of such material gifts, whereas the pagan belief was that the deity literally feasted on the flesh of the victim, as it rose from the altar in the sublimated form of smoke or steam³. In estimating indeed the moral effect of the levitical worship we have to bear in mind, first, the fact that the worshippers were for the most part deeply imbued with the characteristic teaching of the prophets; secondly, the fact that in post-exilic days sacrificial worship necessarily 'ceased to be the expression of everyday religion.' Prof. Robertson Smith appositely remarks that 'the very features of the levitical ordinances which seem most inconsistent with spirituality ... appear in a very different light in

---

[1] Robertson Smith, *Religion of the Semites*, p. 331.

[2] לחם יהוה—a name applied to sacrifice in general. See Lev. iii. 11, 16; xxi. 6, 8, 17; xxii. 25; Num. xxviii. 2; Ezek. xliv. 7; Mal. i. 7. Cp. Wellhausen, *Prolegomena*, pp. 61, 62. The phrase *Bread of God* in John vi. 33 seems to imply that the self-oblation of Christ gives perfect *satisfaction* to the Father. Cp. Eph. v. 2.

[3] See Tylor, *Anthropology*, p. 365. Ps. l. 9 foll. is a protest against this idea. Cp. Iren. *Haer*. iv. 18. 3; Westcott, *Ep. to the Hebrews*, pp. 286-287.

the age after the exile, when the non-ritual religion of the prophets went side by side with the Law, and supplied daily nourishment to the spiritual life of those who were far from the sanctuary[1].'

The above considerations may guide us in our survey of the levitical sacrifices. It only remains to bear in mind *ex abundanti cautela* that the completely-organized system is the result of a long and slow development of traditional usages, each of which had its separate history[2].

We may proceed to deal first with the names and prominent features of the several sacrifices described in the Pentateuch.

The names most generally employed are two: a sacrifice is described in the priestly code as *Qorban* (LXX. δῶρον), 'a gift,' or as *Ish-sheh* (θυσία), 'an offering by fire.' The first is the wider and more primitive designation, and includes every species of oblation. The original meaning of the word seems to be 'something presented' or 'brought near' to a superior, and it corresponds to the most simple aspect of sacrifice as a tribute due to God[3]. The second term, *Ish-sheh*, implies the established use of fire as a mode of consumption[4]. The remaining words for sacrifice become specialized by limitation of their usage. The most important distinction is that between *Minchah* (θυσία), 'gift' or 'present,' which though applied to sacrifice in various passages, and even to an ordinary present[5], is in the priestly code restricted entirely to the meal or vegetable offering; and *Zebach*, 'slain

---

[1] *O. T. in J. C.* pp. 378, 379.

[2] The use of *fire*, for example, as a mode of consumption seems to have been introduced at a comparatively late stage in the evolution of Semitic sacrifice. That it was a subordinate feature seems to be implied in the name of the altar, מזבח, 'place of slaughter.' On the whole subject see Robertson Smith, *Religion of the Semites*, ch. x, and below, p. 238.

[3] Wellhausen, *Prolegomena*, p. 61. The vb. הקריב corresponds to קרב. See Lev. i. 2; ii. 11; iii. 1, &c.

[4] Lev. i. 9, 13, 17; ii. 2, 9, &c.; Num. xv. 3; xxviii. 8.

[5] Gen. iv. 3-5; Num. xvi. 15; 1 Sam. ii. 17; Ps. xl. 6 (LXX. προσφορά), &c. Cp. Gen. xxxii. 13 and 2 Sam. viii. 2, 6.

sacrifice,' which appears to be a more ancient designation than *Minchah*, implying nomadic conditions of life such as would ordinarily precede the settled habits of an agricultural people[1].

From these general names we pass on to consider the three main classes of sacrifice described in the levitical Law: the sin-offering[2], with its special variety, the trespass- or guilt-offering; the burnt-offering[3], which was invariably accompanied by a meal-offering and a libation of wine; and the peace-offering[4], including several species, such as the 'vow,' the 'praise-offering,' and the 'free-will oblation.' Each of these three main divisions of sacrifice is connected with either the renewal or the maintenance of covenant fellowship with Jehovah. The order, however, of their historical development is to be carefully distinguished from that of the detailed treatment in the book of Leviticus. When the three classes are mentioned together, the essential order of thought seems to be observed. First in order stands the sin-offering, implying the necessary expiation of guilt which might have severed the Israelite from the privileges of the covenant; next the burnt-offering, suggesting the idea of renewed self-dedication; and, lastly, the peace-offering, with its sacrificial meal, which was the seal as it were of

---

[1] Robertson Smith, *Religion of the Semites*, p. 226.

[2] Heb. חטאת, 'sin' (LXX. περὶ ἁμαρτίας), Lev. iv. 24, &c. אשם, 'trespass' (LXX. περὶ τῆς πλημμελείας) is scarcely distinguishable from the sin-offering. Cp. Lev. v. 6–8. See below, p. 238.

[3] Heb. עלה (ὁλοκαύτωμα), 'that which ascends.' To this corresponds the vb. העלה; cp. Ps. li. 19. Occasionally the poetical word כליל, 'whole-offering,' occurs (1 Sam. vii. 9; Deut. xxxiii. 10). With the burnt-offering were offered the meal-offering (מנחה) and the drink-offering, or libation of wine, (נסך).

[4] זבח שלמים, 'slain-victim of *Shelamim*,' i.e. 'vows,' from vb. שלם, 'pay' or 'discharge' (Robertson Smith, *Religion of the Semites*, p. 219 note), or preferably 'fullness' of salvation (so apparently Wellhausen, *op. cit.* p. 71, and Schultz, i. 378). The sing. שלם occurs only in Amos v. 22. The name, according to Riehm, conveys the notion of unimpaired and perfect fellowship. The peace-offering is a symbol of peaceful and friendly communion with God (*A Tl. Theologie*, p. 120).

restored fellowship, and the highest expression of perfect communion with deity.

All these classes of sacrifices had three elements in common. In each case there was the ceremony of presentation, the act of slaughtering, and the disposal of the victim.

The victim was to be presented at the door of the tabernacle court by the offerer himself, in token of that willing intention which constituted the acceptable element in the oblation. This act was followed by the imposition of hands (*semichah*), i. e. an actual pressure of both hands upon the victim's head. This rite appears to have implied not so much the idea of substitution, or transference of guilt, though it was ordinarily accompanied by detailed confession of sins, as that of entire self-identification with the victim, or the dedication of it to some special object or office, such as the removal of guilt[1]. The slaughter of the victim next took place. This was performed by the offerer, not by the priest, except in the case of a sacrifice offered for his own sin, or for that of the whole congregation[2]. The slaying[3], which took place on the north side of the altar—perhaps because the north was regarded as the quarter with which judgment or punishment was connected—seems to have had no independent significance; it served simply as a means of obtaining the blood or

---

[1] On the סמיכה see Schultz, i. 391, who seems to give the true account with clearness; cp. Robertson Smith, *Religion of the Semites*, p. 402; Westcott, *Ep. to the Hebrews*, p. 290; Jukes, *The Law of the Offerings*, p. 38: 'This act *in itself* was nothing more than *the expression of the identity of the offerer and offering*.... The offering, whatever it might be, stood for, and was looked upon as identical with, the offerer.' Riehm, *ATl. Theologie*, says that by the *semichah* the victim was made 'Träger der Gesinnungen, die er (the offerer) gegenüber Gott bethätigen will.'

[2] See Lev. i. 5, 9: possibly also the priest slew the victim in the rite for cleansing lepers. See Lev. xiv. 13, 25, and cp. Oehler, i. 411. In 2 Chron. xxix. 24 the slaying by the priests seems to be mentioned as exceptional. Ezek. xliv. 10-16 shows that it was an ignoble office.

[3] The Heb. vb. is שחט. Cp. Lev. i. 11, and see Isa. xli. 25, Jer. i. 14, li. 48. On the general significance of the slaughter see Oehler, *loc. cit.*; Schultz, i. 394; Westcott, *Ep. to the Hebrews*, p. 291.

sacred life. The Law seems to have laid no stress either on the intrinsic fact of suffering, or on the material value of the sacrifice, as is shown by the limited scale of the offerings: neither hecatombs of victims nor human sacrifice were required for the purposes of acceptable atonement. Indeed, it is clear that the significant part of the ceremony was not thought to lie 'in the death of the victim, but in the application of its life blood[1].'

And this brings us to the third point—the disposal of the victim: of its blood and its flesh. The blood of sacrifice was the appointed medium of atonement as being the seat of the sacred life, and could accordingly be presented only through the mediation of the priest[2]. Without going here into special detail it is sufficient to notice that the mode of dealing with the blood varied, the precise variations being minutely specified. Thus in the case of the burnt-offering or peace-offering the blood was thrown or dashed[3] against the sides of the brazen altar; but in the case of a sin-offering part of it was solemnly sprinkled on the horns of the altar when offered for a private person, but within the holy place on the horns of the incense altar when offered for a priest or the whole congregation. On the Day of Atonement there came as it were a climax in the ascending scale. On that day alone the blood was carried within the veil and solemnly sprinkled by the High Priest *upon the mercy-seat and before the mercy-seat* seven times[4]. With regard to the disposal of the flesh the Law required that the victim should be flayed by the offerer and divided, and then consumed by fire upon the altar or elsewhere. It was to be wholly burnt in the case of the burnt-offering, in part only if the sacrifice was a sin- or peace-offering. The use of fire in this connexion is

---

[1] *Religion of the Semites*, p. 319.
[2] Lev. xvii. 11.   [3] Heb. זרק (LXX. προσχεῖν).
[4] Lev. xvi. 14–19. On the disposal of the blood in Semitic sacrifice see Robertson Smith, *Religion of the Semites*, especially lectures v, vi, and ix.

noticeable. In primitive ethnic sacrifices fire would be regarded as a means of conveying food in an etherialized form to the deity; but in the levitic rites it seems to be employed merely as a safe and appropriate method of disposal, when the flesh of the victim was regarded as a thing too holy to be touched, or disposed of in any other way, even by consecrated persons [1]. Through the action of fire the flesh was finally withdrawn from the possibility of profane use or contact.

Besides these general elements common to all sacrifices, there were special features distinctive of each particular class. The *sin-offering* in some sense ranks above the other sacrifices as being 'most holy [2],' that is, entirely withdrawn from ordinary human use. Whether there is any clear distinction between the sin-offering and the trespass-offering is disputed; but one thing seems evident, viz. that the entire complicated system of atonement existed only in relation to minor offences, committed whether through ignorance, carelessness, or infirmity. For open breaches of the ten words—sins *with a high hand* [3]—there was no availing atonement possible; they were to be punished with death. Such sins were theoretically regarded as involving a presumptuous violation of covenant conditions, and a deliberate withdrawal from the sphere in which sacrifice was efficacious. Apparently, however, a distinction was possible in the case of minor transgressions. The trespass-offering appears to have implied some previous act of fraud; some infraction of the rights of ownership; some withholding from God of His due. But any artificial distinction between the sin- and the trespass-offering is precarious [4]. The two species of sacrifice

---

[1] Cp. Schultz, i. 396 note; *Religion of the Semites*, lect. x.
[2] Lev. vi. 17 and 25 foll.
[3] Heb. ביד רמה. Num. xv. 30; cp. xxxiii. 3.
[4] On this point see Willis, *Worship of the Old Covenant*, ch. vii. § 2; Schultz, i. 380. Wellhausen, *Prolegomena*, pp. 74, 75, observes that 'the sin- and trespass-offerings of the Pentateuch still bear traces of

seem, however, to correspond to two different aspects of human sin, regarded as demanding expiation on the one hand, on the other as admitting to a certain extent of reparation.

In the ritual of the sin-offering some special points call for attention: for instance, the exact specification of the victim, which differed according to the grade of the offerer or the dignity of the occasion[1]; and the verbal confession of sins which was uttered by the worshipper leaning upon the victim's head[2]. The most characteristic feature, however, of the sacrifice was the ceremonial sprinkling of the sacred blood at spots to which belonged different degrees of sanctity, implying different stages of nearness to God. On the Day of Atonement, by the sprinkling of the blood on the mercy-seat the highest moment of reconciliation known to the Law was attained: the life of the people being in a representative act of dedication brought into closest contact with the divine presence. Noticeable also is the disposal of the victim's flesh: all the fat, as being the choicest part, was burnt upon the altar *for a sweet savour unto the Lord*[3]; the remainder of the flesh was disposed of in different ways. If the offering was that of a private person it was consumed by the priests within the precincts of the sanctuary[4]; but in certain cases, when the sin-offering was that of a priest or of the entire congregation, it was regarded as too holy to be eaten even by consecrated persons, and it was burned outside the camp, as the safest method of dis-

---

their origin in fines and penalties; they are not gifts to God, ... they are simply mulcts payable to the priests, partly of fixed commutation value (Lev. v. 15).' See 2 Kings xii. 16 for a mention of 'trespass-money and sin-money.'

[1] Lev. iv.
[2] Lev. v. 5; Num. v. 6 foll. Cp. Willis, *op. cit.* p. 141.
[3] Lev. iv. 31.
[4] Thus the sin-offering retains a relic of the ancient sacrificial feast of communion, only the communion is restricted to the priests. Obs. Hos. iv. 8 implies (1) that some form of sin-offering existed in the prophetic period; (2) that the guilty priests, instead of attempting to stem the sinfulness of the people, longed for its increase with a view to fresh gains. See Cheyne ad loc. in *Camb. Bible for Schools*.

posing of a most holy thing. The culminating service of national expiation, which was solemnized on the Day of Atonement, is worthy of special study, because it sums up and interprets the significance of the entire system of piacular sacrifice. In the ordinances of that day we see 'writ large' the conditions of access to God, the method by which the state of covenant privilege for Jehovah's people was renewed. At the same time the mark of imperfection was visibly impressed on the whole procedure of the day, and it had to be yearly repeated, as if to remind the people that their tenure in God's house was not absolute, but renewable only from year to year.

The *burnt-offering*, or holocaust, if we may rely on the early historical notices, was apparently known, but not very commonly practised, in the patriarchal period. There are traces of the yet more primitive slain-sacrifice with its sacred meal in the book of Genesis[1]; and the account in Gen. xxii of the offering of Isaac marks, as we have noticed, a critical epoch in the development of the doctrine of sacrifice. The passage illustrates the way in which ethnic corruptions were purified: it disconnects the spirit of absolute devotion from the necessity of any particular material exhibition of it[2]. Some writers have supposed that the use of fire had its origin in the custom of human sacrifice; the victim was burned in a spot apart from men, as being too sacred to be eaten: but whatever be its origin, the practice of burning the bodies of ordinary animals on the altar very early established itself. The essential idea of the holocaust was probably that of a grateful tribute to God as king. It would be an exceptional form of sacrifice, expressive of man's grateful dedication of himself and his possessions to God. Certainly in its developed form the burnt-offering would present itself to the mind of a devout Israelite as an apt symbol

---

[1] Gen. xxxi. 54; xlvi. 1.
[2] Westcott, *Ep. to the Hebrews*, p. 284; cp. Oehler, § 121, note 1.

of entire self-consecration to God. It would give outward expression to the spirit of perfect devotion, conscious of the infinite gulf that separates the sinful creature from the All-holy[1]. In this connexion it is significant that the principal act of public worship in the days of the second temple was the daily or continual[2] burnt-offering, which consisted in the oblation of a spotless lamb every morning and evening. Around this as a centre were grouped the prayers and the praises of Israel; it formed as it were the foundation of the whole sacrificial system. Probably the offering of incense was kindled in the holy place simultaneously with the burnt-offering, while the assembled congregation stood praying without in the court. Together with the burnt-offering, as a kind of supplement were presented the *Minchah* or meal-offering (a portion of which, called the 'memorial[3],' was burned upon the altar), and the drink-offering consisting of wine. This feature was one common to the Hebrew sacrifices and to those of classic paganism. The name *Minchah* indicates that the notion of the meal-offering was that of a tribute paid by the worshipper to God and wholly given over to Him, whereas in the case of animal sacrifice there was originally at least a communion feast in which God and the offerer shared. The accessories of the burnt-offering are among those many details which are of the nature of survivals in the Mosaic religion. Certainly when sacrifice had become an act of national homage to Jehovah, maintained at the public cost, the daily burnt-offering acquired unique importance and dignity. We may judge of the importance of the *Tamid* or 'continual' burnt-offering by the fact that its cessation was thought

---

[1] Riehm, *A Tl. Theologie*, p. 119: 'Wie die Erhabenheit der Gottheit über die irdische Welt in allen semitischen Religionen stark betont wird, und im Mosaismus in der Idee der Heiligkeit Jahves mit besonderem Nachdruck sich geltend macht, so nimmt auch das Brandopfer im Kultus Israels die Hauptstelle ein.'

[2] Ex. xxix. 42; Num. xxviii. 3.

[3] אזכרה (LXX. μνημόσυνον) Lev. ii. 2.

practically to involve the abolition of public worship[1]. Its maintenance came to be regarded as the absolutely necessary condition of covenant-union between Jehovah and His people, and in daily life the devout Jew followed 'with an inward longing and spiritual sympathy the national homage which continually ascended on behalf of himself and all the people of God in the stated ritual of the Temple[2].'

The levitical system of sacrifice is completed by the *peace-offering*, which is of peculiar interest as reproducing in a higher and more spiritual form the main features of primaeval sacrifice. Originally, when the slaying of animals for food was a comparatively rare event, all slaughter was regarded as a sacrificial act; and, conversely, a sacrifice was habitually connected with a communion feast. Accordingly the *Zebachim* represent the original type of sacrifice out of which all other forms were developed. In early ages sacrifice was a family or tribal action, the object of which was to re-establish the bond of communion or fellowship between the tribe and its god through joint participation in a sacred victim. Such sacrifices followed by feasts were characteristic of a period when religious ideas were of a physical cast, it being the fundamental conception of ancient religion that the gods and their worshippers formed one community united by the tie of kinship[3]. The evidence of the earlier Old Testament books shows that the primitive religion of Israel so far resembled in its general character that of the other Semites, that 'a meal was almost always connected with a sacrifice[4].' 'In ancient Israel,' says Cornill,

---

[1] See Dan. viii. 11 foll., xi. 31; cp. xii. 11. Wellhausen, *Prolegomena*, p 79, says: 'According to 2 Kings xvi. 15, an עלה in the morning and a מנחה in the evening were daily offered in the temple of Jerusalem, in the time of Ahaz.... In the Priestly Code the evening *Minchah* has risen to the dignity of a second '*Olah*; but at the same time survives the daily *Minchah* of the high-priest, and is now offered in the morning also (Lev. vi. 12–16).'

[2] Robertson Smith, *O. T. in J. C.* p. 252.

[3] See *Religion of the Semites*, p. 33.

[4] Cp. Wellhausen, *Prolegomena*, p. 71; Cornill, *Der Israelitische Pro-*

'the worship of Jehovah had always a blithe and joyous character.... It consisted in making merry before God. In the sacrifice, of which God received a definite portion, while the worshipper himself consumed the rest, a man entered into table-fellowship with Deity; he was the guest of his God, and thereby became doubly assured of union with Him.' When, however, the Deuteronomic law of one sanctuary and one altar came into force, the eating of flesh inevitably ceased to be a purely religious act. It is deeply interesting, however, to observe that the crowning sacrifice of the levitical system consecrates, as it were, the very oldest forms of Hebrew worship, and reproduces in an age of heightened spiritual aspiration the mystical idea which underlay the ancient sacrificial meal, viz. that man's highest life consists in living fellowship with God, which is most appropriately typified by a sacred meal [1].

There were some peculiar features in the ritual of the peace-offering. A larger latitude was allowed in the choice of a victim, and there were certain ceremonies of presentation—'heaving' and 'waving [2]'—of which the explanation is somewhat doubtful; but the most prominent feature of the sacrifice was the subsequent meal, in which God, the officiating priest, and the offerer, together with his friends and such poor as he might invite, alike participated. The inner fat portions—those in which the sacred life was believed specially to reside—were burned upon the altar as the

---

phetismus, pp. 38 foll.; Robertson Smith, *The Prophets of Israel* (ed. 1), pp. 98, 99; and *Religion of the Semites*, pp. 236 foll.

[1] Conversely, the sin of 'eating upon the mountains' (Ezek. xviii. 6 foll.) consisted in the fact that it involved holding communion with false gods: the meal was a token of fellowship as a guest with the idol. Cp. the argument of 1 Cor. x. 20.

[2] Heb. תרומה and תנופה. The ceremony probably implied simple presentation to God, the 'waving' being a movement to and fro, the 'heaving' a movement up and down. Rabbinic writers, however, explain it as a recognition of the divine omnipresence. See Oehler, § 133 (vol. ii. pp. 6 foll.); and some interesting details mentioned in Willis, *Worship*, &c., pp. 175 foll.

portion appropriated to the deity; the wave-breast was the perquisite of the whole body of priests, the heave-shoulder of the officiating minister. All that remained was eaten by the offerer and his friends on the day of sacrifice, those who took part in the meal being obliged to be ceremonially clean [1]. The broad conception of the whole ceremony was that God received the offerer at His table, the part returned to the worshipper being made the occasion of a blessing in which others might share. Such was the main characteristic of the peace-offering in all its forms; the special species of such offerings, whether votive, free-will, or eucharistic, it is unnecessary for present purposes to describe in detail.

IV.

Our object in these lectures is to indicate the principles which should guide a Christian student in his use of the Old Testament. Having therefore briefly described the two principal institutions in which the covenant-relationship that subsisted between Jehovah and His chosen people found expression, it remains to consider the symbolic significance of the sanctuary as illustrated by the express teaching of the New Testament, and the spiritual ideas which the sacrificial system was intended to embody.

And here we must proceed with caution. What is called typical interpretation consists in the application of things and incidents described in the Old Testament to those which are recorded in the New [2]. And the question may fairly be asked, How are we to determine in any given instance whether a thing is typical or not?

---

[1] Lev. vii. 19.
[2] 'Typus *historiae* est sensus Scripturae mysticus, quo res gestae vel facta Vet. Testamenti praefigurant et adumbrant res in Novo Testamento gestas.' Glassius ap. Waterland, pref. to *Scripture Vindicated* (*Works*, vol. vi. p. 12). Glassius distinguishes between types historical and prophetical. The ceremonial law is an instance of the first, Jeremiah making yokes and bonds (Jer. xxvii. 2) of the second.

The answer has been given, that since the warrant for typical interpretation is supplied by Holy Scripture itself, we are not justified in going beyond the limits which it expressly sanctions in various instances. In spite of its habitual reserve on such points, there are certain cases in which the New Testament itself indicates that two objects or incidents 'were so connected that the one was *designed* to prefigure the other'; that both were in fact '*fore-ordained* as constituent parts of the same general scheme of providence[1].' Others, while recognizing the necessity of safeguards against abuse of the method in question, plead for a certain liberty of interpretation, 'beyond the precedent, but according to the spirit of Scripture[2].' In the case, however, of the Jewish sanctuary and ritual we are not left destitute of a key which unlocks the spiritual sense of the passages describing them. Moreover, the belief that the ordinances of Hebrew religion were intended to foreshadow the mysteries of the new dispensation may legitimately be inferred from the very notion of inspiration. For inspiration implies a special action of the one Spirit of Him to whom *all his works are known from the beginning of the world*[3], an operation whereby He ever guided and controlled the course of redemptive history, and continuously informed the minds of those who from time to time assisted in organizing the polity, the law, or the ceremonial worship of Israel. At the same time revelation has been progressive, accommodating itself to the actual condition of mankind, through material things and rudimentary institutions indicating its spiritual purpose and goal. Thus it is that the New Testament writers discern in the Law at once a temporary discipline and a prophecy of good things to come[4]. Their general

---

[1] See Marsh, *Lectures on the Criticism and Interpretation of the Bible*, pp. 375, 376.
[2] Newman, *The Arians of the Fourth Century*, ch. i. § 3.
[3] Acts xv. 18.
[4] Iren. *Haer.* iv. 15. 1 : 'Lex et disciplina erat illis et prophetia futurorum.' Cp. Heb. x. 1. A historical sketch of the patristic view of the

view of the Old Testament as a vast prophecy is based on the principle that in revelation as in nature there is continuity; and speaking broadly, their conception has absolutely justified itself in Christian experience. Even the fantastic ingenuity and extravagance in exegesis which occasionally disfigure the writings of the fathers may be regarded as only instances of the misapplication of a principle both simple and true: the unity of Scripture and the continuity of revelation alike bearing witness to the unity of their Author, and of His purpose for mankind. The levitical *cultus* in particular is a product too intricate and mysterious to allow us for a moment to suppose that it was an antiquated and meaningless excrescence upon a decaying system. Further, criticism teaches us that in its developed shape the *cultus* was inspired by thoughts which a Christian knows to be eternally true. It was intended to give outward expression to that thought of divine indwelling which has been realized in the Incarnation and in the experience of the Christian Church. Ezekiel's vision of a city which is Jehovah's dwelling-place is essentially identical with St. John's conception of the heavenly Jerusalem [1]. Accordingly, it is natural and reasonable to discern in every detail of the Jewish ritual a divine thought, a spiritual idea, foreshadowed dimly in the legal type, but manifested in Jesus Christ; *Nihil enim vacuum neque sine signo apud Deum* [2]. As we learn from the Epistle to the Hebrews, the whole system of worship was the pattern and shadow of heavenly realities; the holy places made with hands were *figures of the true*; under material symbols and visible arrangements were continuously disclosed thoughts which the Holy Spirit

---

Ceremonial Law will be found in Diestel, *Geschichte des A. T. in der christlichen Kirche*, § 7.

[1] Ezek. xlviii. 35; Rev. xxi. 3, 22, 23.
[2] Iren. iv. 21, 3. Cp. Orig. *de Princ.* iv. 6 τὸ ἐνυπάρχον φῶς τῷ Μωυσέως νόμῳ καλύμματι ἐναποκεκρυμμένον συνέλαμψε τῇ Ἰησοῦ ἐπιδημίᾳ, περιαιρεθέντος τοῦ καλύμματος, καὶ τῶν ἀγαθῶν κατὰ βραχὺ εἰς γνῶσιν ἐρχομένων ὧν σκιὰν εἶχε τὸ γράμμα.

intended to teach from the first[1]. In fact, we miss the real purport of the minute descriptions of the tabernacle and its worship contained in the Pentateuch if we fail to discern beneath the picture of the ideal sanctuary the outlines of the kingdom of God which is destined to find its consummation in the perfected Church of the redeemed.

For the Mosaic tabernacle seems to give concrete and pictorial expression to three fundamental truths of catholic religion.

First, it was a symbol of the right of access to God vouchsafed by the divine mercy to man. The tabernacle was *the tent of meeting*[2], the spot where God could be approached, and where He deigned, under conditions of His own appointment, to draw near to man. The writer to the Hebrews points out that in Jesus Christ man acquires the right of priestly access to God. In Him as the representative of His redeemed people we can *draw near in full assurance of faith*; we can *come boldly unto the throne of grace*[3]. In union with Him the individual soul may perpetually enjoy that privilege which was imperfectly foreshadowed by the solitary entry of the High Priest, on one day only in the year, into the Holy of Holies. The proof of divine inspiration in the account of the tabernacle lies not necessarily in its actual correspondence with fact, but rather in the ideal anticipations of which it is the product. It bears witness to the consciousness, which ever haunted the Israelite, of his vocation to communion and converse with God.

Secondly, the tabernacle was the abode where God made His dwelling in the midst of His people. Hence

---

[1] Heb. ix. 8 τοῦτο δηλοῦντος τοῦ Πνεύματος τοῦ ἁγίου, κ.τ.λ. Cp. Heb. viii. 5, ix. 24.
[2] אהל מועד. Exod. xxvii. 21; cp. xxix. 42.
[3] Heb. x. 22, iv. 16. Cp. vii. 25, &c., and observe the frequent use of the words προσέρχεσθαι, ἐγγίζειν in the Epistle. See also Rom. v. 2; Eph. ii. 18, iii. 12.

it is frequently called Jehovah's dwelling-place[1], wherein He deigned to walk with His ancient people throughout the days of their pilgrimage in the wilderness. It prefigured that mystery of condescension which was fulfilled in the tabernacling of the divine Word made flesh among men[2]. It was a visible emblem of that body of the incarnate Redeemer which was the 'temple' or tabernacle indwelt by His divine person. The simplicity of the ancient shepherd's tent probably suggested its structure and arrangements. But another name of the tabernacle indicated a more advanced and spiritual conception of the divine indwelling: namely, the phrase *tent of the testimony*[3], which implied that Jehovah's presence among His people was 'a moral fact conditioned by God's covenant grace' rather than any mere local proximity. It was the moral law that was Israel's true glory, and formed the pledge of its special nearness to God.

Lastly, in its structure and characteristic services the tabernacle was an emblem of the inaccessible holiness of Jehovah. Its arrangements and ritual were intended indeed to satisfy man's desire for approach to God, but the privilege of access was jealously restricted. The Jewish worshipper was held, so to speak, at arm's length. He was constantly reminded of the gulf that intervened between sinful man, whatever might be his aspirations, and the all-holy God. The very fact that human approach to God was possible only under the most jealous restrictions served to bring home forcibly to the heart of the Israelite the inherent imperfection of the whole ancient system. 'The inaccessibility,' remarks Dr. Bruce[4],

---

[1] משכן. See Exod. xxv. 8, 9; cp. xxix. 45, 46. The tabernacle was the place of the שכינה.

[2] See 2 Sam. vii. 6 foll. Cp. John i. 14, ii. 19; Rev. xxi. 3.

[3] אהל העדות. Num. ix. 15. Cp. Exod. xxxviii. 21, &c.; and see Schultz, *O. T. Theology*, i. 353 foll.

[4] In an exposition of Heb. ix. 1-10; see *Expositor*, ser. 3, no. lx (Dec. 1889).

'was not absolute, but the solitary exception made the sense of inaccessibility more intense than if there had been no exception. Had entrance been absolutely forbidden, men would have regarded the inner sanctuary as a place with which they had no concern, and would have ceased to think of it at all. But the admission of their highest representative in holy things on one solitary day in the year taught them that the most holy place was a place with which they had to do, and at the same time showed it to be a place very difficult of access.' This indeed seems to have been the true import of the arrangement, *the Holy Ghost signifying this* thereby[1]. It was a perpetual memorial to the Jew of the divine holiness. It was a *tabernacle of the congregation* only in the sense that the people in the person of their divinely-appointed representative there met with God[2]. The structure of the tent and the regulations in regard to entry taught in the most impressive way the truth that *without holiness no man shall see the Lord*[3]; and indeed this was perhaps the most significant of the purposes served by the picture of the ancient sanctuary. It fulfilled a function corresponding to its place in the system of divine education. The restrictions under which approach to God was allowable, qualified the sense of His gracious condescension by laying deep the foundations of holy fear. *Ye shall reverence my sanctuary*, says the Law of holiness: *I am Jehovah*[4]. And it is obvious that only when the immeasurable interval subsisting between the divine nature and the human had been adequately realized, was the foundation prepared for a true doctrine of their union in the person of the incarnate Son of God. The religious idea of God's distinctness from nature was

---

[1] Heb. ix. 8.
[2] The above A. V. translation of '*Ohel Mo'ed* is thus incorrect. See Willis, *Worship*, &c., p. 68.
[3] Heb. xii. 14. See Riehm, *A Tl. Theologie*, p. 88.
[4] Lev. xix. 30, xxvi. 2. On the natural basis of this fear or reverence for holy places see Robertson Smith, *Religion of the Semites*, lectt. iii, iv.

educated by a moral discipline which, while it emphasized the possibility of union between God and man, deepened the consciousness of a barrier which only divine grace could remove [1].

When we turn to the sacrificial system we still find ourselves under the guidance of the apostolic writer who first explicitly draws out the general significance of the levitical sanctuary. In regard to the law of the offerings, his teaching implies that they were divinely intended to foreshadow the mystery of Christ's person and work, and their intricacy and many-sidedness corresponds to the diversity of aspects under which the work of redemption may be contemplated [2]. The analogy of the Gospels illustrates the mode in which a Christian student may use the Old Testament types. Speaking generally, each Gospel gives a separate view of Christ's person, just as each parable in St. Matthew's thirteenth chapter presents some different aspect of the divine kingdom. So it is with the Old Testament sacrifices. When Faustus the Manichaean complains that they are no better than a system of idol-worship in which the Church by accepting the Old Testament becomes a partaker, Augustine replies by explaining their real significance for Christians. Though they do not, he says, form any part of our practice, yet we welcome them among the other mysteries of Holy Scripture as aiding us to understand the things which they prefigured. 'Even these,' he continues, '*were our examples* [3], and

---

[1] On the symbolism of the tabernacle, see Note A at the close of the lecture.

[2] Novatian, *de Trin.* ix: 'Hunc enim Jesum Christum ... et in Veteri Testamento legimus esse repromissum et in Novo Testamento animadvertimus exhibitum, omnium sacramentorum umbras et figuras de praesentia corporatae veritatis implentem.' Cp. Jukes, *The Law of the Offerings*, p. 41: 'The offering of Christ ... was but one, and but once offered; but the shadows vary in shape and outline according to the point from whence, and the light in which they are looked upon. In other words, the one offering had several aspects, and each aspect required a separate picture. Had Christ's fulness and relations been less manifold, fewer emblems might have sufficed to represent them; but as they are many, and each to be variously apprehended, no one emblem, however perfect, could depict them all.'

[3] 1 Cor. x. 6.

all such ordinances in many and varied fashions foreshadowed that one sacrifice whereof we now celebrate the memorial. Hence since it has been revealed, and in due time offered, the ancient rites have been removed from the sphere of frequent observance, but in the way of signification they have remained authoritative[1].' This statement corresponds to Augustine's distinction between Old Testament ordinances as partly *praecepta vitae agendae*, partly *praecepta vitae significandae*. The moral law given to the Jews is of permanent obligation, the ritual directions are of permanent significance. Like prophecy, the ceremonial code laid hold of eternal principles, and in so doing foreshadowed the future developments of the divine purpose. Consequently, as Augustine elsewhere observes, the Apostle speaks not of the abolition of the Law, but of the doing away in Christ of the veil which concealed its true sense[2].

The writer to the Hebrews regards Christianity mainly under one aspect—as the final or absolute religion. It has the characteristic of *perfection* (τελείωσις), inasmuch as it establishes that unimpeded fellowship between God and man which in the levitical system was adumbrated but not attained. The faith of Christ is the religion of *the better hope, whereby we draw nigh unto God*[3]. For Jesus Christ fulfils in Himself two distinct types of priesthood. He is a priest after the order of Melchizedek; His priesthood belongs to an order eternal and supra-national. It is based on divine promises and combines with sacerdotal functions those of royalty; it is the medium of high and heavenly blessings to mankind. But, on the other hand, Christ is the antitype of the Aaronic priest. He fulfils all that was prefigured in the levitical ordinances by offering Himself as a spotless victim, and by entering within the veil of the *true*

---

[1] *c. Faust. Manich.* vi. 5 ; cp. vi. 2.
[2] *de util. cred.* 9 (2 Cor. iii. 14). Cp. Bas. *de Spir. sancto*, 21.
[3] Heb. vii. 11 and 19.

tabernacle[1], there to present Himself in the presence of God on behalf of His brethren and to dedicate them in His own representative person for the life of acceptable service[2]. As the true Melchizedek, Christ bestows blessing, and feeds His people with eucharistic bread and wine: as the true priest of Aaron's line, He purges the whole sphere of man's worship with His own blood; He cleanses the individual conscience from the defilement of sin; *He ever liveth to make intercession*[3].

Such is the well-known teaching of the Epistle to the Hebrews, which gives a sanction to the patristic view of the sacrificial ritual; and having this sanction we may proceed to inquire what were the main ideas symbolized in the *cultus*, and how they were fulfilled in the work of Christ.

We have seen that the informing idea of the levitical sanctuary, as sketched first by Ezekiel and afterwards in the priestly code, was that of Jehovah's presence in the midst of Israel[4]. The thought that inspires the sacrificial ritual seems to be that of maintaining Jehovah's covenant. Thus its fundamental significance is ethical, for the covenant implied on the one side Jehovah's grace, on the other Israel's moral obedience. The sacrifices were full of spiritual symbolism: they spoke of self-surrender and devotion to the will of God; of the need of forgiveness and the blessings of divine fellowship. The prophetic teaching as to Jehovah's requirement gave them a typical meaning which, if we may judge from the language of some of the Psalms, was transparent enough to devout and thoughtful minds. The burnt-offering, for instance, was a vivid type of man's willing self-surrender in a life of unbroken obedience; the sin-offering with its ceremonial sprinkling of blood spoke of the submissive acceptance of penalty by the sinner

---

[1] Heb. viii. 2.   [2] Heb. vii. 27; viii. 3; ix. 14, 26; x. 10 foll.
[3] Heb. ix. 13, 14. 23 foll.; vii. 25.
[4] See Ezek. xxxvii. 26–28; Exod. xxix. 45, 46.

as the necessary condition of forgiveness; the peace-offering with its communion-feast expressed the idea of fellowship between God and man renewed and consummated. Here, then, were prefigured in broad outline the moral conditions of man's reunion with God: but in the fulfilment of them by Jesus Christ even the minor details of the *cultus* were found to possess a previously unsuspected significance.

1. For, in the first place, Christ's life of perfect devotion to the will of God is the antitype of the burnt-offering. His whole life is comprehended by St. Paul in the single word *obedience*[1]—an obedience which was an integral element in the acceptableness of His self-oblation. In Christ man rendered to God that which alone could satisfy Him, a whole-hearted self-devotion, a perfect consecration of every faculty—of will, thought, and affection[2]. That element of voluntariness which from the nature of the case could not be represented by an irrational victim was in the highest measure present in the oblation of Christ's life. He discharged the covenant obligation of obedience which Israel could not render, and crowned it by the surrender of His life. For the death upon the cross cannot be separated from the earthly pilgrimage which it consummated[3]. It was the highest exhibition of that love wherewith Christ *loved us and gave himself for us an offering and a sacrifice to God for a sweet-smelling savour*[4].

The life and ministry of Jesus were in fact prefigured by the *Tamid* or continual offering which was intended to remind Israel of its ideal vocation. Day and night without intermission there ascended from the temple

---

[1] Rom. v. 19; cp. Phil. ii. 8.
[2] Cp. Lev. i. 8, 9; and see Matt. iii. 17, xii. 18, xvii. 5, xxii. 37; John viii. 29. Observe, the fire which consumed the burnt-offering is an emblem of the perpetual devotion of love (cp. John xiv. 31). See Euthymius on Heb. ix. 14 (quoted by Westcott, ad loc.).
[3] Cp. Heb. x. 1–10.
[4] Eph. v. 2. Observe the phrase ὀσμὴ εὐωδίας, which is used also of the burnt-offering and symbolizes divine acceptance. See Gen. viii. 21; Lev. i. 9, 13, 17; cp. Ezek. xx. 41.

court into the clear air the smoke of the sacrifice which lay upon the brazen altar. It was at once a memorial wherein Israel was as it were continually presented before God, and a striking emblem of that to which as a holy people it had pledged itself[1], the whole-hearted and unbroken service of Jehovah. But the daily burnt-offering was a type fulfilled only in the life of Christ—in the perfection of His self-surrender, in the spotless purity and nobleness of what He offered, in the infinite acceptableness and victorious might with which it pleaded, and yet pleads, before God. For the continual offering of the Jewish sanctuary points to a perpetual function of Christ. His perfect obedience has not merely prevailed for man's acceptance in the past; it yet pleads with living power where the great High Priest now presents Himself on man's behalf, and wheresoever on earth the memorial sacrifice of Christendom is uplifted before the Father's face. In that unceasing act of intercession the Israel of God is ever presented before the throne of Heaven, nor is it fanciful to suppose that the meal-offering, and especially the ordinance of the shewbread, was divinely intended to prefigure the mystery wherein the Christian Church shows *the Lord's death till he come*[2]. The least that can be said is that the meal-offerings prepared the Jewish mind for 'the acceptance of that form of sacrifice which was to supersede all others, in which the elements were to be simply bread and wine[3]'; in which bloody sacrifice was to be replaced by the

---

[1] Cp. Exod. xxiv. 7.

[2] 1 Cor. xi. 26. The shewbread (לחם פנים, LXX. ἄρτοι ἐνώπιοι or ἄρτοι τῆς προθέσεως) was set forth as a *memorial*, Lev. xxiv. 7 : ἔσονται οἱ ἄρτοι εἰς ἀνάμνησιν προκείμενοι τῷ κυρίῳ. Cp. Luke xxii. 19. The loaves of shewbread were in fact a kind of perpetual sacrifice (Schultz, i. 355). Cp. Lev. xxiv. 8. Its typical character consists (1) in its being a *Minchah* or non-bloody offering, (2) in its having a memorial significance, (3) in its being wholly consumed by man. It thus combined the idea of *sacrifice* with that of *communion* (Willis, *Worship of the Old Covenant*, p. 166).

[3] Willis, p. 163. The Fathers commonly regard Mal. i. 11 as a prophecy of the Eucharist.

oblation of incense and by the pure offering (*Minchah*) mentioned by Malachi.

2. In the next place, Jesus Christ as the representative of humanity accepts death, in token of His submission to the penalties of human sin. It is noticeable that the burnt-offering was in idea independent of the thought of sin. Its atoning virtue was incidental. Its essential significance was that of self-dedication; it implied the satisfaction not of offended justice, but of a holy requirement[1]. The sin-offering, on the contrary, was piacular; it implied the development of a consciousness of guilt; it witnessed to the reality of retribution and the need of satisfaction; to the impossibility of remission *without shedding of blood*[2]. The antitype then of the sin-offering is the atoning death of Jesus Christ who makes propitiation for sin by His own blood. Moreover, the death of Christ may be regarded as a trespass-offering[3], inasmuch as the second Adam offers satisfaction and makes restitution for the wrong done to the majesty of God by the first Adam.

Here let us pause to consider the meaning of the use of blood in connexion with the ancient sin-offering. There was, as we have seen, but very little significance attached to the victim's *death*; slaughter was simply the means employed for obtaining the *blood*, which was sacred as the seat of life[4]. And it is important to observe that in the transaction which followed the slaughter—in the presentation, and sprinkling of the blood—the dominant idea was rather that of the surrender of life than that of the acceptance of death. The blood was in fact regarded as still living; it was only *liberated* for higher purposes by the act of slaughter; it was conceived as still living and in a real

---

[1] Cp. Lev. i. 4, and see Robertson Smith, *Religion of the Semites*, pp. 329, 330; Jukes, *Law of the Offerings*, p. 52.
[2] Heb. ix. 22.
[3] Obs. אשם in Isa. liii. 10.
[4] Gen. ix. 4; Lev. xvii. 11. Cp. Schultz, i. 392.

sense active beyond death[1]. Tradition tells us that it was usually caught by the officiating priest, as it flowed from the slain animal, in a pointed vessel which could not be set down, and was constantly stirred to prevent coagulation. Quick, warm, alive it was carried to the appointed place and there solemnly sprinkled. The blood thus offered was in fact an emblem of life yielded up in perfect self-surrender, and dedicated to the service of the living God. The act of sprinkling on the horns of the altar or on the mercy-seat typified the reception of human life into the sphere of divine fellowship. The slaughter then of the victim was 'only an initial stage in a great sacrificial transaction; in conformity with the legal type, Christ, living through and beyond death, must needs pass within the veil as our perfected High Priest. The atoning work was not complete until, by His ascension, Christ had passed into the Holy of Holies, which is *heaven itself, there to be manifested in the presence of God for us* as our representative.' There 'the ascended Lord, taking with Him those for whom He died, presents them in Himself to His eternal Father[2].' With His own blood shed on man's behalf He passes into *heaven itself*[3], and there accomplishes what was dimly prefigured in the solemn sprinkling of the sacrificial blood by the levitical priest. He brings the life of man into perfect fellowship with deity.

It will have appeared from what has been said that the complete type of the atoning work of Christ is to be found only in the ceremonial of the Day of Atonement which was regarded as completing the whole cycle of piacular sacrifices[4]. In a sense it 'summed up and

---

[1] Cp. Westcott, *Epp. of S. John*, p. 35 ; *Ep. to the Hebrews*, p. 293.
[2] *The Doctrine of the Incarnation*, vol. ii. p. 313.
[3] Heb. ix. 24.
[4] Cp. Lev. xvi. 21. The Day of Atonement was held to cleanse the people from all their sins, i.e. 'according to the Mishnic interpretation, to purge away the guilt of all sins, committed during the year, that had not been already expiated' (*Religion of the Semites*, p. 388).

interpreted the whole conception of 'sacrifices' in so far as they were divinely intended 'to gain for man access to God¹.' The great feature of the day was the entry of the High Priest into the Holy of Holies, a representative act in which the whole nation was year by year admitted to the presence of Jehovah, but which was only possible in virtue of blood, that is of life, shed, and solemnly offered². In this transaction the life of the people was first symbolically yielded up as a token of submission to the penalty of sin, and afterwards brought within the veil into the immediate presence of God. Israel was first ransomed, then dedicated; first pardoned, then consecrated³. The covenant status of the people was renewed; Israel was restored, by the removal of sin, to the position of a community in which Jehovah could continue to dwell⁴.

But the blood of the sin-offering sacrificed on the Day of Atonement was not only offered on behalf of the people; it was applied. By its presentation at the mercy-seat it was endued with cleansing and sanctifying efficacy. Sprinkled on the floor of the sanctuary, and on all the sacred furniture, it purged them from the defilement they had contracted from the handling of sinful men; it reconsecrated them to holy functions. And *the blood of sprinkling*⁵ may be regarded as a sample of all the Jewish rites of purification⁶, which could purge at least outwardly those who had involved themselves in ceremonial uncleanness and needed restoration to covenant privileges. The writer to the Hebrews, however, draws attention to the contrast between these merely external ordinances and the inward effectual operation of Christ's blood.

---

¹ Westcott, *Ep. to the Hebrews*, p. 279. Cp. Schultz, ii. 402 foll.
² Heb. ix. 7; cp. Lev. xvi. 14, 15.
³ See Milligan, *The Resurrection of our Lord*, pp. 133 foll.
⁴ Cp. Lev. xvi. 16. ⁵ Heb. xii. 24.
⁶ In Heb. ix. 13 the blood of Christ is placed in line with (i) the blood of bulls and goats, i.e. the rites of the Day of Atonement, (ii) the water of sprinkling mixed with ashes of the red heifer (Num. xix).

'The Mosaic rites availed to renew the covenant fellowship between God and His people, which might have been interrupted by sin; they removed the accumulated defilement arising from daily action and intercourse or from contact with death. But their effect was outward and transitory. They hallowed, but could not purge the worshipper. Their effect might be described in the word ἁγιασμός, which implies merely the reconsecration of what had been desecrated or profaned. But the effect of Christ's blood is a true and inward purgation of the character and conscience from moral and spiritual defilement; His blood is a real means of cleansing (καθαρισμός), of actual deliverance from the stain of guilt and from the power of sin. . . . The communication of the blood of Christ, whether in the gift of absolution or in the grace of Holy Communion, is in fact the communication of a divine life, annihilating the stains and reinforcing the frailty of nature[1].'

3. This brings us to the third division of sacrifice and its fulfilment in Christ. He is the slain victim of the peace-offerings, His sacrifice being the groundwork of a communion feast[2]. A meal is the ordinary symbol, according to oriental conceptions, of fellowship and peace. And the eucharistic feast of the Christian Church is the highest realization, under the conditions of our mortality, of the blessedness for which man was created. It typifies the peace which follows upon penitent self-surrender to the will of God. It is a means whereby he becomes a partaker of the divine nature, and a recipient of the divine life[3]. In a real sense it anticipates the consummation towards which the kingdom of God ever tends, the perfect indwelling of the Creator in His creatures. On this point there is no need to dwell at length. It is enough to draw attention to the impressiveness of the circumstance that the earliest and rudest forms

---

[1] *The Doctrine of the Incarnation*, vol. ii. pp. 325, 326.
[2] Heb. xiii. 10.   [3] 2 Pet. i. 4; John vi. 53-57.

of sacrifice foreshadowed a religious idea than which none is more distinctive of Christianity. We are told on high authority that the ancient sacrificial meal had both a social and a religious significance. The primitive notion was that those who ate and drank together were 'by this very act tied to one another by a bond of friendship and mutual obligation'; such an act of worship cemented 'the bond between man and his god, and also the bond between him and his brethren in the common faith [1].' Further, it was a widespread belief in Semitic antiquity that ' by eating the flesh or drinking the blood of another living being a man absorbs its nature or life into his own [2].' How remarkable it is that the great Christian sacrament should embody and consecrate the element of truth which, often in the crudest and most fantastic forms, underlay these ancient ideas! It is true not only in the critical moments of religious history, but also in the development of religious ordinances, that *there are last which shall be first, and there are first which shall be last* [3].

As we look back over the different ordinances of the levitical legislation in the light of their Messianic antitypes we shall recognize the truth of St. Paul's bold assertion that *the law is spiritual* [4]. Under those *carnal ordinances imposed* as a burden *until the time of reformation* [5] lay concealed a spiritual fact which was their basis and presupposition—the fact of Jehovah's electing love. It is true that, speaking generally, ' Israel did not rise to the level of its institutions, but rather brought them down to its ever-lowering standpoint [6]'; we must judge, however, of the tendency of the Law, not by its acknowledged failures, but by its spiritual triumphs. And doubtless in those books of the Old Testament which represent the devotion and

---

[1] *Religion of the Semites*, p. 247.
[2] *Ibid.* p. 295. [3] Luke xiii. 30.
[4] Rom. vii. 14. Cp. Orig. *de Princ.* iv. 6 τὸ πνευματικὸν τοῦ Μωυσέως νόμου ἔλαμψεν ἐπιδημήσαντος Ἰησοῦ.
[5] Heb. ix. 10. [6] Edersheim, *Warburton Lectures*, p. 245.

faith of the spiritual Israel, and the fruit of the discipline through which it had passed, we learn what was the divinely intended outcome of the Law and its appointed worship. Such books as Deuteronomy and the Psalter reflect the spirit which found satisfaction or edification in the services of the sanctuary; they illustrate the religious affections which the Law awakened in chosen souls; their thirst for righteousness, their holy fear, their longing for purity of heart, their passionate desire for union with God. It was this life of the affections which the sacrifices were peculiarly fitted to educate. The ethical foundations of covenant fellowship with God had been firmly laid by the teaching of Moses and of the prophets. The Decalogue and the early legislation, social and moral, were calculated to act as a restraint upon conduct and a discipline of character. But the ordinances of worship in their developed form were at once a school for the heart and a channel of spiritual instruction. In the intention of its priestly compilers no doubt the ceremonial Law was designed to emphasize and elaborate the external holiness of Israel. But the thoughts of God are not man's thoughts, neither are our ways His ways[1]; and the actual effect of the *cultus*, at least in devout hearts, was to deepen the inwardness of their religious life, to stir emotions which only the divine heart could fathom, and to awaken unutterable yearnings which the love of God, manifested in His Son, alone could satisfy.

[1] Isa. lv. 8.

Note A.

The Symbolic Significance of the Tabernacle.

THE following note, based largely upon a chapter in *The Worship of the Old Covenant* (Oxford, 1880), by the Rev. E. F. Willis, is inserted as an illustration of legitimate typical interpretation.

The writer of the Epistle to the Hebrews insists emphatically on the fact that all the arrangements of the earthly sanctuary were, according to the divine injunction, modelled after the pattern displayed to Moses on the mount [1]. It is evident that in his view the description of the sanctuary was an embodiment of divine thoughts, of mysteries which it was the work of the Holy Ghost to partially unveil. Accordingly, to quote Bishop Westcott [2], 'there can be no reasonable doubt as to the symbolism of the tabernacle. It conveyed of necessity deep religious thoughts to those who reverently worshipped in it. It was, however, a natural and indeed a justifiable belief that the spiritual teaching of the fabric was not confined to its ruling features, but extended also to every detail. There are correspondences between all the works of God which deeper knowledge and reflection make clear. The significance attached to the numbers which continually recur in all the relations of the several parts cannot be questioned.' But we have also to remember that the sanctuary 'was not simply an epitome of that which is presented on a larger scale in the world of finite being; the archetype to which it answered belonged to another order; the lessons which it conveyed were given in the fullness of time in a form which is final for man,' namely in the humanity of Jesus Christ [3].

In its general structure it is not difficult to see that 'the tent of meeting' is a type of Him who *was made flesh and tabernacled among us* [4]; and that each several part or chamber is emblematic of a dispensation in redemptive

---

[1] Heb. viii. 5. Cp. Exod. xxv. 8, 9; Acts vii. 44.
[2] *Ep. to the Hebrews*, p. 237.
[3] *Ibid.* p. 240. [4] John i. 14.

history. The outer court with its bleeding sacrifices and its laver of purification symbolizes the preparatory stage of Mosaism with its sacrificial system and comprehensive ceremonialism. The number five, which is the prevailing figure in the measurements of the court, being half of ten, the number of perfection, serves to convey the moral idea of incompleteness, while the inferior metals employed in the construction of the altar and the laver symbolize what is imperfect and rudimentary [1]. The Holy Place entered by the veil which separated it from the court contained three symbolic objects—the golden altar of incense, the table on which stood the pure vegetable oblation of the shewbread, and the seven-branched candlestick with its lamps. Here faith may find a type or representation of the Christian Church with its Eucharist, its sevenfold gift of the Spirit, its perpetual intercession in union with that of its ascended High Priest. But the Holy Place held a position which in itself was parabolic [2], and not merely prophetic. It witnessed indeed to man's true destiny as called to fellowship with God; but the fact that he might not penetrate to the innermost shrine constantly reminded the Jewish worshipper that he could not yet enjoy the fullness of divine communion [3]. In the Holy Place Jehovah was manifested only in condescending grace; in His divine glory and majesty in the Holy of Holies alone. Thus the realities (αὐτὰ τὰ πράγματα) of heaven itself were typified by the most Holy Place. Its very form was an emblem of God's dwelling-place, *for the length and the breadth and the height of it* were *equal* [4]. It formed a perfect cube of ten cubits, as if to suggest the ideal ultimate perfection which the kingdom of God was destined to attain. It was lighted only by the *Shekinah*, the divine glory dwelling in visible manifestation between the golden cherubim, upon the mercy-seat or covering of the ark. The mercy-seat was the sacred place of reconciliation or atonement; the ark was the receptacle of Israel's most sacred possession, namely the tables of the testimony which formed the charter of the divine covenant. Upon the mercy-seat stood cherubim—probably standing figures in human or possibly composite form, representing the most exalted of created beings, nearest to the throne of deity and highest in service, yet reverently stooping as if to gaze into the mysteries of God. The thought

---

[1] See generally Willis, *The Worship of the Old Covenant*, ch. v; Oehler, *Theol. of the O. T.* §§ 115-119.
[2] Cp. Heb. ix. 9.   [3] Cp. Westcott, *Ep. to the Hebrews*, p. 250.
[4] Cp. Rev. xxi. 16.

is thus visibly expressed that the self-revelation of God is at the same time a self-concealment. The cherubim, according to the usual imagery of the Old Testament, at once proclaim the presence of God and veil His essential glory[1].

The materials of the tabernacle, gold, silver and brass, and the colours of the hangings, blue, scarlet and purple, are employed in such a way as to suggest the ideas of gradation, continuity and splendour. The furniture of the outer court is mostly brass; in the Holy Place no brass is used except in the sockets of the pillars at the entrance. Silver, the emblem of moral purity, is used in the foundations of the Holy Place, and it is noticeable that the capitals of the pillars in the outer court are of the same material, as if to show that 'the highest glory of what the court foreshadowed was inferior to the lowest of that which was typified by the Holy Place[2].' The materials employed in the Holy Place and Holy of Holies are acacia wood and gold with which it was overlaid, but the mercy-seat and the cherubim are wrought of solid gold. The colours also are symbolic: white is the emblem of holiness, of soiled robes cleansed from stain. Blue, the colour of the sapphire stone[3], suggested the heavenliness of the divine calling. Scarlet, the colour of blood, signifies created life. Purple, the intermingling of scarlet and blue, is a symbol of the union of two natures, divine and human. All these different materials and colours suggest different degrees of glory and dignity, beauty and excellency: all are emblematic of the holiness, purity and majesty of the kingdom of God. They suggest thoughts of that *glorious body* of which the Apostle speaks[4], of that *glorious church*[5] which Christ purposes to present to Himself.

Once more, the measurements of the different parts of the tabernacle are not without significance. For we cannot but be struck by the stress laid upon number and measure in the Bible[6]. In the account of the tabernacle and of the temple[7], and in Ezekiel's prophetic description of

---

[1] Riehm, *ATl. Theologie*, p. 90. On the mercy-seat (הַכַּפֹּרֶת, LXX. ἱλαστήριον) see Willis, *op. cit.* p. 105; Riehm, *loc. cit.* Cp. Gifford on *Romans*, iii. 25. On the cherubim, see Schultz, *O. T. Theology*, ii. 229 foll. He says (p. 236): 'The cherubim were not angels, but symbolical figures, combining the noblest qualities of the created world—a man being the symbol of intelligence, a lion of sovereignty, an ox of strength, and an eagle of swiftness.' See also Oehler, § 119.
[2] Willis (quoting Rev. H. Douglas), p. 92.
[3] Cp. Exod. xxiv. 10. [4] Phil. iii. 21. [5] Eph. v. 27.
[6] See Schultz, *O. T. Theology*, vol. i. p. 352 note; cp. Willis, pp. 76 foll.
[7] 1 Kings vi and vii.

an ideal sanctuary and city, the dimensions of things are prominently and minutely recorded; and they even find a place in St. John's picture of the heavenly Jerusalem. We have noticed already that while the tabernacle is of oblong shape, the Holy of Holies forms a perfect cube; a contrast which suggests the incompleteness of the visible kingdom of God as contrasted with the ideal perfection towards which it tends. As to the numbers, those which occur most frequently, either singly or in combination, are three, four, five, seven, ten, and twelve. Three is generally recognized as an emblem of what is divine. It symbolizes divine appointment, and corresponds to the revelation of the divine nature and attributes. Accordingly, in the tabernacle we find three main divisions, three veils, three metals used, and three colours. Four suggests the notion of created being, and, as we should expect, the number is very prominent in the structure of the visible sanctuary (ἅγιον κοσμικόν)[1], being impressed upon the general design of the whole building and upon its contents. Seven is the union of four and three; it symbolizes a covenant relationship—the union or reconciliation of man with God. It is not so distinctly characteristic of the tabernacle itself as of the Jewish dispensation and ceremonial regarded in its entirety[2]. It corresponds to the name Emmanuel, *God with us*. The number ten denotes perfection or completeness. Its employment in the measurements of the tabernacle suggests the idea that, though temporal in form and use, the structure was yet perfect of its kind. Five, the half of ten, evidently conveys the idea of incompleteness. Finally, the number twelve, four multiplied by three, corresponds to a more intimate relationship between the Creator and the creature than is expressed in the number seven. It symbolizes the indwelling of deity in the creature, and accordingly we find that the number is characteristic of the Church of God in all the successive stages of its history: there are twelve patriarchs, twelve tribes, twelve stones in the breastplate of the High Priest, twelve Apostles of the Lamb. The number is specially prominent in St. John's vision of the heavenly Jerusalem. It corresponds to the consummation of the mystery of the Incarnation—a state or sphere in which God is not merely *with* men, but *in* them; not merely visits and redeems His people, but possesses them with His indwelling presence.

---

[1] Heb. ix. 1.
[2] In the tabernacle we have the seven-branched candlestick; in the levitical system the number frequently occurs. Cp. Willis, p. 79.

LECTURE VI

And it shall be said in that day, Lo, this is our God; we have waited for him, and He will save us: this is the Lord; we have waited for him, we will be glad and rejoice in His salvation.—Isa. xxv. 9.

THE general results of Old Testament criticism might be summed up in a single sentence in which at first sight two opposite views of the sacred history appear to be contrasted: instead of speaking of 'the Law and the Prophets' we might equally speak of 'the Prophets and the Law.' Now it is to be borne in mind that both expressions are found in the New Testament, either *totidem verbis* or in some equivalent form [1]; but there can be no question that the usual order in our blessed Lord's repeated references to the subject is 'the Law and the Prophets,' and we might naturally infer from this language the priority in time of the Law. A few moments' attention, however, will show in what sense the phrase 'the Law and the Prophets,' though apparently unhistorical, is both perfectly natural and strictly accurate. The history of the growth of the Hebrew Canon supplies the real clue to our Lord's ordinary mode of speech. The formation of the Canon began with the codification, promulgation, and eventual canonization of the book of the Law. The foundation-stone of the work was laid in Josiah's reign, which witnessed 'the dawn of that love and reverence for Scripture with which the true Israelite, whether Jew or Christian, was destined ever afterwards to be identified [2].' The publication of 'the book of the Law'

---

[1] Cp. Acts xxvi. 22, 'the Prophets and Moses.'
[2] Ryle, *Canon of the O. T.* p. 61.

(the Deuteronomic code) was the primary stage in a movement which was carried on during the exile mainly, it would seem, under the influence of Ezekiel. The so-called priestly code seems to have been slowly compiled and elaborated before the return from Babylon, but apparently the work was not finally completed before the mission of Ezra to Jerusalem; it is with Ezra's name that we ought to connect the promulgation of the completed book of the Law, described in the eighth chapter of the book of Nehemiah. All the evidence points to the conclusion that the book publicly read by Ezra on the occasion of Nehemiah's arrival at Jerusalem (444 B.C.) was none other than the Pentateuch substantially in its present form. What had hitherto been a priests' book became a people's book, and thus the Law became the nucleus of the Old Testament scriptures [1].

The 'Prophets' do not as yet seem to have been collected in any authoritative or canonical form. Writings of various prophets were already current, both historical documents which were afterwards classed as 'earlier' or 'former Prophets,' and the books ascribed to most of the 'latter' Prophets themselves. But these did not as yet form a recognized part of Scripture. It was only on the analogy of the Law, and at a considerably later period, that 'the Prophets' came to be regarded as a canonical book, and to be ranked as Holy Scripture by the side of the Law [2]. Now it is most probable that our Lord in speaking of 'the Law and the Prophets' is simply referring to those two great divisions of Hebrew Scripture which were respectively known by these titles. He refers to 'the Law' as the oldest and most venerable portion of the Hebrew Bible, and to 'the

---

[1] Ryle, *op. cit.* ch. iv. It was the Pentateuch which the Samaritan synagogue took over from the Jews in about the year 430 B.C.

[2] Perhaps not before 300 B.C. Prof. Ryle says, 'Before the beginning of the second century B.C., the second stage in the formation of the Canon had ended; and the limits of "the Law and the Prophets" had been determined' (p. 109).

Prophets' as a collection of writings formed at a later date, and probably not regarded by the ordinary Jew as standing entirely on the same level of dignity and authority as the Law. According to His wont, our Saviour is conversing with the Jews on the basis of their own traditions and preconceptions. He is addressing men whose religion was predominantly legalistic; and it is noticeable that two of the passages where the phrase 'the Law and the Prophets' is found occur in the Sermon on the Mount, in which Christ is as it were proclaiming the new law of the Messianic kingdom[1]. He is speaking to those whose religion, whether for better or for worse, had tended to become the religion of a book or even a code, and there can be no question that He speaks not from the critical standpoint, but from the standpoint of one who is concerned with the practical work of religious instruction, and who is dealing with men to whom the Law was the most sacred of possessions and the most authoritative of institutions.

Speaking broadly, the phrase the 'Law and the Prophets' represents two spiritual tendencies, which were not absolutely opposed, or even two distinct periods in the history of Israel's religion, which were not as a matter of fact strictly successive in point of time. So far as we can judge, Prophecy and Law were co-existent and co-operative elements in Israel's spiritual development from the first: but it is evident on a careful study of the Old Testament history, and of the course of events which followed the return from Babylon, that two main epochs are practically distinguishable: the age of the Prophets, which lasted for some two centuries before the exile, and the age in which the Law became the principal factor in Israel's spiritual progress. But, as a recent writer observes, 'No one maintains that the Law first appeared, or first began to exercise its influence, when the prophetic development had already come to a close. The

[1] Matt. v. 17; vii. 12.

existence of the book of Deuteronomy in the seventh, and of the "Book of the Covenant" already apparently in the ninth century, would instantly refute any such assertion. On the other hand, no one denies that Prophecy exercised decisive influence upon the formation and development of the Law. Even the most convinced defender of the traditional view will allow to Moses in his activity as lawgiver prophetic inspiration, and will not deny him a prophetic character[1]. We have already seen that Moses was recognized by later prophets as himself one of the greatest of prophets. The book of Deuteronomy indeed reminds us at its close that *There arose not a prophet since in Israel like unto Moses, whom the Lord knew face to face*[2]; and Hosea expressly teaches that *By a prophet the Lord brought Israel out of Egypt, and by a prophet was he preserved*[3].

Thus the expression 'the Law and the Prophets,' or its converse, was not necessarily intended to emphasize the idea of succession in time; it implies a reference to the Hebrew Scriptures according to their constitutive elements. In any case it cannot be meant to imply that the work of the prophets was in any sense of secondary importance in the development of Israel's religion. On the contrary, when we consider the entire tone and tendency of our Lord's teaching we shall conclude that He, *the Wisdom of God*, sets His seal to the work of the ancient Prophets when He places the moral requirements of God in the very forefront of the new law, and assigns to the fulfilment of legal righteousness a subordinate place: *Except your righteousness shall exceed the righteousness of the scribes and Pharisees, ye shall in no case enter into the kingdom of heaven. Go ye and learn what that meaneth, I will have mercy, and not sacrifice. If ye had known what this meaneth, I will have mercy, and not sacrifice, ye would not have condemned the guiltless. Woe unto*

---
[1] Valeton, *Vergängliches und Ewiges im A. T.* p. 22.
[2] Deut. xxxiv. 10.
[3] Hos. xii. 13.

vi] PROPHECY AND THE MESSIANIC HOPE 269

you, scribes and Pharisees, hypocrites! for ye pay tithe of mint and anise and cummin, and have omitted the weightier matters of the law, judgment, mercy, and faith: these ought ye to have done, and not to leave the other undone[1]. Nay, does not this last passage remind us that He whose Spirit inspired the sacred writers Himself recognized the oneness of divine intention which underlay the teachings of the Law and the Prophets alike. In both of them the Jews were right in supposing that they had eternal life [2]: for man's true life consists in the love of God and the imitation of Him. *Whatsoever ye would that men should do to you, do ye even so to them; for this is the Law and the Prophets.* On two chief commandments *hang all the Law and the Prophets*[3].

It cannot be too often repeated that prophecy is the dominant and distinctive element in Israel's religion. Without it Israel would only have been one of the innumerable nomad tribes of the Semitic race, the very traces of which have perished [4]. Hebrew history has been justly called 'a history of prophecy,' since it is the history of a relation between God and an elect people in which prophets were the principal mediators. The God-ward aspirations of Israel attained in them the highest and most representative expression; through them the message of Jehovah was communicated to His people. All the great turning-points in the history were connected with the appearance of prophets. Their activity was the most decisive factor in the moral and social progress, as well as in the religious development of the nation. In

---

[1] Matt. v. 20; ix. 13; xii. 7; xxiii. 23.   [2] John v. 39.
[3] Matt. vii. 12; xxii. 40. Observe that Christ's references to 'the Law and the Prophets' seem to indicate that to Him these were the most important parts of the Canon. The 'Writings' formed a group, of which the limits were scarcely yet precisely defined. The reference to 2 Chron. xxiv. 21 in Matt. xxiii. 35 appears to imply that the books of Chronicles closed the Hebrew Canon then as now. See Valeton, *Christus und das A. T.* 31 foll.
[4] Darmesteter, *Les Prophètes d'Israël*, p. 210. Cp. Driver, *Sermons on the O. T.* p. 101.

a word, apart from prophecy the history loses all its significance. Consequently, although it cannot be said that our present tendency lies in the direction of underrating or ignoring the influence of Hebrew prophetism, our subject requires that some attempt should be made to estimate anew its unique significance. I run the risk of touching on a good deal that is already very familiar to my hearers, but the theme is one of special importance to all who desire to understand the ideals which make Christianity what it is— the religion of the better hope.

I.

The beginnings of prophetism bear witness to the close connexion that existed between Hebrew institutions and the phenomena of Semitic religion in general. Tradition points to the activity and influence of Samuel as marking a creative epoch in Israel's history, and it is significant that his distinctive work was the regulation and organization of prophetism. The natural soil out of which the prophetic gift was developed seems to have been the tendency to ecstatic religious excitement which is characteristic of the Semitic temperament. Prophetism was in fact an institution which Israel originally shared with its heathen neighbours[1]. The gods of Phoenicia had their prophets; the prophets of Baal we know— fanatical devotees who with wild dancing and music endeavoured to attract the attention or win the favour of their god, by cutting themselves with lancets and knives *till the blood gushed out upon them*[2]. In some respects akin to these Canaanitish *Nebiim* seem to have been the bands of prophets

---

[1] The story of Balaam shows that in a rude form prophetism existed among the Semitic races before the conquest of Canaan. The *Nabhi* of that age was little more than a sorcerer, whose incantations were supposed to operate with infallible effect. See Renan, *Histoire du peuple d'Israël*, bk. ii. ch. 1.

[2] 1 Kings xviii. 28.

described in the first book of Samuel in connexion with the early career of Saul[1], enthusiasts who have been compared, not perhaps inaccurately, to the dervishes of the East[2], displaying in a kind of ecstatic behaviour the effects of special religious exultation. These prophets appear to have lived together in companies or schools; they wore a coarse garment of skin in token of their religious calling; they probably depended for support upon the charity of the faithful, and were objects of mingled contempt and reverence to the multitude. The prophet who was commissioned to anoint Jehu king was despised as *a mad fellow*[3], and the point of the inquiry *Is Saul also among the prophets?* lies in the popular astonishment that so distinguished a man should be found in such strange company. There are incidents in the career even of Elijah and Elisha which imply a similar connexion between prophetic inspiration and physical excitement[4], but apparently these phenomena accompanied only the early stages of a movement to which we owe the noblest figures of Hebrew history, and the most sublime literature ever produced. Nevertheless, we can frankly recognize the rudimentary character of the early stage[5]; and when we attempt to measure the interval that parts the wild and uncouth behaviour of these primitive devotees from the exalted and chastened majesty of men like Isaiah, we shall acknowledge that Hebrew prophetism supplies a conspicuous example of the method of accommoda-

---

[1] 1 Sam. x. 5–13; xix. 23, 24.
[2] Cornill, *Der Israelitische Prophetismus*, pp. 13–15. Cp. Renan, *Histoire*, &c., bk. ii. ch. 13, and Kittel, *Hist. of the Hebrews*, vol. ii. p. 110.
[3] 2 Kings ix. 11.   [4] See 1 Kings xviii. 46; 2 Kings iii. 15.
[5] Riehm, *ATl. Theologie*, p. 203: 'Gehören im ATl. Prophetentum die Zustände bewusstloser Ekstase nur der niedrigsten Stufe seiner Entwickelung an, während in seiner Blütezeit die prophetische Begeisterung immer mit voller Klarheit des Bewusstseins verbunden ist.' Cp. Ewald, *The Prophets of the O. T.* [Eng. Tr.] vol. i. pp. 16, 17. It is noticeable that Amos himself, one of the most striking prophets, seems to have been popularly regarded as one of the class of professional *Nebiim* (Amos vii. 14), but repudiates the suggestion.

tion which marks the entire history of Israel—God condescending to use a defective and rudimentary institution, a rude native outgrowth of the Semitic character, in order to develope therefrom a glorious product of grace. 'We must not be reluctant,' says Cornill, 'to recognize many strange elements in the religion of Israel. We do not set them aside; on the contrary, we regard them as evidence of the highest vitality, and of a most powerful faculty of assimilation. The people of Israel in its spiritual capacity resembles the fabled king Midas, for whom all that he touches turns to gold[1].' Everything indeed which Israel derived from its past or present environment was transmuted into something new and unique, so that it is difficult to recognize in the final result the lowliness of the elements which contributed to it, but which in due time disappeared.

Samuel then it was who revived or re-organized the prophetic office, and we may pause to consider the full significance of his work. What he apparently aimed at was the regulation of the turbulent and boisterous elements in the behaviour and character of the *Nebiim*, in order to enlist the movement in the service of a higher and purer type of religion[2]. There is no reason for rejecting the supposition that the earliest outburst of prophetic enthusiasm was connected with a patriotic uprising against Philistine oppression, but Samuel's main object was probably not political. He discerned that

---

[1] *Der Isr. Prophetismus*, p. 15.
[2] Kittel, *Hist. of the Hebrews*, II. 110. Observe the contrast which is perhaps suggested in 1 Sam. ix. 9 between Samuel himself, calm and self-contained, and the excitable and undisciplined troops of *Nebiim*. He is a 'seer' (Roeh), they are 'prophets' (Nebiim). Montefiore, *Hibbert Lectures*, p. 77, thinks that the two names represent two orders, the one native Hebrew (seers), the other Canaanite (prophets), and that later prophecy is a result of a coalition of the two; a 'grafting of Canaanite prophecy upon the old stock of Hebrew seers.' But he admits that there is little to support his conjecture. The narrative contains a note stating that *Nabhi* is a more recent and *Roeh* an older name for the same thing. Cornill points out that the passage implies the recent and *foreign* (i.e. Canaanite) origin of the *Prophetism* (*Der Isr. Prophetismus*, p. 13).

VI] PROPHECY AND THE MESSIANIC HOPE

the fierce ardour for Jehovah's cause and for the integrity of His land which fired the *Nebiim* might be educated into a powerful religious force. Accordingly, he gathered them into organized schools or guilds in which the prophetic gift might be cherished, and the life of religious devotion cultivated. Possibly also the art of sacred song was studied in these societies, and the historical annals of the nation formed or collected[1]. From this time forward, at any rate, the schools of the prophets occupied a recognized sphere in the religious life of the nation. We hear of the *Nebiim* again in connexion with the reign of Ahab, and it is probable that their renewed activity was occasioned by alarm at the king's syncretistic propensities. It would seem that by this time the ecstatic and fanatical element had been more or less subdued, and that the *Nebiim* were on the point of becoming a regular order. But it was not as an order that they became influential. When they became a professional class they seem to have given way to professional failings[2]. 'First-rate importance cannot be claimed for the *Nebiim*,' says Wellhausen[3], but occasionally there appeared among them 'individuals who rose above their order and even placed themselves in opposition to it.' The first and most eminent of these striking personalities was Elijah. 'Elijah,' says Kittel[4], 'introduced into prophecy that species of categorical imperative which distinguishes him as well as the later prophets; that brazen inflexibility, that diamond-like hardness of character, which bids them hold fast by their moral demand, even should the nation be dashed in pieces against it. For him the demand means to stand by Jehovah as against Baal.' Henceforth, then, the prophets acted on the nation by the

---

[1] This is denied by Wellhausen, *Sketch of the History of Israel and Judah*, p. 64; but there seems nothing improbable in the suggestion. See Kuenen, *Religion of Israel*, ch. iii [Eng. Tr., vol. i. p. 210].
[2] Sanday, *Bampton Lectures*, p. 134.
[3] *Sketch of the History of Israel and Judah*, p. 64.
[4] *Hist. of the Hebrews*, vol. ii. p. 266.

T

sheer force of inspired personality. As individual witnesses for God, steeped in the fundamental ideas of the religion of Jehovah, they proclaimed His word, His sovereignty, His righteousness, His election of Israel, His abhorrence of lip-service, His hatred of social wrongdoing. For aught we know, much may have been accomplished in this way by the banding together of the *Nebiim* in organized companies; but experience shows that the influence of even large and powerful religious communities is unequal to that of a single great religious leader. It was to the influence of personality that Israel's religion owed its persistent vigour, its perpetual upward tendency, and the growing purity and loftiness of its fundamental conceptions.

II.

In order, however, to gain a comprehensive idea of the significance of Hebrew prophecy for the Christian Church, it is necessary to survey briefly the chief aspects of the prophets' work.

1. First, the prophets were inspired men, 'men of the word.' The root from which *Nabhi* is derived can be traced in the ancient language of Assyria and Babylon as well as in Arabic. In Assyrian it has the meaning, 'utter,' 'proclaim.' It appears in such patronymics as Nebu-kadnezar, and Nabo-polassar, and in the title of the Babylonian deity whence they are derived, *Nebo* or *Nabu*, which probably signifies the God of wisdom or wise utterance, corresponding to the Greek Hermes. The word *Nabhi* would thus originally mean 'one who utters.' But in Arabic the root has a more specific connotation: it imports the announcement of a message which the speaker is commissioned to deliver. *Nabhi* would accordingly seem to bear the sense of ' a *commissioned* speaker.' Aaron, for example, is called the *Nabhi* or ' prophet ' of Moses as speaking in his name and by his commission [1].

---

[1] Exod. vii. 1; cp. iv. 14–16.

A prophet, then, is one who speaks as the accredited messenger of Almighty God. This seems a better account of the word than that which some writers prefer, viz. that *Nabhi* means one in whom the flood of divine inspiration 'wells' or 'bubbles up[1]'; one who speaks as the passive instrument of the divine Spirit. In fact the term corresponds rather to the Greek προφήτης than to μάντις: it means *a forth-teller* rather than *one who foretells*; one who announces what has been supernaturally revealed to him as an organ of divine interposition in the affairs of men. And if we wish to understand the essential characteristics and true significance of Hebrew prophetism it is important to rid ourselves of the associations which have gathered round the English word 'prophet,' implying that the essential element in the work of the Hebrew prophets was prediction. This, we shall find, was far from being the case. The vital element in prophetism was the prophet's own consciousness that he was not acting or speaking in his own name, but as the instrument—sometimes indeed the reluctant instrument—of a higher Power.

In two respects the prophets may be distinguished from the ordinary soothsayers (μάντεις) of heathendom, Aryan or Semitic[2]. First, they were conscious and intelligent when they uttered their oracles. Hebrew prophecy rapidly outgrew the ethnic stage of mere possession, or ecstasy. The prophet was no 'unintelligent medium' of divine communications; he spoke under a sense indeed of overmastering moral constraint, but all his faculties were intensified and illuminated by the power of the divine Spirit[3]. So vividly

---

[1] So Kuenen, *Religion of Israel*, ch. iii, note. Cp. Oehler, *Theology of the O. T.* § 161; but see Robertson Smith, *The Prophets of Israel*, lect. ii. note 18; Cornill, *Der Isr. Prophetismus*, pp. 6-11, and Schultz, *O. T. Theology*, vol. i. pp. 264-265.

[2] The Pythia of Delphi is an instance. On the other hand, Homer's Calchas, the Athenian Musaeus, Socrates, and Plato (in his prophecy of the righteous suffering) are instances of phenomena more nearly akin to those of Hebrew prophetism (Riehm, *ATl. Theologie*, p. 204).

[3] Driver, *Sermons on the O. T.* p. 135: 'The psychical conditions

conscious are the prophets of their mission that they ordinarily use the first person when they speak in God's name, but they never lose their sense of the distinction between their own thoughts or impulses and the revealed word of Jehovah[1]. Secondly, the Hebrew prophet stands alone in the character of the message delivered. What was it that distinguished the true prophets from the heathen soothsayers or from the false prophets 'who gave out the dreams of their own heart as God's word'? It was the profoundly moral purport of their message that made the prophets unique. *Truly I am full of power by the spirit of the Lord, and of judgment, and of might,*—so cries Micah, *to declare unto Jacob his transgression, and to Israel his sin*[2]. Prediction, indeed, is an element of comparatively secondary importance in prophecy. The main work of the prophet is to turn men from their sins and to proclaim the sovereignty of Jehovah. Where prediction constitutes the dominant element, prophecy loses its distinctive character and is better described as apocalypse. The book of Daniel, for instance, is an apocalyptic book rather than a prophecy. The predictions of the prophets are the outcome of their unshaken belief in the moral government of the universe, and in the impending fulfilment of the divine purposes; they are the result of inspired insight into

under which God spoke in them, the nature and operation of the initial impulse which brought them to the consciousness of Divine truth, may belong to those secrets of Man's inner life which God has reserved to Himself; but by whatever means this consciousness was aroused, the Divine element which it contained was assimilated by the prophet, and thus appears blended with the elements that were the expression of his own character and genius.' Cp. Riehm, *op. cit.* pp. 212 foll.; Kittel, *op. cit.* p. 317.

[1] Cp. Oettli, *op. cit.* p. 19: 'Nach ihrem sonnenklaren Zeugniss die Quellen ihrer Religion, wie ihrer besondern Erleuchtung, nicht in ihrem eignen Geiste, sondern in einer wunderbar ihnen erschlossenen transcendenten Welt von göttlicher Realität lagen.'

[2] Mic. iii. 8. Cp. Just. M. *Dial. c. Tryph.* vii ἐγένοντό τινες ... μακάριοι καὶ δίκαιοι καὶ θεοφιλεῖς θείῳ πνεύματι λαλήσαντες καὶ τὰ μέλλοντα θεσπίσαντες ἃ δὴ νῦν γίνεται. προφήτας δὲ αὐτοὺς καλοῦσιν. οὗτοι μόνοι τὸ ἀληθὲς καὶ εἶδον καὶ ἐξεῖπον ἀνθρώποις, μήτ' εὐλαβηθέντες μήτε δυσωπηθέντες τινά, μὴ ἡττωμένοι δόξης ἀλλὰ μόνα ταῦτα εἰπόντες ἃ ἤκουσαν καὶ ἃ εἶδον ἁγίῳ πληρωθέντες πνεύματι.

the inevitable tendencies and consequences of human action, and of national or personal wrongdoing[1]. Not that the power of prophecy is any mere apotheosis of human reason[2]: it implies, however, not the supersession or suspension of ordinary human faculties, but the elevation of them to the highest point of intensity. The prophets claim to utter a message from Jehovah, and they know that He who bids them speak enables them by His Spirit, and is with them to strengthen, and if need be to deliver them[3].

2. Such then were the characteristics of prophetic inspiration. It is natural in the next place to consider the sphere in which it was exercised, and the conditions, social and moral, with which it was appointed to deal. From the days of Samuel onwards we find the prophets standing in the closest relation to the political circumstances of their times. They have been called 'watchmen of the theocracy[4],' and undoubtedly they believed it to be their mission to intervene from time to time in politics, with the view of keeping alive in the minds of their fellow-countrymen just and true conceptions of the theocratic state. They made it their business to watch the course of national affairs in general, and specially to control and judge the conduct of the reigning monarch and his counsellors. They steadfastly believed in the fact of Israel's election, and in the spiritual mission with which it was charged. The exalted destiny to which the chosen people had been called

---

[1] Cp. Riehm, p. 206; Bruce, *Apologetics*, p. 242; *Chief End of Revelation*, p. 217. The following striking remarks of M. Darmesteter illustrate the same point: 'Le Prophète ne prédit jamais. Il voit les grandes lignes de l'avenir, parce que, s'étant fait une doctrine et une philosophie du monde, il se fait une idée nette et précise de la destinée qui attend son peuple, suivant la voie où il s'engage : le grand mouvement des choses et des idées, avec leurs conséquences lointaines et nécessaires, est la seule chose qui l'intéresse : le détail, le fait concret, le petit hasard de l'actualité lui échappe ; il l'ignore, il l'abandonne aux charlatans de la prophétie' (*Les Prophètes d'Israël*, pp. 137, 138).
[2] Darmesteter, p. 246 : 'Le Dieu des prophètes n'est que la raison humaine projetée au ciel.'
[3] Jer. i. 8, 19.
[4] Cp. Mic. vii. 4; Jer. vi. 17; Ezek. iii. 17 ; xxxiii. 7. See Oehler, *Theology of the O. T.* § 162 and Ewald, *op. cit.* pp. 28, 29.

could only be fulfilled by continual faithfulness to the great religious ideas which underlay Israel's vocation [1]. Accordingly it was the chief aim of the prophets to keep Israel faithful to Jehovah as He had revealed Himself at Sinai, as a God in whose eyes pure worship, social righteousness, and fraternal charity were of supreme value. Further, they fulfilled their mission not only by their preaching, but by their own lives. As individual 'men of God' they represented typically the realization of that living fellowship with God towards which the theocracy ever tended as its ultimate goal. And in their unbroken moral converse with God, in their pureness of heart, and in the simplicity of their faith and dependence on Jehovah, lay the secret of their influence [2]. It has been said that by producing the prophets Israel realized her vocation [3]. Certainly as 'the servant of Jehovah' the prophet bore a title which was ideally applicable to Israel as a people, and which expressed the actual calling of each individual Israelite. For the ideal of the Old Testament was a dispensation in which all should be prophets: *Would God*, exclaimed Moses when Joshua envied for his sake,—*Would God that all the Lord's people were prophets, and that the Lord would put his Spirit upon them* [4]. The prophets then were examples of the illuminative power of holiness and single-hearted devotion to the will of God. Moreover, their fate was in most cases typical. Their position might vary from time to time according to the disposition of the reigning monarch. Prophets were held in honour by kings like David, Hezekiah, and Josiah, who understood the necessity of maintaining a close connexion between the national life of Israel and the spirit of religious faith; but sooner or later their

---

[1] Cp. Isa. ii. 5.
[2] Cp. Amos iii. 7; Wisd. of Sol. vii. 27. Riehm, *ATl. Theologie*, p. 204, observes, 'Die höheren Stufen prophetischer Begeisterung werden auf eine Gottverwandtschaft der Seele zurückgeführt.'
[3] Bruce, *op. cit.* p. 195; cp. Robertson Smith, *O. T. in J. C.* p. 291.
[4] Prof. Cheyne remarks that this idea is characteristic of the post-exilic period (*Aids to the Devout Study*, &c., p. 151; cp. p. 203).

fearless denunciations of vice could scarcely fail to bring them into collision with royal self-will or with popular prejudice and fanaticism [1]. One and all, in greater or less degree, they were called to suffer for their faith, for their boldness in rebuking sin, or for their devotion to the revealed will of Jehovah. Thus in their isolation from the world, in the intimacy of their relation to God, and in the sorrows which they were called to endure, they typically embodied the ideal vocation of *the righteous nation* [2] viewed in its entirety.

The prophets then were the accredited guardians of the fundamental ideas upon which the theocratic state was based. Their testimony accompanied, so to speak, the historical realization of the divine purpose for Israel, the word of Jehovah constituting a kind of continuous commentary on His acts. Accordingly we find that a considerable element in the prophetic function consists in the elucidation or interpretation of past history and of contemporary events. The prophets trace and proclaim the ruling principles of divine action and governance: and specially it is their work to bring out the moral significance of the Mosaic Law—a task the fulfilment of which necessarily brought them into relation to the priests, who were the official guardians of the law. But while the priests were the permanent teachers of *Torah*, the prophets were occasional messengers of Jehovah. Through the priest the covenant people exercised its privilege of drawing near to God. Through the prophet God drew near to His people. Naturally the priests submitted themselves to the prophets as to extraordinary and direct agents of Jehovah [3]; but there were elements of antagonism in the two orders which were frequently in danger of coming into

[1] Cp. Schultz, *O. T. Theology*, vol. i. pp. 248 foll.
[2] Isa. xxvi. 2; cp. Deut. xxxii. 15 (Jeshurun). Aug. *c. Faust. Man.* iv. 2 says: 'Illorum hominum non tantum lingua sed et vita prophetica fuit.'
[3] Cp. König, *Religious History of Israel*, p. 160. Kuenen, *Hibbert Lectures*, pp. 81 foll., discusses the teaching office of the priests, and the prophetic complaints of their shortcomings.

collision. The history of Israel shows how strong was the tendency of the priesthood to exaggerate the value of ritual, and to change into hard and fast law what originally might be a matter of variable custom. It was obviously the interest of the priesthood to exalt the laws of ceremonial purity; they would be apt to lay stress on details, and to lose sight of principles. But the prophets were more concerned to insist on Jehovah's moral requirement as a whole; and in putting morality on a higher level than ritual, they undoubtedly continue and develope the teaching of Moses himself. They reassert the claims of justice and mercy which the ancient legislation of the Decalogue and the Book of the Covenant had placed in the forefront [1]. Their well-known polemic against sacrifice does not indeed amount to a rejection of the institution, as has been sometimes asserted; but they unquestionably do insist that punctiliousness in sacrifice is no equivalent for civil and social well-doing. What they abhor is 'religion divorced from right conduct,' ritual, however costly and elaborate, combined with neglect of moral obligations [2]. On the whole the attitude of the prophets towards sacrifice is negative. They content themselves with 'condemning such elements in the popular worship as are inconsistent with the spiritual attributes of Jehovah [3].' From an early period, then, in the history of prophecy we find a tendency towards antagonism between prophets and priests, the former reminding the latter that all true

---

[1] Cp. Driver, *Sermons on the O. T.* pp. 113 foll. See also some good remarks in Oettli, *Der gegenwärtige Kampf um das A. T.* p. 9.

[2] See Amos v. 24; Hos. vi. 6; Isa. i. 16 foll.; Mic. vi. 8; Jer. vii. 21 foll. This last passage does not imply that ritual laws formed *no* part of the Mosaic legislation, but it may fairly be used as testimony (1) that in Mosaism the most important element was ethical, (2) that the elaborate levitical code was unknown to Jeremiah. See a note in Riehm, *ATl. Theologie*, pp. 246, 247; cp. Wellhausen, *Prolegomena*, p. 58. Even König (*Religious History of Israel*, p. 168) allows that 'religion and morality were from the beginning the basis of Israel's favour with God.'

[3] Robertson Smith, *O. T. in J. C.* p. 305. Cp. Hos. iv. 6; Zeph. iii. 4.

Torah must move within the lines of Jehovah's original covenant with Israel. In a more awful and momentous form the antagonism ultimately meets us in the pages of the Gospel [1].

But it is time to resume our main theme—the social and political conditions of the period in which the great prophets appeared upon the scene of Hebrew history, and for convenience' sake our survey will be confined to the northern kingdom. The political activity of such men as Isaiah or Jeremiah in the kingdom of Judah exercised so profound an influence on the fortunes of the Hebrew state and on the development of its religion, that it seems better to omit any detailed reference to the work of these great prophets than to deal with it summarily within the narrow limits of a lecture. The eighth century was indeed a critical epoch in Israel's career. Hitherto prophecy had frequently taken the form of an occasional rebuke sternly administered by individual prophets to unrighteous rulers. Thus Samuel had rebuked Saul, Nathan had denounced the crime of David, and Elijah had been the divinely-appointed scourge of Ahab and his house. But with Amos and Hosea the spirit of prophecy comes into collision with the temper and tendencies of the nation as a whole, and in so doing it passes into the wide sphere of social and political activity. The general conditions of the time were in fact rapidly obscuring Israel's sense of spiritual and moral vocation. In the eighth century a new conception was dawning upon thoughtful hearts—the idea of the world and the world-empire. It was an idea that was only to be deeply impressed on the minds of men by 'the pitiless hammer-strokes of fate [2].' And the prophets discerned

---

[1] Consider Luke xxiv. 19, 20. Schultz, vol. i. p. 338, remarks: 'This antagonism naturally showed itself still more plainly where, as in the northern kingdom, the priesthood wished, in spite of the preaching of the prophets, to maintain an antiquated and impure form of religion (Amos vii).' Cp. Riehm, *ATl. Theologie*, p. 208.

[2] Kittel, *Hist. of the Hebrews*, vol. i. p. 242; ii. p. 259. Cp. Riehm, *ATl. Theologie*, pp. 224, 225.

that Israel's appearance in the world-theatre must necessarily seal her destiny as an independent state. It was manifest that she could never hold her own as one of the monarchies of the East. The huge and restless empire of Assyria darkened the distant horizon like a menacing thunder-cloud, but the storm did not immediately burst. Danger from a nearer quarter threatened Israel. In the reign of Jehu's son and successor Jehoahaz (*circ.* 815) the northern kingdom was harassed by the pertinacious hostility of Syria[1]; and although Israel played a valiant part in the ensuing struggle, its deliverance was eventually due to the intervention of the Assyrian power, which had already begun to advance in a westward direction[2]. The war between Syria (Aram) and Assyria ultimately broke the power of Damascus. Israel recovered its strength in proportion as that of Syria declined[3], until in the reign of Jeroboam II the northern kingdom appears to have reached the very zenith of material prosperity. But the social and economic effects of long-continued warfare constituted a growing peril which prophecy was quick to discern. The cessation of hostilities had indeed led to a great increase in Israel's wealth and resources, but the simplicity of pastoral and agricultural life had vanished. The whole conditions of society had given way to the exigencies of military organization. The prolonged struggle with Damascus had impoverished the small landholders to such an extent that they were rapidly sinking into abject poverty and even slavery. Meanwhile the court and a corrupt aristocracy absorbed the land, and exhausted the wealth of the nation; and the gulf between class and class became every day wider and more menacing. On the other hand, the mercantile spirit had received a great impetus from the recent wars; the sins of a growing and insolent middle class began to make their appearance; there was a vast

---

[1] 2 Kings xiii. [2] Cp. 2 Kings xiii. 5.
[3] 2 Kings xiv. 25; Amos vi. 14.

amount of dishonest trading, and considerable harshness in the exaction of debt. Finally, the inveterate curse of oriental life was embittering the social miseries of the time, viz. venality and corruption in the judges, with its inevitable result that the oppressed classes were left without hope and without redress [1]. The social influence of the prophets has sometimes been exaggerated. It is rather misleading to call them, as Darmesteter does, 'a series of religious and political tribunes [2]'; or to speak of their 'programme of reform,' as if they were mainly social agitators, intent upon overthrowing the existing order of society. As Professor Robertson Smith pregnantly observes, their cry is 'not for better institutions but for better men [3].' Beyond doubt, however, the prophets were most conspicuous as preachers of social righteousness. They were champions of the poor and oppressed. The spirit of the excellent priest described in a recent French romance was theirs. 'I am not,' says the *Curé de Canton*, 'a socialist; but I nevertheless admit that I conceive life otherwise than as a continual battle. And if there is such a battle, I shall range myself gladly on the side of the weak rather than on that of the strong [4].' The prophets waged war not with wealth as such, but with 'that reckless and material temperament' in which they recognized 'the completest type of enmity to Jehovah and His religion [5].' In one and the same spirit they denounced the heartless luxury of the wealthy and the material-

---

[1] On the social conditions of Israel and Judah in the eighth century see Kittel, vol. ii. p. 313; Robertson Smith, *Prophets of Israel*, lect. iii, and *O. T. in J. C.* pp. 349 foll.; Darmesteter, *Les Prophètes d'Israël*, pp. 36-40.
[2] *Les Prophètes*, &c., p. 122; cp. p. 141. Cp. Mill, *Representative Government*, pp. 40 foll. (p. 17 in popular edition).
[3] *O. T. in J. C.* p. 348.
[4] *Lettres d'un Curé de Canton*, publiées par Yves de Querdec (Paris, 1895).
[5] Montefiore, *Hibbert Lectures*, p. 153. Cp. Meinhold, *Jesus und das A. T.* p. 90: 'Der Glaube an Gott, den Gott Israels, ist ihnen so stark, dass das Benutzen weltlicher Mittel zur Rettung des Volks als Glaubenslosigkeit erscheint.'

istic aims and self-seeking worldliness of statesmen [1]. Further, what intensified their moral indignation at the prevailing iniquities of the social state was the outwardly flourishing condition of the national religion. Religious worship was an institution at once pleasant and fashionable. There were stated sacrifices connected with the *cultus* of Jehovah, and religious festivals in abundance; the sanctuaries were thronged on these occasions by crowds of enthusiastic and riotous worshippers, who regarded the sacred feasts as a legitimate opportunity for self-satisfied enjoyment and tumultuous revelry [2]. The growth of national prosperity which followed the close of the Syrian wars was popularly accepted as a comfortable token of divine favour. There was a widely-diffused notion that under no circumstances would Jehovah fail to befriend the people of His special choice. Israel was the favourite of God, and His interests—it was confidently assumed—were bound up with those of His people. Enough and more than enough was being done to secure the divine regard by a richly-appointed and well-maintained *cultus*. Thus any prediction, like that of Amos, which threatened Israel with overthrow was regarded as blasphemy against Jehovah. Jehovah must necessarily side with Israel against its foes. To question this was to question the very existence of the covenant relationship established by Mosaism. Accordingly a favourite watchword of the time seems to have been *the day of Jehovah* [3], a phrase which embodied the general expectation of some overwhelming and triumphant display of Jehovah's favour, manifested for instance in the overthrow of Israel's enemies. Failing utterly as they did to recognize the true character and requirement of Jehovah, the people persistently claimed to be special objects of His favour

---

[1] See e.g. Amos vi, and Isa. xxx, xxxi.
[2] Cp. Cornill, *Der Isr. Prophetismus*, pp. 38 foll.; Kuenen, *Hibbert Lectures*, no. 2.
[3] Amos v. 18 foll.

and protection. *Jehovah God of hosts is with us*, they declared: *us only does Jehovah know of all the families of the earth*. But while from this confidently assumed premiss Israel drew the conclusion, 'Therefore Jehovah will take our part and defend us from invasion,' the earliest of the great prophets, Amos of Tekoa, deduced a precisely opposite inference: *Therefore will* He *punish you for your iniquities*[1].

For indeed the primary work of the prophets was to proclaim not salvation but judgment. They were confident that the great social iniquities of the time—the luxury, greed, profligacy, oppression, and practical atheism of the upper and middle classes—were certain to bring upon the sinful nation a crushing retribution. Naturally enough they ranged themselves on the side of the down-trodden and oppressed, but their zeal was inflamed not so much by sympathy for the poor and suffering classes, as by a passionate belief in the supremacy of the law of righteousness. In an age of glittering prosperity and of ostentatious care for the externals of religion, the prophets were not blind to the symptoms of a profound moral corruption, which they knew to be the one fatal obstacle to the maintenance of the covenant relationship between the Holy God and His people. They proclaimed that because Jehovah is what He is, the theocracy in its existing condition must be inevitably doomed. The foundation on which it rested was rotten[2]. Thus in their insistence on the moral requirement of Jehovah for Israel, the prophets were not merely acting as defenders of outraged rights and liberties, or as champions of the poor against their oppressors; they were preach-

---

[1] Amos iii. 2; v. 14. Montefiore, *Hibbert Lectures*, p. 124, makes the striking remark, 'This terrible "Therefore" must have been as a bolt from the blue to the popular religious consciousness in the days of King Jeroboam.'

[2] Darmesteter, p. 48, mentions the 'four axioms' of prophecy: 'What is not founded on righteousness must perish—Jehovah has revealed His righteousness to Israel—Israel is bound to realize and embody this righteousness—It *will* be realized in the future.'

ing 'the august idea of the moral government of the world[1].'

3. This brings us to a third point: the religious function and influence of prophecy. It is often stated that the prophets were the creators of ethical monotheism; the founders of that 'true biblical religion which came to its fulfilment in Christianity[2].' Certainly they proclaimed with burning and passionate ardour the moral element in Jehovah's character. They taught that His anger was not fitful or unreasonable, not lightly arising or falling indiscriminately, but essentially and perfectly righteous. Two remarks, however, suggest themselves in regard to the statement that the prophets were 'creators of monotheism.' In the first place, it is necessary to protest against the idea that the higher conception of God was the outcome merely of human reflection, or the product of a higher phase of moral culture. What the natural evolution of religion leads to we see in the religions of heathendom. The gods of paganism were deified human beings, reproducing the attributes, or at least some one attribute, of their worshippers; heathen deities wear the impress of the national or tribal character which they reflect. But the God of the Hebrew prophets is one who stands in sharpest contrast to His people; indeed it is their unlikeness to Jehovah that is the secret of their threatened ruin. Left to itself the northern kingdom would have chosen Baal, and the worship of Jehovah might have even disappeared but for Elijah in the ninth century, but for Amos and Hosea in the eighth[3]. Secondly, the monotheism of the prophets was no new article of faith. It was the revival of a belief which probably had been the implicit conviction of the best in Israel

---

[1] Kuenen, *op. cit.* p. 124.
[2] Pfleiderer, *Gifford Lectures*, vol. ii. p. 45. Cp. Nicolas, *Des doctrines religieuses des Juifs*, p. 25: 'Les prophètes sont des initiateurs à la vérité divine; les premiers ils ont entrevu ce spiritualisme religieux dont le christianisme a été l'expression la plus élevée.'
[3] Cp. Oettli, *op. cit.* p. 15.

ever since the time of Moses[1]. The vital importance of the prophetic doctrine was that it was a turning-point in the transformation of faith in Jehovah as the national God into a universal religion. Professor Kuenen has pointed out that the doctrine of Jehovah's holiness lifted the whole conception of deity to a new and higher sphere. It was in His holiness that Jehovah was unique, and if holiness were an essential element in the divine character, the God of Israel must be the only God[2]. He cannot belong only to one particular people; every nation that recognizes an ethical standard, whether it be the law of nature written in the heart[3] or some positive code devised by human wisdom, stands in a necessary relation to the Holy One of Israel. Thus while we are not justified in concluding that the idea of monotheism was entirely new in the prophetic period, that idea was undoubtedly proclaimed with fresh emphasis, and under circumstances that gave precision and point to a dimly-realized belief which hitherto had been probably confined to a very small circle of the faithful[4]. For the nation as a whole cannot have been in any strict sense monotheistic. The average Israelite regarded the gods of the heathen as really existing beings who within their own sphere or domain were as powerful as the God of Israel in His. In opposition to this belief the prophets taught that where the law of righteousness was recognized, however defective or rudimentary might be its content, there the sway of Jehovah extended. Right was everywhere right, and wrong wrong. If the God of Israel were once acknowledged to be the God of righteousness, His dominion must necessarily be conceived as co-extensive with the law of righteousness itself, in a word with the inhabited world. The appearance therefore of Amos, the earliest of the

---

[1] Cp. Bruce, *Apologetics*, p. 176.
[2] Cp. Kuenen, *op. cit.* p. 119. [3] Cp. Rom. ii. 14.
[4] See Robertson's criticism of Kuenen, *Early Religion of Israel*, pp. 320 foll.

eighth-century prophets, forms an era in the history of human thought. Amos, says Cornill, 'is the pioneer of a process of development from which a new epoch in humanity dates.' If righteousness is indeed the supreme law of the universe, the God of Israel is the God of the whole earth, and in the creed of Israel are concealed the germs of a world-religion.

Mark how Amos enforces this truth. His prophetic glance extends beyond the borders of Israel itself. The heathen nations are arraigned by him as amenable to the judgment of God for offences against ordinary laws of humanity and international good faith. Damascus, Philistia, Edom, Ammon and Moab—they also are subject to the just sway of Jehovah, though they acknowledge Him not. On them, too, Jehovah inflicts the penalties which are the expression of His necessary resentment against human sin; it is His holiness which is outraged by the wholesale barbarities inflicted by one nation on another; it is He *to whom vengeance belongeth*[1]. What is this but an anticipation of St. Paul's statement, *The wrath of God is revealed from heaven against all ungodliness and unrighteousness of men*[2]? Assuredly in this prophetic view of God, in this conviction that the area of judgment extends beyond the limits of Israel[3], are hidden the elements of a true universalism. The teaching of Amos is still a long way removed from the generous faith which welcomed the nations into the kingdom of God and looked upon them as participating in the privileges and hopes of the chosen people[4]. But that faith was already implicitly contained in the doctrine of Amos that Jehovah was the God who had controlled by His providence the restless movements of the nations, or in that of Micah that the substance of Israel's conquered

---

[1] Ps. xciv. 1.   [2] Rom. i. 18.   [3] Montefiore, *op. cit.* p. 146.
[4] Montefiore has some interesting paragraphs on the growth of the universalist conception, pp. 145 foll. He regards the prediction of Isa. xix. 22-25 as 'the high-water mark of eighth-century prophecy' (p. 149).

foes should be consecrated *unto the Lord of the whole earth*[1].

Corresponding to this primary conception of God is the prophetic philosophy of history[2]. A large share of attention is devoted by most of the prophets to Israel's past career. They delight to trace the course of the divine dealings with the chosen people, and to point out the critical epochs in Jehovah's self-manifestation. In a certain sense, as we have seen, their mission is extended to all the nations in turn. Egypt, Tyre, Asshur, Edom, Moab, Babylon, though outside the sphere of the sacred covenant, were within that of the divine governance. But the real distinction between Israel and the nations consisted in the fact that Jehovah was not to His elect people merely what He was to the heathen—a dimly recognized power making for righteousness, but a covenant God manifesting Himself and making known the laws of His operation in condescending grace. The guilt of Israel was conspicuous in proportion to the degree of divine knowledge, and the measure of divine favour which it had enjoyed. Heathenism, it has been said, 'has neither a religious view of history, nor a philosophy of history; for it knew no absolute final moral purpose to the attainment of which the fates of the nations were to serve as means. Israel, on the other hand, knew such a purpose of history—namely, the realization of a kingdom of God, of a human fellowship and community corresponding to the holy will of God.' It was the belief of the prophets in the purpose of a righteous God that made them for all mankind 'the teachers of the religious view of the world which contemplates all that is perishing, all that is transitory, *sub specie aeternitatis*[3].'

---

[1] Amos ix. 7; Mic. iv. 13.

[2] Cp. Darmesteter, *op. cit.* p. 208: 'La philosophie de l'histoire est née le jour où les prophètes crurent trouver au monde et à la vie un sens et un objet.'

[3] Pfleiderer, *Gifford Lectures*, vol i. pp. 191, 192. Cp. Robertson Smith, *Prophets of Israel*, p. 138.

But other elements were contributed by the prophets to the idea of God. If the ethical doctrine of Amos stood by itself, it might appear to have a certain one-sidedness. The God whom he proclaims is essentially a moral ruler and judge, an object rather of fear than of love or trust[1]. In Hosea we discover that which forms the counterpart to the teaching of Amos. By Hosea a religious, rather than an ethical, aspect of God's relation to Israel is brought into prominence. To Amos, God is Israel's king and judge; to Hosea, her husband and father: to Amos, Israel is a state, *a sinful kingdom*, which has brought upon itself the righteous penalty of sin; to the mind of Hosea, the house of Jacob presents itself as 'a moral individual' or person, whom Jehovah has graciously brought into a close relationship with Himself[2]. The idea indeed of the continuity of this relationship colours Hosea's brief retrospect of history. In the career of Jacob, the progenitor of Israel, who had so manifestly experienced the strength and tenderness of Jehovah's pity and pardoning love, the history of the nation was typically summed up. Punishment and discipline—these had been the great factors in Jacob's life—but they had ever been controlled by an unfailing purpose of grace; they had been the instruments of moral purification; they had been visible proofs of Jehovah's abiding favour. *I will not leave thee*, was the promise to the lonely wanderer at Bethel, *until I have done that which I have spoken to thee of*[3]. Similarly, the entire history of Israel, from the days of the patriarchs downwards, is for Hosea the history of 'a single unchanging affection always acting on the same principles, so that each fact of the past is at the same time a symbol of the present or a prophecy of the future[4].' Hosea then crowns the doctrine of Jehovah's justice by dwelling on the constancy of His love. It is noticeable in this

---

[1] Cornill, *Der Isr. Prophetismus*, p. 48.
[2] Robertson Smith, *Prophets of Israel*, p. 165. [3] Gen. xxviii. 15.
[4] Robertson Smith, *loc. cit.* Cp. Hos. ii. 15; ix. 9; Joshua vii. 24.

connexion that the favourite word of Hosea, *Cheṣed*, 'loving-kindness,' is not found in Amos. The use of it implies that between Jehovah and Israel there exists a relationship of love, involving mutual obligations. This love is sometimes contemplated as marital[1]—Israel is the betrothed spouse of Jehovah, whom He has tended with unwearying faithfulness; sometimes as parental— Israel is the child whom Jehovah has taught to walk in His ways with watchful and considerate tenderness; sometimes as covenantal—Israel being regarded as a single person pledged to observe all the obligations that were involved in covenant-union with God and had been set forth in the ancient *Torah*, the continuous instruction which Israel had enjoyed through the mediation of the priesthood[2]. The word *Cheṣed*, however, is by no means confined to Hosea; it plays a great part in the theology of the Old Testament. But Amos and Hosea may be regarded as the representatives respectively of that twofold aspect of the divine character which is so familiar in the Psalter. Amos is the teacher of God's faithfulness or truth; His entire self-consistency, His essential fidelity to the law of righteousness. Hosea dwells on His mercy; His tenderness and loving-kindness to man—inviting the response of a similar affection on the part of man[3]. The word *Cheṣed* in fact, as employed by Hosea, suggests the truth that 'those who are linked together by the bonds of personal affection or of social unity owe to one another more than can be expressed in the forms of legal obligation[4].' As a term of common life, *Cheṣed* tends powerfully to simplify the thought of God. It anticipates the full disclosure of the New Testament *God is love*.

Thus by combining the teaching of Amos and Hosea we are enabled to form an impression of the epoch-making significance of Hebrew prophecy. For

---

[1] Hos. i–iii. Cp. Jer. ii. 2, iii. 1 foll.   [2] Hos. iv. 6; viii. 1, 12.
[3] See iv. 1; vi. 6; x. 12; xii. 6.
[4] Robertson Smith, *op. cit*. p. 160.

the two characteristic thoughts, one of which each prophet represents, are distinctive and permanent elements in the prophetic conception of God. The one idea, that of Jehovah's righteousness, reappears in the characteristic teaching of Isaiah, to whom Jehovah is *the Holy One of Israel*—not merely separate from the creation which owes its being to Him, but distinct from all that is limited and morally imperfect[1]. It is this attribute of Jehovah which is at once the necessary cause both of the judgments which fall upon Israel, and of the deliverances by which He vindicates His claim to be the hope and confidence of the faithful. The same idea underlies Ezekiel's thought of the greatness and inviolability of Jehovah's name, which in a sense has been profaned both by Israel's unfaithfulness and by the ignominy of their punishment[2]. On the other hand, to the three prophets whose writings are linked together by a common interest in the great passage, Exod. xxxiv. 6 foll., namely Micah, Nahum, and the writer of the book of Jonah, the leading element in God's character is His mercy and loving-kindness; on this they base their hopes, not of Israel's deliverance from foes, but of that spiritual enfranchisement from sin of which any outward salvation was only a distant emblem[3]. And it may be said that in the wonderful book of Jonah, possibly the latest product of the prophetic spirit, the thought of the divine loving-kindness receives its crowning expression. The design of the book, which was probably written in the post-exilic period, was mainly didactic[4]. It appears to have been composed with the aim of correcting the narrow, exclusive particularist idea—peculiar to the Judaism of that period—viz. that the sphere of salvation and grace was confined to Israel alone. Jonah's reluctance to do

---

[1] Cp. Kirkpatrick, *The Teaching of the Prophets*, p. 175.
[2] Ezek. xx. 9 foll.; xxxvi. 22. See Kirkpatrick, *op. cit.* p. 339.
[3] Mic. vii. 18–20. Obs. Mic. vi and vii appear to belong to a later period.
[4] See an admirable account of the book in Hunter, *After the Exile*, part ii. chap. 3.

Jehovah's bidding and his anger at Nineveh's repentance reflect the usual attitude of later Judaism towards heathendom[1]. Jonah for the moment represents the temper of which Tacitus hits the main characteristic: *adversus omnes alios hostile odium*[2]. Such an attitude of mind was indeed in direct conflict with the higher teaching of the prophets. Jeremiah, for instance, had taught that even in the case of the heathen repentance might avert the punishment of sin[3]. And among all other mysterious features which make the book of Jonah one of the most precious in the Hebrew Canon, we should perhaps assign the highest place to its evangelic purport. Whenever God brought Israel into relation with any heathen people it was for the purpose of making Himself known to it as a God of power and grace: to Egypt by Joseph and Moses; to Philistia through the capture of the ark; to Syria by Elisha when he healed Naaman; to Babylon by Daniel; to Persia by Esther. And so in the case of Nineveh, the mission of Jonah had borne witness to a truth which perhaps could only be adequately recognized in a much later age—the age in which the story of Jonah was clothed in a literary form—the truth namely of the universality of God's gracious purpose; the possibility of a natural goodness that implied some hidden operation of divine grace[4]; the fatherly love of the Creator and His compassion for all that He has made, His mercy extended even to the lowliest of all His works. This is the last word of the book of Jonah, and perhaps in that word we have the farewell voice of Hebrew prophecy. Thus the writer of Jonah is linked to Hosea as the preacher of the divine love[5].

---

[1] Cp. Acts xiii. 45; 1 Thess. ii. 16.
[2] *Hist.* v. 5. Cp. Maurice, *The Prophets and Kings of the O. T.* p. 354.
[3] Jer. xviii. 7 foll.
[4] There seems to be an intentional contrast suggested between the conduct of the Ninevites and that of Jonah fleeing from God's presence. The conduct of the heathen sailors is also presented in a very favourable light (Jonah i. 13 foll.).
[5] Meinhold, *Jesus und das A. T.* p. 10. The book of Jonah 'ist gegen

I have said enough at least to illustrate the religious influence of the prophets and the extent of their contribution to wider, purer, and richer conceptions of God. Before passing on, we may, at some risk of repetition, call attention again to the fact that the prophets are striking examples of the power of personality in the development of religion. Each prophet is in his own way and degree a religious genius. And here we have just that factor which is antecedently incalculable, and which any naturalistic account of Israel's religious development tends to ignore or misconceive. For it is in this element of individuality that Israel's religion is so distinct from that of surrounding peoples—an element which, I repeat, is the very core and essence of prophetism. A religious conviction so intense, a faith so glowing and so tenaciously grasped, as to mould or elevate the spiritual life of a nation, cannot have been merely the result of uninspired reflection. We can, as Schultz points out, only be historically just to the Old Testament in proportion as we acknowledge the presence and working in the history from first to last of the element of divine inspiration. The religion of the prophets is in a word the outcome of the operation of the Holy Spirit. The freedom, independence, and force of the prophet's personality results from a fact of which he was invariably conscious—the fact of his being called to his work and enabled for his high function by Jehovah Himself[1].

die Engherzigkeit des Judentums gerichtet und lehrt dass die Juden (Jonas) die Aufgabe haben den Heiden (Nineve) das Wort des wahren Gottes zu verkünden. Denn Gott ist ein liebender Vater auch der Heiden und ein Feind der engherzigen Abgeschlossenheit des Judentums' (Jonah iv. 11). See Cornill's enthusiastic estimate, *Der Isr. Prophetismus*, p. 169. ('One of the deepest and most large-hearted books that have ever been written.') Montefiore, *Hibbert Lectures*, p. 371 (cp. Hunter, *loc. cit.*), thinks that the book of Ruth may have been written with a similar intention. Valeton, *Christus und das A. T.* p. 46, points out that in His reference to it (Matt. xii. 39 foll.) our Lord 'sets His seal to the *spirit and tendency* of the book of Jonah.' He deals with it rather as a prophetical than an historical book.

[1] Cp. Mic. iii. 8.

III.

We now pass to that which many consider to be the most distinctive feature of prophecy—the element of prediction. The Old Testament is a book of hope. It is the record of a constant and growing anticipation, based on a divine promise to humanity, and embracing a future in which the whole race of mankind has an interest. Now the Christian student of prophecy is guided as a rule by one of two objects. He either studies the history of the Messianic hope in the apologetic interest—as a great department of the evidence to which his religion appeals in attestation of its truth; or he investigates it for the purpose of personal illumination and edification, interpreting by the aid of ancient prophecy what is still dark and mysterious in the dealings of God with men or in the primary Christian facts. He uses it in a word for the confirmation and education of his faith in pursuance of the inspired writer's injunction, *We have also a more sure word of prophecy, whereunto ye do well that ye take heed, as unto a light that shineth in a dark place, until the day dawn and the day star arise in your hearts*[1]. In Old Testament prophecy we have *a sure word* and *a light*: a 'sure word' of which the general fulfilment is in large measure an established fact of experience; a 'light' or 'lamp' in so far as prophecy brings to bear on the enigmas of human life the revealed laws of God's moral government. The ordinary conception, however, of the actual development of Messianic ideas has been in some degree modified by the conclusions of criticism. Accordingly my present object is to sketch the history of prophecy in such a way as to indicate the elements which successively moulded the image of the Messiah in Hebrew thought, confining my survey however so far as may be possible within Old Testament limits.

[1] 2 Pet. i. 19. Cp. Tert. *Apol.* xx.

It is possible to trace a chronological order in the stages of Hebrew prophecy, inasmuch as it was rooted in the history of Israel, and events themselves suggested the ideas which we call Messianic. In its onward movement prophecy continually incorporated new elements, of which now one, now another, came to the surface. The peculiarity indeed of Israel's career was that it lent itself so easily to idealistic treatment, and Messianic prediction was to a considerable extent the result of a continuous process of reflection on the history of the past. But it is never a simple or easy task to discover the actual birth of an idea. In general no doubt it is true that advanced spiritual ideas postulate a relatively advanced stage of moral development; but it would be hazardous to overlook the part which the intuitions of spiritual genius have undoubtedly played in the growth of religion. Analogy suggests that at a very early stage of Israel's history, there were leading spirits who though they received not the promises yet saw them *afar off and were persuaded of them and embraced them* [1]. We do not know all that lies hidden in that mysterious saying of our Lord, *Your father Abraham rejoiced to see my day, and he saw it and was glad* [2]. On the whole, however, it is possible to distinguish certain clearly defined stages in Messianic anticipation —periods in which a particular ideal hovers before prophetic eyes and determines their vision of future events.

1. First, then, we observe that the primaeval promise to humanity is that of spiritual victory. 'Antagonism to evil is decreed to be the law of humanity [3]': and it is the essence of the *Protevangelium*, that it promises to man as man—to universal humanity—victory over moral evil. Since the higher life of man is to be the result of an arduous and painful struggle, it

---

[1] Heb. xi. 13.   [2] John viii. 56.
[3] Driver, *Sermons on the O. T.* p. 52. Observe Gen. iii. 15 forms part of the oldest (prophetical) narrative (J).

essentially consists in dominion, in victory. Just as the words *Have dominion* are the charter of man's position in the universe; so the words *I will put enmity between thee and the woman, and between thy seed and her seed; it shall bruise thy head, and thou shalt bruise his heel*, define the general conditions under which man's regal destiny shall be fulfilled. The first stage of Messianic prophecy as embodied in the traditions which are preserved and shaped by the writers of the Pentateuch consists in the further elucidation of this primary idea. The promise to Abraham is in effect a promise of dominion—that he shall be the *heir of the world*[1]. It is renewed to Isaac and Jacob as *heirs with him of the same promise*[2] in terms which suggest that ultimately it will find its fulfilment in an individual[3].

In the so-called 'Blessing of Jacob' we probably possess the earliest testimony to the nature of the hopes in which the expectation of a *personal* Messiah originated. It has been supposed that this very ancient poem is an ode composed of different tribal songs or proverbs; it perhaps formed part of an ancient collection of national poetry, and its original compilation may belong to the period between the Judges and the reign of David[4]. In this song the passages of chief importance are the predictions relating to Joseph and Judah. The figure of Judah is glorified and idealized as the future holder of sovereignty over his people. On him are to depend the destinies and the eventual triumph of God's kingdom. Judah is depicted as a ruler or judge, with the staff of office in his hand; enjoying a dignity which is destined to give way only to a more complete and perfect form of sovereignty; which 'in other words is not to cease at all, but simply to develope into a glorious kingdom of perfect peace[5].' To this

---
[1] Rom. iv. 13.   [2] Heb. xi. 9.
[3] On the phrase 'thy seed' cp. Gal. iii. 16 and the Commentaries.
[4] See Schultz, vol. ii. p. 336.   [5] Schultz, *loc. cit.*

comprehensive picture corresponds the prediction ascribed to Balaam in the book of Numbers (xxiv. 17). This also hints at the sway of an individual which is to proceed from Israel, and is to extend over the other nations of the East. Probably the primary reference is to some historical king; but the prophecy becomes the foundation of more precise conceptions of Messianic sovereignty.

So far prophecy is indeterminate and vague, but we must note that the actual conditions under which alone the world-conquest could be realized, had already been foreshadowed in the historical incidents of Israel's deliverance and formation into a people of Jehovah. The prospect of national triumph, the hope of an age of peace after national struggle, these were visions suggested by the momentous era of the exodus. At the same time the religious separation of Israel from the rest of the nation and the promulgation of the law at Sinai afforded a proof that the future victory of humanity would depend on moral and spiritual conditions. True, the victories of Israel's youth were prophecies of the ultimate exaltation of God's kingdom over all the kingdoms of the earth, but already the prophetic spirit would discern that the historical deliverance was after all only the type of a higher and more blessed deliverance; and that the judgments of God descending on Israel's enemies were declarations of His thoughts in regard to human sin and of the specific character required in those whom He had formed into a holy community for Himself.

Further, Moses himself was a typical figure. He had been indisputably raised up by Jehovah to be the human instrument of a redemptive purpose. *By a prophet* Israel had been brought out of Egypt[1]. As a mediator between Jehovah and His people, Moses had declared the mind of God; he had embodied Jehovah's revealed requirement in a written

---
[1] Hos. xii. 13.

law. The principle was, as it were, laid down that the divine guidance of Israel would be direct but mediatorial. The passage in Deut. xviii. 15 foll. which describes Moses as a 'prophet,' thus contributes an important element to the Messianic idea. No doubt it primarily refers to a class of prophets through whom Jehovah will make known His will as occasion may require. It is implied that prophecy will be an integral element in Israel's development, an essential feature in the true religion. But the figure of the prophet already points to a Messianic counterpart. The consummation of the divine kingdom demands not only a line or order of inspired teachers keeping alive the sense of Jehovah's continual guidance of His people, but a ruler and lawgiver *like unto Moses*, that is, one in whom the divine thought for man will be finally and authoritatively disclosed. The law of God's redemptive action already manifested in the person and work of Moses will find a new fulfilment in an ideal and transcendent form [1].

2. Thus the course of events constantly tended to give greater definiteness and precision to the conception of Israel's future royalty; but it was not until the reign of David that the Messianic idea in its primal and most simple form was expanded and developed by the associations connected with visible sovereignty. Riehm observes that while the institution of the monarchy involved on the one hand a certain perilous materialization of the Mosaic ideal of a theocracy, on the other hand it was a necessary element in the consolidation of the ideal. And the significance of David's rule is that it clearly manifested the compatibility of

---

[1] We do not find the promise of Deut. xviii. 15 connected with the person of Messiah elsewhere in the Old Testament, though possibly it was cherished among the Samaritans (see Westcott, *Introd. to the Study of the Gospels*, ch. ii. note ii), but the expectation of a coming prophet seems to have revived before our Lord's advent. It is implied in Mal. iv. 5. See also 1 Macc. xiv. 41. Cp. Stanton, *The Jewish and the Christian Messiah*, pp. 126 foll.

a human hereditary monarchy with the idea of a divinely ruled polity[1]. In David the hopes of the nation were centred, as in one who had been chosen by God to fulfil and realize the theocratic sovereignty. Certainly the consciousness of such a vocation and destiny seems to find expression in two utterances which sound criticism warrants us in ascribing to David himself—Psalm xviii (2 Sam. xxii.) and the words preserved in 2 Sam. xxiii. 1–8. In these two passages David praises God not only for signal deliverances from his enemies, but also for loving-kindness which is pledged to his house for evermore[2]. The promise which became the foundation of such exalted hopes is indicated in the account of Nathan's oracle preserved in 2 Sam. vii. 4 foll.[3]

It is possible that this oracle has been partially coloured by the associations of Solomon's magnificent reign, but in the main it seems to reflect the hopes which the men of David's own generation connected with his name and family. At any rate it is beyond question that it exercised an important influence on the future direction of Messianic prophecy. Three main ideas are prominent in it: (1) The human descent of a promised king. He is to be a son of David; and so fixed did this belief become that henceforth the title *Messiah*, 'the anointed,' became limited specially to the Hebrew monarchs regarded as lineal descendants of David's house. (2) The everlasting continuance of David's throne and house. The family of David may suffer chastisement and humiliation, but is not to be finally rejected. The hope of everlasting dominion was in fact destined to survive the lowest humiliation that ultimately overtook David's descendants. (3) The dignity of divine sonship bestowed on the theocratic king, who is to stand in

---

[1] *A Tl. Theologie*, p. 194.   [2] Ps. xviii. 50.
[3] See a careful note in Kittel, *Hist. of the Hebrews*, vol. ii. p. 160. Cornill, *Einleitung in das A. T.* p. 104, regards ch. vii as probably not earlier than the time of Isaiah. Cp. Schultz, *O. T. Theology*, vol. ii. 342; Cheyne, *Aids to the Devout Study*, &c., p. 26.

a peculiar relation of privilege to Jehovah Himself; to him, in other words, the sacred vocation of Israel is to be specially delegated. Nothing less is involved in the solemn transference of the title 'son' from Israel[1] to its king than the assumption that henceforth the holder of the promised sovereignty is to be an individual of the reigning house.

This oracle, reflecting the Messianic consciousness of a unique vocation, becomes the starting-point of what is sometimes called 'figurative prophecy,' that is, the ascription of ideal attributes to the reigning monarch. The idealization of David himself and of the period of his reign begins with the narrators of the books of Samuel, and reaches its climax in the representations of the Chronicler. To prophets like Jeremiah and Ezekiel, whose position is intermediate, the name of David became the recognized symbol of Messiah[2]. David's reign came to be regarded as the pattern of Messianic times, a kind of golden age in Israel's history; and amid the calamities of a later period the national hopes were sustained by the promise of a kingdom framed on the Davidic pattern. Prophecy henceforth takes a new development. The king who from time to time sits on David's throne is seen 'in the light of the promise made to David, and in that light he is transfigured[3]' and invested with more than human attributes, whether as victorious warrior (Ps. ii), or as royal bridegroom taking to himself a consort from the heathen world (Ps. xlv), or as monarch reigning in righteousness and peace (Ps. lxxii), or finally as one who combines the functions of royalty with those of priesthood (Ps. cx), the promised dignity of the Davidic prince with the prerogatives of the ancient king who had blessed the

---

[1] Exod. iv. 22.
[2] Jer. xxx. 9; Ezek. xxxiv. 23, 24; xxxvii. 24, 25 (referred to by Cheyne, *Aids to the Devout Study*, &c., p. 70). Cp. a striking passage in Meinhold, *Jesus und das A. T.* p. 99.
[3] Perowne, *Commentary on the Psalms*, Introd. (vol. i. p. 54).

patriarch Abraham himself[1]. Thus prophecy creates a kingly image with ideal attributes—each monarch being in his degree a type of the coming Messiah. It is true that in Palestine, as in the East generally—in Egypt and Assyria and Chaldaea—there was a tendency to deify the king; to regard him as the visible embodiment of the divine majesty[2]. But there is a special significance in the application of the title *Elohim* to the Hebrew monarch. It implies that the divine sovereignty is in a manner actually delegated to a human representative. The theocratic king reigns and feeds his flock in the name and in the strength of Jehovah[3]. He occupies a unique and central position in the kingdom of God—the kingdom of righteousness. He is endued with a full measure of the Spirit of God, executing God's holy will, guided by His wisdom, judging with His righteousness, even revealing His essential attributes[4]. We may observe that circumstances at one time elevated the thought of a theocratic king into prominence, at another time threw it into the background; but the vision was never completely lost. In the days of the disastrous struggle with Assyria, when the world-power attacked the kingdom of God specially in the person of its monarch, the figure of the king naturally became the centre of Israel's hopes; through the king there would be deliverance from the national foe; in allegiance to David's house alone would there be any prospect of salvation for the hardly-pressed northern kingdom[5]. For in an age of distress and decay it was the figure of David that lived in the memory of the nation—David taken from the sheepfolds to feed Jehovah's people; David the ruler of strong hand and powerful arm, wise of heart *as an angel of God*[6]. In the most distressful days faith clung to the covenant established by Jehovah with David and

---

[1] Heb. vii. 4 foll.   [2] Schultz, vol. i. p. 169.   [3] Mic. v. 2–4.
[4] See Isa. ix. 6 and xi. Isa. xi. is called by Darmesteter 'une vision de paix, qui depuis a hanté l'univers' (*Les Prophètes d'Israël*, p. 63).
[5] Hos. i. 11; iii. 5; Amos ix. 11 foll. Cp. Jer. l. 4.
[6] 2 Sam. xiv. 17, 20; xix. 27.

his house. 'Thus,' says Schultz, 'it was a faith in things not seen, a faith in the everlasting significance of this house.' It is a phenomenon without parallel in history that even under the worst disasters of a later period ' the confident hope of seeing the Saviour of the future born of this dishonoured family was never lost [1].'

We may briefly notice some other associations which are never quite absent from the scriptural idea of royalty. David was a typical man of war, and the Messianic ideal did not fail accordingly to include the element of victorious triumph over foes. The title of king was essentially that of a warrior, a leader of hosts in the wars of the Lord. The notion of sovereignty thus implied the deliverance of Jehovah's people from their enemies and a perpetual extension of the boundaries of God's kingdom. Under the title 'king' applied to Messiah we discern 'the potency and promise' of universalist ideas. The Messiah must reign *till he hath put all enemies under his feet* [2]. But this aspect of the Messianic character was not the most prominent. One of the best-known representations of Messiah depicts him as making his entry into Jerusalem in the garb of a prince of peace, *just and having salvation, lowly and riding upon an ass, and upon a colt the foal of an ass:* without the implements of war he extends his righteous sway. *He shall speak peace unto the heathen, and his dominion shall be from sea even to sea, and from the river even to the ends of the earth* [3]. A typical passage which combines the idea of a peaceful rule with worldwide conquest is to be found in the prophecy of Micah (chapter v), which represents the future Saviour as feeding His people *in the strength of Jehovah, in the majesty of the name of Jehovah his God;* and *the remnant of Jacob shall be in the midst of many people*

---

[1] *O. T. Theology*, vol. i. p. 173. Cp. Hunter, *After the Exile*, part i. pp. 225 foll.   [2] 1 Cor. xv. 25.
[3] Zech. ix. 9, 10. The date of Zech. ix-xiv is very uncertain. See Kirkpatrick, *Doctrine of the Prophets*, pp. 440 foll. ; Cornill, *Der Isr. Prophetismus*, p. 166. Schultz, ii. 416, and apparently Riehm, regard Zech. ix-xi as pre-exilic.

as a dew from Jehovah, as the showers upon the grass; but also *as a lion among the beasts of the forest*; while Messiah executes *vengeance upon the heathen, such as they have not heard*[1]. The two conceptions illustrate the effect on the imagination of the prophets of the two primary facts in the historical situation during the time when Micah wrote. The advance of the Assyrian power no doubt gave a stimulus to the conception of a world-monarchy advanced by warlike prowess; but the permanent form of Messianic prediction was mainly determined by visions of a stable and peaceful re-establishment of David's kingdom[2].

3. Another permanent element in Messianic prophecy is the idea of a personal manifestation or intervention of Jehovah to set up His kingdom as sovereign in Zion. The final purpose of the kingdom of God is to manifest Jehovah Himself as supreme over the universe: *for he cometh, for he cometh to judge the earth: he shall judge the world with righteousness and the peoples with his truth*[3]. As we shall see, the prophets do not attempt to adjust or correlate the two parallel lines of thought which pervade their writings. They look upon the Messianic salvation sometimes as the work of a Davidic king, sometimes, on the other hand, as the outcome of Jehovah's personal visitation of His people. But in any case, whoever may be from time to time the instrument in effecting His redemptive purpose, it is Jehovah Himself who is the real and sole source of help and deliverance. Further, the day of divine manifestation is a turning-point in human history, the day of judicial intervention, the day of God's decisive act, *the day of the Lord*. We have noticed the blind confidence with which the mass of Israelites clung to the thought of this day as an object of hope in all

---

[1] Mic. v. 4, 7, 8, 15.
[2] On the significance of Hezekiah's reign in relation to the Messianic hope see Darmesteter, *Les Prophètes d'Israël*, pp. 60 foll.
[3] Ps. xcvi. 10, 13; xcvii. 1; xcviii. 9, &c. Cp. Schultz, vol. ii. p. 354.

VI] PROPHECY AND THE MESSIANIC HOPE

times of distress. It was supposed to be 'self-evident that the crisis would certainly end in favour of Israel[1].' We have seen that it was the special task of Amos to denounce this temper, and to proclaim the unpalatable truth that only through the overthrow of the existing theocracy and the salvation of a mere remnant would the purpose of God be accomplished[2]. It was inconceivable that in view of the moral corruptions of the time there should be deliverance except by the way of judgment. Accordingly, from the rise of prophecy until its close in literature of a definitely apocalyptic type the thought of *the day of the Lord* continually reappears. It was to be a day of outward terror; the ordinary course of nature would be violently interrupted; the sun would be darkened, the moon turned into blood; the earth would tremble; the works of man would one and all be brought low; his loftiness would be humbled to the dust[3]. It was to be a day of moral sifting, a manifestation of divine indignation against wickedness: *cruel both with wrath and fierce anger to lay the land desolate; and he shall destroy the sinners thereof out of it*[4]. It would be a day of judgment in which God would test and refine not only the nations of the heathen world but His own people *by the spirit of judgment and by the spirit of burning*[5]. *Jehovah alone shall be exalted in that day.* With a searching visitation He will vindicate His outraged majesty, He will purge His kingdom of all that offends[6].

This is one aspect of the day of the Lord. But it has another side. It is a day ushering in the blessings of the Messianic age. Though the corrupt mass of the people are warned not to wish for a day which to them shall be *darkness and not light*[7], the true Israel is encouraged to look forward to it with hope and joy. For the day of the Lord will be a day of vengeance on

---

[1] Wellhausen, *Sketch*, &c. p. 83.   [2] Amos ix. 8, 9.
[3] Isa. ii. 12 foll.   [4] Isa. xiii. 9.   [5] Isa. iv. 4.
[6] Isa. i. 24 foll.   [7] Amos v. 18.

Israel's oppressors, a day of release and of consolation. God's people shall *with their eyes behold and see the reward of the ungodly* [1]. Further, we find that the picture of the Messianic deliverance varies according as one heathen power or another is the temporary oppressor of Jehovah's people. 'The prophetic oracles,' says Dr. Bruce, 'were addressed to the present, were rooted in the present, were expressed in language suited to the present, and pointed to a good in the near future forming a counterpart to present evil or to an evil in the near future which was to be the penalty of present or past sin [2].' If Jerusalem is threatened by hostile armies, hard-pressed and compassed about, standing in the midst of a wasted and ruined land *like a lodge in a garden of cucumbers*, the blessing of the future shall be the vision of *Jerusalem a quiet habitation, a tabernacle that shall not be taken down*, an island protected by *broad rivers and streams, wherein shall go no galley with oars, neither shall gallant ship pass thereby* [3]. If Israel is carried away captive, merged and overwhelmed in the sea of nations, cut off from life and hope—the promise is given of a resurrection, a bringing back from the grave, a revival of perished hopes by the renewing might of Jehovah's Spirit [4]. Forlorn, exiled, and scattered as they seem, the children of Zion may look forward to a home-coming more glorious, more amazing even than the exodus from Egypt. The day of the Lord is not merely a terror to the evil; it is to be a day of everlasting joy to the righteous. *The ransomed of the Lord shall return and come to Zion with songs and everlasting joy upon their heads; they shall obtain joy and gladness, and sorrow and sighing shall flee away* [5].

At this point it may be well to notice some limitations in the prophetic vision of Israel's future. We

---

[1] Ps. xci. 8.
[2] Bruce, *Chief End of Revelation*, p. 221; cp. Riehm, *Messianic Prophecy*, pp. 95 foll.
[3] Isa. i. 8; xxxiii. 20.　　[4] Ezek. xxxvii.　　[5] Isa. xxxv. 10.

have seen that two great elements alternate in prophetic thought—the glory of a Davidic king, and the personal manifestation of Jehovah; and that the promised redemption of Zion is connected now with one element, now with the other. But the two lines of thought are parallel, and are nowhere actually combined in the picture of a single divine-human figure. They are continuous and co-existent elements in Messianic prediction. They meet us again in the writings of Jeremiah and Ezekiel. In the last-mentioned prophet the two ideas are found in close juxtaposition. Jehovah Himself is the shepherd of His people, and the Davidic king is a prince ruling in His name[1]. Further, nothing is more remarkable than the adherence of the prophets to the forms and figures suggested by present experience. They picture a kingdom of God visibly founded on earth; they regard Jerusalem as the necessary centre of Messianic government, and as the spot where the divine self-manifestation will ultimately take place. In these representations we recognize the effect produced by the magnificence of Solomon's temple and the worship connected with it. The visible theocratic institutions in fact coloured the entire picture of the future, and though Jeremiah in days of religious and political upheaval was able to rise in a measure above these limitations[2], the prophetic thought of a later period reverted to the earlier conceptions. Thus the prophecy of Ezekiel closes with the vision of the restored temple as the earthly dwelling-place of Jehovah in the midst of His people, while the later Isaiah looks for the restoration of Jerusalem in radiant splendour as the scene of a spiritualized levitical worship in which all nations of the earth are summoned to participate[3]. Again, in predicting future blessings

---

[1] See Ezek. xxxiv. 11, 23, 24, and xxxvii. 22, 24, 25; Jer. xxiii. 3-6, 15. Cp. Schultz, vol. ii. pp. 417 foll.; Kirkpatrick, *Doctrine of the Prophets*, p. 312. Obs. in the apocalyptic writings the two conceptions are united, the figure of the Messiah being invested with a halo of superhuman glory.
[2] Jer. iii. 16 foll.; xxxi. 29-34. Cp. Riehm, *ATl. Theologie*, pp. 220, 221.
[3] Cp. Zech. xiv, and Cornill's remarks on it (*Der Isr. Prophetismus*, pp. 166 foll.). See also Kuenen, *Hibbert Lectures*, pp. 108, 109.

the prophets know not the time or manner of fulfilment. To them the present and future are contiguous and as yet undistinguished. Each prophet gives an independent picture of the future, exhibiting it from his own standpoint and depicting it in terms suggested by the actual experiences of his own time. A living hope indeed is inevitably inclined to hasten the natural course of events; it regards each crisis as final, and the conditions of the moment as ripe for the occurrence of a catastrophe. In general, therefore, the prophets proclaim salvation as a blessing of the immediate future; yet the delay of the promised consummation does not shatter their hope and confidence, partly because they regard even a small and relative measure of fulfilment as a pledge of an ampler and more decisive deliverance yet to come, partly because they are keenly alive to the conditional character of Jehovah's word, since impenitence or apostasy on Israel's part necessarily interrupts or postpones the advent of Messianic times[1]. But whether remote or near at hand, the coming of Messiah was the consummation on which hope was fixed. 'The long vista of expectation was closed with His form[2].' Faith waited for Him that should come and did not *look for another*[3]. As king He would be supreme, as prophet or teacher He would bring a final and authoritative message from God to man[4]. The unclouded light of truth and the blessings of righteous sovereignty were alike connected with His advent. The age of the Messiah was an epoch beyond which prophecy did not look, since it would inaugurate an era of eternal peace and blessedness[5].

4. But to proceed. When royalty in and after the days of Manasseh declined in influence and prestige, and the national fortunes became more and more

---

[1] Cp. Riehm, *A Tl. Theologie*, p. 222.
[2] Stanton, *The Jewish and the Christian Messiah*, p. 148.
[3] Matt. xi. 3. [4] Cp. John iv. 25 (Westcott, ad loc.).
[5] Cp. Stanton, *loc. cit.*

disconnected from those of the reigning house, another Messianic conception, at which earlier prophets had already hinted, rose into prominence—that of the holy remnant or true people of God. It was a period of violent reaction against the teaching of the prophets, which lasted for about fifty years. The contrast between Manasseh's reign and that of his father Hezekiah has been justly compared to that which is presented by the era of the Stuart restoration in its relation to the Puritan ascendency which preceded it. The insolent, materialistic spirit of libertinism revived. Jerusalem again became the scene of strange idolatries; Manasseh himself practised the hideous rites of Moloch worship; the arts of sorcery, magic, and soothsaying amused the indolence of a corrupt court. The living voice of prophecy sank into silence[1], and was only again uplifted when Josiah had ascended the throne. Moreover, from this time onwards an increasing volume of calamity threatened the Jewish state. Before the close of Manasseh's reign (638) the terrible inroads of the Scythian hordes took place. They overran for a period of twenty years the greater part of western Asia, spreading desolation and terror to the very borders of Egypt. Meanwhile Nineveh was tottering to its fall (607); then followed a struggle for supremacy between the giant-powers of Babylon and Egypt, which was decided by Nebuchadnezzar's defeat of the Egyptian army at Carchemish (605). The period was in fact one of almost unbroken excitement, terror, and distress; the effects of Josiah's attempted reformation of worship on the basis of the Deuteronomic law were superficial and soon passed away; it was manifest that for Jerusalem the day of reckoning was close at hand. Zephaniah at the beginning of Josiah's reign had already proclaimed that in the impending deluge of judgment Israel would by no means escape. Habbakuk represents

---

[1] Darmesteter, pp. 65, 66. Possibly, as Ewald and Cornill hold, Micah chh. vi, vii belong to the reign of Manasseh.

the patience of faith waiting on God amid universal convulsion. Jeremiah is the prophet of Jerusalem's fall[1]. He, together with Habbakuk, gives utterance to the distress of that righteous remnant of Israel which in an evil time had set itself to seek God. The whole problem of suffering began to press for solution; and rightly to estimate the spiritual importance of the epoch which began with Josiah's death (about 609) and only ended with the return from exile, we must bear in mind its general character: the entire period was one of judgment, inevitable, crushing, and complete. The sorrows of *the holy seed*, the spiritual Israel, in the land of captivity served to accentuate the problem which perplexed the minds of Israel's prophets and saints. The faithful remnant, conscious of its own integrity of heart and of its newly-awakened zeal for God, was overwhelmed in the common calamity which had overtaken the nation. Old theories of retribution had thereby been proved to be inadequate. A new doctrine of suffering was imperatively needed to account for the new circumstances in which the righteous found themselves placed. And, speaking broadly, it is not inaccurate to say that the lesson which above all others Israel learned in its day of calamity was the real meaning and purpose of suffering.

The principal pictures of the righteous sufferer contained in the Old Testament — for instance, the twenty-second psalm, the fifty-third chapter of Isaiah, the story of Job—seem to embody the deepened spiritual experience of the exile. In these great passages of Scripture tribulation is recognized as being not merely a judgment upon human sin, but an element in the progress of the kingdom of God, a discipline by which the true servant of Jehovah is trained and educated for his unique mission. The thought of the priestly or mediatorial office of God's people comes to

---

[1] Cp. Cornill, *Der Israelitische Prophetismus*, pp. 77 foll.; Montefiore, *Hibbert Lectures*, pp. 171 foll.

the front; and, according to a characteristic tendency of the Hebrew mind, we find a disposition to individualize the nation, and to bring to a focus the characteristic thought of the age in 'the conception of an individual righteous man who as the accepted representative of his nation must needs make atonement by suffering for its sins, and so become a prevailing intercessor with God. In this ideal servant of Jehovah are concentrated the scattered characteristics of God's faithful: their spirit of dependence, their patient devotion, their unswerving faithfulness in the fulfilment of vocation, their brave constancy under trial, their meek acceptance of death[1].' In the fifty-third chapter of Isaiah prophecy seems to rise to this culminating point. It delineates the figure of one who by pouring out his soul unto death can indeed make atonement for the transgressions of his people, and who passes through the gate of death to a new and glorious life of fruitfulness and power. 'This wonderful figure combines in itself,' says Schultz, 'the figure of the Priest who offers Himself up as a sacrifice for the world, the figure of the Prophet who by His knowledge of God brings justification, and the figure of the King who, transfigured and blessed, enjoys the fruits of His sufferings[2].'

During the exile, then, the hope of Israel was finally transferred from the theocratic king to *the servant of Jehovah*, the faithful remnant which still represented the people of God. Conscious as they were of possessing the true knowledge of God, and of vocation to His service, the faithful patiently awaited the issue of the conflict between the true religion and the idolatries of heathenism. The sublime prophet of the exile in fact developes the thought of the mediatorial functions of God's people which the very circumstances of the exile suggested.

In his pages the universalist ideas of earlier

---

[1] Repeated from *The Doctrine of the Incarnation*, vol. i. p. 55.
[2] Schultz, vol. ii. p. 435.

prophecy become deepened and spiritualized. The Israel which he represents recognizes its prophetic and priestly function, its vocation to be *a light to the Gentiles*[1]. It learns that the purpose of grace manifested in Israel's election embraces the entire family of mankind. And in accordance with these ideas, prophecy henceforth displays a new sense of the dignity of priesthood and its functions. Already in his ideal sketch of the age of restoration, Ezekiel assigns special prominence to the Aaronic priesthood. The priests are to be the teachers and judges of the future, and are to represent in their own persons the entire consecration of Israel to Jehovah[2]. In the prophecy of Zechariah, Joshua the high-priest stands on a level with Zerubbabel the theocratic prince. There is a juxtaposition of the offices of priest and king implied in the coronation of Joshua[3]. The high-priest is not as yet identified with the prince; what Zechariah's prophecy signifies is the perfect harmony and unity of two elements indispensable in the newly-established settlement. *The counsel of peace*, he says, *shall be between them both*. Only at a more advanced stage, it would seem, did prophecy rise to the thought of a monarch who as representative of the priestly nation should himself hold the dignity of the priesthood, being made by the oath of Jehovah *a priest for ever after the order of Melchizedek*[4]. In Psalm cx is to be found the combination of two separate lines of prediction.

5. Corresponding to the conception of a people of God charged with a spiritual mission to mankind is that of a new covenant—a covenant of which grace, not law, is the outstanding characteristic. It was a hope to which Jeremiah had already given touching expression[5]. In his days it must have seemed the

---

[1] Isa. xlix. 6.   [2] Ezek. xliv. 10–28; xlviii. 11, &c.
[3] Zech. vi. 11–14. Cp. Schultz, ii. 423.
[4] Ps. cx. See a note in Riehm, *ATl. Theologie*, p. 257.
[5] Jer. xxxi. 31 foll.

only hope that remained for an apostate Israel. In effect Jeremiah appears to have abandoned the expectation of any response to his warnings and denunciations. He renounces the nation which is hastening headlong to its ruin, and apparently devotes himself to preparing the way for a new people that should emerge from the ashes of the old[1]. The hope of a new covenant was indeed the stay of the faithful under continual disillusionment. The experience of ages is embodied in the pregnant verdict of Jeremiah on the final result of the Mosaic dispensation : *which my covenant they brake, although I was an husband unto them, saith the Lord*[2]. Jehovah had purposed to make Israel a kingdom of priests and an holy nation, but the only hope of the ideal being realized lay in the free action of Jehovah's grace. The old covenant was marked by inherent deficiency: it was powerless to secure the obedience it enjoined, it was burdensome as a law of positive precepts and ordinances; in relation to the removal of sin it was hopelessly ineffective. Prophecy therefore recognized that the old covenant was waxing *old and ready to vanish away*[3]. It looked to the future for a new covenant of grace, under which not merely the outward life, but the heart of Israel, should be renewed unto holiness. In the Messianic age the law of Jehovah should be written in the heart; each soul should have immediate knowledge of God and unrestricted access to Him; above all, the clinging burden of sin and defilement should be finally removed. *For I will forgive their iniquity, and I will remember their sins no more*. Thus it was at length realized that the Messiah was not destined to fulfil the aspirations of national ambition, but to satisfy the yearnings of spiritual need : *to preach good tidings unto the meek, to bind up the broken-hearted, to proclaim liberty to the*

---

[1] Darmesteter, p. 67.   [2] Jer. xxxi. 32.   Cp. Heb. viii. 9.
[3] Heb. viii. 13.

captives, and the opening of the prison to them that are bound[1].

In the prophecies of Ezekiel we find a continuation of Jeremiah's teaching. One effect of the exile on the faithful was doubtless a deeper consciousness of sin, and a sense that the mere collective and national access to God provided for in the institutions of pre-exilic worship was incapable of satisfying the thirst of the individual soul for salvation[2]. Ezekiel repeats and emphasizes Jeremiah's doctrine concerning individual responsibility; but he goes further and points to the prospect of an inward renewal wrought by the power of Jehovah's spirit. *I will sprinkle clean water upon you, and ye shall be clean: from all your filthiness, and from all your idols, will I cleanse you. A new heart also will I give you, and a new spirit will I put within you: and I will take away the stony heart out of your flesh, and I will give you an heart of flesh*[3]. Thus the prophets who had been, to quote Wellhausen's striking expression, 'the spiritual destroyers of old Israel[4],' became the pioneers of a new era. They hold out the prospect of a nationality which has renewed its youth; they look for a new creation. *Behold, I create new heavens and a new earth; and the former shall not be remembered, nor come into mind. But be ye glad and rejoice for ever in that which I create; for, behold, I create Jerusalem a rejoicing, and her people a joy*[5].

6. The post-exilic prophets gather up the substance of former predictions, their aim being to deepen those conceptions respecting the Messiah and his work which were already current. In Haggai and Zechariah the idea of Israel's spiritual mission to the world reappears, but in a form moulded by the special circumstances of their time—the rebuilding of the temple and the reorganization of worship on the levitical pattern. The interest of prophecy centres

---

[1] Isa. lxi. 1.   [2] Riehm, *ATl. Theologie*, p. 36.
[3] Ezek. xxxvi. 25 foll.   [4] *Sketch*, &c. p. 122.   [5] Isa. lxv. 17, 18.

in the temple as at no previous period in history. Haggai, for example, points to a new glory of the national sanctuary as the appointed centre of divine self-manifestation in the future. The sudden coming of Jehovah to His temple will usher in the age of Messianic blessings [1]. Thither the desirable things of all nations shall be brought; there the deepest yearnings of man's heart shall be finally satisfied : *In this place will I give peace, saith the Lord of hosts.* Nearly a century later the same thought reappears in Malachi in a somewhat modified shape characteristic of his time. Jehovah will manifest Himself through the mediation of an angel, the messenger of His covenant, and instrument of His righteous judgment. To Malachi, as to Haggai, the temple is the destined scene of the future theophany; and the main object of the divine judgment is to purify the sons of Levi, that there may once more be a faithful priesthood in Israel, and a pure offering acceptable to God [2]. On the other hand, the moral and ethical tone of prophecy, and its insistence on the divine requirement as a condition of covenant communion, is still dominant in the prophets of the restoration. In Zechariah especially we find 'the two correlative aspects of spiritual reformation' enforced: as 'the bounden duty of man, and as the promised gift of God [3].'

It is difficult to trace the process by which it came about, but there can be no doubt that the hopes of later Judaism are of a narrower and more nationalistic cast than those of the exilic period. In fact, as Professor Pfleiderer remarks, in some respects 'the legal religion of the synagogue shows a retrogression from the lofty idealism of the prophets [4].' The universalist

---

[1] Hag. ii. 7-9; Zech. ix. 9 foll. It is noticeable that for a brief space the prince of David's house, which in the person of Zerubbabel emerged from its obscurity, figures once more in the pages of prophecy. See Zech. iii. 8 ; cp. Jer. xxiii. 5.
[2] Mal. iii. 1-5, 16 foll.
[3] See Zech. iii. 4 ; v. 5-11 ; viii. 16, 17. Cp. Montefiore, *Hibbert Lectures*, vol. ii. p. 300.
[4] *Gifford Lectures*, vol. ii. p. 51.

hopes of the later Isaiah fall into the background, and give way before the ambitions of Jewish particularism. The spirit of rigid exclusiveness fostered by the levitical Law displayed itself in an attitude of hatred and contempt towards the heathen world. Cornill observes that the stage was a necessary one in Israel's development, for the life and death struggle with Hellenism was yet to come [1]. The observance of the Law, which sharply separated Israel from the heathen world, formed a kind of defensive armour, which the polished shafts of paganism could neither break nor penetrate. Judaism was a hard shell under which the kernel of true religion was preserved and transmitted unimpaired. Nevertheless, the effect of this period on prophecy was not altogether happy. The book of Joel seems to represent the temper of the new Judaism. Its tone is strongly nationalistic; it regards the heathen as objects only of vengeance, not of grace; it reflects the confidence of the Jew that Israel is a righteous people and the object of a divine favour, which is sufficiently secured by the care bestowed on the temple *cultus*[2]. In fact, it has been thought, though the point is necessarily uncertain, that in the book of Joel we pass from the older type of prophecy to the class of apocalyptic literature, which has peculiarities and merits of its own, but cannot be fairly judged by the same standard as earlier prophetic writings. While prophecy is the mature fruit of ancient Israel's religion, apocalyptic writings are the characteristic product of Judaism. They bear witness, like the belief in the *Bath Qôl*, to the consciousness that Jehovah had ceased to speak immediately to His people [3].

[1] *Der Israelitische Prophetismus*, p. 162.
[2] *Ibid.* p. 163. The book of Obadiah seems to display a similar tendency.
[3] On the distinctive characteristics of the apocalyptic literature see Riehm, *A Tl. Theologie*, p. 389; Drummond, *The Jewish Messiah*, Introd.; Westcott, art. 'Daniel' in Smith's *Dictionary of the Bible*. The last writer points out that the exile 'supplied the outward training and the inward necessity for this last form of divine teaching; and the prophetic visions

The apocalyptic literature, in fact, arose as the result of that passionate aversion to heathenism and grief at its apparent triumph which came to a head in the Maccabaean struggle. The unfulfilled ideals of prophecy were studied afresh with the hope of finding a clue to the past course of history and the future prospects of the nation. With the peculiarities, however, of this literature we are not specially concerned. It is only necessary to remember that it also was used as a vehicle of divine teaching. Its contribution to the Messianic idea was, comparatively speaking, indirect. The apocalyptic writers occupied themselves with the prospects of the divine kingdom in its relation to the empires of this world, rather than with the personal glories of the promised Saviour. Consequently, their works reflect in their comparative silence as to a personal Messiah, the condition of the nation when it had lost its independence and had passed under the rule of a priestly hierarchy. In the extra-canonical literature the Messianic king was generally depicted as a hero of whom it was confidently expected that he would re-establish Israel's national independence and inaugurate a world-wide dominion; but in regard to details old ideas and new were strangely intermingled. The rule of righteousness and peace was to involve 'the full triumph of the law and the law's religion[1].' The universal kingdom of Messiah was destined to manifest the peculiar favour with God enjoyed by Israel.

Perhaps the most significant feature in later canonical prophecy is the stress laid on Messiah's humanity. The book of Daniel speaks of *one like unto a son of man*[2], an expression which in its original context

of Ezekiel form the connecting link between the characteristic types of revelation and prophecy.' On the book of Joel see Hunter, *After the Exile*, part i. ch. xii. Its apocalyptic character is noticed by Cornill, *Einleitung in das A.T.* p. 182.

[1] See Montefiore, *Hibbert Lectures*, No. viii.
[2] Dan. vii. 13. On the probable date and origin of Daniel see Cornill, pp. 176 foll. On the influence of the book see Riehm, *ATl. Theologie*, p. 389.

seems to describe the characteristics of the ideal kingdom of the saints which is destined to supersede the heathen empires founded on brute violence and material force. It was apparently in a later apocryphal work—the book of Enoch—that the title was first restricted to a personal Messiah, but the passage in Daniel may be regarded as marking a new stage in the growth of the Messianic expectation[1]. Apart from this isolated expression, the figure of *the anointed prince*[2] in the book of Daniel is highly significant. The Messiah is numbered with *the saints of the most high* as their head and representative, exercising the universal dominion bestowed on him as his rightful heritage by Jehovah Himself. The conception of a specially close relationship between the Messiah and Jehovah is also found in the later chapters of Zechariah, which depict the expected Saviour as the rejected shepherd of his people, as the *fellow* of Jehovah, and as one in whom Jehovah Himself is pierced[3].

There is no need to extend our survey of Messianic prediction beyond the limits of the Old Testament, since the permanent elements that contributed to the conception of Messiah are already contained in the Hebrew Canon itself. The subsequent period is of great importance in so far as it throws light on the expectations of our Lord's own contemporaries; but this subject lies outside the range of our inquiry[4]. Accordingly, it only remains to point out briefly how the work of Christ, the history of His Church, and the experience of His saints unfold and develop the significance of those great principles which prophecy had learned to trace in Israel's history.

For we have seen that the prophetic visions of the

---

[1] See Stanton, *op. cit.* p. 110; Drummond, *op. cit.* bk. ii. ch. 7.
[2] Dan. ix. 25, 26.
[3] Zech. xi. 15 foll.; xiii. 1-9; xii. 10. On the date of Zech. ix–xiv see Cornill, p. 166.
[4] See Schürer, *The Jewish People in the time of Christ* (Eng. Tr.), § 29; Westcott, *Introd. to the Study of the Gospels*, pp. 94 foll.; Stanton, *op. cit.* pp. 111 foll.

future were for the most part inspired by reflection on the history of the past. The Messianic hope had its roots in the faith that Israel had been originally brought into a special relationship to Jehovah. The expectation even of a personal Redeemer was coloured by vague anticipations that Israel itself would ultimately realize the ideal foreshadowed in the original covenant established with its ancestors. The personal advent and work of the true Messiah only inaugurated the fulfilment of the earliest and most widespread hopes of the nation [1]. Thus the idea of salvation as a work of divine grace visiting the afflicted, or as a victory by which a captivity was carried captive, had been visibly illustrated in the exodus from Egypt; the idea of a kingdom of God had its foundations laid in the polity organized, at least in rudimentary form, by Moses, and was further developed and consolidated by the institution of the Hebrew monarchy; the conception of a people of God charged with a priestly mission to mankind had probably never been entirely absent from the highest spiritual thought of the people. The place, meaning, and function of suffering had from the first been suggested by the recorded experience of righteous men from the dawn of history: Abel had been slain by Cain; Isaac had been laid on the altar of sacrifice; Jacob had been a wanderer ready to perish; Joseph had been rejected by his brethren and *the iron entered into his soul* ere he could become the saviour of his kindred and of Egypt; Moses had been a fugitive and exile before he was raised up to be a captain of salvation over Jehovah's people and to fill the desert *with songs of deliverance*; David had been a persecuted outlaw before he became the light of Israel. Yes; 'the heralds of salvation, the bearers of God's mercy, have to pass through suffering and death before they win salvation for themselves and others [2].' So in later days each of the goodly fellowship of the prophets was in his measure *a man of sorrows and*

---

[1] Cp. Stanton, *op. cit.* pp. 99, 135.   [2] Schultz, vol. ii. p. 353.

acquainted with grief. Finally, the remnant of Israel in exile recognized itself as the suffering *servant of Jehovah* prepared to fulfil its unique mission by meek endurance of affliction. Thus prophecy is faith's interpretation of the past; in the temporary conditions and circumstances of Israel's history lay concealed eternal thoughts of God, which in Jesus Christ were to receive their perfect elucidation[1]. In His passion, death, resurrection and exaltation to the right hand of God, St. John contemplates the supreme triumph which the seed of the woman was from the first destined to achieve[2]; and the writer of the Epistle to the Hebrews points to Him as one in whom the destiny of our race is potentially accomplished. *Thou hast put all things under his feet.* Such is the promise; *now* however *we see not yet all things put under him. But we see Jesus.* In the triumph of the ascension man may behold a pledge of the fulfilment of his own appointed destiny.

Again, in the moral reign of Jesus Christ over the hearts of the faithful we recognize the transfigured kingdom of David; we see the spiritual counterpart of those great ideas which the age of Solomon foreshadowed—a world-wide empire over the souls of men and a universal religion—a catholic Church and a catholic Creed. In the action of the Holy Spirit upon society and individual men, consecrating the peculiar endowments and gifts of each to divine uses, we welcome the fulfilment of prophetic visions of a righteous people of Jehovah sprinkled with clean water, and drawing near to God in acceptable service. Finally, in the overthrow of Israel's enemies Christian faith sees the removal from the true kingdom of God of *all things that offend, and them which do*

---

[1] There is a valuable chapter on 'the use of the Old Testament in the early Church' in Mr. Stanton's *Jewish and Christian Messiah*, with an exhaustive table showing the Messianic use of the Old Testament in the New Testament.

[2] Rev. xii; cp. Heb. ii. 6 foll.

iniquity; and the forthshining of the righteous *as the sun in the kingdom of their Father* [1].

Thus the person, the work, the Church of Jesus Christ explains the many-sided imagery of the Old Testament; and if we believe that the Incarnation is at once the plainest of facts and the deepest of mysteries, we shall feel that no study of Hebrew prophecy can be too painstaking or minute; inasmuch as it embodies the thoughts of God—those thoughts of which the Psalmist says, *How precious are thy thoughts unto me, O God! how great is the sum of them! If I should count them, they are more in number than the sand. Many, O Lord my God, are thy wonderful works which thou hast done, and thy thoughts which are to us-ward; they cannot be reckoned up in order unto thee: if I would declare and speak of them they are more than can be numbered* [2].

Prophecy has been defined as 'the expression of an ideal truth which, just because it contains an eternal law of the order of the world, also finds ever new fulfilment at all times [3].' In it we touch what is deepest and most vital in religion. Prophecy is not merely the judgment of sagacious men on the events of their own day, or on the state of the society in which they were called to move and act; it is an inspired commentary on the phenomena of universal history. Its idealism is the result of God-given insight into the true conditions of human welfare, and into that true order of the universe which has been obscured and perverted by human folly, selfishness, and crime. The optimism of the prophets, says Dr. Bruce, 'does not consist in shutting the eyes to the evil that is in the world. On the contrary, it knows how to take the evil into the ideal as one of its constitutive elements, and transmute it into the highest good [4].' It is their sense of a power pervading human history and

---

[1] Matt. xiii. 41, 43.　　　　　　[2] Ps. cxxxix. 17 foll.; xl. 5.
[3] Pfleiderer, *Gifford Lectures*, vol. ii. p. 42.
[4] Bruce, *Apologetics*, p. 256.

'From seeming evil still educing good'

that makes the study of the prophets at once so necessary and so fruitful. In reading their books we find ourselves fired by the same passion of hope, illuminated and cheered by the same splendid visions.

Thus the study of the Old Testament may most appropriately begin with the prophets, not only because the date of their activity and the authenticity of their works are in the main certain and undisputed, but also because their writings will give us the true point of view from which to approach the entire history and institutions of Israel. They will educate our sense of proportion in dealing with the narrative and legislative parts of the Old Testament. They will imbue us with a consciousness of the gravity of the problems which confront society at the present day. They will develope our insight into those needs and aspirations of human nature which the religion of the Incarnation was destined to satisfy; and, finally, they will awaken and stimulate in us that which is the highest power for good in human life—the passion for righteousness, the love of man, the thirst for God.

LECTURE VII

O God, thou art my God.—Ps. lxiii. 1.

THE age of the prophets had contributed to the religion of Israel all that was most essential to its further development. We may notice two points particularly in which the tendencies of the post-exilic period were already foreshadowed before the return from Babylon. First, prophecy had risen to the conception of a universal religion. The vision of the Messianic age, in proportion as it became spiritualized, enlarged its range. The great prophet of the exile represents the heathen world as waiting expectantly for the salvation of God. Israel is to be the herald of redemption to all the nations of the earth, the centre of a world converted to the service of Jehovah. Secondly, the conception of an individualized religion had already appeared. This can be traced back to the prophet Jeremiah, whose position of peculiar isolation and dependence upon God led him to reflect particularly on the relation of the individual to God. His prolonged experience of the supporting power of divine grace under the pressure of overwhelming difficulties constituted him a link between an old and a new state of things. By his own personal fidelity to God, he rescued as it were the true religion which in those disastrous times was in danger of perishing outright. It is even possible that the inspired picture drawn by the exilic prophet of the faithful servant of Jehovah making atonement and intercession on behalf of his people was suggested by the memory of Jeremiah's labours and sufferings [1]. In his own inner life the prophet realized the efficacy of repentance, the need of personal conversion [2], the yearning for newness of heart. And in Jeremiah's prophecy of the new covenant with Israel, which is to be the characteristic blessing of the Messianic age, we have perhaps the first suggestion of a salvation not merely national but personal. *They shall all know me, from the least of them unto the greatest of them, saith the Lord* [3]. The Law was one day to be written, not on tables of stone, but on human hearts. It was the task of Ezekiel to deepen the impression made by his predecessor, to educate in the faithful a consciousness of personal accountability for sin, and to proclaim the divine promise of a time when consciences should be cleansed and hearts renewed by the gift of the Spirit. These two lines of prediction are distinct, and yet they seem to be mutually connected. A spiritual religion can no longer be a merely national religion; the law that can be written on the single human heart is a law for mankind. On the sense of individual relationship to God a world-religion can be founded, for God is one and His Spirit one. The thought underlies St. Paul's striking argument in the third chapter of Romans: *Is he the God of the Jews only? is he not also of the Gentiles? Yes, of the Gentiles also, seeing it is one God, which shall justify the circumcision by faith, and uncircumcision through faith* [4].

Now in the period that followed the exile these characteristic products of prophetic thought — the idea of universal religion, and that of personal salvation—were destined to be developed, but rather through the stress of the circumstances in which

---

[1] Meinhold, *Jesus und das A. T.* p. 105. Cp. Montefiore, *Hibbert Lectures*, p. 218.
[2] Jer. xvii. 14; xxxi. 18.
[3] Jer. xxxi. 34; Ezek. xxxvi. 26.
[4] Rom. iii. 29, 30. Cp. Pfleiderer, *Gifford Lectures*, vol. ii. pp. 50, 51.

Judaism found itself placed, than through any conscious or deliberate effort to realize the spiritual hopes of prophecy. At first sight indeed the whole epoch wears a retrogressive aspect: religion becomes formal and legalistic, while the wider Messianic ideals give way before a temper of narrow particularism. Nevertheless, looking back upon the period, we are able to discern the providential work of God going on under the unpromising exterior features of the history. The dispersion of the Jews brought them into contact with the culture and thought of heathendom, not without adding to their religion elements of expansiveness which the rigid legal discipline of Palestinian Judaism tended to repress. On the other hand, the troubled conditions under which Jewish nationality struggled to maintain its independence led to a certain religious concentration; sorrow and misfortune became to the Jew a school of the heart.

Let us pause to consider some of the circumstances which gave an impulse to the development of personal religion. First, we notice the depression and sense of disappointment which quickly followed the restoration. The returned exiles, their ears still ringing with the uplifting music of the voice which bade them depart in triumph from the land of captivity, and *come with singing unto Zion*, and with *everlasting joy upon their head*[1], found themselves in their ancient home—in a city ruined, comfortless, unprotected, and surrounded by alien or hostile tribes. The community itself was only a miserable remnant of a once powerful nation. Hopes of revival and recovery seemed to have been blasted at their birth[2]. The foundations of the temple were laid, but the opposition of the Samaritans, combined with the despondent apathy of the exiles,

---

[1] See Isa. li. 11; lii. 7 foll.; lv. 12, &c.
[2] Stanton, *The Jewish and the Christian Messiah*, p. 97, observes: 'It has come to be very generally recognized that illusion followed by the discipline of experience and disappointment played no unimportant part in the formation and definition of the clearest Messianic hope of Israel.' See Hunter, *After the Exile*, part i. chap. v, 'Among the Ruins.'

led to a prolonged cessation of the work. Nor were the prospects of the community materially improved even at a later time, when the temple had been completed and the national worship organized on the levitical system. Jehovah's promises seemed to have come to nought. Things remained as before. In the place of Babylon, the heathen power of Persia had brought Israel under an oppressive yoke. Moreover, the restored worship of the temple provided no effective compensation for the miseries of the time. The book of Malachi bears witness to the prevailing temper of the prophet's contemporaries. Evidently the requirements of Jehovah's service were regarded as an oppressive and costly burden. The strict discipline of the Law provoked a spirit of moroseness, of religious indifference, and even of resentment against God [1]. The community as a whole, and even the priesthood, had apparently sunk into listless apathy and heartless formalism.

Meanwhile, the ideal which reformers like Ezra and Nehemiah set before themselves was that of a holy community, separated by elaborate restrictions from the pollutions of heathendom, and from the semi-paganism of the 'people of the land.' In pursuance of this ideal even the habits and incidents of daily life were brought under the discipline of an all-embracing system, the result of which was a gradual change in men's moral conceptions. The righteousness which the prophets had preached as Jehovah's supreme requirement came to be identified with an anxious and scrupulous legalism, the culminating point of which was eventually reached in Pharisaism.

The tendency to externalism in religion manifested itself most conspicuously in the zeal expended upon the worship of the national sanctuary. The restriction of the levitical *cultus* to the temple tended to make

---

[1] See Mal. ii. 17; iii. 14. Cp. Cornill, *Der Isr. Prophetismus*, pp. 155, 156; Hunter, *op. cit.* part i. pp. 121 foll.; ii. p. 242.

a particular spot the centre of religious interest. Everything came to be regarded from the point of view of Jerusalem, and the sacrificial system by which the nation maintained its covenant-union with Jehovah gradually assumed a disproportionate importance. From this point of view a characteristic product of Judaism is to be found in the books of Chronicles. The writer does more than display a devout and passionate interest in the temple and its services. He makes the legal *cultus* a standard by which the conduct of the Jewish kings in pre-exilic days is judged. This standpoint in fact colours his entire representation of Hebrew history. On the supposition that the levitical system prevailed in the days of the first temple, the chronicler commends or blames the various monarchs according as he believes them to have religiously observed or wilfully neglected the legal observances.

But although the tendency to externalism was no doubt most decidedly pronounced in Jerusalem itself, even among the habitual worshippers in the temple there must have been some to whom the sacrificial *cultus* was the centre of a deeply-rooted spiritual life and a true means of spiritual education. The very calamities of the time would impel devout minds to seek for solace in the services of the sanctuary. Nor must we overlook the very important influence of the synagogue-worship. The synagogues of Judaism replaced the local sanctuaries of the earlier religion, and they became centres of spiritual education—prayer and the reading of the Law being the most prominent features in their services[1]. The effect of such an institution as the synagogue could not fail to be important. 'It actively helped,' says Mr. Montefiore, ' to individualize religion, and to bring it home to the hearts and understanding of all[2].' The synagogue in fact provided a

---
[1] See Kuenen, *Religion of Israel*, vol. iii. chap. 9.
[2] *Hibbert Lectures*, p. 391. Cp. Riehm, *ATl. Theologie*, p. 397; Hunter, *op. cit.* p. 222.

certain spiritual satisfaction for the growing needs of the personal religious life, and while on the one hand it helped to diffuse the knowledge of the Law, thus giving an impulse to the temper of legalism, it could not fail also to suggest more profound ideas of the divine requirement. It served in some measure to counteract the tendency to lay inordinate stress on the sacrificial *cultus* of the temple.

It would accordingly be a serious mistake to suppose that the post-exilic age was a barren period in the religion of Israel. The Psalter alone affords evidence sufficient that the triumph of the nationalistic and legalistic element in Judaism did not fatally impede the growth of personal religion. As a matter of fact it seems to have acted in two ways. In some cases the fervid ecclesiasticism of the time probably tended to produce a temper of sceptical reaction, such as we find reflected in the pessimism of the Preacher: the elaborate *cultus* of the temple may have seemed to exclude the presence or action of the living God. On the other hand, to some the levitical worship seemed rather to bring God nearer [1], and to give vitality to the thought of Jehovah's presence in the midst of His people: to such the *cultus* was full of symbolic teaching, and the study of the *Torah* a great means of communion with God. The Psalter has been said to illustrate ' the combination of prophetic principles with warm attachment to the purified forms in which religion was outwardly clothed [2].' In the Psalms the religion of the prophets is perpetuated: their sacred hopes and fears, their joy in God, their boundless devotion to His service. The Psalter testifies that the discipline of the Law did not necessarily quench the

---

[1] Montefiore, p. 385: 'Spiritual communion with God and the pure joy of a felt nearness to Him were born from participation in the Temple service.' Cp. Schechter, *Studies in Judaism*, p. 292; Kuenen, *Hibbert Lectures*, p. 165.

[2] Montefiore, p. 386. See a valuable passage in Bruce, *Apologetics*, pp. 272 foll., as to the religious significance of the critical view in regard to the origin and date of the Psalter.

life of religious emotion, but rather purified it and imparted to it a new intensity. Nor is it only from the Psalter that we can infer the actual spiritual effects of the period of legalism. In the other writings which complete the Hagiographa we are brought face to face with characteristic products of Judaism. The number and variety of the books composing this group is significant; they bear witness to the zeal, literary culture, and religious devotion of the post-exilic age.

The Hagiographa testify to a growing receptivity of the Jewish mind, a capacity for assimilating ideas derived from Persia or Greece, and for clothing old faiths in new forms. They practically represent the religious life of a people which had passed through many chequered experiences. They comprise the products of religious reason exercising itself upon the problems of life and of religious emotion striving to find for itself adequate utterance. They embrace books so opposite in character as Ecclesiastes, Esther, Daniel, and the Psalms. Thus they embody divergent phases and types of spiritual experience, and give to the Old Testament a peculiarly representative character, making it a book which reflects the needs, perplexities, and aspirations of humanity at large.

As to the Psalms and Wisdom literature, it is sufficiently obvious that they reflect much more than the spirit of one particular age. They do indeed give utterance to ideas and conceptions peculiarly Jewish: the Psalms, for instance, display here and there the characteristic temper of Judaism: its passionate sense of national rectitude, its haunting consciousness of uncleansed guilt, its rigid exclusiveness, its vehement hatred of national foes. But, on the other hand, the Psalms are the product of a spirit which has realized the mystery and blessedness of communion with God; they give expression to its infinite yearnings, its awe, its agonies, its desolation, its exultation. The Old Testament Wisdom also, while it busies itself with the problems of human life, or gathers up the lessons of

age-long moral experience, displays to some extent
the limitations of Judaism. To the Jewish sage,
for instance, the existence of God is an axiom
which lies beyond the range of possible question.
But though Jewish thought always works with a
religious background, it deals with universal problems,
and those the most urgent—the anomalies of human
life, the purpose and meaning of pain, the mystery
of retribution. And if the Hebrew sages do not solve
the problems into which they inquire, it may at least
be claimed that they adequately state them [1].

Again, the sacred histories, Chronicles, Ezra, Nehemiah, Esther, and Ruth, are connected together by the
fact that they are 'studies' of particular periods of
Jewish history, written from a particular point of view,
and dictated more or less by a didactic purpose. The
first three books, which seem originally to have formed
together a single work and are closely connected in
style and method, reflect in a very instructive way the
general effect on thought and character of Judaism in
its earlier stages. Their point of view is purely
religious and particularistic: their aim is to illustrate
the blessings of faithfulness to the requirements of the
levitical code. The book of Nehemiah even displays
some traces of the growth of a doctrine of merit [2], and
a consciousness of personal righteousness which
occasionally meets us in the Psalter also. The book
of Esther has been variously judged. Doubtless it
reflects the fierce passions awakened by the Maccabean
struggle, and so far, in the vindictive spirit which
characterizes it, the story serves the purpose of
practically illustrating a leading defect of the Old
Testament discipline. But though the inclusion of
Esther in the Canon was perhaps designed for instruction rather than spiritual edification, the book is by
no means altogether wanting in religious characteristics [3]. The LXX. translation seems to bring out

---

[1] Cp. Bruce, *Apologetics*, p. 242. [2] Nehem. v. 19; xiii. 14, 22.
[3] Cp. Delitzsch, *O. T. History of Redemption*, § 81. See Luther's verdict,

more clearly than the Hebrew the belief of the writer in God's providential guidance; and other lessons may be derived from it: the 'deep sense of personal vocation to do God's work, faith in self-sacrificing intercession,' courage, patriotism, and a steadfast adherence to the true faith even amid heathen surroundings, which the modern European in India, Africa, or Japan might imitate with advantage[1]. There is no difficulty in recognizing the canonical value of the book of Ruth, which some would regard as a polemical product of Ezra's reforms, marking possibly a tendency to reaction against the puritanical narrowness of the time[2]. If this be a correct account, the book of Ruth fulfils much the same function as that of Jonah. It bears witness to the universality of God's purpose of grace and to His compassion for the heathen who lay beyond the pale of the covenant.

Finally, the book of Daniel, apparently composed as a manual of consolation for the confessors and martyrs of the Maccabean period, is a specimen of prophecy in its later apocalyptic form. With this type of literature the modern western mind can only imperfectly sympathize; but the fact is undeniable that apocalyptic writings exercised a very powerful influence on Jewish thought during the last two centuries before Christ[3]. The book now in question bears witness to the strong hold which Messianic hopes had gained upon the imagination of the faith-

---

ap. Köhler, *Über Berechtigung der Kritik*, &c., p. 31. Cornill's estimate of the book is very severe, *Einleitung in das A. T.* p. 138. Cp. Meinhold, *Jesus und das A. T.* pp. 97, 98; Hunter, *After the Exile*, part i. pp. 237, 238.

[1] See some suggestive notes of Professor Lock in Sanday, *Bampton Lectures*, pp. 222-223. Cp. Ryle, *O. T. Canon*, p. 176.

[2] Cp. Hunter, *op. cit.* pp. 44 foll.

[3] Cp. Drummond, *The Jewish Messiah*, p. 8: 'The authors of the various apocalyptic works... are not justly open to a suspicion of wilful deceit. Our modern taste accords little welcome to this kind of literary inventiveness, and our modern strictness may regard it as not altogether permissible, but I see no reason why it may not have been practised by high-minded and honourable men.' See also Kuenen, *Religion of Israel*, ch. x [Eng. Tr. vol. iii. p. 114].

ful; it shows how effectively they sustained drooping faith under the pressure of persecution. It also illustrates the characteristic religious practices of Judaism, its fervour in prayer and fasting, and its growing sense of the merit of almsgiving[1]. Moreover, the book of Daniel indicates a certain advance in religious thought, due probably in a measure to the contact of Israel's religion with that of Persia[2]. Again, it illustrates the remark of Darmesteter that to the Jewish mind human life and the world's history were a drama. The book is an attempt to grasp the history of the world as a whole[3]. It is dominated, not only by an unshaken confidence in the ultimate triumph of truth, but also by an overmastering sense of a universal divine purpose which overrules all the vicissitudes of human history, the rise and fall of dynasties, the conflicts of nations, and the calamities that overtake the faithful.

Such is a general description, with one or two unimportant omissions, of the contents of the Hagiographa. They display to us in very varied forms the religious mind and character which the teaching of the prophets and the discipline of the Law had brought to maturity. But they also contribute to the Old Testament an element of many-sided sympathy which otherwise it might have lacked, since some of the 'Writings' reflect the experience derived from contact with Gentile thought and life, while others are the product of that habit of direct communion with God by which man gains the power to penetrate the hidden mysteries of the unseen world. The Hagiographa, in a word, give a universal character

---

[1] Cp. Dan. iv. 27. Cp. Riehm, *ATl. Theologie*, pp. 397, 401. On our Lord's references to the book, see Valeton, *Christus und das A. T.* pp. 49 foll.

[2] e.g. in the doctrine of angels, the clearer conception of Satan, and possibly the idea of a resurrection of the body. Cp. Kuenen, *Religion of Israel*, ch. ix. The influence of Persia, however, on Jewish thought must not be overrated. See Hunter, *op. cit.* part i. pp. 82, 83; Nicolas, *Des doctrines religieuses des Juifs*, partie i. ch. 2.

[3] By Jerome, *ad Paulinum*, 14, Daniel is described as 'temporum conscius, et totius mundi φιλίστωρ.' Cp. Kuenen, *op. cit.* ch. x, and Westcott in Smith's *Dictionary of the Bible*, art. 'Daniel.'

to the Bible. 'All the sacred books,' says Origen, 'breathe the spirit of fullness, and there is nothing in them which does not descend from the plenitude of the divine majesty[1].' But these writings especially, both in what they are and what they are not, seem to testify to the presence and operation of the Spirit who bloweth where He listeth, and from whom the secrets of no human heart are hid. It is this remarkable universality of scope which differentiates the literature of the Hebrews from that of other races. Granted that the sacred books of India, Persia, or China display real traces of divine inspiration, or at least of providential guidance, it nevertheless remains true that the Bible alone has proved itself adequate to the task of instructing the ignorance, assuaging the griefs, and ministering to the perplexities, not of one race merely, but of mankind.

In this lecture we are chiefly concerned with the books of the Hagiographa as throwing light on the divine purpose for the individual soul, thereby laying the foundations of personal religion. It seems to be specially their function to prepare the way for three truths which in the New Testament are openly proclaimed: first, the doctrine of immortality; secondly, the mystery of divine providence; thirdly, the fruitfulness of suffering. Christ Himself openly reveals these truths, and in so doing He responds to the most anxious questionings of the human heart. In the Old Testament, however, we are dealing only with the intuitions and presages of holy men, dimly anticipating a future solution of their perplexities. In their searchings of heart we are enabled to study the spiritual needs which God's self-revelation in Christ was designed to satisfy—needs the very consciousness of which was inspired by Him. The function of the Bible in the Church is not so much to originate faith as to aid and educate it: and faith may be helped as well by a sympathetic recognition of difficulties as by

---

[1] *Hom. in Jerem.* xxi. 2.

the solution of them, by actual examples or life-like pictures of faith perplexed not less than by instances of faith triumphant and crowned.

I.

It is natural to deal first with the idea of a future life—an idea which is by no means entirely wanting in the theology of the Old Testament, but which necessarily demanded a moral basis in the human mind. There could be no doctrine of personal immortality at a stage in civilization when as yet the sense of individuality was undeveloped. Amid the conditions of primitive society the individual as such was practically unrecognized. In religion, we are told, as well as in civil affairs, 'the habit of the old world was to think much of the community and little of the individual life. . . . The God was the God of the nation or tribe, and He knew and cared for the individual only as a member of the community[1].' The Old Testament indeed represents the redemptive movement as beginning with an individual man's venture of faith, but it is with a family or tribe, in course of time with an entire nation, that Almighty God establishes His covenant-relationship. We may indeed see a rudimentary recognition of the individual in the doctrine that Jehovah visits the sins of the fathers upon the children unto the third and fourth generation of them that hate Him; this implies that the welfare of a small group of persons within the nation or tribe would depend on the conduct of a single member of the group[2]. But in the main it is obviously true that the *status* and duty of each individual was determined by the character and calling of the nation. Certainly the Israelite is enjoined ever to bear in thankful remembrance the vocation

---

[1] Robertson Smith, *The Religion of the Semites*, pp. 241, 242; R. W. Church, *Discipline of the Christian Character*, Serm. i.
[2] Cp. Riehm, *ATl. Theologie*, p. 28.

and the privileges of his people[1]: and there seems to be, in the pre-prophetic period at any rate, no thought of the salvation of the individual apart from that of the nation. From the Mosaic point of view a man's position depended upon his relation to the covenant people. He was accepted and recognized, so to speak, by Jehovah only in so far as he could claim lawful membership in the elect nation. It is only when viewed collectively that Israel is honoured with the title of Jehovah's son[2]. The individual Israelite had no right to appropriate personally either the style or the privileges of sonship. He enjoyed filial dignity only in virtue of his incorporation into the community which collectively inherited the promises vouchsafed to the patriarchs[3]. An individual and personal sonship scarcely makes its appearance within the confines of the Old Testament.

The utmost that we can clearly discern in the religious history of Israel is a gradual and progressive moral discipline paving the way for a doctrine of personal immortality and salvation, which without such a preparatory education might have appeared incredible and even unwelcome to human thought. Now we find the moral groundwork of the doctrine of immortality, the premisses as it were from which the conclusion might have been drawn, and was in a measure actually drawn, in two great verities—the one characteristic of the age of Mosaism, the other of the troubled period of Israel's later history: (1) the truth of man's relation as an individual soul to God, (2) the truth

---

[1] Cp. Deut. iv. 7; vi. 7-9. König holds an opposite view to that stated in the text, but his arguments fail to carry conviction. See his *Religious History of Israel*, pp. 178 foll. [2] Exod. iv. 22.
[3] Cp. Riehm, *ATl. Theologie*, p. 28: 'Die sittlich-religiöse Bedeutung der Persönlichkeit ist noch nicht völlig erkannt. Gott steht im Verhältniss zu dem ganzen Volke, aber der einzelne nennt ihn nicht Vater. Nur das Volk als solches ist erwählt, und einzig als Glied desselben hat der einzelne an dieser Erwählung teil. Jede Störung des Gemeinschaftsverhältnisses zwischen Gott und Israel wird daher auch von ihm nicht bloss schmerzlich, sondern auch als Störung seiner persönlichen Beziehungen zu dem Höchsten empfunden.' See also Oehler, *Theology of the O. T.* i. 259.

of a fundamental moral order concealed beneath the perplexing anomalies of the world.

To deal with these in order.

1. In the Law, even in its final shape, no doctrine of the soul's existence after death is definitely taught. What is characteristic of Mosaism is its deliberate and entire exclusion of any distinct conception of the state after death. Dr. Mozley points out how favourably this absence of any clear conception contrasts with the false and unworthy notions which we meet with in contemporary paganism. Mosaism is on the whole marked by a chilling, negative idea of death—an idea no doubt in many ways suitable to a dispensation of which the aim and tendency was to reveal the divine holiness and abhorrence of sin. The word *She‘ol*—the place of departed spirits—is variously derived, but perhaps the best account of the word is that it is connected with the verb שׁעל *to be hollow* : it would thus have the primary meaning of 'hollow place' or 'pit.' It occurs even in the earliest writers, and is very frequent in the Psalms and Prophets, being often poetically personified[1]. The only definite statements as to their condition are to the effect that the state of the departed is one of utter privation of all or of most that belongs to life; in *She‘ol* there is darkness instead of light, forgetfulness and sleep instead of waking and conscious thought; there is neither hope nor joy, nor power of praise, nor any longer the solace of communion with God. To descend into *She‘ol* is to go down into the depths of the earth, to a place of corruption and of the worm, to a *horrible pit*, to *the dust of death*[2]. But on the other hand, there is not supposed to be any annihilation of personality in *She‘ol*; the soul exists in a state of consciousness; the identity of personal being continues. In *She‘ol* the dead are

---

[1] Cp. Schultz, ii. 324.
[2] See Job x. 22; Eccl. ix. 5 foll.; Ps. xxii. 15; lxxxviii. 12; cxv. 17; Isa. xiv. 10, 11.

gathered without distinction, in tribes and families; men are said to be *gathered to their fathers* not as sharing necessarily a common tomb, but as having a certain social existence even after death. To some extent there is a reproduction in the place of the departed of the circumstances and conditions of the upper world: kings are thought of as sitting on thrones; the righteous *rest in their beds*. Such ideas contradict the supposition that death to an ancient Hebrew meant annihilation[1]. The dead were believed still to exist, though their condition was shadowy and phantom-like[2]. Moreover, the practice of necromancy implies a belief that the departed have a higher measure of knowledge than the living, and are consequently able to foretell future events[3]. But the prevalent view is that their condition is one of loss, and of final withdrawal from all the activities, hopes and rewards of life. In *She'ol*, according to the Preacher, *there is no work, nor device, nor knowledge, nor wisdom*. There, forgetful and forgotten, the dead *lie like sheep, cut away* from the hand of God[4]. It is evident indeed, without further illustration, that the ordinary Hebrew conception of the state of death, which results from the discipline of the Law, is based on the visible phenomena connected with death. All the effects of dissolution, as they impressed the imagination of the devout Israelite, are of course undeniable, and are intended no doubt to produce a certain impression on the human mind. 'The order of nature,' says Dr. Mozley[5], 'is a melancholy revelation on the subject of death, placing one sepulchral picture before our eyes of generation after

---

[1] See Isa. xiv. 9; lvii. 2; 1 Sam. xxviii. 15; Ezek. xxxii. 21, 24.
[2] They are called רְפָאִים, 'weak' or 'pithless ones,' 'shades.' Cp. the Homeric εἴδωλα καμόντων. Job xxvi. 5; Isa. xxvi. 14, &c. See Oehler, § 78; Renan, *Histoire*, &c., bk. i. ch. 9.
[3] Cp. Riehm, *ATl. Theologie*, p. 190. The practice of necromancy is forbidden in Lev. xix. 31; xx. 6, 27; Deut. xviii. 11. On the other hand, Eccl. ix. 5, 'The dead know not anything,' &c.
[4] Eccl. ix. 10; Ps. xlix. 14; lxxxviii. 5.
[5] *Essays*, vol. ii. pp. 172 foll.

generation of men entirely disappearing, and being heard of and seen no more. Now in the case of the Jew the appeal of nature was as strong as it is now, the opposing one of Scripture much weaker. The consequence was that the order of nature, an order intended to affect the mind in a particular way under all dispensations—for God does not make even appearances for nothing, but intends that joyful ones should duly gladden and mournful ones duly depress us—affected the Jew more strongly than it does the Christian. As such was his lot, he bowed meekly to it and received the whole of that melancholy impress upon his passive soul.' The Old Testament horizon, in point of fact, lies wholly on this side the grave. A continued existence in his descendants—this was the utmost that a pious Israelite could reasonably hope for; the loss of life was in a sense a 'withdrawal of the highest good [1].' Consequently, even devout hearts look forward with dread and unconcealed bitterness of spirit to the monotony and dreariness of *She'ol*. The highest blessedness, the supreme reward of covenant faithfulness, is long life in the land which is God's gift to His people. Nothing that death could give—rest from the storms of life, and final deliverance from suffering, oppression or contumely—seemed to be any compensation for the total loss of the blessings of continued earthly existence, to which the Jew clung with a pathetic eagerness.

What then, it might be asked, did the Mosaic dispensation contribute towards the idea of a future life, of personal immortality for the individual? The answer is—it impressed on the Israelite's mind the truth of man's covenant-relationship to God, his dignity as admitted to the life of fellowship with

---

[1] Stade ap. Schultz, ii. 327. Even after the exile, the pious Jew 'did not as yet venture to express the hope of a life after death, of a resurrection of the body. The utmost he hoped for was *a memorial in Jerusalem* (Neh. ii. 20), a monument within its walls which was better than sons and daughters (Isa. lvi. 6).' Hunter, *op. cit.* i. p. 83.

God. Man's personality was of permanent worth and importance, inasmuch as he was created capable of standing in an essential relation to the source of all good and to the moral law as the reflection of God's being. It is this side of the Mosaic teaching which is developed in the Psalms. Meanwhile, we may notice in passing that Jewish faith was not entirely unvisited by anticipatory gleams of consolation and hope: to sustain this faith there existed the tradition of Enoch, who *walked with God, and he was not, for God took him*; the narrative of Elijah's translation to the unseen world in a chariot of fire; and that of the return of Samuel from the abode of the departed to prophesy the doom of Saul [1]. These are at least testimonies to an anticipation which later reflection was destined to render more explicit. Moreover, the Jew could always find rest in his fundamental assurance that a holy God existed—a truth which implied the reality of an invisible world of which God was the centre. Further, it was certain that Jehovah had willed to make a covenant of grace with men, in order to bring them into a living fellowship with Himself. Jehovah was the Almighty God of the patriarchs; and herein lay an implicit pledge—a latent prophecy—that He would continue through and beyond death the existence of a creature to whom He had displayed such condescending love. Our Lord seems to draw the conclusion which the unbelief of the Sadducees hesitated to deduce in His recorded answer to their captious questioning: *Now that the dead are raised, even Moses showed at the bush, when he calleth the Lord the God of Abraham, and the God of Isaac, and the God of Jacob. For he is not a God of the dead, but of the living; for all live unto him*[2]. In the belief of holy Israelites that God continued to stand in an unbroken and eternal relationship of grace to the forefathers of the nation, lay an implicit sense

---

[1] Gen. v. 24; 2 Kings ii. 11; 1 Sam. xxviii. 11 foll.
[2] Luke xx. 38.

of the enduring dignity and preciousness of human nature—a sense which formed a suitable foundation for the idea of personal immortality[1]. Nor must it be forgotten that the Law itself, in appealing sternly to man's faculty of obedience, implicitly recognized his worth as a being capable of response to moral commands. Mosaism recognizes, so to speak, the theomorphic structure of man; it treats him as a spiritual being; it recognizes his moral freedom, his capacity for perfection and for fellowship with God. Indeed it might be maintained that upon this view of human nature 'the whole religion of Israel, with its idea of the kingdom of God, its worship and its prophecy, is founded[2].'

The Mosaic conception of human nature is inherited and further developed by the prophets and psalmists. In the writings of the prophets the individual relationship of man to God is contemplated from the moral side. Thus Jeremiah and Ezekiel qualify the doctrine of inherited guilt by insistence on the truth of individual accountability. The former prophet in his vision of the future new covenant includes the idea of personal salvation: *In those days they shall say no more, The fathers have eaten a sour grape, and the children's teeth are set on edge. But every one shall die for his own iniquity*[3]. And the thought is expanded in detail by Ezekiel: *The soul that sinneth, it shall die. The son shall not bear the iniquity of the father, neither shall the father bear the iniquity of the son: the righteousness of the righteous shall be upon him, and the wickedness of the wicked shall be upon him*[4]. (It may have been Ezekiel's sense of the heavy personal responsibility

---

[1] Cp. Riehm, *ATl. Theologie*, p. 192 : 'Lag in der Gewissheit, dass der Fromme in der Gnadengemeinschaft mit dem ewigen Gott sterbe, der triebkräftige Keim, aus welchem sich die Hoffnung des ewigen Lebens entwickelen, und in jenem Glauben an Gottes Macht über Tod und Totenreich lag das Fundament auf welches der Auferstehungsglaube gegründet werden konnte.'
[2] Schultz, ii. 263.   [3] Jer. xxxi. 29 foll.
[4] Ezek. xviii. 20. Cp. Kirkpatrick, *The Doctrine of the Prophets*, pp. 340 foll.

involved in his own calling and mission that led him to develope this line of thought.) It was the necessary correction of a view of divine governance which, though it seemed to be the logical outcome of the Mosaic dispensation, had now done its work. Ezekiel, dealing as a divinely appointed watchman or pastor of souls with the despondency and apathy of the exiles, found it necessary to proclaim a truth that formed a new starting-point in the evolution of religion[1].

The psalmists occasionally betray their consciousness of two opposite aspects of human life. *Lord, what is man, that thou art mindful of him, and the son of man, that thou visitest him? Thou madest him lower than the angels, to crown him with glory and worship. Thou madest him to have dominion of the works of thy hands, and thou hast put all things in subjection under his feet*[2]. Of these two views, however, the more ideal one everywhere prevails, and indeed gives its characteristic tone and colour to the Psalter. Consequently, although we find in the Psalms the same chilling and cheerless conception of death which the discipline of the Law had fostered, yet alongside of it we find a conviction, ever growing in clearness and strength, of the subsistence of an indestructible bond between the living God and the creatures whom He has visited and redeemed. The idea has been justly called 'a sentiment rather than an article of faith'; yet it seems to be powerful enough to resist successfully the impression made by the exterior phenomena of death. Thus we have such passages as Ps. xlix. 15, *God will redeem my soul from the power of the grave, for he shall receive me*, the verb used being the same which occurs in the narrative of Enoch's translation (Gen. v. 24), *He was not, for God took—received—him*. With this passage we may compare the outburst of faith in Ps. xvii. 15, *As for me, I will behold thy face in righteousness;*

[1] Cp. Ezek. xxxiii. 7, 10; xxxvii. 11.   [2] Ps. viii. 4, 5.

I shall be satisfied, when I awake, with thy likeness. And to these might be added the sublime verses which close the seventy-third Psalm: *Thou shalt guide me with thy counsel, and afterward receive me to glory. Whom have I in heaven but thee? and there is none upon earth that I desire beside thee. My flesh and my heart faileth, but God is the strength of my heart, and my portion for ever.* The devout Jew was in fact able to feel secure even with the prospect of dissolution before him, in the firm conviction of his relationship to a perfectly holy and loving being. He rested in the *thoughts of peace* which his religion supplied, not inventing, as the heathen did, a definite picture of the future state, but trusting calmly to omnipotent goodness as the one constant and fixed reality amid the decay and change of visible nature[1]. He was not blind to the positive lessons presented by the daily spectacle of human mortality. He doubtless learned to connect the mystery of death with the fact of sin and of God's wrath, as the ninetieth Psalm testifies; and this consciousness of a close relation subsisting between death and sin would certainly be deepened by the ceremonial defilement which under the Law was involved in any contact with death. Nevertheless, the true Israelite could hold fast to his trust in God[2]; he could submit to be gathered to his fathers in peace, secure in the thought of that personal relation to God which he had proved by the experience of life to be a solace and a stay. For the very call to communion with God of which he was conscious would be to him a pledge of uninterrupted life. The character of God—His covenant-faithfulness, His creative compassion for the souls which He had made—could assure the righteous man of protection. Death would be a supreme and trustful self-surrender. Into the hands of God he would com-

---

[1] Cp. Mozley, *Essays*, ii. 173.
[2] See Job xix. 25 foll.; Ps. xcii. 13 foll.; Prov. xi. 7; xiv. 32; xxiii. 18; xxiv. 14; Isa. lvii. 2.

mend his spirit in confidence that a being whom God had so highly favoured would not utterly perish. The hope of the devout Israelite might, in short, be expressed in the words of Augustine: *Junge cor tuum immortalitati Dei, et cum illo aeternus eris*[1]. Without therefore laying too much stress on isolated passages, or reading into them a belief which was not yet developed, there is ground for the statement that at least the foundation was laid in the Mosaic system for a doctrine of immortality, since the Law presupposed and inculcated the truth of man's dignity and worth as a being called to communion with God and capable of rendering moral obedience to His will.

2. The second main foundation on which the doctrine of a future life could be based is to be found in the gradually awakened sense of the anomalies and difficulties of God's moral government, and the apparent uncertainties of divine retribution.

The Mosaic doctrine of retribution is well represented in such a passage as Lev. xxvi, which embodies the general doctrine of the Law that ultimately man's earthly lot will correspond with his desert. It is one of the incidental limitations of Mosaism that it represents the present world as the only scene of God's distributive justice. It almost invariably connects material prosperity with righteous conduct and disaster with wickedness. Certainly there are traces in the Old Testament of something much higher than mere eudaemonism. Earthly blessings are promised to the righteous, but it is taught that they are to be prized mainly as tokens or pledges of divine favour. The psalmists and prophets rise to the thought that in the presence of God is fullness of joy, that He is the hope of the soul, its treasure and its *portion in the land of the living*, its unfailing source of gladness, even although *the fig tree shall not blossom neither shall fruit*

[1] *Enarr. in Ps.* xci. 8. Cp. Cheyne, *Aids to the Devout Study of Criticism*, p. 159: 'Living as he does by prayer, and with a sense of the invisible things which grows every day in strength and purity, he cannot imagine that his intimacy with God will come to an abrupt end.'

be in the vines[1]. And in general it seems to be true that the Old Testament idea of 'life[2]' as the sum of blessing points to something higher than material prosperity, just as the narrative of Joseph sold by his brethren, wrongfully accused and thrown into bondage in Egypt, might suggest the possibility of suffering befalling the innocent. But these are only dim anticipations of a deeper conception of retribution. The simpler Mosaic doctrine was one with which Jewish faith was evidently loath to part. It seems to underlie the treatment of history in the books of Samuel and Kings. In the books of Chronicles the belief appears in an almost unqualified form—the writer's apparent aim being to construct a theodicy[3] rather than a history, based on the principle that the temporal happiness or misery of the nation was entirely determined by its attitude to the moral and ceremonial injunctions of the levitical Law. But it is clear that while this theory might be suitable to the phenomena of a simple and comparatively stable condition of society, it was liable to break down under the strain and stress of troublous times; it would not correspond with men's experience of the actual and visible facts of a highly-developed and corrupt civilization. In such a state of things the invariable association of righteousness with earthly prosperity was not found to hold good. The afflictions of the godly were matters of daily experience. A Josiah was slain in battle; 'a Jeremiah was crushed beneath a thousand woes, and sorrow-stricken psalmists prayed in vain to be delivered from the injustice and oppression of the great. . . . In a word, evil appeared to come purely from a law of nature, absolutely irrespective of moral order[4].'

Now these unwelcome facts of human experience

---

[1] See Ps. xvi. 5 foll.; cxlii. 5; Habak. iii. 17, 18. Cp. W. S. Bruce, *The Ethics of the O. T.* pp. 21, 22.

[2] חיים Deut. xxx. 15 foll.; Prov. viii. 35; xii. 28, &c. Cp. Oehler, § 89.

[3] Cp. Montefiore, *Hibbert Lectures*, p. 448.

[4] Schultz, ii. 209.

were met sometimes with a persistent denial, sometimes with sorrowful expostulation and strenuous assertions of innocence: for we must remember that the Law had not only trained men to the belief that suffering is the result of sin; it had also produced the sense of guilt, and its opposite the consciousness of innocence. This latter spirit was characteristic of post-exilic Judaism. It breathes in many of the Psalms; and a main element in Job's truthfulness and rectitude of character is his steadfast refusal to condemn himself[1]. The same temper finds utterance in the cries of expostulation with God on the apparent injustice of His dealings, which we meet with in Scripture—in the protests and appeals of such typical passages as Psalm lxxiii; Jeremiah, chap. xii; or Habakkuk, chap. i. The fact is that an adequate doctrine of future retribution was as yet lacking. The righteous sufferer of the Old Testament was left to hope against hope that what he had ever believed to be a law of divine governance would yet somehow be triumphantly vindicated. The same sense of injured rectitude also contributes to the impatience and thirst for vengeance which startles us in the imprecatory passages of the Old Testament. Both alike—the expostulations and the curses uttered by godly Israelites—bear witness to the perception of a serious moral difficulty, the attempted explanation of which was to lead to more profound views of the future state, as one in which the anomalies of the present would be corrected.

So far as the Psalms deal with this problem, a solution seems to be implicitly contained in the idea previously noticed, that namely of such a 'saving and indissoluble union with God' as might adequately compensate the righteous man for his undeserved suffering and for the prosperity of the wicked. In the Wisdom literature, however, we seem to be able to trace a continuous and progressive effort to solve the problem. Thus the book of Proverbs, reflecting the

[1] Job xxvii. 5.

experience of a relatively simple state of society, reproduces on the whole the general principles which had been inculcated by the Mosaic discipline. The authors of the Proverbs have a naïve confidence in their belief that sin and suffering, righteousness and earthly prosperity, are causally connected. This optimism, says Professor Cheyne, is 'just what we might expect in a simple and stationary condition of society. The strange thing is that it should have lasted on when oppression from within or hostile attacks from without brought manifold causes of sorrow upon both bad and good. . . . There must have been circles of Jewish moralists averse to speculation who would continue to repeat the older view of providential government even at a time when the social state had completely exposed its shallowness [1].' There are, however, hints here and there in the Proverbs that suggest a more profound moral insight; in some passages, at least, there is a consciousness expressed that suffering may fulfil a probationary and disciplinary function even in the case of the righteous. For instance, in Prov. iii. 11, 12 we discover a view of suffering different from that of the traditional theory: *My son, despise not the chastening of the Lord, neither be weary of his correction; for whom the Lord loveth he correcteth, even as a father the son in whom he delighteth.*

Then follows an 'era of difficulties [2]'—such a period as included the decay and ruin of the Jewish monarchy, the great cataclysm of the exile, and the difficulties of life in Palestine after the restoration. The age of Solomon appeared, in retrospect at least, as a golden age: at any rate, it was believed to have been a period of generally diffused prosperity. Probably there had been in Solomon's reign a strong consciousness of national unity, a fair administration of justice, and

---

[1] *Job and Solomon,* p. 122.
[2] See Dean Farrar's introduction to the Book of Wisdom in the *Speaker's Commentary.*

a sense of order, stability, and security in the conditions of life. But towards the close of the monarchical period, when pastoral habits had to a great extent disappeared and given way to those of commerce and trade, inequalities of social condition became more apparent; the prosperity of wicked men was a patent fact, and the social troubles of a decaying civilization forced the question of retribution again into notice. The miseries of life in Palestine during the time of the Persian domination seem to be reflected in the book of Ecclesiastes. The prevalent evils were 'unrighteous judgment, despotic oppression, riotous court-life, the raising of mean men to the highest dignities, the inexorable severity of the law of military service, the prudence required by the organized system of espionage [1].' But above all, the captivity itself was the crowning example of the undeserved sufferings of the righteous [2]. The figure of the patriarch Job is, as we have noticed elsewhere, a type of the righteous servant of God overwhelmed by unmerited affliction, and there is some reason to connect the composition of the book with the period of the exile [3]. It may be intended to impress upon the godly in Israel a new view of suffering as not merely penal but probationary and disciplinary, testing fidelity and patience. It may be remarked in passing that this was an idea which we find already suggested in the book of Deuteronomy and in some passages of the prophetic writings [4], and that the author of Isaiah liii carries the thought further. He points to the possibility of vicarious or substitutionary suffering; and the traits common to the sublime figure of that chapter, and the representation of Job, make it probable that the same idea is hinted at in the

---

[1] Delitzsch, quoted by Cheyne, *Job and Solomon*, p. 258. See Eccl. iii. 16; iv. 1; v. 8; viii. 9; x. 16 foll. Possibly the book of Joel also illustrates the condition of Palestine during the Persian period. Cp. Hunter, *op. cit.* pp. 238 foll.; Cornill, *Einleitung in das A. T.* § 28.
[2] Cp. Habak. ii.   [3] Cp. Driver, *Introduction*, &c., p. 405.
[4] See Deut. viii. 2; Hos. ii. 8 foll.; Jer. xxxv. 13; Isa. xxvii. 8; Ps. lxvi. 10 foll.

book of Job itself, which teaches that Job's sufferings give him intercessory power[1]. The problem discussed however remains, as Professor Cheyne observes, unsolved in the book itself. Indeed the older doctrine of retribution is expressly confirmed by the issue, according to which Job's fidelity is rewarded with an enlarged measure of earthly blessedness. The net result of the book then is the proved insufficiency of the traditional opinion that *all* suffering can be accounted for by personal sin. In chapters xiv–xix, however, we find a further advance towards a solution of the difficulty, in the hints there given of a supra-mundane justice manifesting itself, if not in this life, then beyond its boundary. It is difficult to determine exactly the significance of the main passage (xix. 26, 27) that bears upon the point in question[2], and it is manifest that the suggestion is left undeveloped, whatever be its precise import. Job himself falls back on the lower standpoint and presses for a solution of his unexplained sufferings on this side of death. And the great lesson of the book is that of patient waiting.

The book of Ecclesiastes, reflecting the sad experience of days when the bulk of the nation was in danger of losing its higher hopes and sinking into listless and sullen despondency, marks an 'era of quiescence.' In the book of Job an appeal is made to the divine omnipotence, the thought being that supreme power implies a supreme righteousness in which the pledge of a further revelation is involved. But in Ecclesiastes the problem of retribution is virtually abandoned as insoluble. The writer is led through the many-sided experience of life, which for him ends only in satiety and despair, to give up his fruitless efforts to comprehend the principles of God's moral government[3]. He evidently realizes keenly the

---

[1] Job xlii. 8.
[2] See Riehm, *A Tl. Theologie*, pp. 360, 361. The idea of Job seems to be that God as a *Goel* or Avenger of blood will some day stand over his grave and vindicate his character. Cp. Schultz, ii. 329 foll.
[3] Renan, *L'Ecclésiaste*, p. 40: 'Cohélet a sa place définie dans cette

untenableness of the traditional view of retribution: but he ultimately arrives at the negative conclusion that trustful obedience, submission to God's known will for man, and steadfast fulfilment of moral duty can alone make life tolerable. There is, however, a suggestion peculiar to the book : it ends with the presage of a judgment, involving a new self-manifestation of God, by which the riddle of the present world will be solved [1]. Moreover, it is noticeable that the writer of Ecclesiastes still clings to that sense of personal relationship to God which differentiates man from the brute [2], and points to a possible continuation of existence after death.

On the whole, then, the last word of the Old Testament is one of resignation not unhopeful. The tendency was already manifesting itself to push the solution of the moral problems of human life beyond the limits of life itself, and to base the justification of God's ways on eschatological doctrine [3]. It is true that in some passages of an apocalyptic character we find a doctrine of resurrection, though still confined within nationalistic limits. The idea of a resurrection of Israel as a nation from its grave is found in Hosea and in Ezekiel [4]. But the author of Isaiah xxiv–xxvii foretells a divine victory over death in the Messianic age, and the awakening to new life of the godly members of the elect nation who have perished. The purport of Daniel xii. 2 is similar.

histoire du long combat de la conscience juive contre l'iniquité du monde. Il représente une pause dans la lutte.' Cp. Kuenen, *Religion of Israel*, ch. x.

[1] Observe this is a point common to the Old and the New Testament. Cp. Ritschl, *Unterricht in der Christlichen Religion*, § 18, note d : 'Die Dichter im A. T. sehen sich durchgehend in ihrer natürlichen Erwartung getäuscht dass es den Gerechten gut, den Gottlosen übel ergehen müsse. Sie müssen sich begnügen, die Auflösung des umgekehrten Thatbestandes für die Zukunft von Gott zu erbitten. Deshalb wird die Herstellung der richtigen Ordnung auf die Erwartung des zukünftigen Gerichtes Gottes fixirt, sowohl im A. wie im N. T.'

[2] Eccl. iii. 21 ; xii. 7.

[3] Cp. Farrar, *ubi supra*, p. 417 ; Cheyne, *Job and Solomon*, p. 201.

[4] Hos. vi. 2 ; xiii. 14 ; Ezek. xxxvii. Cp. Riehm, *ATl. Theologie*, p. 346.

This passage does not imply a general resurrection from the dead, but a rising again of all Israel's dead, good and bad alike, *some to everlasting life, and some to shame and everlasting contempt*[1]. The doctrine of a general resurrection first makes its appearance in some post-canonical literature, e. g. the Apocalypse of Baruch, and the book of Enoch[2]. Only in the New Testament is it proclaimed with such clearness that St. Paul can declare that *life and immortality* have been *brought to light through the gospel*[3].

II.

A presage then, rather than any definite or clear anticipation of a future life, was the outcome of the long period of discipline which began with the legislation of Moses. But, at any rate, the foundation of a true spiritual life was laid; the soul of the godly Israelite learned to possess itself. Conscious of its high calling, Hebrew faith strove to apprehend the significance and privileges of that close relationship with God to which it felt itself summoned. We see the fruit of its endeavours in the book of Psalms.

We shall best understand the true function of this book if we consider the real meaning of religion. The question what in its essence religion is, is an old one, and the history of human thought on the subject is full of solemn pathos, mainly because it is the story of fundamental and most disastrous misconceptions. There was, for instance, an age, and a condition of human speculation about God, when it could be said in bitter earnest—

'Tantum relligio potuit suadere malorum[4].'

And there are those even in the present day whose confidence in their power to survey the whole field of

---

[1] Cp. 2 Macc. vii. 9; xii. 43; and see Nicolas, *Des doctrines religieuses des Juifs*, partie ii. ch. 6.
[2] See *Apoc. of Baruch*, chh. xlix-li, with Mr. Charles' notes. Cp. the same writer's edition of the *Book of Enoch*, p. 52.
[3] 2 Tim. i. 10. [4] Lucr. *de Rer. Nat.* i. 101.

human progress leads them to speak of Jesus Christ as one whose intentions were good, yet who has done infinite mischief to the world [1]. The imperfections and inconsistencies of religious men, the disastrous mistakes into which the Church has now and then been betrayed by the folly and shortsightedness of her own children, the divisions of Christendom—all these have no doubt fatally wounded nascent faith, and retarded the advance of the divine kingdom: they have produced either the impatience which betrays or the despair which abandons the cause of God. And yet when we endeavour to explain to ourselves that overwhelming and heart-piercing fact of the general aversion from religion which is so common in the present as in every age we shall, I think, find that ultimately it is due to a fundamental mistake as to the true meaning of religion. The experience of saints recorded in Scripture shows that religion is, and from the first ever has been, the life of friendship with God; nothing can be clearer than this conception as it is marked for us in each stage in Israel's history [2]. A friendship between God and the soul of man—this is religion. So the Old Testament tells us of Enoch, who walked with God; of Noah, to whom God revealed His secret purpose of judgment; of Abraham, who was *called the friend of God*; of Jacob, the object of divine pity, protection and favour throughout the days, few and evil, of his pilgrimage; of Moses, with whom *the Lord spake face to face as a man speaketh with his friend*; of Samuel, dedicated to the service of Jehovah from his childhood; of David, the recipient of awful and momentous, yet most tender, promises. The prophets too—they are *friends of God* [3]: they repre-

---

[1] The remark is quoted, apparently with approval, by Darmesteter in a review of Renan's *Histoire du peuple d'Israël* (see *Les Prophètes d'Israël*, p. 204).
[2] There is great truth in a striking remark of M. Renan: 'Le peuple juif est à la fois le peuple le plus religieux et celui qui a eu la religion la plus simple' (*L'Ecclésiaste*, p. 28).
[3] Wisd. vii. 27.

sent in their own persons the ideal calling of every individual Israelite; that life of holy intimacy, of upward-looking faith, of unreserved self-surrender which was really involved in the vocation of God's chosen from the first.

But it is chiefly in the psalmists that we find typical representatives of religion—of the life of love. The element that is local, national, temporary in the Psalter is comparatively insignificant. 'What gives the Psalms, even more than the Prophets, their value as classical devotional writings for all times and peoples, is just the withdrawal and partly the total absence of the national theocratic point of view. Cares about the fates of peoples and the future ideals of universal history lay far from the Psalm-poet of the Persian and Greek age; to him the place of the secular state was taken by the religious community[1].' The Psalms describe the converse of the human soul with God—the human soul in its solitariness, its frailty, its aspirations, its yearnings for ideal truth, light, peace, love, and joy. They bear witness, as no human literature has ever done, to the elemental fact of life, that

'God alone can satisfy whom God alone created.'

For to the psalmists God is all in all: the refuge in any trouble, the rock which stands unshaken amid the storms of human life, the supreme solace in loneliness, the living object of the soul's thirst, its richest and most precious portion and possession, the object of its tenderest, most passionate and yet most restful self-surrender, trust, and love. This is the blessedness of the true Israelite's religion: his portion is God, *the living God*[2], more close, more dear, more faithful than father or mother[3], bringing refreshment as the true fountain of life, and gladness as the source of all beauty and light. In the Psalms it is

---

[1] Pfleiderer, *Gifford Lectures*, vol. ii. pp. 57 foll.
[2] Ps. xlii. 2. Cp. Ps. lxxiii. 25; Lam. iii. 24.
[3] Ps. xxvii. 10.

love which breathes, love which awakes and sings like a bird in spring. The whole passion of the human heart pours itself forth in that endless variety of phrase in which it strives to realize what God is to the soul. The psalmists look at all things with the eye of love: at the past history of Israel, the vicissitudes of the soul's life, the troubles of the righteous, the ordinances of temple worship, the requirements of the Law, the solitariness of exile, the mysteries of pain and death. And here we touch on what is most fundamental in human life: the soul's capacity for loving God above all things, and resting in Him as a refuge and home. It is surely for this reason that the Church of God places the Psalter in the hands of her children: she would train them to think the thoughts, to utter the language, to experience the affections of love. There can be no more eloquent testimony as to the true meaning and power of religion; there can be no higher expression of its essential spirit than is contained in the Psalms. Religion—the relationship of love—is here described, is here describing itself, as the supreme satisfaction of man's deepest and most personal needs; and the essential inter-dependence of ethics and religion is implied in the soul's discovery that the highest good is God, and that communion with Him is the only blessedness.

Now the peculiar contribution of the Psalter to the religious life seems to lie in its uniform recognition of the truth of divine providence—of the personal care of God for the soul—that mystery which (as was once said by Dr. Newman in this place) might well 'make us laugh with perplexity and amazement.' *O God, thou art my God*: here is the keynote of the book. The confession marks a wonderful advance in the story of human faith. A devout Israelite did indeed recognize the hand of God in nature and in history. He watched with reverence and awe the operation of an invincible and righteous will in the universe. He acknowledged its supremacy: *Whatsoever Jehovah pleased, that did he in heaven, and in earth, in the sea, and in all deep places.* It was He *who bringeth forth the clouds from the ends of the world;* He *who smote the firstborn of Egypt, both of man and beast*[1]. Jewish faith intuitively perceived that all things were so guided and controlled as to serve the purposes and promote the ends of a moral kingdom. The conception of miracle was unclouded by any speculative difficulty, for to the Jew the idea of the fixity of natural laws was entirely subordinate to the sense of a righteous will bearing all things onward in a divinely predetermined course. The self-revelation of God—this was what gave to history its significance, to human life its dignity, to nature its mysteriousness[2]. But it needed a certain development of subjective religion to prepare the way for the belief which is reflected in the Psalter—the belief in God not merely as the awful ruler of the universe, but as the precious possession of the soul. It is indeed, if we think of it, a new spiritual discovery that underlies the habitual language of the Psalms. That the Creator cares for the single soul, that He answers prayer, that His ear is open to the cry of spiritual desolation or need, that He can dispose and overrule the hearts of men as it pleases Him, that He watches and protects the individual life, shields it from peril and provides for its natural necessities, that His care extends even to the beasts of the forest or of the field, and to the birds of the air—this belief was new. In modern times it is that which seems most to be threatened by the immensities opened to us by science. Yet once realized it is the very foundation-truth of religion. *He that cometh to God,* says an apostolic writer, *must believe that he is*[3]; and he surely who prays and longs to love God, must believe that He hears, and cares for

---

[1] Ps. cxxxv. 6 foll.
[2] It is noticeable that the later Psalms are full of the thought of God's immediate presence and handiwork in the ordinary processes and incidents of nature.
[3] Heb. xi. 6.

the soul. The Psalms testify to the fact that the Jew equally with the Christian, so far as each is true to his faith, lives in the sense of divine providence[1]. It is a belief which must in any case follow from any vivid realization by man of God's personality, and of his own. The restoration in our time of the lost sense of a Father's providence, which watches and tends and guides the individual soul, depends upon the measure in which the Christian Church can bring home to men the truth of the divine personality, and by its active ministries can re-awaken the consciousness of a love which works behind the veil, though obscured by the unlovely struggles, the harsh competitions, the agonies, disasters, degradations, and failures incidental to the march of civilization.

It is unnecessary to enlarge on this point; but it is worth while to notice that the general teaching of the Psalms on this subject pervades other books of the Hagiographa. In a sense the Psalter gives a character to the entire division of the Hebrew Scriptures in which it occupies the foremost place. Its importance corresponds to its apparently accidental position, and to the fact that the entire collection of Hagiographa seems to be occasionally quoted by the title of *The Psalms*[2]. All the books may be said to be connected by the common conception of religion as not merely a covenant relationship between God and the chosen people, but as a personal possession and stay of the individual soul. The dramatic Song of Solomon, in its primary acceptation, may be regarded as a divine consecration of human love. Incidentally, in so far as it makes for purity in the relation of the sexes, it serves to emphasize an element in the religion of Jehovah which sharply distinguished it from the nature-worship of Canaan. But the usage of the New Testament and the traditional practice of interpreters

---

[1] Consider Ps. xxxiii. 13–15. See generally Weill, *Le Judaïsme, ses dogmes et sa mission*, troisième partie, chh. 1, 2.
[2] Luke xxiv. 44.

warrant us in regarding the Song as a description of the mystical relationship between God and the individual soul. Hengstenberg has pointed out that the New Testament is pervaded by references to the Song of Songs, and all of them are based on the supposition that it is to be interpreted spiritually. 'Proportionately,' he says, 'no book of the Old Testament is so frequently referred to implicitly or explicitly in the New Testament as this one [1].' The song is in fact an idealized representation of that relationship of love between the soul and God which in the New Testament is so often described under the metaphor of a bridal [2]. The power of using the book with spiritual profit is a great test both of proficiency in the spiritual life, and of purity of heart; and its general significance seems to be independent of difficulties in regard to its arrangement and exposition. When we consider its place in the Hebrew Scriptures, and the close connexion of some of its language with that of the Psalms, we shall feel that the allegorical method of interpretation which prevailed both among the Jews and the Christian Fathers, though it has been modified in detail by a critical investigation of the book, is yet in the main a true mode of dealing with it. In any case its ethical value has been vindicated; but we may also truthfully recognize in it a spiritual and mystical purport [3].

Something of the same personal character seems to distinguish the historical books of the Hagiographa. The book of Ruth and the book of Esther seem to describe in conspicuous instances the way in which the providence of God works through individuals and guides their fortunes. The book of Ruth is not only of historical importance as recording the ancestry of Israel's first king. It also bears witness to the

---

[1] See passages collected in *Comm. on Eccles.*, &c., pp. 297–303.
[2] e.g. John iii. 29; Eph. v. 27; Apoc. iii. 20; xix. 7 foll.
[3] Cp. Keil, *Introduction to the O. T.* vol. i. p. 506; Driver, *Introduction*, &c., pp. 423, 424; A. Réville, *The Song of Songs* (Eng. Tr.).

reality of a divine love which welcomes, accepts, and crowns with a fitting reward, humble and trustful obedience to the laws of natural affection. It describes the fulfilment beyond expectation of the blessing pronounced by Boaz, *The Lord recompense thy work, and a full reward be given thee of the Lord God of Israel, under whose wings thou art come to trust*[1]. The book of Esther shows us the providence of God acting with the same individual and discriminating tenderness, but on a grander stage. In Ruth, God's guidance of the soul is illustrated; in Esther, His providence overruling the destinies of His Church. There are of course defective moral elements in the book which lie upon the surface; but its deeper teaching is not prejudiced by these [2]. Again, the historical portions of the book of Daniel seem designed to illustrate God's willingness to manifest Himself even to the heathen, and the reality of His lordship and sovereignty *in the kingdom of men*[3]. Once more, in the large historical work which comprises the books of Chronicles and their sequel Ezra and Nehemiah, it would be a mistake to assume that the *historical* interest is uppermost. In Chronicles the aim is very clearly moral and didactic. We may question the accuracy of the Chronicler's retrospect of Israel's history, but we must acknowledge the general truth of the lesson which he aimed at enforcing, namely, the reality of God's disciplinary dealings with His people. A leading feature indeed of the book seems to be the tendency to refer all effects to the direct causation of God—to bring out vividly and directly the reality of God's moral governance in

---

[1] Ruth ii. 12.
[2] Dalman, *Das A. T. ein Wort Gottes*, p. 13, remarks: 'Steht das Esterbuch im losesten Zusammenhang mit dem Zweck der Sammlung, nicht weil von Rache darin die Rede ist, . . . auch nicht, weil der Gottesname darin fehlt, . . . sondern weil das Purimfest, welches es motivieren will, kein wesentlicher Bestandteil des Gottesdienstes des nachexilischen Israel der vormakkabäischen Zeit war, wie es ja auch niemals in das Tempelritual Eingang gefunden hat.'
[3] Cp. Dan. iv. 17, 25, 32.

history, especially in that of the Hebrew nation. It need not be a stumbling-block to us that the writer 'consciously or unconsciously shapes the facts to suit the theory' if the theory be in itself plainly true, though we may think that it is somewhat artificially conceived and illustrated. An essential element in true religion is the conviction that God's will is in very truth the supreme force, the one ever-present cause in history and human life, working indeed on lines less simple than the Chronicler perhaps imagined, but still acting ceaselessly in judgment, in retribution, in far-seeing providence, in the overruling of evil for purposes of universal good. The books of Ezra and Nehemiah are also plainly more or less subjective in character. In these the personality of two conspicuous men is very prominent; but in both cases the thought of a providential mission underlies their recorded experiences; the moral value of such a sense of mission and its effect on conduct and character could hardly be more plainly exhibited. The two pictures together present us with two types of individual devotion, inspired by a consciousness of divine guidance, and of a task providentially imposed. It was the work of Ezra and Nehemiah to establish and organize a Church, on such principles as would guard Israel's distinctness from the heathen world and preserve its national unity. In the broad fact that these books describe the reorganization of the temple worship and the endeavour of the Jewish leaders to secure a more general faithfulness to the conditions of the divine covenant, we are to discern the element which gives them a place in the Hagiographa. The instruments whom God raised up to carry His purpose to fulfilment were men who were themselves penetrated by the thought of the blessedness of covenant fellowship with God.

III.

There is a third element in the life of personal religion which the Old Testament Hagiographa bring into prominence: namely, the sense of the fruitfulness and blessedness of suffering. This theme, treated under various aspects, is especially characteristic of the Wisdom literature—the books of Proverbs, Job, and Ecclesiastes.

The importance of these writings is due to various causes, but the most obvious and striking feature in them is the spirit of universalism. They are the products in large measure of the contact between Judaism and heathen, especially Hellenic, thought; and they have an enduring interest as forming a link of connexion between Judaism and the philosophy of other nations. In its exile and dispersion Israel became conscious of its missionary function in the world, but it probably also began to realize the religious capacities of alien races and to take wider views of the divine government[1]. And so far as the Wisdom literature reflects the spiritual experience which Israel had thus acquired, it marks a stage in the advance of Judaism from being a national faith to being a world-religion. What is it then that gives to the Wisdom of the Hebrews its universalistic character?

First, no doubt, we should place the very conception of divine Wisdom. It was a conception by which Hebrew thought bridged over the gulf between God and the created universe; and what was primarily regarded as an attribute of God became poetically personified as an objective power working in the universe, at once reflecting and executing the creative thoughts and purposes of the Most High. Wisdom thus personified has been admirably described as constituting 'a middle term' between the religion of Israel and the philosophy of Greece. The Jewish

[1] See some interesting remarks on this point in Stanton, *The Jewish and the Christian Messiah*, p. 105.

use of the word was calculated to suggest that 'the life of righteousness might be identified with the life of true wisdom.'

Secondly, we notice in the Wisdom literature a tendency towards the systematic study of ethics. It is the nearest approach to philosophy exhibited by the Hebrew mind. It starts indeed with religious presuppositions: it bases the theory of life on a high and pure conception of God; it approaches problems from the standpoint of Hebrew religion[1]. But there is a certain absence of religious warmth and a certain freedom of treatment which are not distinctively Hebraic. The book of Proverbs, for example, treats the subject of ethics as resting on an independent ground of reason, common sense, and experience, apart from the teaching of revelation. It shows that the Jewish thinker learned, through his contact with the wise and cultured of other nations, that there was a common ground on which he might stand side by side with them; while, conversely, in the sacred books of Israel, a Greek would find shrewd and homely practical teaching on the subjects of life and duty, virtue and vice, wisdom and folly, which would be analogous to that which was traditional among men of his own race[2]. Indeed, in translating the book of Proverbs the compilers of the Septuagint version would find themselves compelled to borrow equivalent terms from Greek ethics. The book is, in short, a monotheistic treatise on practical ethics, its distinctive feature being the idea of wisdom as something transcendental, as a gift from God, manifested in a supreme degree in Israel's Law, and attainable by man only on condition of reverence and submission to the revealed will of God. It is true that Ecclesiastes shows little trace of religious ideas. On the contrary, the writer seems to have lost his interest in religion; it may be he had been repelled and alienated by the exces-

---

[1] Cp. Schultz, ii. 83, 84.
[2] Cp. Prov. viii and ix with Xenophon, *Memorabilia*, ii. 1.

sive systematization of religion in the temple *cultus*, or possibly his contact with Hellenism had raised in his mind misgivings and questionings which his traditional belief failed to allay or answer. Nevertheless, if the book is to be treated as a unity, it must be said to end with a religious solution of the problem of human life. Its notion of duty is the fear of God and obedience to a will supposed to be known. So far the book recognizes a special divine revelation vouchsafed to Israel.

But the most striking proof of the universalist standpoint of the Wisdom literature is to be found in the nature of the problems discussed in it: the worth of life, the reality of God's providential government, above all the meaning and purpose of suffering. Hence is derived a certain catholicity of tone in these books which has often attracted attention. Thomas Carlyle speaks of the book of Job as 'a noble book—all men's book,' and Professor Froude comments on its remarkable freedom from nationalistic elements. 'The life, the manners, the customs,' he observes, 'are of all varieties and places. Egypt with its river and its pyramids is there; the description of mining points to Phoenicia; the settled life in cities, the nomad Arabs, the wandering caravans, the heat of the tropics and the ice of the north—all are foreign to Canaan, speaking of foreign things and foreign people ... as if in the very form of the poem to teach us that it is no story of a single thing which happened once, but that it belongs to humanity itself and is the drama of the trial of man [1].'

There is no doubt a national reference in the narrative of Job. The book contained teaching

---

[1] *Short Studies*, &c., vol. i. pp. 296, 297. In view of the freedom of the book of Job from specially Hebrew characteristics, and specially the fact that it illustrates the action of divine grace outside the pale of the covenant people, Bishop Wordsworth observes that 'The reception of the book into the Hebrew canon was a generous and large-hearted act of genuine sympathy and comprehensive liberality and love. It was like a kiss of peace given by Israel to its brother the Gentile world' (*Commentary on the Bible*, Introd. to the *Book of Job*, p. vi).

peculiarly adapted for Israel during the period of its humiliation and suffering in a strange land. It may be regarded as 'a new reading' of Hebrew history. For the hero seems both in his circumstances and in the tone of his thought to represent the afflicted remnant of Israel, which appears to have had a history marked by severe trials, borne with great constancy of faith; and some have supposed that Job's wife, who appears as a temptress endeavouring to seduce Job from his allegiance to God, represents the multitude of Jews who apostatized or lapsed into indifference under the stress of trial and persecution. In any case there is a certain idealistic character in the sufferings that fall upon Job, which cannot fail to suggest a connexion between them and the calamities threatened in the book of Deuteronony in the event of Israel's disobedience to the divine warnings[1]; moreover, as has already been pointed out, the figure of Job corresponds with the ideal sufferer of Isaiah lii and liii. Accordingly we may discern in the epilogue of the book a word of consolation for the true Israel: a promise of glorification after suffering patiently endured[2]. The writer very probably intended his fellow-Israelites to see in Job's history a representation of their own misfortunes, and to trace in the issue of them a forecast of their own future restoration. We may also discern a corrective intention in the book of Job. The form of the picture was probably designed to act as an antidote to the temper of self-righteousness, and to expose the deficiencies of the current notion of retribution. But it is in its contribution to the Messianic idea that the special importance of the book seems to lie. In one of his essays Dr. Mozley has pointed out that the book of Job virtually stands in an 'interpretative' relation to the general body of

---

[1] Cp. Deut. xxviii. 27, 35 with Job ii. 7.
[2] Isa. lxi. 7 speaks of Israel as receiving double; cp. Job xlii. 12. See also Isa. liv. 1; lx. 7; and cp. Job xlii. 10 with Ezek. xxxvi. 10 foll.

Messianic prophecy. If the Jew with his growing expectation of a brilliant, prosperous, and victorious Messiah was ever to accept a Messiah who should lead a life of sorrow and abasement, and ultimately be crucified between two thieves, 'it was necessary that he should be somewhere taught that virtue was not always rewarded here, and that therefore no argument could be drawn from affliction and ignominy against the person who suffered it.' This function is evidently fulfilled not only by isolated passages in prophecy, but by an entire book in which the lesson is enforced, the book of Job[1]. To those who like Job's three friends pertinaciously insisted on an invariable connexion between suffering and sin, the cross could not fail to be a stumbling-block[2].

But apart from all reference to the particular circumstances of Israel, the book of Job has a catholic aspect and function, in that it discusses a problem which in one form or another is *the* problem of the universe—the mystery of pain. The Hebrew tendency to individualize Israel's national experience, so familiar a phenomenon in many of the Psalms as well as in Job, falls in with the entire movement of man's moral education as described in the Old Testament. The sorrows of the nation led to deeper reflection on the function of pain in the life of the individual. Suffering was gradually recognized as a necessary element in the evolution of higher life. What the Christian learns from the example of his Saviour, the devout Jew was taught to discover in the collective experience of his people. It was a difficult lesson. 'It came into collision,' says Schultz, 'with everything which a superficial faith was wont to regard as most certain. When Israel was first brought face to face with the idea that suffering might fall upon a saint without being deserved as a punishment, it was only after a hard struggle, and many

---

[1] See Mozley, *Essays*, vol. ii. pp. 227 foll.
[2] Cp. Luke xiii. 2; John ix. 2, 34.

a bitter trial that it succeeded in making this thought its own[1].' The book of Job bears witness to the truth of this remark; and it might be added that an historical example of the agony which accompanied the gradual dissolution of the traditional idea of suffering is to be found in the experience of Jeremiah. Almost startling is the expostulation of the afflicted prophet: *I sat not in the assembly of the mockers, nor rejoiced; I sat alone because of thy hand, for thou hast filled me with indignation. Why is my pain perpetual, and my wound incurable, which refuseth to be healed? wilt thou be altogether unto me as a liar, and as waters that fail*[2]*?* It was only by a discipline which involved the righteous in the calamities brought upon themselves by sinners that a new conception of suffering could be awakened. It had to be recognized that pain might have an educational function in the personal life of the soul: that it was the necessary condition of spiritual power, that it equipped men for the task of raising, blessing, and saving their fellows, that it imparted new gifts of character, and heightened the faculty of moral intuition, that it was in short a necessary element in the personal religious life.

It is not fanciful to discern a somewhat similar line of teaching in the book of Ecclesiastes. Into its origin and character it is needless to enter particularly. It is certain, however, that it belongs to a time when Hellenistic influences had deeply penetrated the higher thought of Israel[3]. It is also generally agreed that the book is in some sense an autobiography—perhaps a record of the conflicting moods and experiences of a child of Israel who had travelled far and observed much, had perhaps utterly lost and then painfully recovered, at least in a rudimentary form, the faith of his childhood. A more detailed examination of this book seems likely at the present time to

---

[1] *Old Testament Theology*, vol. i. p. 319.   [2] Jer. xv. 17, 18.
[3] The date of the book seems to be not much earlier than 200 B.C. See Cornill, *Einleitung in das A. T.* p. 252.

be fruitful. In the past it has certainly provoked curiously different estimates. Luther, for instance, calls it 'a noble book which it were well worth while for all men to read with great carefulness every day.' On the other hand, a modern German critic declares that 'the end of all the preacher's admonitions is recommending ease and enjoyment of life.' And while Cornill compares the writer to Thersites, and another critic describes the book as 'the work of a morose Hebrew philosopher, composed when he was in a dismal mood and in places thoroughly tedious,' M. Renan has described it as 'livre charmant! le seul livre aimable qui ait été composé par un juif[1].' Perhaps the more common impression formed of Ecclesiastes is that expressed by von Hartmann. The book, he says, is 'the breviary of the most modern materialism.'

Now considering the probable date of its composition and the place which it holds in the canon, we are probably right in considering that the main lesson of the book relates to the mystery of pain. But first we should notice the fact that it has a place in the literature of Israel because it has a theological or redemptive significance.

It is not inaccurate to describe the book of Ecclesiastes as a divine comment on the life and thought of the Gentile world. Consider St. Paul's description of that world as it lay open to his experienced and penetrating gaze. Its leading characteristic was vanity, aimlessness,—a life in which no faculty was directed aright, in which all labour seemed profitless and mean, all unselfish effort valueless, all worship emptied of satisfaction or hope. The Gentiles walked *in the vanity of their mind*[2]; and St. Paul bids his Ephesian converts remember what and where they had been: *Gentiles in the flesh, with-*

---

[1] *L'Antichrist*, p. 101 (quoted by Cheyne, *Job and Solomon*, p. 242). Cp. the same writer's *L'Ecclésiaste*, p. 24.
[2] Eph. iv. 17. Cp. Rom. i. 21.

out Christ, aliens from the commonwealth of Israel, and strangers from the covenants of promise, having no hope, and without God in the world[1]. These last words, ἐλπίδα μὴ ἔχοντες καὶ ἄθεοι ἐν τῷ κόσμῳ, concentrate in a single phrase the sum of human misery, yet how appropriately they would form the motto of Ecclesiastes. From this point of view the interest of the book is almost unique. It stands on a level with the prophetic narrative of Jonah, and fulfils, if we may so speak, an equally indispensable function in the literature of revelation. In this book a pagan worldling, sated, despairing, and weary of life, would find himself not merely described but understood: he would find his own hatred of life[2], his alienation from God, his cynical despondency expressed and interpreted. Thus the presence of the book in the canon may be regarded as a token to the Jew that the Gentiles, wandering in vanity and moral darkness and seeming to be beyond the pale of divine care and covenant grace, were after all not forgotten, not altogether abandoned. The book is a pledge of coming good even for them, and this not only because it describes so truthfully the conflict of passionate moods that might distract the undisciplined Gentile heart, but also because it recognizes the fundamentals of natural religion to which such a heart might half unconsciously still adhere. It speaks of God, the God of Israel's faith, only by titles which the heathen would acknowledge, avoiding the sacred name as was customary in the later period of Judaism, and describing the deity only as 'Creator' and 'Judge.' And in the key-word of the book, *All is vanity*, the writer seems to cast up the sum-total of man's life and labours apart from God; nay, he expresses the condition of the whole visible creation in its state of alienation from

---

[1] Eph. ii. 11, 12.
[2] Eccl. ii. 17, 'I hated life.' Renan, *L'Ecclésiaste*, p. 90: 'Le pessimisme de nos jours y trouve sa plus fine expression.' On the relation of the book to *modern* pessimism see Wright, *The Book of Koheleth* (Donnellan Lectures), ch. vi.

its Maker; he describes the inherent emptiness and nothingness of all that has not God for its end and object[1]. Solomon, in whose person the author describes his own experiences, is taken as the type of universal wisdom, which had put to the test all that life had to offer of temporal good—pleasure, wealth, power, knowledge—and had found a resting-place for heart and mind nowhere but in God. But though ascribed to the Hebrew monarch, the book reflects the condition of a paganism that is practically bankrupt[2].

But it is in relation to the problem of suffering that Ecclesiastes marks a moment in the education of humanity. It deals with pain, first, as a difficulty to be discussed on the basis of traditional ideas; secondly, as a disease to be ministered to, and if possible healed. For the pain which it contemplates is not merely that which affects bodily life and well-being, but that which arises from contemplation of the anomalies of the world in its totality. The book reflects a spirit of far-reaching scepticism which calls in question not merely the dealings of God with the righteous, but the very existence of any providential plan or government in the universe at all. Consequently, Ecclesiastes may be said to have a twofold aim: philosophic and didactic. First, it contributes something to the philosophical or moral problem of retribution already noticed. We have already observed that its standpoint is that of quiescence. It practically renounces the fruitless effort to comprehend the mystery of God's dealings with

---

[1] Cp. Rom. viii. 20; and see Greg. Nyss. *Hom. i. in Eccl.* ματαιότης ἐστιν ἢ ῥῆμα ἀδιανόητον ἢ πρᾶγμα ἀνόνητον ἢ βουλὴ ἀνυπόστατος ἢ σπουδὴ πέρας οὐκ ἔχουσα ἢ καθόλου τὸ ἐπὶ παντὶ λυσιτελοῦντι ἀνύπαρκτον. Cp. Hugo de S. Vict., *Hom. in Eccl.* i.
[2] Riehm, *ATl. Theologie*, p. 33, says: 'Das Heidentum als solches, das sich durch die Trübung jenes Gottesbewusstseins durch das Weltbewusstsein charakterisiert, kann sonst nur negativ auf das Christentum vorbereiten, sofern es mit sich selbst im Widerspruch steht und das religiöse Bedürfniss des menschlichen Herzens unbefriedigt lässt und darum mit Bankerott endet.'

men, in view of the fragmentariness of human knowledge. This, as Cornill remarks, is a signal triumph of Old Testament piety. The writer of Ecclesiastes, he says, is so penetrated and dominated by the spirit of Hebrew religion that he escapes the apparently inevitable conclusion of his reasoning, viz. that the world is subject to a blind and relentless Fate, and falls back upon the belief in a personal God in whose light the human race will see light [1]. Besides the voice of pessimism, or 'malism' as Professor Cheyne prefers to calls it [2], we discern tones in the book which contain 'the germ of a higher optimism'; for it ends with the prediction of a judgment to come—a judgment which will solve the perplexities of the present, and which because it is personal and particular, will be relative to the opportunities of individuals, and will involve the manifestation of every secret thing in its true character.

Again, the book of Ecclesiastes has a didactic import. Just as it seems to indicate the care and compassion of God for the seemingly unregarded millions of heathendom, so it is a welcome token of divine sympathy with the mental perplexities and spiritual sorrows of individual men. From this standpoint we can even ascribe to the book an evangelical function. It is an instance of the simple law that in order to minister effectually to perplexity, we must show that we understand it. Here, as occasionally in the Psalter and in the book of Job, Scripture addresses itself to an abnormal mood—perhaps the very darkest which the human soul is capable of entertaining; in order to give a proof of its complete power of understanding and even sympathizing in some degree with every phase in the life of the human spirit [3]. But Scripture only depicts the dark mood

---

[1] *Einleitung*, p. 251.   [2] *Job and Solomon*, p. 20.
[3] So Augustine says of Ps. xciv that it speaks comfortably to the perplexed soul, *Enarr. in Psalm.* xciii. 9: 'Compatitur tibi et Psalmus, quaerit tecum, non quia nescit, sed ideo tecum quaerit quod scit, ut in illo invenias quod nesciebas. Quomodo qui vult aliquem consolari, nisi

in order that the soul may be educated out of it and lifted into the light of faith. Ecclesiastes ends by pointing to the certainty of judgment, and to the life of obedience. In these lies the only hope of attaining to further light in regard to the problems of existence. Thus while the Old Testament finds a place for the cry of perplexity, and shows its compassion for the agony of doubt, it teaches that a remedy or alleviation is to be found only in fidelity to known moral duty. Our Lord practically endorses the admonition with which the book of Ecclesiastes concludes when He plainly says, *If any man will do his will, he shall know of the doctrine whether it be of God, or whether I speak of myself*[1].

We have reason then to be thankful that, owing apparently to the liberal and large-hearted spirit that prevailed in the school of Hillel, Ecclesiastes was allowed to find a place in the Hebrew Canon[2]. For it is undoubtedly a book of peculiar value to those who have to deal with the mental ailments, often so subtle and so complex, that are peculiar to the present bewildering stage of modern civilization. It illustrates the manner in which the temper of paralyzing scepticism may be most efficiently treated, and it points to a simple creed as the best antidote to hopelessness, aimlessness, and heedless oblivion. Its characteristic lesson is the need of strenuousness in the life of the soul—a lesson concisely summed up in the words of St. Peter: *Gird up the loins of your mind, be sober, and hope to the end for the grace that is to be brought unto you at the revelation of Jesus Christ*[3]. The last word of the Old Testament Wisdom is a warning that human life must be ennobled by moral purpose,

---

condoleat cum illo, non illum erigit. Prius cum illo dolet, et sic eum reficit sermone consolatorio.' Cp. *Enarr. ii. in Psalm.* xxi. 4: 'Intelligat homo medicum esse Deum, et tribulationem medicamentum esse ad salutem, non poenam ad damnationem.'

[1] John vii. 17.
[2] See Cheyne, *Job and Solomon*; and Ryle, *Canon of the O. T.* pp. 195 foll.
[3] 1 Pet. i. 13.

brightened by hope, and sobered by perpetual recollection of the end.

I have endeavoured to show that the Hagiographa are pervaded by certain ideas which bear directly upon the spiritual life in man. These ideas were suggested by the actual experience of Israel's history; they were developed and confirmed by the discipline of the Law, and they have been transmitted to Christianity as permanent elements in the religious character. It is a remarkable characteristic of the Hebrew genius that it clings closely to concrete facts and historical traditions, without apparently possessing the plastic power to create, as the Greek and Teutonic spirit created, a purely imaginative literature. 'The mind,' it has been said, 'which feeds eagerly on the evidences of an actual Providence will not care to live in a world of its own creation[1].' The Jew stood alone in his persistent sense of a vocation to the life of communion with God. The thought possessed him and absorbed him; it awakened memories, it quickened imagination, it roused emotion, it trained the faculty of spiritual insight. A passionate conviction of the divinely-ordained dignity of human nature stirred him to self-consecration. He recognized that man was in nature only a little lower than the angels, that dominion over the creatures was his birthright, that God had verily put all things under his feet.

From the sense of human worth and dignity the Jew advanced slowly and tentatively to a presage of his own immortality. A being so favoured, so aspiring, so richly endowed, so precious in the sight of God, could not be *made for naught*[2], could not be destined to pass into nothingness. But the longings and intuitions of the devout Israelite were not left to exhaust themselves in vain speculations: they rested upon the solid basis supplied by an historical revelation. The

---

[1] R. H. Hutton, *Essays Literary and Theological*, vol. ii. p. 211.
[2] Ps. lxxxix. 47.

tradition of ancestral faith testified to the existence of a God of redeeming grace who had actually entered into a covenant relationship with Israel, and whose supernatural guidance of its fortunes was a reality testified by age-long experience. This faith gave strength and consistency to the hope of a life beyond the grave, since it suggested the idea of a watchful providence which, while mindful of national destinies, was yet careful of the single life. The Israelite could commend his parting soul into the hands of a faithful Creator, who had tended and guided him throughout the days of his pilgrimage, and could be utterly trusted not to forsake him in his passage through the valley of the shadow of death. It was a dim faith, but it sufficed till the day of a new revelation should *break, and the shadows flee away*[1].

But advancing experience, while it deepened the Jew's assurance of an overruling providence sustaining and guiding the individual, gave rise to a new perplexity. There came a period when the Israel of God, conscious of its zealous devotion to Jehovah and its fidelity to His revealed will, found itself in exile—comfortless, afflicted, persecuted. In their efforts to comprehend the meaning of a calamity that seemed to contradict their most cherished convictions, godly men were led to a more profound view of the mystery of suffering. Israel's history suggested dimly at least the great part which sorrow had played in the development of God's purpose; it had been the purifying discipline through which the ancient heroes and saints had passed. And the teaching of history was to be supplemented by personal experience. The Jewish saint possessed his soul in patience, and as the result of endurance learned to say, *It is good for me that I have been in trouble, that I may learn thy statutes*[2]. So there arose a religious philosophy of suffering; it was seen to be in great measure the chastisement of human sin, but it was also a manifest dis-

---

[1] Cant. ii. 17. [2] Ps. cxix. 71.

cipline of human character, and the needful probation of human fidelity. Much was still left unexplained: there were perplexities which no reasoning could solace, and no analysis could satisfactorily explore. Such perplexities are reflected in the book of Ecclesiastes, and they seem to be intended to recall the soul to its primary intuitions—to its faith in God, duty, and human accountability. In this record of the experience of 'a child of Israel, a child of God' the sorely troubled spirit may recognize itself; it may be comforted or at least touched by the discovery that however far it has wandered from light and love, it is not forgotten, it is understood, it is followed, it is pitied. For to the heart of man God is a refuge in any trouble; in the thought of His creative compassion there is hope; in the revelation of His goodness there is a pledge of love which will deign to subject itself to the conditions of our mortality, there is the implicit promise of a divine self-sacrifice. The perplexities which overwhelmed the heart of the Hebrew sage press not less heavily upon us. With the apostolic writer, we can only say concerning man, *We see not yet all things put under him.* But we Christians possess in our creed a key to the dread mystery of existence. *We see Jesus*[1]. We see the Son of man exalted to the throne of God. The Gospel of the risen and ascended Christ suffices to sustain and reassure the hearts that shrink and the spirits that faint:—

> 'Beyond the tale, I reach into the dark,
> Feel what I cannot see, and still faith stands.
> I can believe this dread machinery
> Of sin and sorrow would confound me else,
> Devised,—all pain, at most expenditure
> Of pain by who devised pain,—to evolve
> By new machinery in counterpart
> The moral qualities of man,—how else?
> To make him love in turn and be beloved,
> Creative and self-sacrificing too,
> And thus eventually God-like.'

[1] Heb. ii. 8, 9.

LECTURE VIII

Open thou mine eyes, that I may behold wondrous things out of thy law.—Ps. cxix. 18.
Then opened he their understanding, that they might understand the scriptures.—Luke xxiv. 45.

IN my first lecture it was pointed out that Scripture has a twofold character corresponding to the dual nature of Christ; and it would seem that erroneous ideas about the Bible and its inspiration have often been the direct result of forgetting the analogy that subsists between the written and the incarnate Word of God.

The self-manifestation of God in Jesus Christ was the answer to an age-long prayer; it presupposed human aspirations and human faith; it appealed to ideas of God which a divine discipline had already moulded and purified. The Gospels in fact show us that the power to discern the true nature and to apprehend the teaching of Christ depended upon the temper and attitude of individual minds. Mere intellect and human learning were of little avail; as often as not they proved to be obstacles in the way of true discernment. Christ's manifestation of Himself was addressed to faith and to the consciousness of need. He was the saviour of the lost, the physician of the sick, the rewarder of humility and perseverance. The Pharisee with all his zeal for the law of God, the Sadducee with all his supposed superiority to antiquated prejudices, the scribe with all his learning, saw in Jesus Christ nothing more than a human teacher [1]. In a word, men found in Him what they were prepared to

---

[1] Cp. John iii. 2; Luke vii. 39; xx. 41.

find; some listened to Him, some admired Him, some hated and feared Him, some *received him*; and to these last *gave he power to become the sons of God*[1]. No man could come unto Him in a saving sense except such as were drawn to Him by the Father who had sent Him[2]. And that the written word comes to men under similar conditions has been proved by experience. We cannot too often remind ourselves that of all the faculties with which we seek God and apprehend His will, one only brings the soul into actual contact with Him—namely, that which St. Paul calls *faith working by love*[3]. It follows that the right understanding of Scripture is a reward by which persevering faith is crowned. In the upper chamber He who had Himself inspired the Hebrew prophets and guided the pen of chroniclers, poets, and sages, answered the prayer to which the Psalmist gives utterance: *Open thou mine eyes, that I may behold wondrous things out of thy law. He expounded unto His disciples in all the scriptures the things concerning himself*[4]. He enabled them to penetrate through the veil of the letter to the Messianic sense beneath; He taught them to regard the Old Testament as a vast and continuous prophecy of Himself; and in so doing He gave His sanction to that method of interpreting Scripture which corresponds to its two-fold character: the method which finds unsuspected spiritual meaning, eternal and ideal teaching, concealed beneath the exterior form which meets the eye. Thus the anticipations of an earlier age were justified. For the Psalmist's prayer illustrates the effect produced on devout hearts by the study of the sacred Law, which formed the earliest canon of Hebrew Scripture. It testifies to the growth of a consciousness that the written word embodied a spirit which had ceased at least for a while to be a living force in the hearts of men. For the voice of prophecy in its strict sense was

---

[1] John i. 12. [2] John vi. 44.
[3] Gal. v. 6.   [4] Luke xxiv. 27.

silent. It had been succeeded by the learned labour of the scribes—teachers who no longer based their claim to attention on any personal divine commission, but were content to appeal to the authority either of the written word[1], or of the unwritten *Halachah*, or law of custom by which the *Torah* was supplemented and almost superseded. The 119th Psalm, however, is evidently the fruit not of mere traditional instruction orally received, but of personal study and contemplation of the sacred law. It witnesses to a rising sense of the depth, the mystery, and the many-sidedness of a book which the spiritual experience of the faithful had recognized as God's word to His people. It reminds us that even the most perfect methods of literal and historical exegesis may fall short of appreciating the full significance of Scripture. The search after God and after a true knowledge of His ways implies not only a temper of constant dependence on the guidance of His Spirit, but a continual recollection of the limitations and defects of even the highest faculties, and the most skilled methods of research[2]. No one who contemplates in the spirit of Pascal or of Butler the infinite mystery that surrounds human life and divine revelation will deny the reasonableness and necessity within limits of a spiritual or mystical interpretation of Scripture. To despise the use and results of a method which has undoubtedly been sometimes employed in an arbitrary and fantastic fashion, is to incur a serious spiritual and mental loss[3]. A true

---

[1] Oettli, *Der gegenwärtige Kampf um das A. T.* p. 10: 'An die Stelle des lebendigen und begeisterten Prophetenwortes tritt der heilige Kodex, der die Religion normiert und bindet.' Cp. Hunter, *After the Exile*, part ii. ch. 16; Kuenen, *Religion of Israel*, ch. ix.

[2] Cp. Aug. *de util. cred.* 4: 'Sed praesumo quod et in hac spe, qua spero vos viam sapientiae mecum obtenturos, non me deseret ille cui sacratus sum; quem dies noctesque intueri conor; et quoniam propter peccata mea propterque consuetudinem plagis veternosarum opinionum sauciatum oculum animae gerens, invalidum me esse cognosco, saepe rogo cum lacrymis.'

[3] Cp. Westcott, *Introd. to the Study of the Gospels*, p. 458: 'It may be as unfair to disparage the symbolic interpretation of Scripture by Origen's

element in spiritual perception is the sense of mystery. Just as many common words have a long history behind them, and are charged with associations reaching far back into antiquity, so many incidents of ordinary human experience, and *a fortiori* the facts recorded in sacred history, are rightly regarded as embodying and illustrating eternal truths and principles. On this subject it would be premature to enlarge at this point. It is enough for the present to draw attention to the significance of St. Luke's statement, *Then opened he their understanding, that they might understand the scriptures.* It was after the resurrection, when the Lord Jesus had passed into the world of mystery that lies beyond death—it was then that He opened the eyes of His chosen disciples to the infinite depth of Scripture, teaching them that the things of the Spirit can only be *spiritually discerned*[1], and that the written word contains a revelation which needs to be approached with the same sense of insufficiency wherewith in the days of His flesh Christ would have had men approach Himself. We know by sad experience that the mere literary or scientific study of Scripture has often left us utterly dark and barren. The real moments of insight and spiritual elevation, when our hearts burned within us, were those in which we were conscious that we were walking with the risen Christ in the way, and holding communion with Him, *while he opened to us the scriptures*[2]. Thus we have proved the truth of St. Paul's aphorism, *If any man think that he knoweth anything, he knoweth nothing yet as he ought to know. But if any man love God, the same is known of him*[3].

Our task in the present day seems to be that of mediation between opposed methods of Scriptural interpretation. While we welcome gladly and eagerly, in spite of the temporary pain and perplexity which it

errors in detail as to judge of the capabilities of inductive science from Bacon's "Theory of heat."'

[1] 1 Cor. ii. 14.   [2] Luke xxiv. 32.   [3] 1 Cor. viii. 2, 3.

costs us, all the light that historical research and critical learning can throw upon the structure and literary form of the Old Testament, we shall reverently endeavour to do justice to methods of using Scripture which the apostles and saints of Jesus Christ have taught us to be profitable and based on true conceptions of the character of the written word. In this concluding lecture of our series we shall consider, first, the light which is shed on the Old Testament by its employment in the New; and, secondly, the function which the Old Testament seems designed to fulfil under our present circumstances. In a word, we shall attempt an inquiry into the present use of the Old Testament in the Christian Church.

I.

Speaking generally, the New Testament seems to ascribe to the Old Testament three main characteristics :—

1. First, it insists on the *fragmentary* character of the revelation contained in it. The divine self-communication to man was made *in many parts* ($\pi o \lambda v \mu \epsilon \rho \hat{\omega} s$). It was a process which had many different stages, in each of which however the continuity of revelation was maintained. This is tantamount to saying that the New Testament embodies what has been called 'a strictly historical conception' of the Old[1]. The new religion recognized that it was rooted in the ancient dispensation, and that each epoch in the sacred history of Israel had been a preparation for the next. There was no single stage at which the ultimate purpose of God for the world was discerned in its completeness. Types and prophecies were alike fragmentary: each foreshadowed one aspect of a vast and intricate scheme yet to be disclosed, a scheme complex as the universe and wide as human life. At

[1] Sanday, *The Oracles of God*, p. 141.

each point in the progressive movement of the world's education faith might have discerned a divine thought. Accordingly the New Testament constantly draws attention to the fact that the utterance contained in the Old Testament is the voice of God. What proceeded from the mouth of the prophets was *spoken of the Lord*[1]; the promises to the patriarchs, the tokens of guidance which they followed, were alike vouchsafed by Him[2]; the commandments of the Mosaic Law came from Him[3]; by Him were foretold the blessings of the Messianic age[4]. Indeed throughout the whole period of the preparatory dispensation there was a continuous self-communication of the Holy Spirit to man, a progressive unveiling of His purposes, a constant indication of His requirement[5]. But revelation was at each stage only partial and incomplete. It has been well said that the Bible supplies a rule that is constantly improving on itself, and that later editions of the rule are intended to antiquate the earlier[6]. The New Testament in fact already sets us the example which modern criticism has enforced—that of reading the Old Testament with discrimination, with readiness to judge the part in the light of the whole, and to recognize in each fragment its true, but not more than its true, value and function in relation to the entire organism of which it forms a part.

2. Again, the New Testament contrasts with the simplicity and singleness of God's self-revelation in His incarnate Son the *variety of methods* by which He manifested Himself to His ancient people. God spake to the fathers in many fashions (πολυτρόπως) as well as in many parts; and this statement implies that the different portions of the Old Testament are not all to be used in the same way: we are not to confound law with history, prophecy with fact, dreams with waking

---

[1] Matt. i. 22; ii. 15.   [2] Acts iii. 25; vii. 2, 3.
[3] Matt. xv. 4.   [4] 2 Cor. vi. 16 foll.; Heb. i. 5 foll.; v. 5 foll.; vii. 21.
[5] Acts xxviii. 25; Heb. iii. 7; ix. 8; x. 15.
[6] Bruce, *Apologetics*, p. 323. Cp. the language of Heb. viii. 13.

VIII] THE OLD TESTAMENT AND CHRISTIANITY 379

realities, poetical anticipations with typical events. Accordingly, we have to be careful as to the extent to which we insist on the historical element in the Old Testament as literal fact. We may occasionally be in danger of misusing what was given us for another purpose. Anticipations of the Messiah and of His work may not only have been foreshadowed in historical fact, but may also have inspired literary creations. Thus there are incidents recorded in the Old Testament respecting which a large latitude of opinion is surely desirable. Some, for instance, may regard the story of Jonah as literally true; others see good reason for finding in it an allegorical narrative written with a didactic purpose. In any case it is certain that the word πολυτρόπως warns us against dogmatic statements as to what *must be* the nature of different Old Testament books, and also against unintelligent and undiscriminating employment of them. The different modes of divine self-manifestation—through dreams, visions, prophecies, oracles, and types, or through the ministry of an angel—will repay study, and will quicken our sense of the condescension with which Almighty God in His communications to mankind has adapted Himself to very varied types of mind and stages of moral development. We are far too apt to make the modern western mind the standard of what is credible not only in the content, but in the manner and methods, of revelation.

3. Once more, the New Testament everywhere presupposes the *rudimentary character* of the old dispensation. Our blessed Lord Himself draws attention in the Sermon on the Mount to the inherent defects of the ancient religion, its self-accommodation to the low moral standard of those whom it was designed to instruct, discipline, and elevate [1]. His example and that of His apostles teaches us that we are to consider the drift of the whole bible in judging the Old Testa-

[1] Matt. v. 19 foll.; xix. 8.

ment; we are to be filled with the spirit of the Gospel, and make it the one standard of measurement in estimating conduct and character, frankly recognizing defect where it exists[1], and not explaining away what obviously conflicts with Christian principles, but attending fairly to the difference of time and circumstances which made imperfect character relatively good and admirable. We must remember how just is the distinction between immorality and crude morality, between transgression of a high standard and conformity to a low one[2]. I have already pointed out that no Christian writer has a stronger sense at once of the continuity of revelation and of the moral imperfection that characterized its earlier stages than Irenaeus. As he truly says: *Una salus et unus Deus. Quae autem formant hominem praecepta multa, et non pauci gradus qui ducunt hominem ad Deum*[3].

One point is worthy of particular attention in this connexion—viz. the general character of the New Testament verdict on the Mosaic Law. The question has been raised 'how far the transposition of the Law as it lies before us in the Pentateuch, from the time of Moses to the time of Ezra,' affects the New Testament estimate of Mosaism[4]? Now we have already seen reasons for supposing that legal discipline of some kind was a constant element of Mosaism, present in it from the first. What is to be noted here is that the critical conclusions which assign a relative inferiority to the Law on the ground of its comparatively late codification entirely fall in with the teaching of apostolic writers as to the place and function of law in Israel's education. Professor Bruce points this out with great force. If we bear in mind St. Paul's teaching in

---

[1] e. g., the '*philo-levitical*' spirit of the chronicler, which is a religious defect in view of such a passage as Heb. vii. 18 (Bruce, *Apologetics*, p. 324). Bruce draws attention to other defects, for instance the spirit of vindictiveness, the hatred of foreigners, the tendency to self-righteousness, &c., which were characteristic of Judaism.
[2] Bruce, *op. cit.* p. 329.   [3] *Haer.* iv. 9. 3.
[4] Bruce, *op. cit.* pp. 275 foll., 308.

VIII] *THE OLD TESTAMENT AND CHRISTIANITY* 381

regard to the temporary and economic purpose of the Law, or that of the writer to the Hebrews in regard to the *weakness and unprofitableness thereof*[1], we shall be prepared to admit that the critical theory tends entirely to confirm the apostolic view of the Law. If the verdicts of the New Testament 'hold good as against a law emanating from Moses, *a fortiori* they hold good against a law which came into force nearly a millennium later. . . . The important principle enunciated by Paul, that the law was subordinate to the promise and came in after it and between it and the [fulfilment of the] promise, obviously holds on the critical hypothesis.' Our general conception of the Law is the same. Accepting the critical view however, we recognize that the rigid legal discipline to which Israel was subjected came at a period in its history later than was formerly supposed; and the words of St. Paul apply even more forcibly to the Judaistic than to the Mosaic stage of Hebrew history. *Before faith came we were being kept in ward, shut up under the law unto the faith which should afterwards be revealed*[2]. The rudimentary purpose and function of the Law is a truth practically unaffected by critical disputes; and certainly we have no reason to be surprised that the legal discipline was so protracted in duration, when we consider how effective it was in its final result.

The New Testament then recognizes the fragmentary character of the old dispensation, the variety of the methods observed in the divine self-revelation, and the rudimentary nature of the discipline which gradually prepared Israel for the coming of its promised Saviour. At the same time we cannot overlook the fact that Christ and His apostles assign to the Old Testament a unique and inviolable authority[3].

---

[1] Heb. vii. 18. [2] Gal. iii. 23.
[3] Cp. Dalman, *Das Alte Testament ein Wort Gottes*, p. 9: 'Bei Jesus wie bei Paulus geht offenbar Hand in Hand mit einer klaren Einsicht in die Unzulänglichkeit der alttestamentlichen Offenbarung eine dadurch nicht erschütterte Ueberzeugung von der göttlichen Autorität nicht nur

I am not come to destroy, but to fulfil. For verily I say unto you, Till heaven and earth pass, one jot or one tittle shall in no wise pass from the law, till all be fulfilled¹. The scripture cannot be broken². Even its smallest fragment must be *fulfilled*; i.e. it must be shown to occupy its rightful place; must be brought under the true point of view, and its significance in relation to the whole vindicated. The same truth is implied in the apostolic vindication of prophecy. The distinctive character of the prophetic word of God is that *no prophecy is of any private interpretation*³. It has more than one application; it has a deeper and wider reference than is apparent on the surface. A careful study does indeed show us that for Christ there was to some extent 'a Bible within the Bible⁴.' The books to which He most commonly refers are Deuteronomy, the Psalms, and Isaiah—those in a word which are most full of the Messianic element. His first public discourse at Nazareth was based on a passage of the later Isaiah; the ministry of teaching and healing placed Him as it were in line with the ancient prophets; the martyr-spirit numbered Him with the righteous men of old whose sorrows and hopes breathe in the Psalter; His consciousness of Messiahship and His passion for righteousness found expression more often in the utterances of the saints and prophets than in those of the historians or legalists of ancient Israel. There can be no doubt however as to the general attitude of Christ towards the Jewish Scriptures. He speaks freely of Moses, perhaps we might say more often as a supreme authority than as an author; He refers to him as leader, legislator, and writer⁵, but always, it would seem, and necessarily, in

der im A. T. ausdrücklich als von Gott stammend bezeichneten Worte, sondern des Schriftwortes überhaupt.'

[1] Matt. v. 17, 18. [2] John x. 35. [3] 2 Pet. i. 20.
[4] Cheyne, *Aids to the Devout Study of Criticism*, p. 155 note. Cp. Bruce, *Apologetics*, p. 363. Cheyne notices that the O. T. Canon was 'not finally settled in all its parts in our Lord's time.' Cp. Valeton, *Christus und das A. T.* p. 30.
[5] Cp. Mark xii. 29; Luke xvi. 29; John v. 46; vii. 19.

accordance with the current literary conceptions of His time, and with the declared purpose of His mission[1]. We are not at present concerned with the manner of our Lord's quotations, but only with the general character of authority which He attributes to the ancient Scriptures. He speaks of them as if they discharged an organic function, and must ever hold a permanent place, in the religion of which He was the founder[2]. While He points out the defective elements in the old dispensation, and supersedes the detailed precepts of the Law by principles of far-reaching simplicity, He never fails to give the impression that He recognizes in the Old Testament the abiding word of God. As *the author and finisher of our faith*[3] He points us to the ancient Scriptures as the food which nourished His own spiritual life and gave due expression to His own Messianic consciousness; as the soil in which the gospel of salvation had its roots, and in which the treasure of eternal life lay hid. *Salvation*, He declared, *is of the Jews*[4].

We may now pass to the consideration of the principles which appear to guide our Lord and the New Testament writers in their references to the Old. And here it is important to remember that in the time of Christ there already existed among the scribes traditional rules of interpretation, which were of high antiquity and unquestioned authority. The scribes were in fact

---

[1] Cp. Köhler, *Über Berechtigung der Kritik des A. T.* p. 13. Christ, he says, must have used the ordinary literary language of His day if He was to make Himself intelligible to His hearers, and if He was not to exceed the limits of His Messianic vocation by giving instruction on points of natural knowledge. The references to Daniel (Matt. xxiv. 15) or to David (Matt. xxii. 41 foll.; cp. Acts ii. 24 foll.) are most reasonably explained on this principle. To the same effect Valeton, *Christus und das A. T.* p. 37; Delitzsch, *New Comm. on Genesis* [Eng. Tr.], vol. i. p. 21.
[2] John v. 39.
[3] Heb. xii. 2. Cp. Valeton, *Christus und das A. T.* pp. 20, 21. See also an admirable lecture by Prof. G. A. Smith, *The preaching of the O. T. to the Age*, pp. 11, 12.
[4] See Oettli, *op. cit.* p. 22. Valeton, *Christus und das A. T.* p. 12, remarks that so close is the inner connexion and correspondence between the words of Christ and the language of the O. T. as almost to justify the paradox, 'In His teaching there is nothing new but Himself.'

guided in their treatment of the canonical Scriptures by two chief aims: first, the systematic development and establishment of the Law, which had now become the central shrine, so to speak, of Jewish religion; second, the didactic manipulation of the historical books. Hence there arose on the one hand the *Halachah*, or customary law, the general object of which was to protect the Law, by a fence of minor restrictions, from even the chance of infringement; and on the other hand the *Haggadah*, i.e. narrative or legend by which the Old Testament history was enlarged, illustrated, or homiletically enforced. The basis of both methods was *Midrash*, or regular exegesis of the biblical text, and they presupposed the principle that inspired writings can contain nothing that is arbitrary, fortuitous, or indifferent, since Scripture both in its organic unity and in the diversity of its contents reflects the infinite being of its Author. And indeed if it be granted that Scripture comes from God in a special and unique sense, it is only reasonable to suppose that even single words of Scripture may conceal a multitude of thoughts and contain truths of inexhaustible significance.

Two methods then of dealing with the sacred text were already current. By the time of our Lord the *Halachah*, or exegetical expansion of the Law, had already resulted in the formation of a vast body of casuistry under which the original Law of Moses was in danger of being practically buried, while the *Haggadah* had produced a mass of legendary accretions by which the biblical history was expanded, for purposes of moral and religious instruction [1].

[1] For an account of the *Halachah* and *Haggadah* see *The Literary remains of Emanuel Deutsch*, ch. 1. Also his article, 'Versions, ancient (Targum),' in the *Dict. of the Bible*. The description of *Haggadah* merely as 'narrative' needs some qualification. It really implies the *amplification* or *imaginative development* of the Old Testament history, especially of that which is not directly expressed in the text, but is supposed to be indirectly hinted at. Edersheim, *Life and Times of Jesus the Messiah*, vol. i. p. 11, n. 2. remarks that *Halachah* might be described as the apocryphal Pentateuch, and *Haggadah* as the apocryphal prophets.

The Chronicles supply an example of *Haggadah* in dealing with the history of the Jewish kings. The Chronicler enlarges the material contained in earlier sources by a whole class of narratives intended to illustrate his favourite thesis, viz. the merit acquired by monarchs who zealously maintained the priestly ritual of the temple. He was doubtless actuated in his treatment of the history by a desire to meet the actual needs of his age, but the result is that his work, as we have already seen, has only a quasi-historical character[1]. It is a didactic work, which is inspired by a purely religious and moral aim, and in which imagination is allowed large play.

It will suffice to mention another method of interpretation which undoubtedly plays a large part in apostolic exegesis, and may be illustrated from Christ's own teaching, namely the method of *Sodh*, by which the mystical or allegorical sense of a passage was elicited. This seems on the whole to have been more characteristic of Hellenistic than of Palestinian Judaism. The Hellenists in their endeavour to amalgamate Greek thought with Hebrew ideas of revelation, found the allegorical method ready to their hand, since it was already in use both among Platonists and Stoics. The true principle that underlies this method will engage our attention presently.

Now a careful study of our Lord's usual mode of teaching makes it evident that in the matter of scriptural interpretation and exposition, as in other points, He occasionally condescended to adapt Himself to the customs of His time. We cannot fail to observe, however, a wide difference between the teaching of our Lord and of the scribes in two main respects—indeed the divergence was already obvious to those who first

---

[1] Schürer, *The Jewish People in the Time of Christ*, § 25. Observe the references to *Midrash* (A. V. *Story*) in 2 Chron. xiii. 22, xxiv. 27, the latter passage embracing the entire history of the kings. 'The compilers of chronicles seem to have used such promiscuous works treating of biblical personages and events, provided they contained aught that served the tendency of the book' (Deutsch, *l. c.*).

listened to His discourses. In the first place, Christ appears to set aside the method of *Halachah* as quite secondary, whereas with the scribes it had become of primary importance. 'Legal Judaism,' says Schürer, 'laid the chief stress upon correctness of action, and comparatively free play was therefore permitted in the sphere of religious notions[1].' The scribes in fact represent a tendency diametrically opposed to that of true prophetism. What Frederick Maurice has said of the scholastic theology of the Greek Church in the seventh and eighth centuries might well apply to the scribes: 'Notions about God more or less occupied them, but God Himself was not in all their thoughts[2].' With them holiness was too often treated as something merely technical and external, and the religious life was cramped and fettered by innumerable petty restrictions. In a word, the scribes represent that reactionary spirit which at first sight seems to give a discouraging aspect to the post-exilic stage of Israel's religion. Jesus Christ, on the other hand, was recognized by the conscience of His contemporaries as a prophet of God. He lifted high once more the standard of prophetism; righteousness and the love of God, *judgment, mercy, and faith*[3]—these were the theme of His preaching. He left the *Halachah* untouched, and scarcely noticed. To Him the one thing of supreme importance was that men should have true thoughts about God and His requirement. Accordingly—to notice the second point—the teaching of Jesus was authoritative, and not like that of the scribes. It was characteristic of the *Haggadah* that though it practically represented what we should call the

---

[1] *The Jewish People in the Time of Christ*, § 25. Deutsch in the *Dict. of the Bible*, s. v. 'Versions' (vol. iii. p. 1641), says: 'The aim of the *Haggadah* being the purely momentary one of elevating, comforting, edifying its audience for the time being, *it did not pretend to possess the slightest authority*.' Schechter, *Studies in Judaism*, p. 420, says: 'The theological side of Judaism, as well as its ideal aspirations and Messianic hopes, find their expression in the *Agadah*.'
[2] *The Religions of the World*, p. 23.
[3] Matt. xxiii. 23; cp. Luke xi. 42.

dogmatic and moral theology of Judaism, it was nevertheless comparatively unauthoritative. It was nothing more than oral instruction; it represented the acumen and insight of individual teachers, and possessed only the weight which might happen to attach to their utterances. It was taken by the hearers in fact for what it was worth. But the very teaching which the scribes made matter of *Haggadah* was in our Lord's view essential and primary. Consider His first discourse in the synagogue of Nazareth. It opens with a proclamation, ineffably gracious and tender, of God's character and ways of working. Its theme is grace; its character prophetic; its illustrations are taken not from the Law but from two episodes of Hebrew history speaking the one of judgment, the other of mercy[1]. In the manner of *Haggadah* is the brief comment on each, illustrating the method of God's redemptive action. But most significant is the personal reference to Himself as the anointed of Jehovah, and the calm majesty of the declaration, *Verily I say unto you.* No wonder that in Jesus men instinctively recognized *a teacher come from God*[2], whose *word was with power*[3]. The theme of His teaching imparted its own sublime simplicity to His method of expounding Scripture. He freely employed the Old Testament as illustrating the truths which He revealed about God, but He spoke on the strength of an immediate knowledge of Him whose glory and kingdom He proclaimed; He taught not on authority, but with authority; not as a professional teacher who has studied religious traditions, but as a prophet who by direct intuition knows God.

Thus, speaking generally, the very object of our Lord's coming determined the method in which He employed the ancient Scriptures. To Him all that made for righteous conduct and for truer conceptions of the divine character was of primary importance; to all that the scribes had overlooked or treated with indifference He assigned its rightful prominence.

[1] Luke iv. 18-27.　　[2] John iii. 2.　　[3] Luke iv. 32.

Haggadah was in a word His favourite method of teaching, but while 'the rabbins interpreted the Scriptures to accord with the traditions of the elders, Jesus interpreted them to accord with the mind of God their author[1].' The sacred liberty which is the characteristic gift of the Holy Spirit[2] appears in the very manner of Christ's citations from the Old Testament. And herein lies another point of contrast between Him and the scribes, whose anxious enslavement to the letter not only blinded them to the inner sense of Scripture and to the daily and hourly fulfilment of it which was going on before their eyes, but actually robbed them of essential reverence for the word of God. They honoured Jehovah *with their lips, but their heart was far from him*[3].

It is clear then that our Lord and His apostles freely sanctioned by their own example the current principles of exegesis, but it is also manifest that both in the subject-matter of their teaching, in modes of illustration, and in the observance of moral proportion, they produced an impression on their hearers different in kind from that which was derived from the teaching of the scribes. In endeavouring, however, to elicit principles from the practice of Christ and the New Testament writers, we have to bear in mind that they used the current methods of exegesis in the way most suitable to the capacity of each particular class of hearers and most appropriate to the subject of their discourse. Moreover, the apostles display differences corresponding to their individual temperament and training: St. Peter, St. James, and St. Jude inclining to the method of *Haggadah*; St. Paul to that of *Halachah* with free use of allegorism; while St. John and the writer of the Epistle to the Hebrews are distin-

---

[1] Briggs, *Biblical Study*, p. 314. I wish to express my obligations to this useful work, on which some of the following paragraphs are largely based.
[2] 2 Cor. iii. 17.
[3] Matt. xv. 8. See Valeton, *Christus und das A. T.* pp. 13 foll.

guished by their preference for this latter method, whether in its Palestinian or in its Hellenistic form.

What, then, are the most striking features in the New Testament exegesis of the Old?

1. First, we notice its remarkable breadth and freedom. Our Lord and His apostles adapt their use of the Old Testament to the requirements and capacities of those whom they address. They deal with Scripture in ways which the popular teaching of the scribes had already rendered familiar. There are passages in the Gospels which are at least closely analogous to the method of *Halachah*. Such would be the *a fortiori* argument of St. John x. 34–36: *Is it not written in your law, I said, Ye are gods? If he called them gods, unto whom the word of God came... say ye of him, whom the Father hath sanctified and sent into the world, Thou blasphemest, because I said, I am the Son of God?* Such again is the illustrative combination of references to the Law and to the former and later Prophets in St. Matt. xii. 3 foll., where our Lord is defending against the Pharisees the action of His disciples in plucking the ears of corn on the sabbath day[1]. On the other hand, there is nothing in our Lord's teaching that corresponds to the casuistry of the scribes; indeed it is only in controversy with the learned that He even appears to use the method of *Halachah*. The large majority of His references to the Law are intended to enforce great principles of morality, and seem calculated to qualify the paramount estimation in which the Law was held by the Jews. Thus many of the quotations, especially from the book of Deuteronomy, are ethical rather than legalistic, and it is significant that in dealing with a lawyer, our Lord takes occasion to enunciate in two passages from the *Torah* the law of love in its widest form, adding to them the comment that on the two commandments of love towards God

---

[1] Aug. *de util. cred.* 6 refers to this passage as a simple use of Scripture *secundum historiam*.

and love towards one's neighbour *hang all the law and the prophets*[1].

Of the apostolic writers, St. Paul especially shows partiality for *Halachah*. Thus in Rom. iv. 3-6 we have an argument on the subject of faith, applying a general principle to an individual case, which is in the manner of *Halachah*[2]. So in 1 Cor. ix. 9 (cp. 1 Tim. v. 18) a passage of Deuteronomy (xxv. 4) is appealed to as implying the acknowledged rule of equity, that service merits reward. Again, such a combination of passages as is used to illustrate or prove a point in Rom. iii. 10 foll. is in accordance with the principles of the *Halachah*[3].

More suitable, however, than *Halachah* for purposes of popular teaching would be *Haggadah*, that is expansive comment on passages of sacred Scripture, or free imaginative application of them. There can be no doubt that the apostolic writers were divinely guided in their use of this method, so markedly do they avoid the idle or absurd legends which the *Haggadah* of the scribes had woven around the sacred story. Thus St. James illustrates the nature of faith from the cases of Abraham and Rahab, and enforces the lesson of patience from the experience of Job[4]. Indeed it may be said generally that all references to Old Testament passages and incidents as typical or prophetic of Christ and His kingdom are in the style of *Haggadah*. Conspicuous instances would be the Messianic citations in St. Paul's Epistles and the description of Melchizedek, or the catalogue of the heroes of faith in the Epistle to the Hebrews, so far as these

---

[1] Matt. xxii. 35-40; cp. Luke x. 25-28. On Matt. xxii. 40 Valeton, *Christus und das A. T.* p. 16, remarks: 'Hier ist mehr als ein einfaches Zitat aus Deut. 6. 5 und Levit. 19. 18; hier ist wieder eine kleine Probe von der göttlichen Freiheit, die nicht *auflöst*, sondern *erfüllt*.'

[2] A somewhat similar argument from 'the law' (in this case Isa. xxviii. 11, 12) is found in 1 Cor. xiv. 21 foll. It is possible that the word διδασκαλία in the N. T. signifies *Halachic* teaching.

[3] Compare a somewhat similar combination of passages to prove a point in James ii. 8-13.

[4] James ii. 21 foll.; v. 11.

enforce or illustrate principles of moral conduct and laws of divine action [1]. In these cases passages of the Old Testament are employed not strictly speaking as predictive, but as illustrative of New Testament facts or truths. A great number of St. Paul's references to the Old Testament are of this description: for instance, the argument in the Epistle to the Galatians which turns upon the use of the phrase *Abraham and his seed*[2], or the quotation from the 68th Psalm in Eph. iv. 7, 8. St. Paul is not here using the Old Testament passage as a proof-text, but as a free illustration of a particular principle of the Christian system[3]. It should be added that in one passage of St. Paul and in two other passages of the New Testament we find reference made to legends supplementary of the Old Testament history and probably already embodied in extra-canonical books [4].

In view of the fact that the parable (*mashal*) is commonly found in the ancient *Midrashim*, it may be questioned whether our Lord's habit of teaching in parables may not be regarded as a particular application and transfiguration of the *Haggadah* method; for His aim ever appears to be didactic, the parables and the direct references to the Old Testament being intended to illustrate the redemptive action of God, or laws of His moral government. Such is his reference to the story of the flood and the fate of Lot's wife, which are used to enforce a solemn spiritual lesson [5]. Indeed, generally speaking, our Lord's references to the incidents of Old Testament history do not enable us to judge how far He lays stress on their historical importance. He is not concerned with

---

[1] See especially Rom. x. 18 (Ps. xix. 4), and Rom. x. 6 foll. (Deut. xxx. 11 foll.).
[2] Gal. iii. 16 (Gen. xvii. 7). Cp. Driver in *Expositor* for Jan. 1889, pp. 18 foll.
[3] See Driver, *Sermons on the O. T.* pp. 198, 199.
[4] 1 Cor. x. 4; 2 Tim. iii. 8; 2 Pet. ii. 4; Jude 9 foll. Cp. Acts vii. 22, 53; Gal. iii. 19; Heb. ii. 2. So Gal. iv. 29, 'persecuted' seems to be based on a Midrashic development of Gen. xxi. 9. See Lightfoot, ad loc.
[5] Matt. xxiv. 37; Luke xvii. 32.

history as such; and the analogy of His silence on points of science would suggest that He neither endorses nor repudiates the ordinary conceptions of His time in regard to the quality of the ancient narratives. In any case it is clear that He only employs them homiletically for purposes of spiritual edification. He does not apparently intend to teach positively on points which belong to the domain of scientific criticism [1]. But there is something significant in the fact that the employment of the Old Testament history by Christ is supplemented by the system of parabolic instruction, while His perfect simplicity in teaching tacitly discountenances the extravagance which often characterized the *Haggadah* of the scribes. He avoids such subjects as would divert the minds of His hearers without instructing them; He has an eye to their moral and spiritual needs; He uses that form of teaching which is best adapted to make great truths understood by the meanest capacity [2].

The freedom of the New Testament writers in their use of the Old is most strikingly displayed in their tendency to employ the method of *Sodh* or allegorism, a point which needs passing illustration. Instances in St. Paul's epistles will immediately occur to our minds [3]; we shall recall the Hellenistic colour of the

---

[1] On this difficult subject the writer would practically agree with the following statement: 'He who came from heaven in order to reconcile us to God, speaks in regard to the things of ordinary earthly life—and to these belongs the formal side of Old Testament knowledge—the speech belonging to His earthly environment, to His time and to His people. He does not move at an inaccessible height above the heads of men, but lives in their very midst. The eternal becomes a child of His time.... He had a task quite other than that of busying Himself, or instructing men, in regard to questions which are discussed in the schools and for the specialist may be of the highest importance, but which are unprofitable for the life of the soul, and in view of His life's work are so infinitesimally small, indeed are scarcely worth even mention.' Valeton, *Christus und das A. T.* pp. 28 foll.

[2] See some wise and beautiful thoughts on preaching in Bp. Wilson's *Sacra Privata* (ed. Oxford, 1840), pp. 243 foll.

[3] St. Paul uses it specially in the Epistles to Corinth, possibly owing to the connexion of that Church with Apollos. See e.g. 1 Cor. x. 1 foll. Cp. Gal. iv. 22 foll.

Epistle to the Hebrews, with its skilful treatment of the figure of Melchizedek, and its insistence on the symbolic structure and ceremonial of the ancient sanctuary; we shall remember the predominance of symbolism in the Apocalypse. Our blessed Lord may be thought to give sanction to this method in the general tenour of His teaching, which implies that the whole of the Old Testament is prophetic and figurative, foreshadowing the mysteries of His person and kingdom. But it cannot be said with truth that He freely employs the method of allegory as generally understood. He rather confines Himself to setting before the Church an open door, in pointing to the essential mystery of Scripture as the work of the Wisdom of God; and in accepting or ascribing to Himself titles bearing far-reaching Old Testament associations, such as *Lamb of God, King of Israel, Son of David, Prophet of Nazareth, Son of Man, the Good Shepherd, the True Vine, the Corner-Stone, the Messiah, the Wisdom of God.* It is indeed sometimes difficult to distinguish between the allegorical use of the Old Testament to illustrate a fact, and the *Haggadistic* use of it to enforce a spiritual law. Augustine only gives one instance of allegorism from our Lord's own teaching: namely the reference to Jonah's deliverance as a sign or type of the resurrection[1]. But no writer is more conscious of the typical and symbolic character of the Old Testament viewed as a whole.

2. Enough has been said to illustrate the freedom of the New Testament in its references to the Old. The next point that claims our attention is the moral import of the quotations. Our Lord, it has been said, deals with the words of Scripture as 'living words of God to man bearing upon human conduct[2].' It is scarcely accidental that His first recorded quotation is from Deuteronomy viii. 3: *Man shall not live by bread alone, but by every word that proceedeth out of the*

---

[1] Matt. xii. 39, 40; xvi. 4. Cp. Aug. *de util. cred.* 8.
[2] Briggs, *Biblical Study*, p. 315.

mouth of God[1]. In the hands of the scribes the Old Testament religion was not indeed a dead thing, but it had lost any capacity of further development and expansion. It could not in any way satisfy the desire of the true Israel for a new word of God, a fresh revelation of truth. Our Lord and His apostles, on the other hand, quickened the very letter of Scripture by pointing to the living personality behind it. The words of the living and eternal God were shown to be full of enduring vitality and continuous significance. The phrase *It is written* in our Lord's mouth implies that each scripture appealed to is not a lifeless formula of law, but the revelation of a living personality and character[2]. What the living God inspires lives in Him, lives unto Him, lives for all who abide in communion with Him. St. Paul even speaks as if Scripture were endued with personality. From the first it foresaw the purpose of God; it preached the gospel beforehand unto Abraham[3]. It accompanies the people of God through the ages as a monitor and witness, sustaining the spirit of patience, quickening expectation, and kindling hope[4]. Like the incarnate Word Himself, the written word reveals its true character only to those in whom faith lives and the sense of need has been awakened. To the Pharisee and the scribe Scripture was practically a fetich; to the cold and critical wisdom of this world it is a dead thing to be dissected and analyzed, or a common thing that may be rejected and despised, or approved and patronized; to faith and the spirit of prayer Scripture is the very voice of God which warns or encourages, the very eye of God which watches and guides the soul. As employed indeed by our Lord and His apostles, the function of Scripture

---

[1] Matt. iv. 4.
[2] Cp. Valeton, *Christus und das A. T.* p. 18: 'Durch ihn jedes Teilchen der Schrift auf seinen rechten Platz kommt: das Kleine, vielleicht lange überschätzt, wird klein: das Grosse, vielleicht wie der von Gott auserschene Eckstein (cp. Matt. xxi. 42), lange von den Menschen verachtet, wird gross. Er bringt Leben und Bewegung: er bringt κρίσις; die Schriften werden "erfüllt."'
[3] Gal. iii. 8. [4] Rom. xv. 4.

stands in close relation to their entire system of dealing with human souls. The tendency of Pharisaism was to bring men into leading-strings, 'to leave as little as possible free to the individual conscience, but to bring everything within the scope of positive ordinance[1].' The free play of individuality, the development of personal character, was utterly remote from the range of their ideas. Even the ideals of prophecy were to them of secondary interest. Their one aim was to secure by a comprehensive discipline the principle of technical holiness. They were *blind leaders of the blind*[2] inasmuch as they had lost all sense of proportion in their estimation of Scripture. They clung to what was temporary and transient; they made what was little great, what was morally indifferent all-important, while they overlooked the broad tendency of Scripture as a whole, and thus lost any sense of a continuous divine utterance, and of a law written not on tables of stone but in the heart of man. Of our Lord, on the contrary, it is a truism to say that He cherishes and reverences personality, that He ever aims at awakening and cultivating individuality. He founded a Church that was to be a school of individual character, in which the diversified capacities of each soul were to be freely developed[3]. And the usage of the New Testament generally, to say nothing of the explicit teaching of Christ, shows that in the work of moral and spiritual education the study of the Old Testament discharges a necessary function. It is the light of the individual conscience; it ministers to individual needs; it is an aid to individual perfection[4]. But such a use of Scripture presupposes a living relationship to God, correspondence with the gift of His Spirit, and an earnest purpose to ascertain His mind and will[5]. And thus the ulti-

---

[1] Wellhausen, *Sketch of the History of Israel and Judah*, p. 186.
[2] Matt. xv. 14; xxiii. 16.   [3] Cp. Col. i. 28; Eph. ii. 10.
[4] 2 Tim. iii. 17.
[5] Aug. *de util. cred.* 13 : 'Quidquid est, mihi crede, in Scripturis illis altum et divinum est : inest omnino veritas, et reficiendis instaurandisque animis accommodatissima disciplina; et plane ita modificata, ut nemo

mate proof that a divine voice speaks in Scripture lies in the region of spiritual experience.

The central point, however, of Christ's teaching is that the revelation recorded in the Old Testament is mainly a revelation of human duty. If we set aside those instances in which our Lord reasons with the learned, and accommodates Himself apparently to their standpoint and to their preconceptions, it is striking how closely analogous His teaching is to that of the prophets. The doctrine of God's Fatherhood stands in the forefront of His teaching, but He ever brings out its moral import as implying an ideal of sonship by which the ethical law of the Old Testament is transfigured. The old obligations are not abolished, but are spiritualized. The eternal principles of righteousness are extricated from their temporary kernel. Christ recognizes the element of accommodation in the ancient Law, and His main work is to impart to His hearers a point of view which will enable them to discern for themselves between the provisional and the permanent elements in the old dispensation, and to teach them that the supreme requirement of God is not the righteousness of conformity to outward law, but the holiness of a heart purified by love towards God and towards man. The lost sense of spiritual proportion was for ever re-established in the statement that this, the law of love, *is the law and the prophets* [1].

3. Once more, Christ Himself and the New Testament writers represent the Old Testament as constituting an organic whole, to which the Messiah and His kingdom are the key. They look upon the entire preparatory dispensation as a shadow of good things to come. The ordinances imposed under the ancient system and the incidents described by sacred historians were divinely overruled in such a way as to prefigure

---

inde haurire non possit quod satis est, si modo ad hauriendum devote ac pie, ut vera religio poscit, accedat.'

[1] Matt. vii. 12; cp. xxii. 37 foll.

the mysteries and circumstances of the new covenant. It was of Christ that Moses wrote[1]; it was the sufferings and glories of Christ that prophets unconsciously described[2]. Of the apostolic writers each one seems to give special prominence to one particular aspect of the prophetic character ascribed to the Old Testament. St. Paul discerns in the history of Abraham the assertion of that principle of faith which preceded the discipline of the Law, and lies at the root of the relationship between God and man which is revealed in Christ[3]. St. Peter claims for the Christian Church titles which imply that she is the heir of the covenant-promises and privileges of God's ancient people[4]. The writer to the Hebrews points to the fulfilment in Christ both of the law of sacrificial worship and of the purificatory rites of Judaism. The ancient ceremonial system was a shadow or outline-sketch of heavenly realities manifested in Christ[5]. In the Apocalypse St. John invests the incarnate Son with the glories of the Messianic kingdom, unfolds the judgments of God and the fortunes of the Church in symbolism derived from the prophets, and describes the bliss of the redeemed in imagery transferred from the earthly Jerusalem to the heavenly sanctuary and the city of God.

In this case again the justification of the method employed in dealing with the Old Testament lies in the appeal to spiritual experience. The prophetic character of the ancient Scriptures is vindicated by the skill which so applies them. 'The spiritual sense,' it has been said, 'is its own proof, as a key by opening a complicated lock sufficiently proves that it has been designed for it[6].' There is no need to enlarge on this point, which will be dealt with later. Let it suffice to

---

[1] John v. 46. Our Lord's references to the fulfilment of the Old Testament in His own person and in the conditions of His earthly life are amply illustrated by Valeton, *Christus und das A. T.* pp. 22 foll.
[2] 1 Pet. i. 11. [3] Rom. iv; Gal. iii.
[4] 1 Pet. ii. 9. [5] Heb. x. 1.
[6] Jukes, *The Types of Genesis*, p. xv.

observe that this character of the old covenant corresponds to the predominance of prophetism in Israel's religion. For the creative element in Hebrew religion was a real and continuous self-communication of God to men; the one Spirit was ever at work, enabling those whom He inspired to anticipate His purposes, and to read, each in his measure, the divine thoughts for mankind [1]. Thus 'there is not one New Testament idea that cannot be conclusively shown to be a healthy and natural product of some Old Testament germ, nor any truly Old Testament idea which did not instinctively press towards its New Testament fulfilment [2].' It is indeed characteristic of a divine religion that its main ideas do not suddenly break in upon human thought; the wisdom of God prepares the soil in which these ideas shall take root and flourish; it fosters anticipations which may welcome the truths ultimately to be disclosed; it impresses even upon external incidents and ordinances tokens of what is to come. The stage of promise, preceding that of law, is a comprehensive prophecy, real though dimly understood, of the goal towards which the whole religion tends. And there is truth in the suggestive remark of Augustine that the whole Old Testament is a promise in figurative form [3]. It is only when we endeavour to grasp the meaning of St. Paul's phrase *the fulness of Christ* [4] that we can do justice to the many-sidedness of the Old Testament. In it the various aspects of the Incarnation are presented in fragmentary forms, 'Christ in His offices; in His character; in His person; Christ in His relations to God and man; Christ in His body the Church; Christ as giving to God all that God required from man; Christ as bringing to man all that man required from

---

[1] Cp. Schultz, *O. T. Theology*, i. p. 54.
[2] *Ibid.* p. 52.
[3] *Serm.* iv. (*de Jacob et Esau*) 9: 'Vetus enim Testamentum est promissio figurata; Novum Testamentum est promissio spiritaliter intellecta.'
[4] Eph. i. 23.

God; Christ as seen in this dispensation in suffering; Christ as seen in the next dispensation in glory; Christ as *the first and the last*, as *all and in all* to His people [1],' in whom *all the promises of God are yea, and in him Amen* [2].

Enough has been now said to illustrate the method observed by our Lord and the New Testament writers in their use of the ancient Scriptures. Their example teaches us that the true key to the Old Testament is possessed only by those who have *the mind of Christ* [3], and who are guided by the same Spirit that 'spake by the prophets.' There are indeed one or two passages in which our Lord seems to suggest principles of scriptural interpretation which could be safely employed only by Himself. Such is His answer to the Sadducees *as touching the dead that they rise* [4]. Here we have an instance of interpretation that necessarily transcends any human method, and that raises far-reaching questions as to the degree in which ordinary minds can penetrate the significance of Scripture. Only He who knew God with an absolute knowledge could thus reveal a mystery necessarily involved in covenant-relationship to Him.

The authoritative tone with which both here and in the Sermon on the Mount Christ elucidates the inner meaning of the ancient law constitutes an element in His claim to be more than man, and it may well check the temper of confidence with which men pass judgment on the contents of the Old Testament, or criticize the reasoning of the New. We cannot for a moment suppose that with His unique spiritual insight our Lord could mistake the real character of the Scriptures to which He so solemnly appeals. That He penetrates to the very heart of their meaning, that He assigns to each part of them the exact significance they were

---

[1] Jukes, *The Law of the Offerings*, p. 10. Cp. Rev. i. 17; Col. iii. 11.
[2] 2 Cor. i. 20. [3] 1 Cor. ii. 16.
[4] Mark xii. 26 foll. Valeton, *Christus und das A. T.* p. 43, makes some good remarks on this passage.

divinely intended to convey, that He grasped unerringly their general drift and their precise bearing on His own work and mission, it is simply impossible to doubt. And although, as we have seen, He does not discard methods of interpretation which were in general use at the period of His active ministry, He so employs them as to rescue the Old Testament from the misuse it had suffered at the hands of the scribes, and to restore to the written word its rightful vitality and authority. Thus to His Apostles and to His believing Church Christ is verily ' the light of all Scripture.'

By way of summary it may be said that both Christ and His apostles use the Scriptures with a certain prophetic freedom. In the contrast between their teaching and that of the scribes is implied the revival of the spirit of prophecy. The word of God again comes to Israel, again has free course. It is significant indeed that the Old Testament is not expressly called ' the word of God' in the New. In the Gospels 'the word of God' means the oral delivery of the gospel. It is not something written, but a living seed implanted by the preaching of the divine message in the heart of the hearer. Nay, Jesus Christ Himself is in utterance and act the living *sermo Dei*[1]. In the Old Testament the Word or Wisdom of God lives as the soul in the body; and *every scribe instructed unto the kingdom of heaven* must *bring forth out of his treasure things new as well as things old*[2]. Accordingly the apostolic writers display a certain flexibility in their use of exegetical methods and in their practical applications of Old Testament Scripture, as if to teach us that those who cling to rigid rules of exposition may fall far short of ascertaining the mind of the Spirit. Practically the New Testament points us to the *unction from the Holy One*[3] as the only unfailing source of spiritual truth.

---

[1] Cp. Meinhold, *Jesus und das A. T.* p. 60. Consider the use of λόγος in James i. 18; 1 Pet. i. 23.
[2] Matt. xiii. 52. [3] 1 John ii. 20.

II.

What has been said respecting the use of the Old Testament in the New is after all only introductory to the main subject under consideration in the present lecture. Our aim is to ascertain if possible the present value and permanent function of the Old Testament in the Christian Church, especially in view of those critical conclusions which have so largely modified traditional opinions respecting the character of the ancient Scriptures.

First however, in view of these conclusions, there is yet a final word to be said bearing upon the historical character of the Old Testament records, and upon the existence of a so-called 'mystical' sense in Scripture.

We have already dealt at some length with the historical element in the Old Testament, its nature and its extent. But the point now to be insisted on is that we must recognize frankly the impossibility of precisely determining the historical value of the narratives in which Israel's history is contained. When the character of the different materials is carefully sifted, and when ordinary historical tests are employed, it is manifest that elements are present in the Old Testament which are historical only in form, and that the history has been in part coloured by a poetical imagination, in part interspersed with semi-historical matter, with legal precedents in narrative shape, and even with free creations of fancy[1]. The modern historical spirit arrives on different grounds at general conclusions which were already reached by a somewhat more subjective process in early times. In the fourth book of the *de Principiis* Origen defends his theory

---

[1] The caution conveyed in some wise words of Prof. Valeton is important: 'A historico-critical verdict upon a *narrative* is not equivalent to a decision upon the historical character of the *events narrated*. Even though all the accounts relating to the foundation of Rome are relegated to the sphere of legend, yet none the less Rome was founded.' (Quoted from an Academical address in *Christus und das A. T.* p. 40.)

of the spiritual sense of Scripture by a free criticism of the Old Testament narratives. It may be worth while to illustrate his position by a few quotations. 'The Scripture,' he says, 'has interwoven in the history what did not actually happen; in some places what could not possibly have happened; in others what might possibly have happened, but certainly did not happen[1].' In a subsequent passage Origen points out that the narrative of the fall is purely figurative. It conveys spiritual truths under the appearance of history[2]. It is true that the strictly historical narratives are more numerous than the figurative[3]; but a fruitful cause of error is the temper which refuses to penetrate beneath the letter to the inner mystical sense of Scripture[4], beneath the corporeal or fleshly husk to the spiritual kernel[5]. It is clear that Origen attached no special value to the purely historical study of Scripture, though he does not by any means overlook the literal sense. What is chiefly to be noticed is his readiness to acknowledge the presence of a non-historical element in the Old Testament. He recognizes, however, that even the semi-historical portions of Scripture are full of inspired teaching, and that their very existence in the Old Testament proves that the purpose of the Bible is not to impart natural knowledge that may be otherwise acquired, but to teach spiritual truth[6]. Now modern criticism is chiefly concerned to determine the character and value of the literary materials contained in the Old Testament;

---

[1] *de Princ.* iv. 15. Cp. similar statements in chh. 19, 20, and a strong passage on the ceremonial law in *hom. vii. ad Levit.* § 5.

[2] *Ibid.* 16 διὰ δοκούσης ἱστορίας καὶ οὐ σωματικῶς γεγενημμένης.

[3] *Ibid.* 19 πολλῷ γὰρ πλείονά ἐστι τὰ κατὰ τὴν ἱστορίαν ἀληθευόμενα, τῶν προσυφανθέντων γυμνῶν πνευματικῶν.

[4] *Ibid.* 9.

[5] *Ibid.* 11 (σὰρξ τῆς γραφῆς); 14 (τὸ σωματικὸν τῆς γραφῆς).

[6] Orig. *in Gen. hom.* xv. 1 describes Scripture as 'secundum disciplinam divinae eruditionis aptatam, neque tantum historicis narrationibus quantum rebus et sensibus mysticis servientem.' Cp. *in Jerem. hom.* xxxix: οὐκ ἔστιν ἰῶτα ἐν ᾗ μία κεραία γεγραμμένη ἐν τῇ γραφῇ ἥτις τοῖς ἐπισταμένοις χρῆσθαι τῇ δυνάμει τῶν γραμμάτων οὐκ ἐργάζεται τὸ ἑαυτῆς ἔργον. Cp. Aug. *de util. cred.* 9 s. fin.

it considers indications of date and authorship; it estimates the time that separates the origin of a document from the events recorded therein; it examines the inner consistency of the narrative, and its harmony with facts otherwise ascertained: and no Christian student of the present day can afford to neglect the ascertained conclusions of critical science. But on the other hand, when he has frankly recognized the distinction between what is historical and what is semi-historical or imaginative, he will place himself on a level with ancient Christianity in his endeavour to ascertain the spiritual and personal bearing of what he reads. Augustine had little or no opportunity of acquiring linguistic or critical knowledge, but there is something strangely modern in the tone of the following passage taken from the first chapter of the *de Genesi ad literam*. 'In all the sacred books,' he says, 'our duty is to examine what eternal truths are intimated therein, what facts are narrated, what future events foretold, what duties we are commanded or advised to perform. Accordingly in the narrative of actual facts inquiry is made whether all things are to be accepted only in a figurative sense, or whether they are also to be maintained and defended as having literally occurred. For that there are not things which must be figuratively understood, no Christian will venture to affirm, if at least he pays heed to the apostle's words *Now all these things happened unto them in a figure* (1 Cor. x. 11); and to the text in Genesis, *and they twain shall be one flesh*—a text which presents to us the great mystery of Christ and of the Church[1].' Here Augustine recognizes the need of discrimination between what is historical and what is merely figurative. From a different starting-point the modern Christian student arrives at a similar point of view. In detail the conclusions of the ancient and of the modern student would differ. But both, in so far as they were true to the limitations of their knowledge, would surely admit that it is not only a great

[1] *de Gen. ad lit.* i. 1.

blunder, but a serious failure in truthfulness, to insist overmuch on the historical element in the Old Testament, and to build indiscriminately on narratives which have been conclusively shown to be utterly different in literary quality and in historic worth. This cautious position is entirely consistent on the one hand with a profound and reverent sense of the spiritual preciousness of all, even of what is only apparently and not really historical, and on the other with a frank suspense of judgment in regard to details. We have already pointed out that it is possible to overrate the importance of certainty on many points of criticism; indeed, it appears probable that some questions now in dispute will practically prove to be beyond the range of satisfactory solution. It is enough that we can use the Old Testament narratives for purposes of moral illustration; while those which are true to fact teach us what Almighty God has actually wrought or allowed, those which are parabolic or imaginative reveal sometimes the anticipations and ventures of faith, sometimes the thoughts of the inspiring Spirit. Like the parables of our Lord, they illustrate the dealings of God with men, or the progress of man's spiritual education, or the workings of divine providence, or the judgments that fall on sin and the blessings which crown righteousness. It is *a priori* probable that in the literature of a religion of which prophecy is the characteristic feature, there should be a considerable element of what is simply parabolic and figurative. If we follow the method of the New Testament writers we shall use the Old Testament stories mainly for the purpose of spiritual and moral edification, considering (to use Augustine's phrase) *quae ibi aeterna intimentur*; the spiritual depth and sublimity of such narratives as that of Jacob's dream at Bethel, or that of the heavenly feast and vision by which the divine covenant with Israel was sealed, is practically unaffected by considerations as to their precise character. It suffices that they convey intimations of God's character, His discriminating providence, His purposes for mankind, His ways of dealing with the individual soul, which have formed an integral element in the spiritual education of our race. These and such-like things are written for our admonition, and as Augustine elsewhere says, we must diligently ponder their meaning 'until the interpretation is brought to bear upon the kingdom of love [1].' For the end of God's ways is the sanctification of man through a saving knowledge of Him.

The existence and *rationale* of a 'secondary' or 'mystical' sense in Scripture next claims attention. This is a question forced upon us not only by the universal habit and tradition of the Catholic Church—a fact which it would be supremely foolish and presumptuous to ignore—but also by the express teaching of Scripture itself [2]. In their vindication of the claims of biblical criticism and exegesis the humanists and the early reformers insisted upon the principle that 'Scripture should be its own interpreter, and that it was not to be interpreted by tradition or external authority [3].' Now it is this very principle that justifies the recognition of a mystical sense in the Old Testament. It is not merely the case that the New Testament writers habitually treat the ancient Scriptures as symbolic and prophetic in the widest sense. There is a certain constancy in the employment of imagery derived from nature or from Israel's history which implies that both are sacramental, that is, that they embody in local, visible, and material forms and incidents the realities which belong to a spiritual and eternal order. We have already noticed that the spiritual sense of Scripture is practically its own proof, but it is desirable to indicate

---

[1] *de doc.* iii. 15 : 'Servabitur ergo in locutionibus figuratis regula huiusmodi, ut tam diu versetur diligenti consideratione quod legitur, donec ad regnum caritatis interpretatio perducatur.'
[2] See an article on 'The mystical interpretation of Holy Scripture,' in the *Church Quarterly Review*, no. 43 (April, 1886) ; the *Bampton Lectures* for 1824, by the Rev. J. J. Conybeare, on 'The history and limitations of the secondary and spiritual sense of Scripture'; Stanton, *The Jewish and the Christian Messiah*, pp. 184 foll.
[3] Briggs, *Biblical Study*, p. 331.

briefly two independent grounds of reason on which the practice of mystical interpretation ultimately rests.

Now it might be fairly argued that the very fact that the Jewish mind displayed a tendency to allegorize points to the presence of a considerable element of allegory in the Hebrew writings themselves. But in order to escape a possible charge of *petitio principii* it is better to defend the method now in question by other considerations. And first, there evidently underlies it a sense of the inexhaustible significance of language when applied to subjects of spiritual contemplation, or when employed as a medium of divine self-communication to man. Human language is obviously inadequate as a vehicle of the thoughts of God; it is at best a sign pointing to the thing signified and leading us back at one step to the sphere of nature and human life, in which God reveals Himself by means of the concrete language of outward fact[1]. The fault of the rabbinical methods of dealing with the letter of Scripture—methods which culminated in the system of the *Cabbala*—was twofold: on the one hand they ignored the human element in the Old Testament, forgetting that the letter was human though the spirit was divine; on the other, they were content with the manipulation of the letter instead of passing beyond it into the broad fields of nature and history[2]. The extravagances of mystical interpretation have in some instances perhaps been due to these mistakes; in others, doubtless, to a defective perception of the progressive character of revelation[3]. Moreover, extravagance was closely allied to arbitrariness, which even Origen appears to recognize in his admission that the mystical sense is not always certainly or safely ascertainable[4]. The fact is that the study of the

---

[1] Cp. Newman, *University Sermons*, p. 268, and the suggestive remarks of Mozley, *University Sermons*, pp. 134 foll.
[2] Cp. Briggs, *op. cit.* p. 302.
[3] e.g., Aug. *de doc.* iii. 12 insists that the morally defective actions of Old Testament characters are all figurative.
[4] *de Princ.* ix ὅτι μὲν οἰκονομίαι εἰσί τινες μυστικαὶ δηλούμεναι διὰ τῶν

written word, regarded as a revelation of the divine mind, needs to be supplemented by devout contemplation of the things and facts which human language only imperfectly symbolizes. Augustine, after carefully distinguishing between *signa propria* and *signa translata*, that is, between language literal and language metaphorical, insists that a deeper knowledge of things is necessary for comprehending the significance of scriptural terms. *Rerum ignorantia*, he says, *facit obscuras figuratas locutiones*[1]. In the language of Scripture a real though imperfect impression is conveyed to man of the works in which the *eternal power and godhead* of the Creator are made known. And possibly one of the reasons why our Lord adopted the parable as His chosen method of instruction was that while His words were often perverted or misunderstood owing either to the malignity or to the literalistic habit of mind of His different hearers, His parabolic teaching was calculated to direct attention to the correspondence between two classes of *facts*, between the processes of nature and the operations of grace. It implied that all the works of God are words, and that nothing is unspiritual or void of signification in a universe the Creator of which is a living spirit [2].

A sacramental view of the universe, then, seems to be everywhere presupposed in Scripture, the visible

θειῶν γραφῶν, πάντες καὶ οἱ ἀκεραιότατοι τῶν τῷ λόγῳ προσιόντων πεπιστεύκασι. τίνες δὲ αὗται οἱ εὐγνώμονες καὶ ἄτυφοι ὁμολογοῦσι μὴ εἰδέναι.

[1] *de doc.* ii. 16. Cp. T. Aquinas, *Summa Theol.* i. q. 1, art. 10: 'Auctor sacrae scripturae est Deus in cujus potestate est ut non solum voces ad significandum accommodet (quod etiam homo facere potest) sed etiam res ipsas.'

[2] Cp. Trench, *Notes on the Parables*, Introd. p. 18. I cannot refrain from quoting a striking statement of a divine whose cautious and scholarly temperament inclined him to distrust anything like the play of imagination in the exegesis of Scripture. The late Dr. Hatch in his *Hibbert Lectures*, pp. 83, 84, points out the permanent principle which underlies the method of mystical or allegorical interpretation. 'It is based,' he says, 'upon an element in human nature which is not likely to pass away. Whatever be its value in relation to the literature of the past, it is at least the expression in relation to the present that our lives are hedged round by the unknown; that there is a haze about both our birth and our departure, and that even the meaner facts of life are linked to infinity.'

creation being a type of the spiritual world. Thomas Aquinas indeed finds the *rationale* of different senses in Scripture not in the nature of the written letter, but in the concrete realities behind them. *Ipsae res significatae per voces*, he says, *aliarum rerum possunt esse signa*[1]. The *Cabbalistic* manipulation of the written word is not only discredited by the stubborn facts of textual criticism; it is based upon a shallow and unphilosophical view of the nature of language. The curiosities which it brings to light are of that unprofitable kind which *minister questions rather than godly edifying which is in faith*[2].

A second justification of mystical interpretation is to be found in the relation subsisting between Judaism and Christianity. The new religion clearly has an organic connexion and essential continuity with the old. Both rest on the same foundation, namely, a self-revelation of God resulting in new religious experiences and a new standard of human duty. Both are dominated by the idea of the kingdom of God as the consummation of history and the goal towards which nature tends. In both the divine requirement is the same. Faith is essentially the same quality in both dispensations, in spite of the fact that the object-matter of faith is not in all respects identical[3]. Finally, the idea of salvation is the same in both, with the difference that in the Old Testament God condescends to moral immaturity by embodying His promises in material and transitory forms[4]. From the unity of the Author of

---

[1] *Summa*, i. q. 1, art. 10. Cp. Waterland, pref. to *Scripture Vindicated* (*Works*, vol. vi. p. 7): 'The words properly bear but one sense, and that one sense is the *literal* one; but the thing expressed by the letter is further expressive of something sublime or spiritual.'

[2] 1 Tim. i. 4; cp. vi. 4.

[3] Cp. Riehm, *A Tl. Theologie*, p. 34.

[4] Aug. *de pecc. mer. et remiss.* i. 53: 'In illis [libris V. T.] quod occultatur sub velamento velut terrenarum promissionum, hoc in Novo Testamento praedicatione revelatur.' Cp. *c. duas epp. Pelag.* iii. 13: 'Ideo in illo sunt promissa terrena, in isto promissa coelestia: quia et hoc ad Dei misericordiam pertinuit ne quisquam vel ipsam terrenam qualemcumque felicitatem nisi a Domino creatore universitatis putet cuiquam posse conferri.'

VIII] THE OLD TESTAMENT AND CHRISTIANITY 409

revelation follows the New Testament principle that *no prophecy is of private interpretation*[1]. It has been repeatedly made manifest in the course of redemptive history that Scripture has successive applications which correspond to different stages in the work of God. Spiritual laws declared by prophecy, or set forth in typical institutions, or in the personal discipline of Hebrew saints and heroes, were seen to be continuously in operation, and from time to time working themselves out afresh. Accordingly, what had been originally spoken of the chosen nation, such as the passage *Out of Egypt have I called my son*, found a fresh and ideal fulfilment in Him who embodied in His representative humanity the people from which, as touching the flesh, He sprang, and who recapitulated in His own life the experience of all the ancient saints. And what was truly accomplished in Him necessarily had a mystical reference also to the true spiritual Israel of God of which He was the founder and archetype[2]. Finally, the individual Christian, in so far as he realizes his union with Christ, discerns in the narrative of Israel's fortunes and in the institutions of its polity or worship a kind of picture, writ large, of his own spiritual course, and of the truths by which he lives. He recognizes the application of the history to himself in his own religious experience. He finds that 'it is true of himself in virtue of his relation to the Church, and as one member of that redeemed body[3].' Indeed, the very

---

[1] 2 Pet. i. 20.
[2] Valeton, *Christus und das A. T.* p. 25, makes a striking remark: 'Ich glaube, die Schriften werden nie mit mehr unmittelbarer Anwendung auf den Leser selbst gelesen und durchstudiert worden sein als von dem Herrn. Was nach Ausweis der Schriften Gott zu verschiedenen Zeiten und auf mancherlei Weise in und mit dem israelitischen Volke gethan hat, an sich selbst sieht er es erst zur vollen Verwirklichung herangereift; ... was Israel sein sollte, Jesus ist sich bewusst es wirklich zu sein: er ist der Messias, der Menschensohn, derjenige, der da kommen soll,—Gottes Ratschluss ist in ihm erfüllt.'
[3] This principle is of course recognized by Augustine in his discussion of the 'Rules of Tichonius'; see especially *de doc.* iii. 34. Cp. Jukes, *The Mystery of the Kingdom*, pp. 17, 25. Observe, the application of Scripture

distinction between Israel after the flesh and Israel after the spirit, between the seed of Abraham literally understood and the children of Abraham by promise, implies that there is a necessary spiritual application of the Old Testament to those who constitute the spiritual Israel[1]. What in the letter belongs to the ancient people can only be figuratively or mystically applicable to the Church. That it is so applicable is warranted by the express teaching of the New Testament and attested by the universal experience of Christians. The mystery of solidarity in the kingdom of grace is the basis and justification of the mystical interpretation of Scripture. The facts of redemptive history point beyond themselves in so far as they illustrate living laws of the divine government and self-manifestation; in so far as they are moments in the forthcoming of the eternal Word 'whose path is and ever must be one[2].' If the Incarnation was indeed a great 'recapitulation' of the past[3], the manifestation in its fullness of a divine purpose predestined from the beginning, it is not surprising that the actions and experiences of ancient prophets, saints, priests, martyrs, and kings should have been prophetic; that in these should have been foreshadowed different aspects of Christ's office and person. Such partial and fragmentary indication of good things to be fully revealed in the future is consistent with all that we know of the divine character and methods.

Again, the typical element in the Old Testament dispensation seems to follow from the constancy of spiritual

---

to the individual soul seems to constitute the *moral* or *tropological* sense, or 'soul' of Scripture. Thus Orig. *hom. i. in Exod.* § 4 (speaking of Joseph's history) says: 'Sed et *moralem* in his non omittamus locum; *aedificat enim animas auditorum.*'

[1] Gal. iv. 29. Aug. *enarr. i. in psalm.* xxi. § 25 explains 'semen Israel' as 'omnes ad novam vitam nati, et ad visionem Dei reparati.'

[2] Cp. Jukes, *The Mystery of the Kingdom*, p. 18: 'Whether it be Israel of old, or one of Israel, or Christ, or the Church, or the believer, each, if faithful to his calling, is or has been a vessel for the manifestation of the Word whose path is and ever must be one.'

[3] Eph. i. 10.

law in the universe. The relation of faith to God and to the facts of life is essentially the same in every age. There are facts and circumstances in history which have a representative character, which exemplify the operation of a moral principle and are accordingly prophetic[1]. A particular spiritual experience necessarily repeats itself because the needs and trials of human nature in successive generations remain constant and unchanged, and because God is eternally self-consistent in His character and in His dealings with mankind. And it may be observed, in conclusion, that the typical character of Israel's history corresponds to the prophetic character of its religion. In a typical transaction, object, or person a law of the spiritual world is to be observed in actual operation. In prophecy the intellect of man, guided by the divine Spirit, lays hold of the law and brings it to the light. Thus, while the continuity of revelation makes the institutions and the history of Israel actually typical or symbolic, it is the office of the prophetic faculty to exhibit its inner significance. There is every reason *a priori* to suppose that the sacred writers or compilers were controlled by the Holy Spirit in their selection, and even in their omission[2], of particular incidents and events. They were guided 'to record them in such a way that over and above the direct moral and spiritual instructiveness they should be susceptible of a parabolic interpretation too[3].'

[1] Alexander of Hales in his *Summa Theologiae* (i. q. 1, mem. 1) makes a striking remark: 'In sacra scriptura ponitur historia non ea ratione seu fine ut significentur singulares actus hominum significatione sermonum, sed ut significentur universales actus et conditiones pertinentes ad informationem et contemplationem divinorum mysteriorum significatione rerum.... Introducitur ergo in historia sacrae scripturae factum singulare ad significandum universale.'
[2] Thus the writer of the Epistle to the Hebrews argues from the *silence* of Scripture in vii. 3, not surely, as Prof. Hommel insists, from another version of Genesis, now lost. The remark of Augustine about the Gospel narratives may be applied to those of the Old Testament: 'Tanta facta sunt quanta tunc fieri debuerunt; tanta scripta sunt quanta nunc legi debuerunt' (*serm. in dieb. Pasch.* ccxl).
[3] See art. in *Ch. Quart. Review*, above mentioned.

Having dealt with these preliminary points we may turn to the consideration of the permanent function which the Old Testament seems designed to fulfil in the education of Christian faith. In discussing this subject, we shall naturally bear in mind the peculiar needs and circumstances of our own day.

1. The main purpose of the Old Testament is to be inferred from consideration of the primary element in our Lord's own teaching. He came into the world for the express purpose of revealing to men the mind, the character, and the will, of Almighty God. He pointed men to the Scriptures as a true source of divine knowledge. Their readiness to accept Himself would be proportionate to the anticipations they had already formed of God. If they read the ancient Scriptures aright they would be prepared for a disclosure of the divine life and character, crowning and not contradicting the recorded revelations of the past. Diligent search of the Scriptures would train and develope certain preconceptions, which were likely to welcome the manifestation of the incarnate Son. The study of Israel's history under the guidance of the prophets would prepare the Hebrew mind for a revelation of grace transcending, but strictly consistent with, the wonderful dealings of God in the past.

In the Old Testament, then, we find a revelation of God's nature and character which justifies and interprets to us our faith in Christ. The message of the Old Testament, it has been said, is summed up in one word—the word God[1]. A personal, holy, spiritual, and gracious Being there manifests Himself. We can study His dealings with men in almost every stage of development and culture; we can watch Him educating His elect people and nurturing the heathen; we see Him as a Judge punishing sins, as a Father disciplining His children. What is the great truth which the history of Israel enforces, and which is a necessary element in the religious view of the world?

---

[1] G. A. Smith, *The Preaching of the Old Testament to the Age*, p. 57.

The answer to this question is that the Old Testament impresses upon us the thought that in His moral government of the world Almighty God sets before Himself one aim, that of bringing His creatures to the highest degree of perfection of which their nature is capable. The moral perfection of man—this is the goal of human history. In the divine view of the world all else appears to be of subordinate importance. The tremendous discipline to which Israel was subjected is a measure of the supreme place assigned in the universe to moral law. The Old Testament exhibits to us the Creator taking in hand that one among His creatures which is capable of holding communion with Him and of wearing His image and likeness, carrying him through all the stages of an agelong discipline, and finally bringing His purpose to accomplishment. Nor is there anything perhaps more necessary in our day than a revival in men's minds of a just conception of the divine purpose which is slowly working itself out in national history. From the Old Testament history we learn what is the meaning of the stern discipline of war, pestilence, and famine, of national distress and signal public catastrophes, of the vicissitudes and shocks which darken the lives of individual men. All these things are divinely intended either to heighten the standard of national righteousness, or to advance the work of personal sanctification. Nothing can more forcibly bring home this lesson, at least to the generality of men, than the inspired record of God's dealings with His people in the time of old. In legend and allegory, in narrative and song, in the homely wisdom of proverbs and in the inspired interpretations of history, the spirit of faith reads one continuous lesson: *This is the will of God, even your sanctification*[1]. The passion for moral beauty, the thirst for righteousness, which fired the Puritans of the seventeenth century, was to a great extent nourished by the zealous study of the Old Testament; and in

---

[1] 1 Thess. iv. 3.

these days of paralyzing moral scepticism and frequently misdirected moral energy it is well to learn once more from its pages what are the things best worth living for, and what is the consummation on which the Lord of all the earth has set His heart: namely, the exaltation of humanity into moral fellowship with the divine life.

But the Old Testament does not merely reveal and illustrate the aim of God's moral government; it also exhibits the methods and laws of His action. God is manifested as one who bears with man in his present condition in order to raise him to a higher level. God separates man from the sphere of sin and corruption in order to make him a co-operating agent in the execution of a world-wide purpose of grace; He uses man's social instincts and tendency to corporate life as the main instrument in his moral development. A kingdom of God is planted upon earth, a sphere within which the quickening forces of the divine Spirit visibly work, a centre of life and light amid the darkness of universal death. And the Old Testament history anticipates and prefigures the fortunes of the Messianic kingdom. For it is the history of an elect people, of a Church invested with a mission to mankind. In the story of Israel's lapses and revivals, distresses and failures, advances and conquests, we have a divine commentary on 'the chequered annals of Christendom[1].' The broad principles of redemptive history do not change with the ages, since they reflect the very being of God and correspond to the comprehensive unity of His plan; they manifest themselves anew in the kingdom of the Incarnation, they finally triumph in the consummation of all things.

Once more, while the Old Testament history illustrates the diversity of the means by which the divine will is ultimately accomplished, we are nevertheless struck by one special feature in the narrative, namely the prominence of suffering. It has been justly observed

---

[1] Westcott, *Ep. to the Hebrews*, p. 494.

that Scripture is a record of human sorrow; certainly the Old Testament teaches more emphatically than any other literature the moral necessity of suffering as a factor in man's development and in his progress from *that which is natural* to *that which is spiritual*[1]. In the culminating vision of prophecy, the exilic picture of the afflicted servant of Jehovah bearing the sin of his people, we see disclosed 'the innermost secret of the divine way of salvation[2].' The sober solemnity which pervades the entire history of the Old Testament corresponds to the dominant aspect of human life; it is the story of faith passing through days of warfare and trial. So too the poetry and the wisdom of the Hebrews give utterance to the complaints, or reflect the perplexities, of righteous men suffering without a cause. In every part of the Old Testament the Hebrew mind is as it were being prepared for the appearance on the stage of human life of the *Man of sorrows*. The trials of Abraham and Isaac, the sorrows of Jacob and Joseph, the discipline of Israel in the wilderness, the wrongs endured by the first true king, the persecutions that befell holy men of God—psalmists, prophets, martyrs, and saints; the afflictions of the righteous remnant in exile—a moment's reflexion will show us how large a part these played in the slow fulfilment of the divine purpose, how constant an element they formed in the spiritual education of mankind. Man, like Joseph, dreams of rule: he is sustained by the light of the divine blessing which whispers to him of dominion; but it is only by the way of sorrow that he attains that for which he was intended from the first. In the Old Testament the whole warfare of man upon earth is set forth. The law of man's glorification is already clearly exhibited: *If we suffer with him we shall also reign with him*[3].

Thus the study of the Old Testament tends to

---

[1] 1 Cor. xv. 46. [2] Schultz, *O. T. Theology*, vol. ii. p. 430.
[3] 2 Tim. ii. 12; cp. Rom. viii. 17.

deepen our impression of the constancy and perpetuity of those great spiritual laws which govern and guide the development of mankind. In its fullness the divine character makes itself known only in the life and teaching of our Saviour; but there are elements in that character which seem to emerge, so to speak, at different intervals and on critical occasions in the history of Israel: the holiness of God revealing itself in the promulgation of the moral law and in the ordinances of the levitical sanctuary; His long-suffering and readiness to pardon being manifested in His dealings with those who provoked and disobeyed Him in the wilderness, and in the providential tenderness with which He *bare* and *carried* His people *all the days of old*[1]; while His patience and tenacity of purpose is exhibited in the restoration of His exiled people to their own land, and in the revival of His work in the midst of a dreary waste of years[2]. Every student of the Old Testament can fill up these outlines for himself; but speaking generally, the point of chief importance is that we should regain and deepen the sense of what is most fundamental in the teaching of the ancient Scriptures, namely the reality of God's eternal purpose—the perfection of man; the method of His action—taking man as he is in order to make him what he is capable of becoming; the means He employs in the execution of His will—the discipline of suffering. We are to get into the habit of reading modern history in the light of the spiritual purpose revealed in Scripture, and to judge of movements social and political by their effects on human character. We are to learn from the prophetic philosophy of history that 'the fates of nations are conditioned by their bearing towards the moral purpose of God[3].'

2. A second great purpose of the Old Testament Scriptures is comprehensively described in our Lord's

---

[1] Isa. lxiii. 9.   [2] Hab. iii. 2.
[3] Pfleiderer, *Gifford Lectures*, vol. ii. p. 42.

declaration to the Jews: *they are they which testify of me*[1]. Christ in all the varied aspects of His person is the final cause and ultimate explanation of the Old Testament, nor can we understand even imperfectly what is meant by His 'Messianic self-consciousness' without its aid. Origen indeed observes that the very proof of its inspiration lies in the fact of Christ's advent[2]. Certainly the true character of the ancient Scriptures is only manifest in the light of the Incarnation. A product so vast and wonderful can only be supposed to stand in vital relation to some unique event in human history, for which it prepares the way. In this connexion it is unnecessary to do more than direct attention to the organic unity of the Old Testament regarded as a history of redemption. The fact of this unity is presupposed in the science of Old Testament theology, which assumes that every element and institution in the discipline of the Hebrew nation had a direct bearing upon the fulfilment of a single divine purpose. If the idea of redemption is the keynote of the Old Testament, the advent of a Redeemer is its goal and consummation. But just in proportion as the idea of redemption is profound and complex, the unity of aim that marks the Old Testament implies an infinite variety in the character of its component parts. Jesus Christ came not to destroy but to fulfil the teaching of the Old Testa-

[1] John v. 39.
[2] *de Princ.* iv. 6. It is scarcely necessary to say that in the early Church the Old Testament was chiefly valued for apologetic and controversial purposes. The argument from prophecy was 'the one formal method of proof' employed by the first Christians. Stanton, *The Jewish and Christian Messiah*, p. 176. The argument from prophecy has gained in force by being restated in accordance with our wider critical knowledge. In its modern form it is parallel to the argument from design, laying less emphasis upon particular predictions and resting rather on the broad general correspondence between prophecy and fulfilment. For a contemptuous but somewhat belated estimate of prophecy, see Mr. Goldwin Smith's recent *Guesses at the Riddle of Existence*, pp. 167 foll. The writer's general point of view will be plain from the following extract: 'The Messiahship of Jesus is a question with which we need practically concern ourselves no more. The Messiah was a dream of the tribal pride of the Jew to which ... we may bid a long farewell.'

ment; but His person was so mysterious, His work so many-sided, that each portion of the book which fore-announced His coming may reasonably be supposed to have reference to some aspect of His person or some element in His work. Thus if, as St. Paul teaches, Christ is the second Adam, it is evident that the mysterious narrative of man's origin in some way prefigures the work of the new creation exhibited in the life of the incarnate Son. The titles *Lamb of God* and *Our Passover* recall the solemn associations connected with Israel's deliverance from bondage, and its formation into an elect people of God. The name JESUS points back to the ministry and achievements of Joshua. The word *Saviour* recalls the memory of the deliverers under whose auspices Israel gained secure possession of the land of their inheritance. The name *David* or *Son of David* appropriates to Christ the experiences of the first true king and his godly successors on the throne; in Christ the mystery of the kingdom finds its fulfilment. The title *Messiah* embraces the spiritual counterpart of all offices discharged by those on whom under the old Law the sacred unction had been bestowed; it includes the dignity of kingship, and in a subordinate degree the functions of prophecy and the grace of priesthood. So, again, when our Lord refers to *the temple of his body*, or to His blood as *the blood of the new covenant*, or to His death as *a ransom for many*, or to His sacred flesh as *meat indeed*, it is obvious that He points to the entire sacrificial system and the very structure of the ancient sanctuary as typical of Himself. Finally, when He refers to Himself as *the Wisdom of God* He seems to bring within the range of the Messianic element in Scripture the whole *khokmah* literature; while His comparison of Himself to a *Bridegroom* justifies the symbolical application of Solomon's Song. Our Lord's teaching in fact suggests and implies much more than it explicitly declares; namely, that in His own person and work all that was limited, shadowy, fragmentary, or disconnected in the writings and characters of the Old Testament, was harmonized, developed, and completed. His life and teaching, His death and exaltation, formed together or singly the key to the true interpretation of Scripture, and the principle of its unity. In narrative, symbol, prophecy, and song, Christians may discern the outlines of His living form; in every righteous hero, in every innocent sufferer, in every steadfast martyr, in every victorious king, in every prisoner of hope, in every ministering priest, in every dispenser of blessing, we may see Christ Himself. In every typical ordinance some aspect of His Messianic office is prefigured, in each judgment on sin His coming is anticipated, in every prophet His Spirit speaks, in every conqueror of God's enemies He is the victor, in every afflicted saint He complains, in every godly king He reigns [1].

What has just been said suggests the further remark that the Messianic quality of many Old Testament passages depends on their idealistic character. It has been said that the true justification of many New Testament quotations from the Old is simply the broad principle that what is ideal is Messianic. Thus the writer of the Epistle to the Hebrews in his employment of the eighth Psalm, and St. Peter in his reference to the sixteenth [2], seem to base their argument on a definite law of scriptural interpretation. Christian teachers would doubtless gradually accustom themselves to read highly idealistic passages of Scripture in the light of the Messianic expectation, and ascribe to them a certain secondary or mystical meaning, thus expanding and spiritualizing their original sense. The

[1] Cp. Aug. c. Faust. Man. xix. 31: 'Quod [sc. regnum caelorum] ori ejus etiam nominandum servabatur quem regem ad regendos, et sacerdotem ad sanctificandos fideles suos universus ille apparatus Veteris Instrumenti in generationibus, factis, dictis, sacrificiis, observationibus, festivitatibus, omnibusque eloquiorum praeconiis et rebus gestis et rerum figuris parturiebat esse venturum; qui plenus gratia et veritate et ad praecepta facienda adjuvando per gratiam et ad promissa implenda curando per veritatem, venit legem non solvere sed adimplere.'
[2] Heb. ii. 6 foll.; Acts ii. 25 foll.

idealistic tendency indeed, like other peculiarities of the Hebrew writers, was doubtless ever under the control and guidance of the divine Spirit and was made to minister to His purposes. The prophet or psalmist was thus led to use language the full scope and application of which was hidden from himself, but which had a divinely intended reference to distant events concealed in the foreknowledge of God[1]. This habit of the Hebrew mind did not necessarily imply that it *spiritualized* the persons or events which it invested with ideal dignity or significance. On the contrary, it delighted in concrete imagery; it described even spiritual realities in terms of the non-spiritual; it regarded the material universe as the sphere of divine self-manifestation; it linked physical nature to the lot of man, and to the purposes of God. And in the interpretation of prophecy we have to remember how hyperbolical and highly-coloured is the symbolism used to express or prefigure spiritual truths or events. The most awful phenomena of nature foreshadow solemn crises in the spiritual history of mankind. So St. Peter, describing the gift of Pentecost, tells his hearers that *this is that which was spoken by the prophet Joel*[2]. The pouring out of the Spirit was an event so momentous that it could only be described in terms of fearful natural phenomena. *I will show wonders in heaven above and signs in the earth beneath, blood and fire and vapour of smoke. The sun shall be turned into darkness and the moon into blood before that great and notable day of the Lord come.* The same general principle of interpretation, viz. that everything ideal

---

[1] The hyperbolical and transcendental language of some of the psalms (e. g. Ps. xxii) seems dictated by a consciousness in the writer that the spiritual principles discernible in the facts of the present were destined to find a more complete expression in the future. See the article in *Ch. Quart. Review* already cited. Stanton, *The Jewish and the Christian Messiah*, p. 98, well remarks: 'On the ground of this divine intention, those who start from the full Christian idea of the Messiah are justified in noting as Messianic every element of thought in the Old Testament which was eventually taken up into the complete idea.'

[2] Acts ii. 16 foll.

VIII] THE OLD TESTAMENT AND CHRISTIANITY 421

has reference to the Messiah and His kingdom, seems to guide St. John's use of Old Testament imagery in the Apocalypse. It is, however, enough to have briefly indicated a rule observed by New Testament writers in the Messianic application of prophecy, which is very simple and comprehensive, but which we might easily overlook. It seems to give us a clue to the freedom and boldness with which the ancient Scriptures are applied to the person of Christ and the fortunes of the Church. All forms of nobleness or loveliness, all types of excellency or majesty, are seen in the light of the Incarnation to be only shadows of the uncreated beauty: *but the body is of Christ*[1]. The song of the redeemed claims for Him all that excites the wonder or merits the praise of man: *Worthy is the Lamb that was slain to receive power, and riches, and wisdom, and strength, and honour, and glory, and blessing*[2].

3. A third great function of the Old Testament is that of forming and training human character. This function it discharges partly by its explicit and formal teaching, partly by presenting living patterns of humanity by which we are taught *how to walk and to please God*[3]. 'The morality of the Old Testament' is a phrase to be used with discrimination. There is the morality which God tolerates as the best that can be attained under the rudimentary conditions and circumstances of those with which He is dealing. There is the morality which He approves and delights in because it rises above the average level of the age in which it appears. There is the morality at which He aims— the final or perfect morality which is disclosed in the spotless life of Jesus Christ. On the other hand, there is the morality recognized or allowed by the standard generally prevalent at a particular time, but retrogressive in so far as it falls short of a higher standard

---

[1] Col. ii. 17.   [2] Rev. v. 12.
[3] 1 Thess. iv. 1. See Aug. *de doc.* ii. 9: 'In his omnibus libris timentes Deum et pietate mansueti quaerunt voluntatem Dei'; iii. 10: 'Non autem praecipit scriptura nisi caritatem, nec culpat nisi cupiditatem, et eo modo informat mores hominum.'

already acknowledged. And it is this which is plainly described as hateful to God, and as bringing down upon men the fire of His judgment. Take the great sin of David for instance—a sin of which it was truly said that it had *given great occasion to the enemies of the Lord to blaspheme*[1]. The man after God's own heart falls into deeds which might have been matters of every-day occurrence in an ordinary oriental court. David acts as any eastern monarch might have acted who was not restrained by a conscience educated under the discipline of a recognized moral law. But in one single sentence the true character of David's deed is declared—*the thing that David had done displeased the Lord*[2]. And his subsequent history is the divine commentary on his crime; the sword never departing from David's house, the rebellion of his favourite son with all its fatal consequences, the outbreaks of lawless passion by which the royal household was subsequently defiled, the over-clouded and sorrow-laden old age of the king himself. Thus even in the historical narratives the eternal requirement of God for man and His thoughts concerning human sin are made abundantly manifest. Augustine indeed insists that the sins of the ancient saints of God are described in order to teach us humility. 'There is not a page,' he declares, 'in the sacred books which does not ring with the truth that *God resisteth the proud, but giveth grace unto the humble*[3].' If evil is described, it is described in its nakedness and loathsomeness; if it is denounced as by the prophets, it is denounced in words that burn, in sentences that might well 'make mad the guilty and appal the free'; while, on the other hand, the great outlines of religious character and the primary elements of human duty are everywhere set forth, with a continual tendency (as in the more humane injunctions of the Law) to raise the whole standard of morality, and to encourage the growth of that inwardness, that purity

---

[1] 2 Sam. xii. 14.   [2] 2 Sam. xi. 27.
[3] *de doc.* iii. 23. Cp. Jas. iv. 6.

of motive which is the distinguishing mark of Christian goodness.

In two respects Old Testament morality transcends the ordinary level of pagan ethics; it is theocentric, and it is altruistic. It is theocentric: *Thou shalt love the Lord thy God with all thy heart, and with all thy soul, and with all thy might* [1]. This is the fundamental and regulative commandment. As we have already noticed, the characteristic feature in Israel's conception of God was that it gave vitality and substance to the thought of the divine personality. God was a person capable of relationships of love—the true and adequate object of devotion, trust, gratitude, obedience, and service. He was one with whom and before whom man might walk; whom to know was man's glory [2], whom to serve was his joy. How strange and complete is the contrast between such a conception of deity and those vague and undefined notions which are characteristic of Semitic paganism. The religion of the Old Testament marks a forward step in the spiritual development of humanity which can never be retraced. It represents man as standing in an intelligible and moral relationship to God; as linked to Him not by the mere accident of birth, carrying with it the obligation to perform correctly certain stated observances [3], but by community of moral nature. For the theocentric idea of morality which pervades the Old Testament corresponds to a theomorphic view of humanity. Man was created in God's image; in other words, his very constitution made him capable of communion with God and of progressive assimilation to Him. From the first the Old Testament sets before man not merely his obligations, but the personal relationship, the tie of kinship to God, on which they rest. Already moral good presents itself to man in the shape of a personal appeal: *Be ye holy, for I the*

---

[1] Deut. vi. 5; x. 12; xi. 1, &c.   [2] Jer. ix. 24.
[3] Cp. Robertson Smith, *The Religion of the Semites*, pp. 29 foll.

Lord your God am holy[1]. Already morality is suffused with emotion: the coldness of a mere abstraction disappears, and the moral law is seen to be the expression, the very essence, of the living personality behind it. Obligation is set before man as dependent on a tie of vital relationship between persons. Thus the revealed morality of the Old Testament marks an epoch in the history of man's ethical progress, inasmuch as it exhibits with absolute clearness the fundamental characteristic of moral action. For it has been justly said that 'Morality begins with the relation of person to person, and all moral government—pre-eminently the government of God—is founded upon and legislates for this relation[2].'

Secondly, the morality of the Old Testament is altruistic. Its essential feature is no longer the self-regarding performance of stated rites calculated to secure the favour or avert the anger of jealous deities, but the fulfilment of duty as a member of the human brotherhood. A conspicuous feature both of the Law and of the prophetic teaching is that in both great practical prominence is assigned to duty towards one's neighbour. It is social righteousness which is preeminently the theme of the prophets. Integrity, justice, faithfulness in every relationship of life, compassion for the oppressed, the friendless, the poor, self-restraint towards an enemy, humanity even to animals, mercifulness in dealing with slaves, reverence for the marriage tie and for the laws of hospitality, habitual respect for age and station, fidelity in the matter of oaths and promises, and strict administration of justice—these are the distinctive points in Israel's moral law; and the sum of them, as St. Paul teaches, is briefly comprehended in this saying, namely, *Thou shalt love thy neighbour as thyself*[3]. It is in fact a sense of the

---

[1] Lev. xix. 2; xx. 7.
[2] See Bp. Ellicott, *The Being of God*, p. 120 note.
[3] Lev. xix. 17, 18; cp. Rom. xiii. 9. See Fairbairn, *Religion in History and in Modern Life*, lect. ii. pp. 123 foll., especially the admirable passage, pp. 132-134.

dignity and worth of human personality as made in the image of God that underlies the moral precepts of the Pentateuch : and it is in its recognition of this principle that the law of the old covenant is of permanent and eternal validity. At the same time the prophetic denunciations of hypocrisy, of formalism, and of the false externality that preferred ceremonialism to righteousness, anticipate those utterances of our Lord in which He distinguishes between the false and true types of goodness. There was much indeed in the Old Testament system that might foster the tendency to serve God in the anxious and timid spirit of a servant; but a corrective element was contained in the injunction to love God: and Hebrew saints and psalmists illustrate the power of this love to chasten and refine character, even when moulded by the stern discipline of the Law.

Speaking generally, the characters delineated in the Old Testament are marked by features which give them typical significance and permanent value as examples. We may admit that the heroic figures of antiquity are idealized, but they are the more valuable on that account as patterns, the qualities ascribed to them being precisely those which are essential parts of the noblest human goodness—fidelity, kindness, self-respect, hospitality, domestic affection, patience in trial, self-restraint, disinterestedness [1]. These are qualities which are constant elements in religious character, because they spring from the root of faith in a living God, the *righteous Lord who loveth righteousness,* who calls men to walk before Him and to be perfect, who delights in trustful obedience, and in that fidelity to obligations which is the reflection of His own unchanging self-consistency and covenant-faithfulness. Thus we habitually turn to the Old Testament for lessons of human duty; we regard it as 'a family album of the saints of God [2].' 'In a certain sense they are all

[1] Cp. Driver, *Sermons on the Old Testament,* pp. xii, xiii.
[2] Valeton, *Vergängliches und Ewiges im A. T.* p. 13.

types; but certainly men of flesh and blood, men in whom we can recognize ourselves, and whose spiritual life, in spite of the immense interval of place, time, and circumstances between us and them, is the same [in its general conditions] as ours, and therefore can serve us as a mirror¹.' In a word, one of the most important functions of the Old Testament is to teach us a knowledge of men and of the human heart—its possibilities of nobleness, its strange self-deceits, its variable hold on moral law, its haunting sense of a vocation to know and love God.

4. Akin to the function of the Old Testament Scriptures just described, is the office which it fulfils as a manual of the spiritual life, *profitable for doctrine, for reproof, for correction, for instruction in righteousness: that the man of God may be perfect, throughly furnished unto all good works*². The word of God, whether written or orally delivered, adapts itself to the requirements of individual men. Thus it is sometimes described as the food of souls—food which is milk or strong meat according to the capacity of him who feeds upon it. It claims to be a lantern or lamp—a light of the conscience—setting before men, whether in the incidents of personal biography or in the annals of national life, the dealings of God with nations and with individual souls. It reveals to them His requirement, it unveils His character, it unfolds His judgments, it encourages them by the splendour of His promises and by the special tokens of His presence. The value of the letter of the Old Testament in this connexion is great; it is, so to speak, a pledge of the continual providence which 'ordereth all things both in heaven and earth.' 'Most precious is the letter,' says a devout writer, 'as showing ... how the path of lonely men, if they walk with Him, their wells, and sheep, and feasts, and wars, are all His interests; that not a marriage, or birth, or death,— not the weaning of a child, or the dismissal of a maid,—

---

¹ Valeton, *Vergängliches und Ewiges im A. T.* p. 13.   ² 2 Tim. iii. 16, 71.

not the bargain for a grave, or the wish respecting the place of burial,—but He watches and directs it[1]. The literal sense of the Old Testament is indeed a consecration of the natural life of men, just as the New Testament is the witness of their spiritual calling and destiny. This seems to be the point of Augustine's observation that the Old Testament belongs to the old man, with which human nature must necessarily begin, while the New Testament concerns the new man, into which human nature ought to pass over from its old estate[2]. Again, Scripture is a mirror—such is the striking thought of St. James—a glass in which the child of God may behold himself, not only in his imperfection and frailty, but in the ideal manhood towards the attainment of which he tends. In the word he may, if he pleases, ascertain what manner of man he was in the divine thought for him. There he can discern to what he is called; what religion essentially is— the life of ever-growing friendship with Almighty God; what is the end of all things—the appropriation and penetration of nature and humanity by the divine Spirit.

Once more, to the writer of the Epistle to the Hebrews Scripture is a *sword*: a weapon of defence for the spiritual man engaged in his inevitable conflict with ghostly foes. So our blessed Lord used the Old Testament in the stress of His temptation, and thereby taught us to do the same. To Him it was the written record of God's unchanging will for man, and His thoughts concerning him. To the Bible viewed in this aspect St. Paul's words apply: *The weapons of our warfare are not carnal, but mighty through God to the pulling down of strongholds*[3]. And it is to be noted in passing that through disparage-

---

[1] Jukes, *The Types of Genesis*, p. xvi.
[2] Aug. *c. duas epp. Pelag.* iii. 13. So *Enarr. i. in psalm.* xxi. 1, Augustine speaks of Christ as 'personam servans veteris hominis, cujus mortalitatem portavit.'
[3] 2 Cor. x. 4. Observe this aspect of Scripture is very prominent in Cyprian. See his *de orat. dom.* i; *epp.* xxxi. 5, lviii. 7.

ment or neglect of the Old Testament, men may find themselves defenceless in the day of strong temptation or mortal fear. *The sword of the Spirit* is to be grasped by habitual study of Scripture, and by really putting it to the proof[1].

In one memorable passage St. Paul indicates the special character of the support which the study of the Old Testament lends to faith. He tells us that *whatsoever things were written aforetime were written for our learning, that we through patience and comfort of the scriptures might have hope*[2]. When we consider the stress which our Lord and His apostles lay upon the necessity of endurance, it is easy to understand how wisely the Old Testament is adapted to our spiritual needs. For it is a book of hope, teaching in every part of it the faithfulness of God, and the meaning and expediency of those delays and trials by which promised blessings are hindered or postponed[3]. The Old Testament is the history of a promise, the fulfilment of which was earnestly awaited and often despaired of by those who were its heirs; a promise only accomplished under circumstances undreamed of and in days when its essential nature was well-nigh forgotten. Further, the Old Testament is a history of grace. It teaches the capacities of that human nature which God condescends to train and discipline. It traces the steps by which the Israel of Egypt and the wilderness became the people of the star and sceptre, the holy nation, the kingdom of priests, the mother of saints, the people prepared for the Lord. It records miracles of national recovery, irresistible awakenings of conscience, the continual overruling of disaster for good, the regenerating force of personal character, the healing influences of the Spirit of God. In a word, the Old Testament witnesses to the continual advance, even through periods of fear,

---

[1] See Heb. v. 12; 1 Pet. ii. 2; 2 Pet. i. 19; Jas. i. 25; Eph. vi. 17; John v. 39.
[2] Rom. xv. 4.   [3] Cp. Jas. v. 11.

depression, and degeneration, of a victorious purpose of good; nor does it fail the human spirit in its hours of overwhelming fear or perplexity. It is a book of hope because it faces the anomalies and enigmas of life which overcloud and baffle so many minds. It teaches us that though we cannot understand the ways of God, at least He understands us. The Psalmist comforts himself by the simple reflection that when his spirit was in heaviness God knew his path[1]. The problems of existence have not been essentially altered by the immense changes of circumstance that part one period of history or one stage of human culture and experience from another. But the Old Testament is a pledge to us that all things—our needs, our perplexities, our failures, our aspirations, our struggles for existence, our toils on behalf of others, our joys and griefs, our hopes and fears—*are naked and opened unto the eyes of him with whom we have to do*[2].

Spiritual edification then is one important function discharged by the Old Testament. It is at once a manual of moral instruction and a book of devotion. It teaches us how to please God, and how to approach Him. It illustrates the close connexion between obedience, faith, and worship. In regard to this point it is instructive to mark how large a place the study of the Law appears to occupy in the thought of those to whom we owe some of the deepest and most spiritual of Psalms. We learn from this circumstance that the free temper of religious devotion can only have its root in a long and patient spiritual education: that the severe schooling of the will must precede the awakening of religious emotion and affection. It was the discipline of the Law that awakened in man's heart the consciousness of what God really was in Himself, and in His relation to man. And in two respects the Psalms seem to embody the entire spiritual teaching of the Old Testament: first

---

[1] Ps. cxlii. 3.   [2] Heb. iv. 13.

in their recognition of the individuality of the soul, of its loneliness in its conflict with spiritual enemies and of its dignity as a creature made by God and for God; secondly, in the thought of the all-sufficiency of God, who is to the soul of man all that it needs, all that it longs for. 'The principle of devotion,' says a writer on the spiritual life, 'is that God being the one source and the one author of holiness, the reasonable creature ought to depend on Him in everything and be absolutely governed by the Spirit of God[1].' This may indeed be described as the final lesson of the Old Testament, by which it is fitted to give expression to man's highest spiritual yearnings. Its office is not only to confirm personal faith by witnessing to the truth of God in the fulfilment of prophecy[2], but to guide it by continuous revelation of the divine will[3].

5. The Old Testament may be studied in the next place as an instructor in social righteousness[4]. It exhibits the moral government of God as attested in His dealings with nations rather than with individuals; and it was their consciousness of the action and presence of God in history that made the prophets preachers, not merely to their own countrymen, but to the world at large. The study of prophecy cannot but deepen our sense of the continuity of national life, of the reality of national vocation and responsibility, of the principle of judgment visibly at work in national history. Israel's career, as interpreted by the continuous commentary of prophetism, obliges us to

---

[1] Grou, *Manual, &c.* p. 2.
[2] Cp. Tert. *Apol.* xx : ' Quicquid agitur, praenuntiabatur; quicquid videtur, audiebatur, &c. . . . Idoneum, opinor, testimonium divinitatis veritas divinationis. Hinc igitur apud nos futurorum quoque fides tuta est, jam scilicet probatorum, quia cum illis quae quotidie probantur, praedicebantur.' So Aug. *c. Faust. Man.* viii. 2: ' Non in servitute facimus quae jussa sunt ad nos praenuntiandos, sed in libertate legimus quae scripta sunt ad nos confirmandos.'
[3] Aug. *de doc.* iii. 1 : 'Homo timens Deum voluntatem ejus in scripturis sanctis diligenter inquirit.'
[4] See G. A. Smith, *The Preaching of the O. T. to the Age*, pp. 19 foll.

consider the light thrown upon social arrangements and institutions by the revelation of the moral will of God. *Behold, the eyes of the Lord God are upon the sinful kingdom,* cries Amos, *and I will destroy it from off the face of the earth* [1]. It was their hold upon law, their inspired sense of the claims of an objective moral order embracing all nations in its scope, that enabled the prophets to predict. It is in their abhorrence of insincerity, in their consciousness of moral proportion, that they are so uniquely qualified to guide Christians whose lot is cast amid the complex conditions of the modern social system. There is indeed significance in the fact that in spite of their ardent zeal for social reform they did not as a rule take part in political life or demand political reforms. They desired, it has been justly said, not better institutions but better men. They were in fact conspicuous as *religious* leaders—men who, feeling themselves commissioned to speak in God's name, were deeply convinced that the divine purpose must be commensurate with human life, must cover the whole field of social action and interest. They were perpetually rebuking that strange self-deceit which besets human nature in every age—the supposition that the province of religion can be severed from that of social life and duty, and that there are departments which lie outside the regulative influence of faith. The prophets were the spokesmen of a righteousness which is everywhere valid; they proclaimed the supremacy of an irresistible will, not to be ignored either by men or nations except at their own infinite peril.

Two points are noticeable in the social doctrine of the Old Testament regarded as a whole. First, it is to be observed that the polity of ancient Israel is not based on individualism. It has lately been maintained that the Old Testament is dominated by the conception of collectivism [2], and it is at least true that to the prophets the nation and not the individual

---

[1] Amos ix. 8. [2] W. S. Bruce, *The Ethics of the O. T.* p. 22.

is the recipient of promises, the possessor of covenantal *status* and privileges. Their tendency is to individualize the nation, and to represent its corporate vocation and responsibility as dependent on a quasi-personal relationship to Jehovah. Certainly the idea of individual rights remained for a long period undeveloped. The highest prayer of the devout Israelite was that he might *see the felicity of* God's *chosen, and rejoice in the gladness of* His *people, and give thanks with* His *inheritance*[1]. The salvation for which he looked was national rather than personal; the highest good for which he waited was a kingdom, the kingdom of God. The thought of personal well-being was overshadowed by 'the contemplation of the divine sovereignty[2].' The sense of belonging to the true Israel has in the later history of Judaism sustained individuals under the pressure of untold disasters, and has perhaps even mitigated the sense of personal shortcoming[3]. The whole tendency of the Old Testament is in harmony with the revelation of nature and with the social ideals now dawning upon us: its main thought is the comparative insignificance of the individual life in relation to the divine purpose for humanity as a whole. Secondly, it is evident that the idea of a spiritual kingdom took deep root in the Hebrew mind, and the conviction that no material forces could either help the fortunes of the elect people, or hinder the supremacy of God's righteous will. The contact of the Hebrew state with the great world-powers was an epoch in religious history. It taught Israel to realize its own special vocation; it also proved that forces were at work in the world more effective and enduring than even the highest products of human ambition, energy, and skill. As one after another the vast empires which had been founded on violence fell into decay and vanished from the scene,

---

[1] Ps. cvi. 5.
[2] Westcott, *Social Aspects of Christianity*, p. 86.
[3] See Montefiore, *Hibbert Lectures*, p. 514.

the spiritual leaders of the elect nation came to understand that what is eternal and heavenly must owe its being to God; that the true kingdom of humanity must be based not on forces of this world—greed, self-assertion, or the right of the strongest, but on the foundation of faith, justice, and truth. And certainly one chief office of the Old Testament is to teach the modern mind to read history aright, by showing what are the true factors that mould, sustain, and perfect human society; that they are moral and spiritual, not material; that character is the most powerful social force, that courage, mercy, and self-control are the real instruments of lasting social amelioration. The chequered story of Israel's career carries with it the lesson that while the kingdoms of this world are built up by the natural energies of man, and must inevitably 'have their day and cease to be,' the kingdom of God is the *city which hath foundations, whose builder and maker is God*[1]. The fruit of the Spirit in man accomplishes what the excellences and virtues of nature cannot achieve. The transfiguration of society can only result from the indwelling of God Himself in individual souls.

6. I must be content with a very brief allusion to one more function of the Old Testament, namely, to assist us in the right interpretation of the New[2]. It is an important aid in tracing the history of ideas, and in determining the significance of particular terms. Augustine somewhere observes that a Christian ought to study the prophets in order that he may not forget *why* he believes[3]. It is equally necessary to read the Old Testament to gain an intelligent idea of *what* we believe. The *content* of our faith, as distinguished from its form, is largely revealed in the Old Testament. Such terms as *the Christ* or *the kingdom of God* are charged with the

---

[1] Heb. xi. 10.
[2] Cp. Kirkpatrick, *The Divine library of the O. T.* p. 126.
[3] *c. Faust. Man.* xiii. 18.

memories and associations of a long religious history. The ideas of 'righteousness,' 'atonement,' 'redemption,' 'propitiation,' which play so large a part in New Testament theology, have their roots in an immense and complicated system of mediation, apart from which their significance can only be imperfectly understood. The full connotation of such a phrase as *the Son of God* can only be ascertained in the light of Hebrew and Judaistic thought and feeling. Nor must we forget that there are many points of contact between the language of the New Testament and the Talmud—that vast 'microcosm,' as it has been called, which is the most characteristic product of post-exilic Judaism [1]. Some of the leading ideas of the New Covenant were 'household words' of Talmudic Judaism. 'It is the glory of Christianity,' says Emanuel Deutsch, ' to have carried those golden germs, hidden in the schools and among the "silent community" of the learned, into the market of humanity [2].' It is unnecessary to multiply instances in illustration of this point [3]. But it is an important consideration that our estimate of the New Testament revelation as a whole will depend upon the idea we have gained from the Old Testament of the needs and weaknesses of human nature. We have to read the New Testament in the light of our knowledge of Hebrew modes of thought, and also with a due sense of the cravings that needed satisfaction, the sorrows that lacked assuagement. Some of our Lord's own utterances, such as the promise of rest to the heavy-laden, or of living water to the thirsting soul, or of life to the dead, or of dominion to the meek, imply wants and experiences in the spiritual life of His hearers which need to be patiently studied before the true significance of His words, who spake as *never man spake*, can be

---

[1] Nicolas, *op. cit.*, pref. p. vii, says very justly: 'Il importe, dans l'intérêt même de la parfaite intelligence de l'œuvre de Jésus Christ, *de pénétrer le plus profondément qu'il est possible dans l'histoire religieuse et morale du judaïsme immédiatement antérieur.*'
[2] See his *Literary Remains* (London, 1874), p. 27.
[3] See Valeton, *Vergängliches und Ewiges im A. T.* pp. 8 foll.

understood. Whatever enables us to understand the historical conditions under which the writings of the Old Testament were produced gives us a deeper insight into the nature of New Testament ideals, and the meaning of evangelical faith. For if it be true, as Wellhausen has said, that 'the Gospel develops hidden impulses of the Old Testament[1],' it is clear that any real advance in comprehending the genius of Christianity depends to a great extent upon more accurate knowledge of Hebrew religion and literature and also of the boundless and little-explored field of Talmudic Judaism and Rabbinic theology. Closer acquaintance indeed with all pre-Christian systems will heighten our sense of the assimilative power of the Gospel. It will reveal to us the useless or corrupt elements which were excluded by Christianity, the forms which perished because they were rotten, the systems which could not stand the test of that *fire* which Christ *came to send upon the earth*[2]. But it will also make manifest the truth and nobility of that which the new religion claimed as its own, or used, and transfigured in the using[3]. And here lies the peculiar value of those historical and critical studies which have enabled us to distinguish between the different elements contained in early Christianity—between ideas carried forward from Judaism and ideas transplanted from the sphere of Hellenic thought. We have learned, partially at least, what elements Christianity found ready to its hand in the teaching of prophets and psalmists, what it owed to Alexandria and to Greece, and what is due to the work and personality of its Founder[4]. Thus we shall come to recognize more

---

[1] *Prolegomena*, p. 509. [2] Luke xii. 49.
[3] See a noble sermon of Mr. Stopford Brooke, *Christ in Modern Life*, no. iv.
[4] Cp. Sanday, *The Oracles of God*, serm. ix. Valeton, *op. cit.* p. 9, observes: 'Mit dem Christenthum auch eine neue Sprache entstanden ist, und zwar eine Sprache, die ebensoviel griechisch ist wie israelitisch. Wir haben ja allerdings jedes Dogma nur in einer mehr oder minder philosophischen Form, die der griechischen Welt entlehnt ist; der religiöse Kern aber ist aus Israel genommen.'

perfectly the inexhaustible significance of the Catholic creed, and its fullness and depth as an interpretation of life. Doubtless the criticism of the Old Testament is a gift which brings with it large responsibilities and special anxieties and trials. But our gains are not less considerable. If Christ is, as Irenaeus expresses it, the treasure hid in the field of the ancient Scriptures [1], we may expect to discover there mysteries which we shall never completely fathom, to find, as knowledge advances, new aspects of truth constantly disclosed, and fresh beams of light cast upon elements in Christian faith and life which as yet we only dimly apprehend. The historical study of Scripture reverently pursued with the aids which modern research places within our reach, will certainly not evacuate the Old Testament of mystery; rather it will make us more modest in our judgments, more humble in the estimation of our powers. We shall say with not less conviction than Augustine himself: *Quidquid est in Scripturis illis altum et divinum est: inest omnino veritas* [2].

My task is now drawing to a close, and I need not say much by way of summary. In the first lecture I stated those presuppositions, doctrinal and critical, with which the subject of the lectures has been approached. The general aim was to show that there is a point of view from which the results of criticism, so far as they are satisfactorily established, may be cordially welcomed. In the second lecture we considered generally those aspects of the Old Testament which were afterwards discussed separately. In the third we endeavoured to estimate the nature and extent of the historical element which pervades the Old Testament, regarded as a history of man's redemption. Our conclusions were necessarily somewhat general, but we saw reason to suppose that in all its main outlines the traditional view of Israel's history is not discredited by sound criticism; on the other hand, there appears to be much more of the subjective

---

[1] *Haer.* iv. 26. 1. [2] Aug. *de util. cred.* 13.

element in the history, much more play of religious feeling and imagination, than had been allowed for in the pre-critical period. The fourth lecture dealt with the self-revelation of God which accompanied the historical movement. We attempted to illustrate the distinctive features of Israel's religion regarded as a progressive moral education and a continuous self-manifestation of deity. In the fifth lecture the spiritual purpose and meaning of the Mosaic dispensation was discussed, the traditional view of Israel's covenantal relation to Jehovah considered, with special reference to the moral obligations involved in it and the typical system of worship by which the covenant-union was maintained. In the sixth lecture the function of prophecy occupied our attention, the element which it contributed to Israel's religious history, and the nature of the Messianic hope which it served to keep alive. The seventh lecture dealt with the divine purpose for the individual, and the main elements contributed by the Old Testament to the idea of personal religion. At this point the universalistic tendency of Hebrew religion became more apparent; we found that its outlook embraced not merely the interests of an elect nation, but the spiritual needs and yearnings of universal humanity. In the eighth and last lecture we have considered what light is thrown upon the Old Testament by its employment in the New, and the important functions which Old Testament study has to fulfil in the present-day life of the Christian Church.

It seems advisable to conclude with two reflections intended to reassure those who either view the critical movement with dismay and suspicion, or are tempted to suppose that its results are necessarily hostile to Catholic Christianity.

1. In the first place, I trust it will have appeared that no Christian believer needs to cast away his faith because a new conception of the Old Testament challenges his attention and perhaps commends itself to his mature judgment. I have attempted to show

that a man who believes in the truth of historic Christianity with all his heart, and who finds in it the only adequate solution of 'the riddle of existence,' is not so committed to any traditional view of Hebrew literature as to be precluded from revising it in the light of advancing knowledge. To an increasing number of Christian students it appears that the view of Israel's history and religion provisionally adopted in these lectures immensely reinforces the claim of Christianity to be the final or absolute religion; it conspicuously illustrates the profound axiom of St. Paul, *Howbeit that was not first which is spiritual, but that which is natural; and afterward that which is spiritual*[1]; and it falls in with very much that we have ascertained in other fields of knowledge concerning the ways of divine wisdom and providence. Accordingly the attempt has been made in these lectures, not so much to support or commend a particular solution of the difficult problems connected with Old Testament research, as to mediate between opposed, but not mutually exclusive, points of view, or at least to discriminate between what is essential and what non-essential to faith. We have seen that a believer in the divine Incarnation has no reason for sharing the rooted dislike of miracle and prophecy, or the contempt of the idea of divine revelation, which is sometimes justly attributed to certain schools of continental criticism [2]. But, on the other hand, a thoughtful Christian will bear in mind that the knowledge necessary for forming a judgment on the complicated questions raised by modern historical science and the trained judgment and true sense of proportion indispensable for duly appreciating the results of criticism, are qualities attainable by few. He will also remember that in every age faith has been tried not only by the direct attacks of its professed foes, but by an enlargement of human knowledge which was ultimately destined to enrich men's conceptions of God. There cannot be

---

[1] 1 Cor. xv. 46.
[2] Cp. Stanley Leathes, *The Law in the Prophets*, p. 271.

mental growth, readjustment, or self-adaptation without perplexity and pain ; without *the removing of those things that are shaken, that those things which cannot be shaken may remain*[1].

In regard to the Old Testament particularly we shall recognize the danger of using *a priori* methods, and the folly of insisting on hard and fast conditions as those under which alone inspiration is possible. It is sufficiently manifest that our highly-developed notions respecting literary morality, and our scientific conceptions of what history means, are out of court when applied to the ancient Scriptures. As Wellhausen tersely remarks : ' What *must* have happened is of less consequence to know than what actually took place[2].' We shall have to revise our notions of what it is absolutely necessary to know. And it is evident that we shall have to be content with something very far short of certainty in regard to some points which we have hitherto supposed to be indisputable. Advancing experience will show us how large a part suspense of judgment must play in our present controversies, but at the same time it may be safely maintained that the matters likely to remain in dispute are, speaking broadly, neither many in number nor of crucial importance. For after all, the field which remains unaffected, or which, to speak more accurately, has been thoroughly explored and illuminated by criticism, is for all practical purposes of religion very extensive. Necessary uncertainty in regard to the nature of the earliest historical narratives does not rob us of ' the revelation of God, the writings of the Law, the oracles of Prophets, the music of Psalms, the instruction of Proverbs, the experience of histories[3].' On the contrary, modern research only reinforces the characteristic teaching of the Prophets and the Psalmists ; it imparts new vividness and clearness to what is demonstrably historic, while it in no degree impairs the spiritual and edu-

---

[1] Heb. xii. 27. [2] *Prolegomena*, p. 46.
[3] Bp. Andrewes, *Devotions* (First Day).

cational function of those portions of Holy Writ, the character of which cannot at present be precisely determined. We must not be too impatient to draw necessary and just distinctions. We must cordially acknowledge our obligation as students of God's holy word to those illustrious scholars, whether English or foreign, whose learned labours, patient sagacity, reverent insight, and trained judgment have achieved such fruitful and deeply interesting results.

2. Those, however, who do not feel the force of the appeal made by the historical criticism of our day, need to beware of an exaggerated or one-sided conception of the function discharged by the Bible as a source of divine knowledge. It is unquestionable that one principal cause of the suspicion with which many devout persons regard the critical movement is the fear of anything that seems to threaten or tamper with the foundations of faith. They are apt to speak of the higher criticism with ill-advised and shallow vehemence as 'an assault on Christian faith.' But apart from the vitally important duty of making an intelligent distinction between the witness of the Old Testament and that of the New, such persons ought to consider whether they have not assigned to Scripture in general a position of inordinate importance in the system of religion. If the Church of God be anything, if human reason and conscience be anything, if the Holy Ghost be a living power in the life of redeemed humanity, we must not overlook or underestimate the sources of divine knowledge other than Scripture which God has placed within our reach. The Church and the Bible certainly co-exist in the world as two great sources of authority, mutually corroborative of each other, and to some extent mutually corrective of each other [1]. Both of them have a share in leading us to the knowledge of God in which consists eternal life: but the mistake is not uncommonly made of overlooking the true function of either one or

---

[1] Cp. Forbes, *The XXXIX Articles*, p. 95.

the other. By the teaching of the New Testament we are encouraged to put ourselves under the guidance of the Church so far as it extends, looking to it for the form or outline of sound words, which it supplies to us in the Creed. To Scripture, on the other hand, the Church bids us look as filling in and giving substance to the outline of faith which we have already received in the Creed. But within and beyond the Bible and the Church there is a guide of whom we in practice think too little. We ought to trust to that *unction from the Holy One* which rests on Christians, unveiling to us as we are able to bear it the inexhaustible significance of our holy faith and illuminating for us the Scriptures which enshrine it. 'We have a Lord,' says Chrysostom, 'who loves mankind, and when He sees us anxious and strongly desirous of understanding the divine oracles, He does not leave us destitute of ought besides, but straightway enlightens our understanding, bestows that illumination which proceeds from Himself, and according to His benign wisdom communicates all true doctrine to our souls [1].' Thus the means which God has placed within our reach are all to be used in combination: we are to hear the Church, and then to diligently search the Scriptures; but above all, we are to remember that God will give the Holy Spirit to them that ask Him. This simple reflection is intended to reassure us in view of the great complexity of all human questions, and the obvious fragmentariness of even the highest human knowledge. We may be confident that the Spirit of Truth will not allow us to be deceived in any essential matter if we diligently ask Him to enlighten us and to guide. *Where the Spirit of the Lord is, there is liberty* [2]. It is remarkable that this statement occurs in connexion with St. Paul's complaint that a veil is upon

---

[1] *Opera* [ed. Ben.], iv. p. 216. Cp. Orig. *hom. xii. in Exod.* § 4: 'Non solum studium adhibendum est ad discendas literas sacras, verum et supplicandum Domino, et diebus et noctibus obsecrandum, ut veniat Agnus ex tribu Juda, et ipse accipiens librum signatum dignetur aperire.' To the same effect Aug. *de doct.* iii. s. fin.

[2] 2 Cor. iii. 17.

Israel's heart *in the reading of the old testament*. That veil *is done away in Christ* through the power of the converting Spirit. And we Christians need Origen's caution that it is possible for a veil to be on our hearts if we are either negligent in the study of Scripture, or if we take no pains to acquire the knowledge necessary for a true comprehension of its teaching [1]. We stand over against Holy Scripture, not as literalists, or slaves of the letter, but as children of God guided by the same Spirit who possessed and inspired the sacred writers. We do not doubt the truth of our Christianity because we see in part, and know only in part; because in this world of half-lights and impenetrable shadows our knowledge is at best fragmentary and imperfect. On the same principle we have no reason to be dismayed or perplexed at the blending of human frailty with the unearthly majesty and mystery of the Scriptures. *We have this treasure*, the word of God, *in earthen vessels* [2]; and while it is a sign of levity to overlook the treasure and throw it away because the vessels are of earth, it is a mark of narrowness to ignore the distinction between the vessels and the treasure they contain. Just as the remarkable religious revival of the last half-century has enabled us to realize the power and presence of the Holy Spirit in the public life and active ministry of the Christian Church, so questions respecting the inspiration and character of the Bible remind us of His continuous work in the immediate guidance and edification of individual souls [3]. An era of difficulties, mental and

---

[1] Orig. *loc. cit.* 'Manifeste si negligenter audimus, si nihil studii ad eruditionem et intelligentiam conferimus, non solum Legis et Prophetarum scriptura, sed et Apostolorum et Evangeliorum grandi nobis velamine tegitur.'

[2] 2 Cor. iv. 7. For what follows see some remarks of Frank quoted by Köhler, *Über Berechtigung der Kritik des A. T.* pp. 48, 49.

[3] Tyndale, *Works*, vol. iii. p. 139 [Parker Society], quoted by Briggs, *Biblical Study*, p. 163, says: 'For though the Scripture be an outward instrument and the preacher also to move men to believe, yet the chief and principal cause why a man believeth or believeth not is within; that is, the Spirit of God leadeth His children to believe.'

spiritual, is meant to reawaken in men the spirit of dependence on Him whose real presence in souls is the source of present consolation and of unquenchable hope for the future. The modern student may heartily endorse the noble words of Origen: 'We cannot declare that anything in the literature of the Holy Spirit is otiose or superfluous, even though to some it appears obscure. But our main concern should be this: to turn the eyes of our mind to Him at whose bidding these things were written, and to beg from Him the capacity to understand the same; that whether there be infirmity in our own soul, He may heal us who heals all its sicknesses; or whether we be limited in comprehension, He may be present with us as a Lord protecting His little ones, and may so nurture us as to bring us to the full stature of spiritual manhood[1].' Yes; the secret of liberty, of largeness of heart and of steadfastness in the faith is with Him. *Ye have an anointing from the Holy One, and ye know all things. ... And as for you, the anointing which ye received of him abideth in you, and ye need not that any one teach you; but as his anointing teacheth you concerning all things and is true, and is no lie, and even as it taught you, abide ye in him* [2].

[1] Orig. *in Num. hom.* xxvii. 1.   [2] 1 John ii. 20, 27 (R. V. *marg.*).

INDEX

Abraham, history of, 111, 118; idealization of, 125; place in the thought of St. Paul, 397.
Achan, 175.
Adonai, 186, 192.
Aeschylus, 217.
Allegorism, its employment in the New Testament, 392.
Amos, teaching of, 288.
Andrewes, Bishop, quoted, 439.
Anthropomorphism, anthropopathic expressions, 107, 194.
Apocalypse, the, 393, 397, 421.
Apocalyptic literature, 317.
Aquinas, T., quoted, 408.
Archaeology and the Old Testament, 105.
Assyria, 282.
Athanasius, quoted, 58.
Atonement, Day of, 237, 239, 256.
Augustine, quoted, 63, 186, 219, 250, 343, 393, 403, 405, 407, 422, 427, 433, 436.

Baal, the name, 193; prophets of, 270.
Baethgen, 111.
Balaam, prophecy of, 298.
Baruch, Apocalypse of, 350.
Bath Qôl, the, 316.
Bible, the, its analogy to the incarnate Word, 15 foll.; to nature, 98 foll.
Blood, use of, in sacrifice, 237 foll.; 255 foll.
Briggs, C., quoted, 405.
Browning, E., quoted, 352.
Browning, R., quoted, 15, 370.
Bruce, Dr. A., quoted, 13, 62, 111, 139, 165, 179, 229, 248, 306, 321, 381.
Bruce, W. S., quoted, 193, 223.

Burnt-offering, the, 235, 240; daily, 241; fulfilled in Christ, 253.
Butler, Bishop, 165.

Cabbala, the, 406.
Calf-worship, the, 221.
Canaanites, slaughter of the, 178.
Canon of the Old Testament, its formation, 100, 265 foll.
Carchemish, battle of, 309.
Catholic, the term, 1 foll.
Channing, quoted, 133.
Chesed, 199, 291.
Cheyne, Prof. T., quoted, 203, 346.
CHRIST, authority of, in relation to the Old Testament, 46 foll.; sacrifice of, 228, 253 foll.; on priesthood of, 251; His view of the Old Testament, 381 foll.; His person and work the key to the Old Testament, 396 foll.; parabolic teaching of, 391, 407.
Chronicles, Books of, 102, 149, 223, 327, 344, 385; teaching and purport of, 357.
Chrysostom, quoted, 441.
Church, doctrine of the, 51 foll.; relation to the Bible, 441.
Church, Dean, quoted, 81, 118.
Circumcision, 167, 222.
Corinthian Church, 6.
Cornill, quoted, 242, 272, 288.
Covenant, idea of the, 79 foll., 207 foll.; the new, 227, 312 foll.
Covenant, Book of the, 138, 171.
Creation, story of, 57 foll.
Criticism, the higher, results of, 33 foll.; defects pointed out in, 41.
Cultus, the Hebrew, its purpose, 228.
Curé de Canton, 283.

INDEX

Dalman, quoted, 66.
Daniel, Book of, 276, 317, 331.
Darmesteter, quoted, 33, 41, 206.
David, character of, idealized, 127 ; reign of, 299 foll.
Day of Jehovah, the, 284, 304.
Death, Hebrew conception of, 336.
Deborah, song of, 155.
Decalogue, the, 75, 172, 215 foll.
Delitzsch, quoted, 347.
Deuteronomy, Book of, 123, 133, 145, 169, 173, 219.
Deutsch, E., quoted, 434.
Driver, Prof., quoted, 65, 120, 296.

Ecclesiastes, Book of, 190, 347 foll. ; relation of, to the problem of suffering, 364, 367 foll.
'El, 'El 'Elyon, 183 foll., 189 foll.
Election, the idea of, 64 foll. ; rejected by Kuenen, 116.
Elijah, 273.
'Elilim, 72.
'Elohim, 183 foll., 189 foll. ; applied to King, 302.
Elohist writer, the, 119.
'El Shaddai, 185, 191 foll.
Enoch, Book of, 318.
Esdras, Fourth book of, 76.
Esther, Book of, 330, 356.
Eucharist, the, 254, 258 foll.
Evolution, the idea of, 43.
Ewald, quoted, 19, 28, 75, 101.
Exile, literary activity during the, 121 ; effects of the, 310 foll.
Exodus, the, importance of, 69 foll., 134 ; evidence of, 94.
Exodus, Book of, its teaching and purport, 93 foll., 138 foll.
Experience, function of Christian, 49 foll.
Ezekiel, 144 ; teaching of, 201, 307, 314, 324, 340; *torah* of, 224, 230.
Ezra, 266, 326.
Ezra, Book of, 149, 358.

Fall, account of the, 59 foll.
Fatherhood of God, 204.
Fire, use of in sacrifice, 238, 240.
Firstborn, sanctification of the, 136, 222.
Flood, the, 60 foll.
Froude, Prof., quoted, 361.
Future life, Old Testament doctrine of a, 334 foll.

Genesis, Book of, narratives in the, 113 foll. ; value of, 131.
Gideon, 155.
Girdlestone, quoted, 131.
Grace, idea of, in historical books, 151.
Green, J. R., quoted, 158.
Grou, quoted, 430.

Habakkuk, 309.
Haggadah, 124, 149, 384, 386 foll.
Haggai, 314.
Hagiographa, the, 95, 329 foll.
Halachah, 384, 386.
Hebrews, Epistle to the, 225, 227, 246, 250 foll., 393.
Hengstenberg, quoted, 356.
Hexateuch, narratives of the, 101.
Historical documents in the Old Testament, their character and value, 102 foll.
Historical element in the Old Testament, 97 foll., 401 foll.
Holiness, idea of, in Old Testament, 72 foll.
Holocausts, 240.
Holy One of Israel, 196.
HOLY SPIRIT, the, in relation to the Bible and the Church, 441.
Hosea, teaching of, 200, 290.

Idealistic language of the Old Testament, its significance, 419.
Idealization in the Pentateuch, &c., 119 foll.
Image worship, 174.
Immortality, *see* ' Future life.'
Incarnation, the, its relation to Scripture, 12 foll. ; analogy suggested by, 15 foll.
Individuality, idea of, in the Old Testament, 90 foll., 175.
Inspiration, meaning of, 22 foll. ; prophetic, 274 foll.
Irenaeus, 3, 81, 436 ; quoted, 65, 166, 213, 246.
Isaac, sacrifice of, 177.
Isaiah, teaching of, 292.
Ishsheh, 234.
Israel, early history of, 134 ; social condition of, in eighth century B.C., 282.

Jacob, the blessing of (Gen. xlix), 297.

Jahveh, Jehovah, 185, 193 foll.; his character displayed in the exodus, 139; attributes of, 198 foll.
Jahveh Tsebaoth, 186, 203.
James, St., references of, to the Old Testament, 388; view of Scripture, 427.
Jashar, Book of, 103.
Jealousy, the divine, 200.
Jehovist writer, the, 109, 119.
Jeremiah, teaching of, 307, 313, 323.
Jeroboam, 154.
Job, Book of, 347, 361 foll.
Joel, Book of, 316.
John, St., his use of the Old Testament, 388, 397.
Jonah, Book of, 292 foll.; narrative of, 379.
Joseph, history of, 112.
Josephus, 84.
Judah, 297.
Judaism, 316.
Jude, St., references of, to the Old Testament, 388.
Judges, the, period of, 155.
Judges, Book of, 102, 147.
Jukes, A., quoted, 129, 131, 397, 426.
Justin Martyr, 30.

Keim, quoted, 84.
Kingdom of God, the, 86 foll.
Kings, Books of, 102, 148.
Kingship, Hebrew idea of, 86.
Kittel, quoted, 132, 140, 273.
König, 205.
Kuenen, quoted, 72, 116, 134, 152, 215, 286.

Language, inadequacy of, 406.
Law, the, its doctrine of retribution, 343; New Testament verdict on, 380 foll.
Legislation, earliest Hebrew, 171.
Liddon, Dr., 26.
Lock, Prof. W., quoted, 331.
Lucretius, quoted, 350.
Luther, quoted, 365.

Magee, Abp., quoted, 10, 22.
Malachi, Book of, 315, 326.
Manasseh, reign of, 308 foll.
Martensen, Bishop, quoted, 60.
Maurice, F., 386.
Mazzoth, feast of, 136.
Melchizedek, 251.

Messiah, the title, 300.
Messianic hope, 82 foll., 296 foll.
Micah, Book of, 303 foll.
Midrash, 149, 384.
Minchah, 234, 241.
Miracle in the Old Testament, 61 foll., 107 foll.
Moloch, 176.
Monolatry, 69.
Monotheism, 286.
Montefiore, C., 11; quoted, 122, 145, 174, 204, 215, 327, 328.
Morality of the Old Testament, progressive, 165 foll.; an ambiguous phrase, 421 foll.; features of Old Testament ethics, 423 foll.
Mosaism, 33, 132; its ethical tendency, 138.
Moses, prophetic work of, 33, 131, 298; song of, 137; legislation of, 141.
Mozley, J. B., quoted, 178, 337, 363.
Mystical sense, the, 405 foll.

Nabhi, Nebiim, 272, 274 foll.
Name of God, 182.
Nature, analogy suggested by, 98 foll.
Nehemiah, 326.
Nehemiah, Book of, 149, 330, 358.

Oehler, quoted, 218.
Oettli, quoted, 78, 79.
Old Testament, various aspects of, 53 foll.; employment of in the New Testament, 383 foll.; functions fulfilled by, 412 foll.; its final cause and ultimate explanation, Christ, 417; social doctrine of, 431 foll.
Origen, quoted, 21, 26, 30, 223, 225, 333, 402, 406, 417, 442, 443.
Origins, the, narrative of, 57 foll.

Parables of Christ, the, 391, 407.
Passover, the, 136, 222.
Paterson Smyth, quoted, 45, 50.
Patriarchal narrative, 109 foll.
Patriarchs, the, 110 foll.
Paul, St., 5 foll., 20; his use of the Old Testament, 388 foll., 397.
Peace-offering, the, 235, 242; its significance, 258 foll.
Pentateuch, the, leading ideas of,

INDEX   447

93 foll.; its significance for Christians, 143; narratives of the, 144.
Persia, influence of, on Hebrew thought, 332.
Personal religion in the Old Testament, 325 foll.
Personality, Hebrew conception of, 338 foll.
Peter, St., his use of the Old Testament, 388, 397.
Pfleiderer, quoted, 289, 315, 321, 352.
Pharisaism, relation of, to Scripture, 394 foll.
Philo, 30.
Piacular sacrifice, 232.
Post-exilic period, 323 foll.
Priesthood of Christ, 251.
Priestly document, the, 120 foll., 141.
Prophecy, fulfilment of in Christ, 318 foll.; importance of studying, 430 foll.
Prophetism, origins of, 270 foll.
Prophets, the, former and latter, 95, 266.
Prophets, Hebrew: their attitude towards ritual, 221; their view of sacrifice, 230; functions of the, 275 foll.; sphere of their activity, 281 foll.; preachers of monotheism, 286; their philosophy of history, 289; limitations, 306.
Protevangelium, the, 296.
Proverbs, Book of, teaching on retribution, 345.
Providence, doctrine of a personal, 353 foll.
Psalms, Book of, 328; teaching of the, 341; on retribution, 345; relation to religion, 352, 429; Psalm cxix, 375.

Qorban, 234.

Religion, meaning of, 351.
Renan, E., quoted, 365.
Resurrection, doctrine of, in Old Testament, 349.
Retribution, Old Testament doctrine of, 343.
Revelation, the Old Testament a record of, 66 foll.; progressive character of, 162 foll.; Hebrew idea of, 187.

Riehm, quoted, 167, 229.
Robertson, Prof., quoted, 157.
Robertson Smith, Prof., quoted, 8, 49, 65, 70, 94, 122, 138, 229, 233, 242, 283, 334.
Royalty, Hebrew idea of, 303 foll.
Ruth, Book of, 331, 356.
Ryle, Prof., quoted, 265.

Sacrifice, human, 176.
Sacrifices, the levitical, 227 foll.; names of the, 234; symbolic meaning of, 250 foll.
Samson, story of, 157.
Samuel, 272, 281.
Samuel, Books of, 102, 147.
Sanday, Prof., 32.
Sayce, Prof., quoted, 39.
Schechter, quoted, 159.
Schultz, H., quoted, 23, 25, 71, 82, 114, 167, 303, 311, 319, 340, 344, 363, 398.
Schürer, quoted, 386.
Scribes, 383 foll.
Scythians, the invasion of the, 309.
Secondary sense, *see* 'Mystical.'
Semichah, the, 236.
Semitic religion, character of, 182.
Servant of Jehovah, the, 88, 311.
Sheʻol, 336 foll.
Shewbread, the, 254.
Sin-offering, the, 232, 235, 238; fulfilment of, in the sacrifice of Christ, 255.
Smith, Prof. G. A., 130; quoted, 160.
Sodh, the, 385.
Solomon, age of, 346.
Song of Solomon, the, 355.
Sophocles, quoted, 10.
Spiritual sense, the, 397. *See* 'Mystical sense.'
Stanton, Prof., quoted, 308.
Stoicism, 92.
Synagogues, 327.
Syncretism, 153.
Syria, kingdom of, 282.

Tabernacle, the, 120, 226 foll.; symbolic significance of, 247 foll., 261 foll.
Tacitus, quoted, 293.
Talmud, the, 434.
Tamid, 241, 253.

Tatian, 30.
Temple, the, in prophecy, 315; worship of the second, 326.
Teraphim, 113.
Tertullian, quoted, 205.
Testament, Old, New Testament view of the, 377 foll.
Theocracy, 84, 140 foll.
Thomson, quoted, 322.
Torah, 213, 222, 279.
Trespass-offering, 238.
Types in Genesis, 126.
Typical interpretation, 244 foll., 410 foll.

Unity of God, 70 foll.

Universalism, 288.

Valeton, quoted, 267, 425 foll.

Wars of Jehovah, Book of the, 103.
Wellhausen, quoted, 14, 86, 87, 90, 150, 214, 226, 273, 395, 435, 439.
Westcott, Bishop, quoted, 179.
Wisdom literature, the, 329 foll., 359 foll.
Wordsworth, quoted, 4.

Zebach, 234, 242.
Zechariah, Book of, 312, 315, 318.
Zephaniah, 309.
Zerubbabel, 312.

www.ingramcontent.com/pod-product-compliance
Lightning Source LLC
Chambersburg PA
CBHW070837020526
44114CB00041B/1415